Visible Learning and the Science of How We Learn

On publication in 2009, John Hattie's *Visible Learning* presented the biggest ever collection of research into what actually works in improving children's learning in schools. Not what was fashionable, not what political and educational vested interests wanted to champion, but what actually produced the best results in terms of improving learning and educational outcomes. It became an instant bestseller and was described by the TES as revealing education's 'holy grail'.

Now in this latest book, John Hattie has joined forces with cognitive psychologist Gregory C. R. Yates to build on the original data and legacy of the *Visible Learning* project, showing how its underlying ideas and the cutting edge of cognitive science can form a powerful and complementary framework for shaping learning in the classroom and beyond.

Visible Learning and the Science of How We Learn explains the major principles and strategies of learning, outlining why it can be so hard sometimes and yet easy on other occasions. Aimed at teachers and students, it is written in an accessible and engaging style and can be read cover to cover, or used on a chapter-by-chapter basis for essay writing or staff development.

The book is structured in three parts: 'Learning within classrooms'; 'Learning foundations', which explains the cognitive building blocks of knowledge acquisition; and 'Know thyself', which explores confidence and self-knowledge. It also features extensive interactive resources including study guide questions to encourage critical thinking, annotated bibliographic entries with recommendations for further reading and links to relevant websites and YouTube clips. Throughout, the authors draw upon the latest international research into how the learning process works and how to maximise impact on students, covering such topics as:

- teacher personality
- expertise and teacher–student relationships
- how knowledge is stored and the impact of cognitive load
- thinking fast and thinking slow
- the psychology of self-control
- the role of conversation at school and at home
- invisible gorillas and the IKEA effect
- digital native theory
- myths and fallacies about how people learn.

This fascinating book is aimed at any student, teacher or parent requiring an up-to-date commentary on how research into human learning processes can inform our teaching and what goes on in our schools. It takes a broad sweep through findings stemming mainly from social and cognitive psychology and presents these findings in a useable format for students and teachers at all levels, from preschool to tertiary training institutes.

John Hattie is Professor and Director of the Melbourne Education Research Institute at the University of Melbourne, Australia, and Deputy Director of the Science of Learning Research Centre. He is the author of *Visible Learning* and *Visible Learning for Teachers*, and co-editor (with Eric Anderman) of the *International Guide to Student Achievement*, all published by Routledge.

Gregory C. R. Yates is a Senior Lecturer in Education at the University of South Australia. He is on the editorial board of *Educational Psychology* and has contributed a number of papers in the area of cognitive information processing and social learning theory.

Visible Learning and the Science of How We Learn

John Hattie and
Gregory C. R. Yates

 Routledge
Taylor & Francis Group

LONDON AND NEW YORK

First published 2014
by Routledge
2 Park Square, Milton Park, Abingdon, Oxon OX14 4RN

and by Routledge
711 Third Avenue, New York, NY 10017

Routledge is an imprint of the Taylor & Francis Group, an informa business

British Library Cataloguing in Publication Data
A catalogue record for this book is available from the British Library

Library of Congress Cataloging in Publication Data
A catalog record for this book has been requested

ISBN: 978-0-415-70498-4 (hbk)
ISBN: 978-0-415-70499-1 (pbk)
ISBN: 978-1-315-88502-5 (ebk)

Typeset in Bembo and Helvetica Neue
by Florence Production Ltd, Stoodleigh, Devon, UK
Printed and bound by CPI Group (UK) Ltd, Croydon, CR0 4YY

Contents

Acknowledgements   ix
Introduction   xi

PART 1   Learning within classrooms   1

1 Why don't students like learning at school? The Willingham
   thesis   3

2 Is knowledge an obstacle to teaching?   11

3 The teacher–student relationship   16

4 Your personality as teacher: can your students trust you?   26

5 Time as a global indicator of classroom learning   36

6 The recitation method and the nature of classroom learning   44

7 Teaching for automaticity in basic academic skill   52

8 The role of feedback   64

9 Acquiring complex skills through social modelling and explicit
   teaching   72

10 Just what does expertise look like?   84

11 Just how does expertise develop?   93

12 Expertise in the domain of classroom teaching   103

Part 2   Learning foundations   **111**

13 How knowledge is acquired   113

14 How knowledge is stored in the mind   126

15 Does learning need to be conscious, and what is the hidden
     role played by gesture?   136

16 The impact of cognitive load   146

17 Your memory and how it develops   157

18 Mnemonics as sport, art, and instructional tools   166

19 Analysing your students' style of learning   176

20 Multitasking: a widely held fallacy   187

21 Your students are digital natives. Or are they?   196

22 Is the Internet turning us into shallow thinkers?   201

23 How music impacts on learning   206

Part 3   Know thyself   **213**

24 Confidence and its three hidden levels   215

25 Self-enhancement and the dumb-and-dumber effect   228

26 Achieving self-control   243

27 Neuroscience of the smile: a fundamental tool in teaching   259

28 The surprising advantages of being a social chameleon   271

29 Invisible gorillas, inattentional blindness, and paying attention   281

30 Thinking fast and thinking slow: your debt to the inner robot   290

31 IKEA, effort, and valuing   306

Glossary   315
References   321
Index   343

Acknowledgements

The major theme in the *Visible Learning* books is making learning visible. This book is entirely devoted to the concept of learning. It is not a book about theories of learning, not about cognitive psychology, not a standard development of models of learning – but rather we discuss what learning looks like, how we can advance it, and some of the fascinating studies that have informed us about learning. The core notions of learning in this book relate to developing skills and strategies in concentration, deliberate practice, persistence, and knowing what to do when one does not know what to do – and emphasise that these skills can be taught (there is no need to drug our children if they do not have these skills).

There are three major sections: 'Learning within classrooms', 'Learning foundations', and 'Know thyself'. The individual chapters evolved from many discussions between us, and through the magic of Skype and Dropbox we have had wonderful debates about how best to present ideas that are core to our thinking about learning. Greg is based in South Australia and John in Melbourne (an eight-hour driving distance), but we started this over a six-month period when both of us were based in Auckland, New Zealand. Then to the details, the writing, the choice of themes and studies, and decisions about how best to present in a writing style aimed to entice readers into the delights of the world of learning.

Many people contributed to the development of this book. Foremost are our partners – Janet and Shirley – it was their support, their constant imperatives to get on with it, their tolerance of two codgers spending hours on a machine talking and dwelling in their esoterica – while they pursued their own esoterica. Also thanks to those we learnt most from – Joel, Kyle, Kieran, Bobbi, Jimmy, Milton, Richard, Catherine, and Trenton.

Others read various chapters, made suggestions, and provided other studies – we thank Terry Bowles, Debra Masters, and Debbie Price. Patricia Alexander prompted us in many discussions over wine and good food (as well as singing 'Summertime' at John and Janet's recent wedding, held after their 27 year courtship). Janet Rivers, as with the other two *Visible Learning* books, provided stupendous editing of our final draft and once again provided insights, flow, and changes that seemed so obvious once she advised us. Bruce Roberts from Taylor and Francis gave us support throughout and once again made the whole process from the publishing side seem easy. Of course, we are responsible for any errors in this book – and yes, they can be opportunities to continue to learn.

Introduction

The overarching theme introduced through the initial *Visible Learning* (VL) book is that achievement in schools is maximised when teachers see learning through the eyes of students, and when students see learning through the eyes of themselves as teachers. In the second book, *Visible Learning for Teachers* (VLT), these themes relating to learning were expanded to identify the major aspects of school life that lead to this maximising learning.

These aspects started with the mind frames of the adults in the school (the leaders, teachers, paraprofessionals) with a particular emphasis on a mindset of '*Know thy impact*'. That is, when teachers focus on their impact it begs a set of operating questions: for instance, '*Impact on what?*', '*What magnitude of impact, and impact with how many students?*'

The VL synthesis asks for teachers to see themselves as evaluators of their impact, and as change agents purposely setting up conditions to impact on learning. This approach entails teachers seeking feedback about their impact and then modifying actions in light of this feedback. In turn, this will create dialogues to 'hear' learning as it is happening, so as to create the following agenda:

a to encourage teachers to set appropriate challenges based on a clear understanding of where the student is currently and where they next need to accomplish;

b to have high expectations that *all* students can learn;

c to welcome error as opportunities to learn; and

d to be passionate about, and to promote, the language of learning.

These overarching themes are clearly a learning agenda with the focus on the learner – the learner being both the student and the teacher.

One part of developing this language of learning is for teachers to be critical planners, using learning intentions and success criteria, aiming for surface and deep outcomes, and ensuring they communicate these notions of success to the students. Both teachers and students can share in the learning task, moving from where they are towards where they want to be. As important, VLT emphasised the role of teachers as adaptive learning experts – by inviting them to create trusting environments between them and the students and between the students as well, to teach students to use multiple strategies, to develop skills in deliberate practicing, to know when and how to concentrate, to develop confidence in learning, to have multiple learning strategies, and to give and receive feedback about learning.

These themes are emphasised throughout the present book, and especially through examining and interpreting what the scientific research literature is able to inform us about optimal learning processes. The depth and extent of this contemporary research is one aspect that made an impression on us as we began reading the literature and gathering information for this book.

It should be clear that learning is a common denominator. It is in the title of the two earlier books and is emphasised again in this current one. But this theme is too often absent from discussions about schooling. Instead the focus of discussion is too often about teaching; this is not to say that teaching is unimportant, but the purpose of teaching surely relates to learning – learning by the student and by the teacher. The decline of educational psychology in many teacher education programs, the more recent emphasis on curriculum and assessment, and the lack of a debate about models of learning in our teacher literature does not help. It seems that many of those involved in our profession would struggle to name two competing learning theories, let alone defend a notion of learning (and by this we do not mean defending activities that students 'do' but how they learn). Perhaps the jargon of learning theories has not helped, and we have tried not to use some of this jargon in this book. But as argued in the first two VL books, the analysis of learning lies at the heart of our business.

Within the recent past educators have been able to improve the conditions under which we teach our students, and thus have provided greater opportunities for more students to achieve and even exceed their expectations. But the nature of learning has barely changed. Learning involves developing sufficient surface knowledge (an idea or ideas) to form conceptual understanding (by relating ideas and extending ideas). Many times, this learning comes out of conflict, such as confronting the unfamiliar, being in challenging situations, and when we are invited to resolve problem situations. Such problem solving can lead to learning more, learning different, learning connections, and overlearning (such that what we do and think becomes automatic).

Learning starts from what we already know, and proceeds toward where we want to be. The argument in VL is that the more teachers understand the prior status of the student, and the more they are aware of the nature of success (and if this is communicated to students so much the better), then the greater the probability of learning happening. The process of teaching therefore is providing ways of moving from the prior or starting position to the success criteria. This process may involve exposing students to new knowledge, engaging students in problem solving, playing with new concepts, exploring new relations, confronting misunderstandings, and correcting errors in ideas or understanding. It also involves deliberate practice, rehearsal, error, reteaching, listening, trying, exploring, and so on.

Of course, it helps when students want to learn, want to be challenged, and want to attain the success criteria from the series of lessons (e.g., putt one stroke less than current; differentiate an equation), and have an intention to implement the power of thinking. This invokes the Goldilocks principle of not making the challenge or success too hard or too easy relative to where the student currently is, or in fancier language we need to have strategic processing in learning towards success.

This book contains 31 separate chapters about learning and each can be read independently or stand alone. This book strives to build upon the foundation outlined in VL and VLT by moving more directly into what is known about learning. The science of learning has steadily progressed over the past century, and many firm findings have been documented. As noted, one essential message stemming from the VL synthesis is that teachers become more effective when they begin to see the learning process through the eyes of their students. Such a notion itself presumes that teachers possess and can act upon a strong understanding of what it means to learn. We hope that this book can contribute toward such an understanding.

While each chapter is relatively self-contained, there are many themes that run strongly through the various chapters. We can express these in terms of nine underlying principles:

Principle 1 *Explanations of human learning in terms of native ability, talent, or intelligence are severely constrained by one consistent and persistent finding: that substantial investments of time, energy, structured tuition, and personal effort are all required in order to develop mastery in all knowledge domains investigated. Notions such as talent, ability, and intelligence exist as useful descriptive terms. But they are not sufficient to explain learning or achievement.* This theme is embedded within the following chapters: 1, 5, 7, 9, 10, 11, 12, 13, 14, and 19.

Principle 2 *We naturally learn from exposure to information detected by our senses. But to increase our knowledge base, this information has to possess a level of organization which matches how our minds are structured and organised — and our minds change in how we structure and organise as we age.* This powerful theme, concerning the role of prior knowledge in learning, is found in Chapters 1, 5, 6, 7, 8, 9, 12, 13, 14, 16, 17, 18, and 20.

Principle 3 *Our mind has severe and inherent limitations, as built-in characteristics. When these limitations are reached, through experiences or depletion, deep and meaningful processing becomes impossible, and only shallow learning will occur from that point.* The cognitive load principle is reflected in Chapters 1, 6, 9, 14, 15, 16, 17, 18, 20, 21, 26, 29, and 30.

Principle 4 *Human learners benefit enormously from social examples, from directed instruction, and from corrective feedback. Learning from exposure to the information provided by other people represents a fundamental aspect underpinning human* *adjustment and evolution; the more expert these 'other people' are in understanding the progression of learning, the more effective is the learning.* This idea, basic to social learning theory, runs through Chapters 3, 4, 5, 6, 7, 8, 9, 11, and 26.

Principle 5   *We will exert strong efforts to perform at a high level, calling upon hidden and guarded reserves of effort, once we become confident that worthwhile goals are achievable in the short term.* This basic motivational principle, that effort is a difficult trait to activate, and that its dynamics are poorly understood by many, is found in Chapters 1, 9, 24, 25, and 26. We are optimistic, however, that enhancing the confidence to invest effort can be taught and learned.

Principle 6   *Short-term goals are highly motivating. But they may exist in conflict with other long-term values we harbour. Hence, one of the key aspects of personal development and happiness involves learning and activating strategies that enable us to control impulses and delay gratification.* The key notion of personal regulation through self-control is highlighted in Chapters 26 and 30.

Principle 7   *Learners possess human traits requiring a consistent level of maintenance. These include ego esteem needs, as well as the need to synchronise actions with other people within the immediate social context.* This powerful idea runs through many chapters, including 1, 2, 3, 4, 24, 25, 26, 27, 28, and 31.

Principle 8   *Neurologically, we possess a remarkably social brain. This evolved organ becomes a tool enabling us to react to the physical presence of others, to learn from information they dispense, and to become familiar with the characteristics of up to 150 individuals within our wider social world.* The social brain hypothesis surfaces in different guises within chapters 3, 4, 15, 17, 27, 28, and 30.

Principle 9   *Within both public and professional domains, fallacious ideas of human learning continue to be promoted despite being contradicted by available scientific opinion and evidence. Many such fallacies are potentially destructive and driven by false promises, pecuniary interests, or an over-reliance on anecdotes.* We highlight several such fallacies in Chapters 19, 20, 21, 22, and 23.

How to use this book

Each chapter provides a review of a topical area of research. Emphasis is not upon the traditional literature review as you would expect to find within professional journals. For instance, readers quickly will note how we have attempted to relegate actual researchers' names to the *Reference Notes* section (to be found at the end of each chapter), but then, within the chapters, focus on actual findings. The chapters provide commentaries that best reflect the existent body of scientific research as we read this literature. This claim is based on our collective experience of some 75 years in the field, teaching and researching within educational psychology and allied disciplines.

In writing, stress was placed on identifying what is securely known about a given phenomenon, what has been discovered or uncovered over time but which constitutes information meaningful from the perspective of an instructor.

We conceive of instructors as people charged with responsibilities involving deliberate social and educative influence over other human beings. An instructor could be a classroom teacher, a teacher educator, a school principal, a university lecturer, a textbook writer, a parent, a computer tutoring program, an office manager, a military trainer, a factory supervisor, a manager, a company executive, or a counsellor.

Giving and receiving instruction is an inevitable aspect of human life. Yet it is strange just how few of those centrally involved in teaching others to learn actually know about the interpersonal and psychological processes that underscore successful learning in the natural world. Nevertheless, an impressive body of scientific research published within the past decade has uncovered many aspects to the process that went unrecognised previously. Many of the findings give considerable support to the VL synthesis: that learning proceeds soundly when instructors become demonstrably aware of the learning needs and goals of the individuals expected to benefit from the interaction.

This book provides a perspective based upon contemporary evidence-based analyses. This is not a monograph on 'how to teach'. Instead it reviews what we know about processes that underpin learning. The VL notion is not a new brand by any means. Instead, it attempts a synthesis based on valid, tried, and perhaps traditional approaches, as aligned with mainstream scientific thinking and publishing. Hence, we highlight and draw upon many key notions such as social learning theory, motivation theory, and information processing theories as representing the finest summary statements of known findings. We also draw upon notions such as the social brain hypothesis and evolutionary thinking that stem more from biological considerations.

The reference notes provide a detailed listing of citations to the scientific literature. We specifically sought to identify readings that are accessible, well-written, and that represent contemporary knowledge within each topic area. We favoured more accessible papers over more 'academic' materials wherever this was possible. We wrote each chapter in the belief that it can be used as a summary statement of existing knowledge, but also as a source of reference to the wider known literature.

The three parts of this book

The *first part* delves straight into learning within the classroom. We start with the challenging notion that the mind may not designed for thinking, as it is slow and effortful and outcomes of thinking are often uncertain. Excellent teachers therefore need to understand thinking, realise how difficult many tasks are for beginners, and find ways to encourage students to build confidence and invest effort to learn various strategies to thus think and learn. It is less about the 'knowledge' to be learnt but more about the ways to progress from not knowing to knowing. This means that many of us as learners need a trusting, fair and safe environment to acknowledge that we 'do not know' and will make errors in learning. Such learning takes time but one of the teacher's roles is to maximise the efficiency of the time available, to provide many opportunities to learn the same ideas over time, and to ensure time is spent on learning and not merely doing 'something'. It can be most powerful for teachers to construct dialogues in classrooms if for no other reason than they can then 'hear the learning', whereas, too often, classrooms are dominated by monologue and recitation.

It may seem ironic, but we are successful in learning when we forget our learning! Most of us forget how we learnt to walk, talk, and do arithmetic. Good spellers 'know' when a word is misspelled but forget how they learnt to make these distinctions. This underscores the importance of overlearning, or teaching for automaticity. Because we can only place so much load on our cognitive skills, we need much overlearning before we can learn more complex tasks. This is a major reason why we need explicit teaching to not only learn the ideas but also to relate these ideas and see connections, relationships, or 'coat-hangers' between the ideas. Complex learning rarely happens by osmosis, discovery, or having a 'guide on the side'.

There is expertise in those who can teach others to learn, and expertise should not be confused with experience. There is a long and rich history of evidence about expertise that is reviewed, and we emphasise the importance of deliberate practice, which generally requires an expert teacher or coach to ensure it is leading to success and not a mindless skill exercise. We take particular interest in expertise in teaching and show how experts differ in many attributes from other competent teachers. Perhaps the most important finding is that experts, compared to experienced teachers have more success in deeper, as compared to surface, outcomes.

The *second part* outlines many of the major ideas that we know about learning. There is much agreement about various aspects of acquisition, memory retention, mental storage, and overload. We note that learning does not have to be conscious, that we have major limitations in how much we can think about at once, particularly when we are novices to a new set of ideas, that we need to develop a language and vocabulary of learning, and that we need multiple strategies of learning. Some of the more common notions often heard in our communities, however, are seriously questioned. These include learning styles (that different people think spatially, verbally, or kinaesthetically), Mozart effects, multitasking, digital natives, and overstated claims about how the Internet is changing how we think.

While the theme in the first two VL books is 'Know thy impact', the *third part* of the present book moves to 'Know thyself' with respect to learning. After decades of research, there are many key findings relevant to such a notion. Higher self-esteem, we note, follows success more clearly than it predicts success, and we need to place more emphasis on building the learner's *confidence* in being able to attain the success criteria. One of the dilemmas is that most of us have positive views of ourselves. When we do not know something, how to do something, or struggle to learn then we can build explanations for this so as to maintain our positive view of ourselves (e.g., I am not *able*, rather than I did not put in enough *effort*). Sometimes our beliefs about our learning can inhibit further learning and we need others who can show that we indeed can invest in learning although we may need much safety as our beliefs about ourselves can get in the way of this investment.

There are many social aspects of learning – the climate of trust to welcome errors in learning, the teacher and peer relations, and the beliefs about ourselves and confidence to succeed. This entails developing an ability to delay gratification, to create space to 'not know', and to develop aspects of self-control to see learning as not about me as '*a personality*', but about me as '*a learner*'. This involves how we set mood, how much our personal goals relate to the learning goals (often imposed by others such as teachers), how much we want to mimic others who are learners, and how successful we are at attending to the learning.

There are so many distractions in most learning situations and thus learning and knowing how to attend is important. But we cannot devote our mental resources to attending all the time – it is tiring. There is a skill in knowing when to think, what to attend to, and when to stop thinking to save cognitive resources. We need to know when to think fast and when to think slowly. Often struggling students are asked to think slowly for too long and become over taxed, and they can then fall further behind those who know when to think slow or think fast. Like all of us, struggling learners then build up ways of learning that may be inefficient, but keep using these ways because they know how to apply them – even when these ways of learning can be inefficient, not adaptive to the situation, and the outcomes of this inefficient learning can then confirm why they are not strong learners, at least within the classroom!

This book is based on the fundamental premises of the VL and VLT books: learning is optimised when teachers see learning through the eyes of the learner, and when learners see themselves as their own teachers. As the songwriter Phil Collins noted: in learning you will teach, and in teaching you will learn.

Learning within classrooms

1

Why don't students like learning at school?

The Willingham thesis

Why don't students like school? This simple question was posed by noted educational writer Daniel Willingham in his 2009 book of the same title. A simple question, yes. But as we attempt to answer it, we can learn a good deal about the human condition, about learning, about how motivation works, and also about our own minds.

It is important to recognise that Dr Willingham was not suggesting that students actively dislike school. In fact, there is no serious evidence indicating that students, on average, dislike going to school. This aspect has been known since the 1920s, when research surveys were first carried out in this area. The findings remain much the same today. Researchers ask students how much they like school by inviting them to respond to items on a survey instrument. Surveys typically allow responses along a 5-point scale such as −2, −1, 0, 1, and 2, where, minus 2 means *strongly dislike*, 0 stands for *neither like nor dislike*, and 2 means *strongly like*.

There is always an inevitably wide spread of scores, with about 10 per cent to 20 per cent of students ticking the negative or minus side. However, the mean comes out somewhere between 0 and 1. That is, on average, students neither love nor hate school. They tolerate school, or are mildly positive towards the experience. School remains an important aspect of their lives that provides numerous benefits. Overall, the picture is slightly more positive than negative.

A thesis close to the bone

Even so, Dr Willingham's question cuts disturbingly close to the bone. Teachers are frequently disappointed by the lack of student response to what ought to be richly stimulating activities and experiences. Student apathy and lack of motivation are frequently cited as factors underlying teacher stress, burnout, and lack of job satisfaction. Teachers work hard to provide engaging learning sequences designed to challenge young minds and make them think skilfully. This manifest apathy becomes a serious professional issue, faced by teachers every day, and which, on the individual level, stretches coping resources severely.

It is frustrating for teachers when the level of student response to carefully organised instructional materials is underwhelming compared with the time and effort invested in their preparation. To the beginning teacher, this is a hard lesson to learn. Whether we like it or not, we are human and depend on feedback we get from our students. How we interpret this feedback can determine how well we teach in the future, how motivated we are to go that extra mile. Every teacher has sacrificed a good deal to get to his or her position, and needs to affirm the journey has been worth the effort.

Surely, students ought to appreciate school more?

So let us view Willingham's question from a different perspective by asking: (a) Why do students not like school more? (b) Why does the average student naturally orient towards the middle attitudinal point? and (c) Why is learning at school so effortful for many students? As teachers and educators, the authors and likely readers of this book tended to enjoy school and its collateral benefits. Collectively, we understood what this game was about, how it was played. When we were students, many of us witnessed undesirable practices. So our generation of professional educators has worked hard to have such practices overturned. Our current crop of students have benefited from reforms and developments in modern attitudes and democratic practices. Such ideas ought to have made the experience of schooling more enjoyable, more stimulating, and considerably more positively affirming, than the experience of previous generations.

Whenever there are deceptively simple questions, there will be a multitude of answers that become possible. Some of these can be acknowledged quickly. Liking for school is aligned with social and emotional factors such as personality and social factors such as the number of friends the individual student has at the specific location. Being at school has numerous benefits. Schooling is an inherently social process, and the attitudes of peers exert a strong impact upon the individual. We tend to align our attitudes to the attitudes of people we perceive as similar to ourselves.

Similarly, family background and parental pressures will play a significant role. For example, in one South Australian study, it was found that students tended to report higher levels of enjoyment at school when their mothers had endorsed a parental style that encouraged children to take greater responsibility. This makes sense in that schools expect students to accept responsibility, so consistency between home and school appears to play a role. Girls often report liking school more than boys and higher ability students more so than lower ability students. Attitudes to school may dip as students move through the high school years, but have often been found to increase again in the senior school years.

Making them think: the demands of the classroom

The answer that Dr Willingham offers, however, in accounting for why students do not like school, is that the human brain does not naturally want to think. Indeed, he notes 'The mind is not designed for thinking' (2009, p. 3). This is a provocative argument that initially appears at odds with human characteristics. Thinking is supposedly one key attribute that makes us human. It is what we do naturally and spontaneously. It is the attribute that separates us from other species. Surely, we were born with this massive cerebral cortex specifically so that we could use it to think? From an idealistic view, thinking ought to be fun. Or, if not exactly fun, it ought to be at least inherently rewarding. We all can experience the pleasure in thinking well, in becoming competent, in solving problems, and taking pride in the successful outcomes of our mental work.

However, the notion that thinking is not great fun fits with a sizeable body of opinion within cognitive psychology. Indeed, this theme emerges in a later chapter about being in two minds (thinking fast and thinking slow), referred to as System 1 and System 2 (see Chapter 30). Thinking is a product of System 2, but this system is clunky, and its outputs can involve high levels of uncertainty.

So just why is thinking not much fun? For a start, it requires effort. Human beings are naturally resistant to squandering resources whenever effort is involved. However, do not think of this trait as laziness. Instead, it relates to a careful allocation of personal energies. Effort is a factor that has to be consistent with one's personal motivation and committed goals. Further, it is tied to one's **self-efficacy** level or confidence that we can succeed. To ask someone to invest effort is never a simple request. It involves a cost that they must consider in relation to other demands being placed upon the mind at the same moment in time. We are resource-limited creatures, but thinking uses up resources remarkably quickly. So to resist an invitation to think is not necessarily an indication of laziness. It could reflect a decision to be economical, cautious, or even prudent with our personal resources.

Thinking also involves high levels of uncertainty. There are too many unknowns in this deal. The dominant motive is often to conserve energy and so to avoid initiating actions when outcomes are uncertain. Since there is never any guarantee that thinking will result in a satisfactory result, any invitation to think brings along with it an invitation to be punished through failing to live up to expectations.

Avoiding failure is a robustly strong motive, several times stronger than the motive to obtain an objectively similar level of positive success or reward. Such notions are expressed in terms of two well validated cognitive principles: (a) whenever called on to commit to decisions we are risk-averse and (b) bad is stronger than good.

Difficulties in using the knowledge in our heads

Furthermore, there is the interesting problem of mental **availability**. Such availability refers to the mind's ability to have appropriate information on hand and sufficient cognitive resources to deal with the problem at hand. Thinking relies directly on our ability to access information held within long-term memory. Our judgements are linked into, and will be strongly biased towards, whatever information we can immediately recall. But one of the most important attributes of any stored information is the *ease* that it can be accessed with and then processed. When information is not easily forthcoming, people feel uncomfortable, less confident, and less motivated to act.

Whenever the mind is stressed by difficult recall demands then the fact that difficulties are experienced itself becomes a factor determining how people use the information recalled. As shown in the research of social psychologist Norbet Schwarz, **ease of access** can produce strange effects. For instance, in one study he asked people to recall past incidents when they were assertive, and then asked them to rate how assertive they were themselves. Half the people were asked to recall 6 incidents, but the other half was asked to recall 12 incidents. People who recalled 6 incidents rated themselves as *more* assertive than those who recalled 12 incidents. Why? Because it easy to recall 6 such incidents. It is hard to recall 12. Within your mental world, the difficulty of recall determines the value and meaningfulness of the experience. Difficulty of recall becomes more important than the volume recalled. It is known that as information becomes difficult to recall, it becomes unlikely to influence one's active thinking. Much validity can be expressed in the popular adage 'out of sight, out of mind'.

We are motivated by knowledge gaps, but put off by knowledge chasms

Central to Dr Willingham's argument is the role played by curiosity. We are naturally curious animals, well motivated to find out more about our world. While this sounds wonderful, there is a huge constraint placed upon such motivation. *We are highly selective in what we pay attention to.* This selectivity creates a major problem whenever we expect another person to exert effort in learning or thinking. Any such thinking, as driven by natural curiosity, has to involve successful levels of comprehension, skill mastery or problem solving. There simply is no such thing as 'general curiosity'. It is something that works only when turned on.

We cannot be curious about all possible things: instead, we are attuned to **knowledge gaps**. We will seek out and pay attention to things we already know about in an effort to increase our personal knowledge base. But we do so provided the knowledge gap itself is perceived as bridgeable within the short term. In allocating our personal resources, this factor is critical. We strive to close worthwhile gaps, but not chasms. Most of us have little interest in how devices such as computers and radios work. We are unmotivated to find out since the perceived knowledge gap is too high to stimulate interest. We are not motivated by relative ignorance, or by our general lack of knowledge. This lack of motivation to learn things we know little about has been demonstrated even in intelligent college students in laboratory studies.

But we become curious when we can see both (a) a knowledge gap relevant to us, together with (b) the means by which it can be closed. Paradoxically, having some prior knowledge provides impetus for wanting to acquire even more knowledge. This effect is strong if the new knowledge can be acquired in the short term with relatively low cost. Metaphorically speaking, when we build our knowledge, we invest effort most strongly when foundations are already securely laid down. But we show disinclination to start construction when there is nothing to build upon.

We rely on memory, rather than thinking

One major plank of the Willingham thesis is that much human functioning relies on activating memory, rather than thinking. By nature, we try to avoid thinking but strive to solve problems by using our memories. As Willingham bluntly put it, 'The mind is not designed for thinking' (2009, p. 3). So what is the mind designed for? It is possible to note several areas in which the brain naturally excels. This curious list includes (a) the bipedal gait and balancing the moving body over undulating terrain, (b) using visual information to make complex assessments and judgements involving time, distance, and space, (c) developing a receptive vocabulary of about a quarter of a million words, (d) instantly being able to name between 20,000 and 30,000 common objects, (e) being able to recognise and attach names to several thousand individual faces, (f) being able to use social cues to accurately assess the mental states of others, along with (g) being able to hold a conversation taking into account another person's orientations, timings, dispositions, and intentions. Note how (e), (f), and (g) are consistent with the **social brain hypothesis**. This is the notion that we have evolved large brains that enable us to establish and maintain crucial social relationships, an idea that will resurface in several chapters of this book (specifically Chapters 3, 4, 8, 15, 17, 27, 28, and 30).

The ability to think well, to learn efficiently, and solve problems successfully are attributes that do not figure in most descriptions of natural human adroitness. A philosopher might argue that some do think well. But this is not an argument that can be pushed far. Certain individuals can be seen as the products of a well-socialised 'thinking community', such as highly intellectual families or institutions that have sponsored high levels of academic achievement. But this is not the general human condition. Instead, humans naturally assimilate the vast bulk of their knowledge through direct social influence processes that do not make great demands on thinking capabilities.

This notion is taken up by the science writer, Michael Shermer, who, in summarising the research into how we think, described the brain as a 'belief machine' (2011, p. 5). We form beliefs through social learning factors, and then learn how to defend them, particularly if we perceive them to be under attack from other social agents who do not share our same views. In jocular vein, Shermer noted that Homo rationalis – the species that carefully weighs all decisions through hard logic and rational data analysis – 'is not only extinct, but probably never existed' (p. 343).

How schooling differs from previous social learning

We can see where these ideas are leading. Although mental work is a natural human capacity, nevertheless, many students are unlikely to be comfortable thinking for themselves. From their earliest years, their home backgrounds required them to copy adults and learn closely from them. While they have mastered a complex language, the focus of life has been to assimilate the tools of the culture in such a way as to store vital elements of information within their personal memory banks. This has been the major effort in their lives, and a singularly important goal: to build a repository of social and interpersonal skills enabling them to read human interactions with great sensitivity and intelligence. Thus, instead of attempting to *go beyond the information given*, the major achievement has to be able to *assimilate the information given*. Suddenly asking young students to begin to think beyond what is immediately visible is a request out of sync with their personal developmental histories.

IN PERSPECTIVE: Evaluating the Willingham thesis

We can summarise the Willingham thesis in the following six ideas: (a) your mind is not naturally well-suited for thinking, (b) as an activity involving the brain, thinking is slow, effortful, and has uncertain outcomes, (c) deliberate or conscious thinking does not guide most people's behaviour in the real world in which they have to interact and survive, (d) instead, our brains rely on memory, and follow paths that we have taken before, or seen others undertake, (e) although we are curious creatures, our interests are restricted to areas in which we have some prior knowledge coupled with confidence in our ability to learn, and finally (f) we are unwilling to invest any serious level of effort in thinking activities until we can perceive the link between immediate effort expenditure and likely success.

In addition, we can also note that when thinking occurs, its content is influenced strongly by whatever the working memory can access immediately. The quality of thinking drops away quickly once **cognitive load** increases beyond four items (see Chapter 16). Not only is the human brain relatively unaccustomed to thinking, but its ability to do so well is very much limited by the ease it can retrieve items from the long-term memory system. This scenario is then further complicated by the average student's lack of confidence. Not only is the student (a) unsure that it is worth investing mental resources in activities that may or may not be successful, but (b) the awareness of substantial knowledge gaps between what he knows currently and what the teacher wants him to know can become a recipe for discouraging any natural curiosity.

To state the Willingham view bluntly: teachers are confronted with a roomful of students whose minds are designed not for thinking, but for saving themselves from needing to think. The thesis is not that students cannot think. It is that thinking in a 'school way' is not what comes naturally or happily for many individuals. Asking them to think about issues becomes an uncomfortable experience. But when it comes to complex learning and thinking, we err in assuming students will do so with enthusiasm and aplomb. Thinking means considering different perspectives. It means withholding impulses and avoiding making judgments in the absence of data. It means allowing evidence and research to overtake prejudice and opinion. It means an openness of mind to ideas that your students may never have encountered before. For many students, these are heavy expectations that may well stand in direct contrast to what their homes have expected of them to this point.

Throughout this book we draw upon a cognitive theory of the human mind consistent with Dr Willingham's basic ideas. One key notion (covered in Chapter 30) is that our brains are set up with two operating systems, a fast-operating System 1 that relies upon well learned habits and routines, and a slow-operating System 2 that can be brought into play when the automated system fails. But, System 2 brings with it costs, uncertainties, and discomfort. It is much easier to travel the path of least resistance, and remain within one's comfort zone. Many struggling students are asked to invoke System 2 thinking often throughout the day, and this is tiring, threatening, and does not always lead to sufficient 'overlearning' that would then allow the faster System 1 to be used. As Dr Willingham would assert, expecting students to stop relying on their fast acting system (System 1) and getting them to use effort to change anything already stored in their minds, or to add to what is already there, represents a substantial challenge for any teacher.

Study guide questions

1 Do students like school? What has been the answer to this question, one that seems surprisingly constant over some 90 years of research, ever since survey research was invented?

2 Notwithstanding the traditional answer to the above question, just what professional issue was Dr Willingham addressing?

3 Willingham alleged that 'the mind is not designed for thinking'. How easy or difficult is it for you, as a professional educator, to accept such an apparently dismal proposition?

4 The present chapter extends this notion by noting that thinking is an activity demanding high levels of effort. Since effort is a limited resource, an invitation to think implies precisely what?

5 Besides effort, an additional issue is referred to as mental availability. The mind wants to use and act upon only that knowledge which it can access immediately. How does this factor work against our educational goals?

6 Although all people are naturally curious, this motive will hit its head against a hugely constraining factor. What is this?

7 If one accepts that the mind is not designed for thinking, then just what is it designed for?

8 Overall, the Willingham thesis provides an interesting perspective on how teachers' goals naturally differ from the goals of their young students. So is the way forward to try to dispute the Willingham thesis, or to recognise its perspective and what it is telling us about student needs?

Reference notes

■ Dr Daniel Willingham is a significant writer within educational research and frequent contributor to the *American Educator*, the house journal for the American Federation of Teachers, writing under the banner 'Ask the cognitive scientist'. His 2009 book, *Why Don't Students like School?* (Willingham, 2009) is a stimulating read.

■ Students tolerate school, or are mildly positive. Support for such a notion is found across many studies including an Australian study (Ainley, Batten, Cherry, & Withers, 1998), a large British survey (Attwood, 2011), and a New Zealand study (Wylie, Hipkins, & Hodgen, 2008).

■ Student apathy creates stress for teacher (Geving, 2007; Tsouloupas, Carson, Matthews, Grawitch, & Barber, 2010).

■ South Australian study into mothers' support (Annear & Yates, 2010).

■ By default, we protect what we have. We are risk averse, and strongly avoid placing assets under threat (Kahneman, 2011). Bad is stronger than good (Baumeister, Bratslavsky, Finkenauer, & Vohs, 2001).

■ Ease of availability in cognition produces strange effects (Schwarz *et al.*, 1991).

■ Motivation through perceivable but closable knowledge gaps (Litman, Hutchins, & Russon, 2005; Loewenstein, 1994).

■ The brain as a belief machine (Shermer, 2011).

2

Is knowledge an obstacle to teaching?

To teach a topic or a skill, it is important to know the topic thoroughly. This idea would seem axiomatic, a virtual truism. The kindly mentor who teaches you chess must be familiar with the game, its goals, and basic moves. It makes inherent sense to assume that knowledge of a topic will enable an individual to teach that topic to others. This principle has been used in industry and virtually all forms of employment for several hundred years. Many areas of employment involve considerable levels of training, and instructors are drawn from the ranks of individuals deemed successful in plying their craft. Such ideas are incorporated in the rich notion of apprenticeship. The apprentice learns the craft through direct interpersonal contact with a master or expert. Within many fields, it is mandatory for experts to share their knowledge with newcomers.

But does disciplinary content knowledge really enable you to teach? A curious finding that has emerged repeatedly from the scientific literature is that teachers' actual depth of knowledge of the content of what is being taught bears little relationship to the attainment level of their students. This finding surely contradicts the underlying ideas expressed in the preceding paragraph?

We suggest you read this chapter in connection with Chapter 12, which describes expertise in the domain of teaching. This present chapter will take a different tack since expertise in teaching is distinct from expertise in knowledge about content material being taught. In reviewing the literature in this area, two strangely negative aspects appear to stand out:

a It is **not** the case that one can be a reasonable teacher when ignorant about what is to be taught.

b Possessing a high level of knowledge about a topic *does not* automatically bring with it the ability to teach this topic well. In fact, all too often, it is the reverse. The more you know about an area, the more difficult it can be to see the same area from another person's position.

Experts underestimate task difficulty for novices

A number of research studies have shown how experts in a field often experience difficulties when introducing newcomers to that field. For example, in a genuine training situation, Pamela Hinds (1999) found that people expert in using mobile phones were remarkably less accurate than novice phone users in judging how long it takes people to learn to use the phones. Experts can become insensitive to how hard a task is for the beginner, an effect referred to as the 'curse of knowledge'. Dr Hinds was able to show that as people acquired the skill, they then began to underestimate the level of difficulty of that skill. Her participants even underestimated how long it had taken themselves to acquire that skill in an earlier session. Knowing that experts forget how hard it was for them to learn, we can understand the need to look at the learning process through students' eyes, rather than making presumptions about how students 'should be' learning.

Experts can be poor in cueing and communicating

David Feldon (2007b) reviewed many studies indicating that experts frequently are poor communicators of what they are doing. Experts possess knowledge that is well organised but encapsulated in ways that can be understood only by people already familiar with their field. Experts can become great communicators once they follow highly structured and sequential procedures, but this is rarely the case. Their expertise has a basis in high levels of tacit knowledge that can be difficult to convey to another party. In this sense, tacit means unspoken, and possibly unknown. For instance, you can ride a bicycle quite expertly, but be absolutely unable to explain to someone just how you can do this. As has been demonstrated in controlled studies, people are unable to explain to others how to catch a ball.

Experts may not know exactly what they are doing since their skill is automated and unconscious. Indeed, Dr Feldon found that possessing a high level of expertise within a domain may become a *disadvantage* within a teaching context. Even when attempting to make it easy, experts still tend to leave out information a novice would find valuable. They fail to convey information in a step-by-step manner. They will employ a vocabulary that is relatively unfamiliar. Several studies have shown experts find it remarkably difficult to gauge how much knowledge a novice possesses.

In one laboratory study, Hinds, Patterson and Pfeffer (2001) asked senior graduate-level students in electronics (as experts) to design and record instructional materials for beginners on a circuit testing task. Another group was asked to do the same, but these people were less advanced students and hence were relative novices. The experts were found to teach using abstract statements and advanced-level ideas since these terms define their customary vocabulary. The novices taught at a more basic or procedural level, using concrete, and direct statements. The effect of these instructional differences was remarkable in that (a) the novices' instruction was *more effective* in teaching the task to total newcomers and (b) these newcomers then rated the experts as less effective teachers.

However, when it came to a task of transfer, those instructed by the experts were able to transfer their new skill to a second different task more quickly (but not any more accurately). It seems that the level of abstraction and complex language inherent in the manner experts talk and instruct other people can create initial problems in learning, although the effect is not always negative.

Students do appreciate knowledgeable teachers

What should we conclude about teacher subject knowledge as a determinant of student learning? First, it is a positive influence, as was found in the research as reviewed in VL (Hattie, 2009). However, its overall effect appears low.

Second, it is likely that its effect appears relatively greater in specialist curriculum such as science. This finding could reflect the fact that students do appreciate being taught by knowledgeable and motivated individuals, especially those who demonstrate passion for their subject matter. It has been established that students will rate their best teachers highly on traits such as competency, credibility, and fairness. Such traits appear more strongly linked to student motivation than to actual learning. Notably, students value the interaction and feedback received from teachers they recognise as clever and knowledgeable adults.

Studies under laboratory conditions have found that children learn less from adults they view as relatively ignorant individuals. After all, if a person knows only as much as you, or is incompetent, then he or she cannot serve as a source of learning. Although it is not crucial to be able to represent yourself as the 'know all' teachers or 'guru', nevertheless, it helps considerably when you can show strong levels of mastery coupled with a willingness to learn and increase your knowledge. It is apparent that one advantage of demonstrating clear and coherent knowledge, together with positive attitudes toward developing your knowledge further, is that your students will regard you as a credible and motivating teacher.

But as the research has now shown, there is a flipside. Problems can emerge when your strong depth of knowledge of a specific topic creates a gap between (a) what you know, how you can think, and what you can do, and (b) your students' current instructional needs. Mathematics educators have referred to such a discrepancy as the **expert blind spot effect**, since individuals who excelled at mathematics were found in one project to make poor judgements as to how mathematics content can to be taught within high school lessons. In itself, your mastery of subject matter does not allow you to easily teach this same content to others who are at a beginning point. At times your expertise will create obstacles that can make you less sensitive to students' needs.

IN PERSPECTIVE: What content knowledge does for a teacher

Despite what common sense and the industrial apprenticeship model suggest, knowing a topic thoroughly and deeply does not automatically translate into knowing how to present and teach that topic well in the first instance to beginners. A particular type of cognitive empathy gap can become apparent (see the next chapter for further analysis on the notion of empathy gaps between people).

However, it is not all bad. While you do not need to know everything, students still appreciate that their teachers are clever and capable people, and they will devalue any adult they see as lacking in basic competency. In particular, your depth of knowledge about a subject is of immense value when giving feedback to students and in evaluating the quality of their work. When your knowledge of an area is shallow, it is so much harder to detect and correct for errors, or to provide extra depth and elaboration when helping individuals develop in their understanding.

Hence, rather than being an essential prerequisite for conducting high quality group-level instruction, curriculum knowledge helps you to identify what is needed for an individual student to improve. Your curriculum knowledge enables you to diagnose individual learning problems, provide corrective instruction, and set new achievable goals. In short, depth of knowledge of the curriculum becomes critical in any situation calling for individual remediation and guidance. It is within this context that you can become sensitive to just how an individual is experiencing problems in understanding. As a knowledgeable teacher, when dealing with individuals, you are able to perceive knowledge gaps that are difficult to identify when teaching large groups.

Study guide questions

1   The apprenticeship model developed in the Middle Ages as a means of accomplishing several goals, such as maintaining and developing new crafts, accomplishing complex projects that demanded division of labour, inducting the new generation to take over, and ensuring that cultural knowledge and inventions would be transported across the entire society rapidly. The model still exists in teacher training. What are the assumptions that underpin the placement of preservice teachers in schools today?

2   In studying how instructors taught mobile phone skills, Pamela Hinds found direct evidence for the 'curse of knowledge'. What is this effect? What are the implications for how we may teach something that we ourselves can do so well?

3   After reviewing many studies, David Feldon noted that experts often have acute problems in communicating with beginners. What specific problems were found?

4 One study found that experts and novices do tend to teach in different ways. Just what are such differences? Did the learners prefer to be taught by experts or novices?

5 It has also been found that students clearly do value knowledgeable and competent teachers. In fact they resist trying to learn from any adult they see as incompetent. So where is the balance in all this? What traits should you strive to exhibit?

6 Although there is no necessary connection between knowing an area well and being able to teach it well within a whole class situation, nevertheless, there are many times when the depth of your curriculum knowledge is of incredible importance to you as a teacher. Just when is this the case?

Reference notes

■ Teacher's content knowledge predicts student learning only weakly, if at all. See VL, pp. 113–115 (Hattie, 2009).

■ Experts underestimate how difficult a task is for beginners (Hinds, 1999).

■ Experts are often poor communicators (Feldon, 2007a, 2007b; Hinds, Patterson, & Pfeffer, 2001; Nückles, Wittwer, & Renkl, 2005; Wittwer, Nückles, & Renkl, 2008).

■ The difficulty of explaining to another person how to catch a ball: not only do you not know how you do it, but instructions you give to others will fix upon incorrect variables (Reed, McLeod, & Dienes, 2010).

■ Young children resist learning from people they see as ignorant (Sabbagh & Shafman, 2009; Sobel & Corriveau, 2010).

■ Students appreciate having knowledgeable teachers: see the Longitudinal Survey of Australian Youth (Underwood, Rothman, & ACER, 2008).

■ Experts have blind spots (Nathan & Petrosino, 2003; Wittwer & Renkl, 2008).

■ The role of teacher knowledge in diagnosing individual progress and adjusting instruction (Wittwer, Nückles, Landmann, & Renkl, 2010).

3

The teacher–student relationship

Before looking into the teacher–student relationship, it is useful to consider findings from the study of interpersonal relationships in general. In particular, one key phenomenon studied has been the *empathy gap*. An empathy gap occurs when people are relatively unable to put themselves in the place of another person. When warm and secure, it is difficult to conceive of another person's pain and insecurities. If you have never been bullied, it is hard to imagine the pain. People who have been bullied, or socially rejected, rate these experiences as severely painful. Others, who have not had such experiences, underestimate the level of hurt. It is not easy to empathise with someone whose shoes you have never walked in.

Similarly, individuals in powerful positions underestimate how others can be affected adversely by their decisions. Studies into aggression have shown that perpetrators are adroit in using a number of powerful defences. Aggressors excuse themselves, justify the actions undertaken, underestimate how much hurt they have inflicted on the other party, and blame the victim for his or her situation. On the other hand, their victims view perpetrators with resentment, anger, and experience a desire for retribution that may increase over time.

Such gaps in perceptions create the basis for deterioration in relationships through **negative escalations**, sometimes called **snowball effects** or **negative cascades**. A minor hurt leads to a retaliation, which is seen by the original instigator as out of proportion to his sin, which thereby justifies further aggression. We have all witnessed unfortunate situations where relationships break down due to escalations. Indeed, consequences can be tragic. Where people are locked into relationships, such as parent–child, then escalations can take the form of becoming so highly aversive towards the other party that havoc, social pathology, or self-damage may ensue.

Toward positive relationships

Thankfully, coercive relationships are rare. For the most part, we can work on the positive side. Behavioural escalations readily work to establish and maintain rich social relationships of mutual benefit. There are sound reasons for teachers to be concerned with developing high quality relationships with their students. A sizable body of research studies has found that the early years of school represent a critical period in the development of an individual's life adjustment pattern. Establishing positive relationships between young students and their teachers has been shown to cascade and so result in lasting benefits involving trust and affection.

For example, Erin O'Connor and others (2011) tracked 1,364 students across the school years into early adolescence. Teachers rated the quality of their relationships with each student in terms of closeness, warmth, and absence of conflict. Positive teacher–student relationships in the early years (a) predicted reduced levels of externalising and antisocial behaviour in these students, and also (b) served to prevent students who began school with initial levels of internalising (such as worry and emotional problems) from developing long-term trajectories of behavioural problems.

The notion that teacher–student relationships have enduring effects was supported by a recent American study that used a professional development training model to induce teachers to focus on improving relationships with their students at the high-school level. It was found that marked improvements in student achievement occurred not in the year the program was carried out, but in the year *following* the intervention, with student grades improving nine percentile points in the targeted students. The trained teachers were observed to improve the way they interacted with their classes, and this was found to have a deferred, rather than immediate, effect upon student learning and motivation.

Closeness and conflict

The work of Dr Robert Pianta has indicated that teacher–student relationships in the early school years can be described in terms of two dimensions: **closeness** and **conflict**. Closeness refers to the emotional context of teaching interactions. A sample item from the research questionnaire, as completed by teachers, is 'If upset, this student will seek comfort from me'. Closeness appears more under the teacher's control. It has been established that when teacher–student relationships are characterised by closeness, students show greater levels of overall school adjustment relative to peers rated as scoring at the lower end of this dimension.

On the other hand, conflict refers to the teacher's tendency to endorse such items as 'Dealing with this student drains my energy'. The research has found that teacher-reported conflict correlates with students' school avoidance, unwillingness to undertake school-like tasks, decreases in pro-social behaviour, as well as increases in aggressive behaviour. Besides such clear findings, we must add that, virtually by definition, conflict adds considerably to levels of teacher stress and reduced job satisfaction. It has also been found that teachers who report lower levels of professional satisfaction, and also those who are observed to provide lower levels of emotional support for students, do report considerably higher overall levels of conflict than other teachers.

Of course, we must be careful not to over interpret this type of child developmental research finding. Although such studies display relationships, we must be ever cautious about assigning cause and effect. It would be unfortunate to hold that teacher–student relationships cause poor social and academic adjustments within the student population. When a teacher reports a child as 'draining my energy', then the teacher is likely to be responding to a genuine context, possibly associated with the child's presenting characteristics. The teacher's dilemma is not to overreact to students who present with such traits. The existence of the difficult-to-teach child is well recognised in educator's parlance, but does not justify negative escalations.

Developing positive and close relationships becomes difficult if the focus is on responding to uncooperative individuals. There is danger in moving into punitive mode too quickly. Research into social psychology has found that when people disguise emotions, a good deal of **emotional leakage** still occurs. Efforts to hide emotions often fall short, and even when striving to be polite to someone you find uncooperative, some level of leakage may occur. For instance, your tone of voice may be inflected (unwittingly) high, suggesting anxiety, sarcasm, or insincerity.

No major theory of learning recommends moving into punitive modes in response to students' lack of cooperation, and this strategy is counter-indicated by a large body of findings. For instance, one Australian survey found that when high school students are disciplined, they attribute the event to the teacher ('teacher hates me', 'teacher picks on me') rather than accept personal responsibility. This is not the place to delve into classroom management research, and citations to this literature are found in the reference notes for this chapter. But the simple, thoroughly validated, proposition is that aversive control methods such as punishment, criticism, shouting, sarcasm, belittlement, or overt rudeness, are tactics that produce only a superficial level of student compliance.

In terms of managing your classroom, negative tactics are ultimately self-defeating. Compliance is not a strong educational goal, especially if achieved to the detriment of other more important educational goals. Application of aversive methods in any interpersonal situation triggers strong emotions and motivations in recipients. Such motivations take the form of resentment, anger, general negativity, helplessness, and passivity, which thereby provide impetus for on-going negative escalations.

School as a buffer

The quality of the relationship that a student has with you is likely to be an important factor in that student's well-being. Clinical research has often reported that children who present with developmental problems tend to be relatively more dependent than others on the available adults within their wider social worlds. Close and supportive relationships with teachers have the potential to mitigate the risk of negative outcomes for children who may otherwise have difficulty adjusting and succeeding in school. Surveys have shown that relationships with teachers can serve to operate as a protective factor against risk for a range of problems, including anti-social predispositions.

When a child has an unsupportive home environment, the school context becomes a major source of social and cultural learning. It is within this scenario that teacher–student relationships exert a strongly influential role in personal development. Individual teachers, without realising it, can serve as effective role models for students who experience less than adequate adult models within their wider social and family life.

School as moderator of developmental trajectories

A sensible perspective on what the research into relationship factors reports is inherent in the notion of *moderation*. Metaphorically, the idea of moderation is that of a switch. When the switch is in one position, good things tend to happen with relative ease. One good thing can flow directly onto another good thing. Further, certain aspects that seem heading toward negative directions may be slowed or stopped altogether, i.e., the buffer effect kicks in. A student who presents with relatively poor developmental traits may encounter positive teacher–student relationships that then reset the likely trajectory pattern of his or her life. Finding positive factors operating within the school environment buffers the child from otherwise predictable but adverse life patterns.

But what if that switch has *not* been set into the more favourable position? Then opportunities are missed, positive events are less likely to interact with, and support each other, and developmental trajectories can proceed as though nothing of importance has happened. In the absence of positive relationships, the student may fail to identify with the goals and purposes of schooling. Our goal as educators is to have a positive impact. Hence, we strive to set the moderation switch away from passive or neutral mode, and into positive agency mode. Actively working towards developing positive teacher–student relationships becomes a primary goal, one that establishes your professional standing, and allows you to have a strong effect on the lives of your students.

Shifting the switch across

Is it possible to shift the switch to a position where good things happen? The most direct answer is that this is what excellent teachers do all the time through their positive interpersonal behaviour. Positivity can apply in dealing with the class in general, but also in particular whenever a teacher interacts with individual students. As noted earlier in this chapter, professional development can be used to focus on developing teacher–student relationships.

Another interesting approach was investigated in an experimental study by Driscoll and Pianta (2010). Over a six-week period they asked early childhood teachers to spend additional time, just several minutes each day, with individual at-risk students. These were brief sessions devoted to non-directive child-centred activities. Although this short-term intervention study did not show any immediate effects on the students, the study found that the teachers' views on the students changed in the positive direction. In addition, the researchers found positive changes in the teachers' self-reported closeness with these targeted students. It makes much sense to conclude that the quality of teacher–student relationships can depend on how much time teachers interact with individual students in a non-coercive and friendly manner. A few minutes regularly listening to individual students can make a major difference in their lives.

Thus the evidence shows that positive school relations can buffer the child from the likely effects of less than optimal experiences in their homes. It is also important to acknowledge, however, another side to this coin. It is also known that positive attitudes and expectations from parents will affect their children in a manner somewhat independently from teacher effects. In one American study into educational achievement outcomes in students from low income families with young adolescents, it was found that positive family support and expectations generated by mothers counteracted the effect of low expectations expressed by their teachers. The researchers noted directly and dramatically the 'evidence that even in the face of low teacher expectations, some youth fare well. For these youth, mother expectations play a critical role in buffering some of the negative effects of low teacher expectations' (Benner & Mistry, 2007, p. 151).

So we find that (a) positive student–teacher relationships can buffer effects associated with poor home background factors, and (b) good home and parental factors can buffer effects associated with less-than-optimal teacher–student relationships. But furthermore, Benner and Mistry established that students with the most favourable educational outcomes enjoyed congruence between the home and school. That is, positive relationships and expectations stemming from *both* parents and teachers predicted just who the most successful students were. The worst outcomes were associated with low expectations from both parents and teachers. Such research findings give strong support to the notion that *every child needs a significant adult* to express positive regard in him or her.

IN PERSPECTIVE: Why teacher–student relationships are important throughout childhood and adolescence

The existence of the inevitable empathy gap can make us less sensitive to the reality that students place value on their relationships with the immediate people who teach them. When relationships are positive so are developmental patterns over time. One of the surprising findings stemming from Dr Pianta's extensive research programme concerns the impact of initial student–teacher relationships over the entire schooling period. Follow-up studies show students who have the advantage of establishing positive relationships with their teachers from their initial contacts with the school

---

system continue to show such advantages a decade later. The benefits of positive teacher–student relationships are persistent and profound, and appear to follow positive escalation patterns. Positive relationships produce good experiences, and good experiences promote positive relationships.

A major reason for developing closeness and reducing conflict is to build the trust needed for most learning. Learning requires considerable investment. It requires confidence that we can learn, it requires an openness to new experiences and thinking, and it requires understanding that we might be wrong, we may make errors, and we will need feedback. Learning for many students is a risky business. The positive teacher–student relationship is thus important not so much because this is worthwhile in itself, but because it helps build the trust to make mistakes, to ask for help, to build confidence to try again, and for students to know they will not look silly when they don't get it first time.

We began this chapter by noting the empathy gap research. We will close by citing other pertinent findings that stem from this same area in social psychology. It is a common finding that people will quickly extend a level of empathy to people they perceive as similar to themselves, but not to those seen as different. People's feelings of empathy closely follow group allegiances, social identities, and cultural alliances. But it is also known that people can shift allegiances quickly once they join a new group. It appears we come built with a natural ability to 'switch sides' with remarkable ease. We may be team players, but have no problem in joining a new team when a better offer comes along.

It is also known that although young children will express empathy for others, they still have immense difficulty seeing the world from another's perspective. We noted earlier how students are inclined to blame the adults in their world for the punishments they receive, even though the adults are striving to be fair and just in applying an agreed-upon system of rules and conventions. The ability to deeply understand others' viewpoints is not evident until late adolescence or early adulthood.

New evidence concerning adolescent (im)maturity

In the scientific literature there has been much recent discussion about brain development maturity requiring an extended period through the adolescent years. While cognitive capacities and reasoning skills are well developed by early adolescence, considerable development still has to take place in terms of social and emotional maturity. Consider, for example the need for older adolescents to develop risk management skills. It used to be thought that adolescents believe themselves to be relatively invulnerable. They may drive fast, or experiment with dangerous drugs, feeling they are unlikely to be harmed. Although appealing, this explanation generally lacks mileage. The evidence was not strong in the first place, and differences between adolescents and adults in such beliefs appear minimal. On the verbal level, most adolescents will show a mature capacity to understand and reason about costs and benefits of choices and decisions that flies in the face of the invulnerability hypothesis.

Recent research indicates that accuracy in assessment of risk continues to develop through the entire adolescent period, and even later. Teenagers know a line is to be drawn, but are unsure where to draw it. Such judgements hinge substantially on the availability of sensible adult models. Adolescents are characterised as sensation seeking, and as having strong approach tendencies unlikely to be reined in by fears. For instance, analysis of adolescent gambling patterns (under simulated laboratory conditions) reveals the tendency to accept bets seen as too risky by adults. Adolescents are strongly influenced by peers who are seen to value risky behaviour (see Box below).

Left to themselves, adolescents often display poor judgement in areas such as social responsibility, risk management, and future planning. Taking genuine risks can be one means of establishing one is no longer a child: but the paradox is that teenagers need guidance in risk management. During the adolescent years, large differences between individuals in their social competencies become apparent. Those who begin this period with high social competency and strong bonds with adults become even more competent. The psychosocially rich become richer, and the psychosocially poor become poorer.

We continue the theme of teacher–student relationship in the next chapter through looking further into the characteristics of teachers who have a positive effect on their students. More specifically, we attempt to answer the question: *Just what aspects of a teacher's personality will make a difference in the classroom context?*

ADOLESCENTS IN THE DRIVING SEAT

Researchers Margo Gardner and Laurence Steinberg asked people from three different age groups (14, 19, and over 24 years) to participate in a driving simulator game, discretely assessing for level of risk in their driving. When people were tested individually, the three age groups showed similarly low levels of risk taking. However, half of the people in the study participated in the presence of two same-aged peers. Having peers watch made no difference to the driving performance of the adults. But with peers present as onlookers, older adolescents showed a 50 per cent increase in risk taking, and the younger adolescents took twice as many risks. There were no gender differences.

These effects were found with peers being mere silent observers, without interaction. Do such laboratory findings translate into real life? Expensive research using cameras and other recording equipment (such as gravitational force sensors) installed into the motor cars of 42 drivers at 16 years of age, of both genders, over the course of a year, has revealed dramatically different patterns of driving contingent upon the nature of the passengers being carried. More dangerous driving became likely with certain friends in the vehicle. However, other peer friends, and adults, facilitated safer driving, which stands surely as a most reassuring finding.

It is well established, from decades of accident research around the globe, that incidents (such as fatal accidents peaking at driver age about 18 years), become more likely through a combination of elements such as powerful cars, late nights, young inexperienced male drivers, and peer influence. This phenomenon was described by one team of researchers as 'the perfect storm' (Allen & Brown, 2008, p. 289).

One curious fact emerging from traffic research is that the accident rate over the first 250 miles of a driver's career is three times that of the next 250 miles. Younger drivers do continue to have accidents, and it takes another four years for the accident rate to settle down to the adult population level. This settling down appears to tie in with a personal goal shift from 'learning driving skills', to 'driving safely and defensively', which is substantially a matter of minimising risk (i.e., one of the key indicators of maturity).

Study guide questions

1 If there is one universal characteristic concerning human interaction, it has to be the notion of the empathy gap. Is it possible to ever put yourself in someone else's shoes? What obstacles exist?

2 A good deal of pathology is implicated in the type of interaction called the negative cascade. What are some other terms used to describe such effects, and just what are the mechanisms at work in such interactions?

3 To what extent does early school experience play a role in establishing positive patterns?

4 And specifically what teacher traits and characteristics have been implicated in maintaining these continuing effects?

5 Robert Pianta's work has mapped student–teacher relationships in terms of two dimensions: closeness and conflict. Which dimension is more directly under the teacher's control?

6 Is it possible to interact with people whilst suppressing your inner emotions? What has been your personal experience in so doing?

7 When students are disciplined, quite fairly, then just what do they attribute (blame) the experience towards?

8 One key notion in this area is that the school can serve as a buffer against adverse societal influences. Can you express this idea in terms of social learning concepts (such as identification)?

9 Another key idea is that the school is able to moderate the relationship between unhealthy backgrounds and otherwise unfavourable outcomes. What mechanisms are involved here?

10 One curious finding from the social psychology literature is that people seem to possess the ability to form new social groups instantly. We have an ability to 'change sides' with ease. (Classic examples being individuals, groups, and even whole nations, who change sides during the course of a war.) Just what does this tell us about human relationships? And what does this say about the way groups form at school?

11 The research indicates that even older adolescents may lack the knowledge needed to thrive well in modern society. They may possess intellect, but still need to develop in many other ways. Do you think there is any advantage in trying to grow up fast?

12 Just why do young drivers display unfortunate levels of car accidents? What is the known database? How should we prepare adolescents for the responsibility of controlling a car?

Reference notes

■ Empathy gap research (Nordgren, Banas, & MacDonald, 2011). Aggressors and victims see things differently (Kearns & Fincham, 2005).

■ How situations deteriorate: negative escalations in teacher–student relations (Demanet & Van Houtte, 2012).

■ Study tracking 1,364 students across the school years into early adolescence (O'Connor, Dearing, & Collins, 2011).

■ American study that used a professional development model (Allen, Pianta, Gregory, Mikami, & Lun, 2011). The program used is described in Pianta and Allen, 2008.

■ Conflict with students produces teacher stress (Chang, 2009; Spilt, Koomen, & Thijs, 2011; Tsouloupas et al., 2010). Teachers who provide little emotional support present with more problems of conflict with their students (Hamre, Pianta, Downer, & Mashburn, 2008).

■ Emotional leakage and the illusion of transparency (Gilovich & Savitsky, 1999).

■ Classroom management tactics: handling uncooperative students (Evertson & Weinstein, 2006; Good & Brophy, 2008). Australian study into how disciplined students attribute their situation to teacher dispositions rather than accept responsibility (Lewis, Romi, & Roache, 2012).

■ Clinical studies indicate children with developmental problems depend strongly on support and relationships with teachers (Little & Kobak, 2003; Myers & Pianta, 2008).

■ Positive relationships can buffer against anti-social dispositions (Meehan, Hughes, & Cavell, 2003). Relationships with teachers have the potential to mitigate the risk of negative outcomes for children who may otherwise have difficulty succeeding (Baker, 2006; Benner & Mistry, 2007; Hamre & Pianta, 2005; H. K. Wilson, Pianta, & Stuhlman, 2007).

- Closeness and conflict as underlying dimensions (Pianta & Stuhlman, 2004).
- Increasing time spent with individual children promotes teacher–student relationships (Driscoll & Pianta, 2010).
- For further information from empathy gap research: in-group vs out-group effects (L. T. Harris & Fiske, 2006). The ability to change sides rapidly (Van Bavel & Cunningham, 2009).
- Uneven mental development during adolescence (Choudhury, Blakemore, & Charman, 2006). While cognitive capabilities are well developed by early adolescence, much growth still takes place in emotional and social maturity (Steinberg, 2007).
- Adolescents are often poor in assessing risk and exhibit weaknesses in planning (Albert & Steinberg, 2011). During these years the psychosocially rich become richer, while the psychosocially poor become poorer (Monahan & Steinberg, 2011). Adolescents take risky bets in gambling (Cauffman *et al.*, 2010).
- Box: Mere presence of peers may induce adolescent drivers to increase risk (Gardner & Steinberg, 2005). Research using sophisticated recording equipment to monitor driving in 16-year-olds over a year (Simons-Morton *et al.*, 2011). 'The perfect storm' (Allen & Brown, 2008). This paper reviews the psychology of adolescent driving, is most readable and suited for parents, teachers, and young drivers alike. For sensible discussion on young drivers shifting their goal from driving 'skill' to driving 'safely' see Keating and Halpern-Felsher, 2008.

4

Your personality as teacher

Can your students trust you?

At all levels of education, students actively rate and evaluate their teachers. These ratings relate not to your personality, but more to how your students feel they are being treated. Your students need to define you as an acceptable, warm, and competent human being, even though they may be relatively uninterested in you as a person. Whether or not you are an introvert or extravert, an optimist or pessimist, nervous or easy-going, is irrelevant to your capability as a teacher, or even your students' attitude towards you. To become a fine teacher, you do not have to have a particular type of personality. Over the past 90 years, with studies stemming back into the 1920s, attempts to describe the ideal teacher in terms of personality traits have proved unfruitful. If there is any secret to becoming a fine teacher, it does not lie in the type of personality you have brought to the profession, as least as defined by traditional measures of personality.

It is communication and action, not personality

It is crucial to be able to manage a successful learning environment, which, in itself, entails your exhibiting attributes that promote positive and open human communication. Students value being treated with (a) fairness, (b) dignity, and (c) individual respect. These threefold aspects have emerged strongly in all studies in which students are interviewed and surveyed as to what they expect of their teachers. One particular finding that emerged from studies conducted with young adolescents is that, at this stage, students need to form a rudimentary belief in a just world, and it is their teachers who play a critical role in representing fairness and justice.

Links have been reported between how students feel they are being treated at school and a range of distress indicators. These have included poor school performance, deficient motivation, and significant medical symptoms. Obviously, the hypothesis that being treated unfairly by teachers will cause students to become ill cannot be investigated: but this linkage is supported by several medical research studies into adolescent illness symptoms.

Universally, it has been found that students form strong views as to what they want from schools, and how they expect teachers to behave. These general criteria are then used to evaluate individual teachers on the extent to which they measure up. But exactly how do students make such ratings? How can you create a favourable persona? One answer is that you can acknowledge your students as individuals with names, histories, interests, and personal goals. The degree of personalisation is an important component in determining satisfaction in all interpersonal relationships.

Another key lies in your nonverbal behaviour, most directly in how you are seen to treat other people. There is much power invested in your role, but it has been found that children lose respect for any adults who do not know and respect basic social rules, who exhibit cruelty or misbehaviour, or who otherwise, break agreed-upon conventions. The teacher is positioned as an inevitable role model, the visible representative of the adult worldview. The adult who goes against accepted standards of basic interpersonal conduct is disqualified from standing as a credible role model.

Many studies show that even young children possess an unflinching sense of what is 'right and wrong' (or good versus bad) – they have a deep sense of fairness. This robust sense of moral righteousness is developing well before the preschool years. As students move into the upper primary years they develop the capacity to think deeply about social and moral issues. Of course, children do not always behave in accordance with what is right. Also, maturity in social judgement and risk assessment will not occur until late adolescence, or later (as noted in the previous chapter). Nevertheless, there are no glaring gaps in the young child's basic knowledge about what is right and what is wrong.

Telling lies is universally seen as a culpable act. Studies within interpersonal psychology indicate that the one immediate way to undermine all positive relationships is to be caught out lying. Despite the fact that lying occurs relatively frequently, any person or child exposed as a liar faces considerable loss of credibility and social status. Lying undermines the level of social credit or trust that an individual had secured previously. Similarly, it has been found that teachers' authority in being able to manage students is considerably eroded when they are seen to break promises made earlier.

The blink effect at work in schools

However, the nature of interpersonal interaction is more subtle than complying with social conventions. Studies show that students begin to evaluate teachers after exposure to them for remarkably short durations, as brief as 10 seconds. This phenomenon is one aspect of the *blink effect* as described by science writer, Malcolm Gladwell. Within the classroom context, students have more time to study you and so develop and amend their perceptions. The key aspects, as described by a significant body of research, involve the teacher's positive open gestures when dealing with the class, physically moving around the room, relaxed body orientation, frequent use of smiles, direct eye contact, and using a variety of friendly and encouraging vocal tones, especially when dealing with an individual student.

When it comes to interpreting verbal information, students are highly sensitive to how teachers speak, specifically to the manner in which words are stated, and the tone of voice being used. Many times, students will focus attention on such presentation mannerisms, rather than what is being stated. As noted by Elisha Babad in summarising her key studies into the classroom impact of teacher nonverbal characteristics and how students will read such cues, 'Although the behaviours are subtle, implicit and seemingly invisible, their influence on students is intense' (Babad, 2009, p. 825).

The notion that students are immediately sensitive to the emotional climate of teacher–student relationships is a well-established finding. In an Israeli study, high school students were shown brief 10-second films of teachers they had not met and were able to rate these teachers on how they would teach. These ratings correlated with what the teachers' own genuine students had reported. In a French study, it was found that 7-year old students increased their scores on academic tests when administered under friendly and warm conditions, as compared to less friendly testing conditions. This effect did not hinge upon student ability level. In that study the emphasis was on the examiner deliberately using warm and inviting body language, direct eye contact, and deliberate use of friendly vocal intonation.

The notion that interpersonal judgements occur quickly and inevitably reflects the blink phenomenon as discussed in Chapter 30 and also in the box at the end of this chapter.

Can we detect when students tell porkies?

Once you succeed in developing strong and positive relationships with your students, can you always trust them? There are some clear and disturbing research findings. When we are on the receiving end of narrative information, there is no mechanism in our head for detecting when people we deal with fail to tell the truth. Developmental studies show that children learn how to convey untruthful statements from about 4 years of age. The skill of deceit is acquired in the context of avoiding restrictions or punishment, thus providing fertile learning conditions. Ironically, the ability to tell a lie well, and hold the story consistently over time, is a characteristic of bright intelligent children with developed metacognitive skills. Teachers soon learn that even their most capable students can become convincing truth-twisters under pressure. Whenever a story is to be relayed, we can move from truth, to embellishment, to untruth, seamlessly – a skill we learnt about 4 years of age.

As caregivers, parents, or teachers, we do not possess the ability to tell when a child in our care is lying. By default, we accept whatever is said as truthful. One well-controlled study, with teachers watching videos of students either lying or telling the truth, found that accuracy for detecting lies was 60 per cent. Other studies found that accuracy in detecting lies at best may approach 65 per cent as against the chance level of 50 per cent in these studies. A conclusion of a number of literature reviews is that on average, people are unable to detect lies above the chance level.

A few individuals have been identified whose ability to detect lies is strong, although never perfect. But these are rare individuals, often involved in forensic work, and they seem to be reading minute facial twitches (or microbursts) that people give out as they lie. We detect emotions, and it is **emotional leakage** that communicates messages suggesting an individual is lying. But this is a poor indicator. Truth-tellers have been found to show signs of anxiety when quizzed about their possible untruthful behaviour. On the other hand, most individuals, children included, are fully able to utter untruthful statements without obvious emotion surfacing. As the history of drug use in elite sports well shows, people anticipate questions likely to surface, and present well-prepared answers.

Help-seeking behaviour: an index of trust in the classroom

When a student needs help in understanding difficult material, what is likely to happen? Some students react passively, exert low effort, and are motivated to disengage. Others react with resourcefulness and determination to overcome hurdles. One key aspect is the willingness to seek help, and to do so from available resources, notably teachers. Seeking help is a viable cognitive strategy promoting resilience. It ought not to be confused with dependency, which means relying on a single source excessively over time. But in all learning situations, wherever and whenever obstacles exist, well-motivated learners will access whatever resources are available, and use them to advantage. There is evidence that students rated by their teachers as seeking help do achieve higher grades.

We know that help-seeking, as a cognitive strategy, is more likely to be seen in students who present with strong levels of intrinsic motivation. This is often referred to as **mastery goal orientation** in that such students are relatively more oriented towards learning new skills and becoming involved in tasks for reasons that involve understanding and acquiring knowledge. Such motives are often contrasted with **ego or performance orientation**, which is the goal to perform, look good, or otherwise outperform one's immediate peer group. It is possible to have two students sitting side-by-side, working away feverously, where one is motivated to gain a deep understanding of the material, while the other sees the material more as a medium for use in proving his or her ability.

It is simplistic, however, to think of these as different types of students since the two orientations (mastery and ego) co-exist in all students. Since students are human, there is always an inevitable level of ego-based motivation. The issue within classroom life is one of keeping ego factors to a relatively low level, while striving to provide an environment in which students feel confident in their ability to achieve through principles of natural progression.

Students' trust in their teachers

One key factor known to influence student help-seeking is you, the teacher. A number of surveys across many classes in primary, middle and high schools have indicated that students sense the extent to which their teachers will personally support their knowledge-building needs when they get into trouble. These surveys reveal that, in some classrooms, help-seeking is discouraged. One American survey found that as students get older, they begin to equate question-asking behaviour with low ability. It has been found that lower ability students ask fewer and fewer questions with increasing grade level, with the implication that these students were learning that asking questions is a dangerous activity likely to expose one's vulnerabilities.

It has also been found that when students perceive their teachers are highly supportive, students will associate question asking with positive aspects such as mastery goals, building their abilities, and with less focus on competition between students. On the other hand, when they perceive teachers as unsupportive, students become far more likely to associate question asking with low ability.

Recent studies into such effects have found that teachers vary in the type of goals they endorse for their own teaching practices. Students appear to be remarkably sensitive to the teachers' goals and intentions. In one Israeli study, Dr Ruth Butler surveyed 53 upper primary classrooms and found linkages between the notions teachers reported about their teaching aims, and their students' ratings about their teachers. Teachers who endorsed statements reflecting mastery (e.g., 'Today I learned something new about teaching or about myself as a teacher, and I tried hard to solve a problem I was having in class and eventually succeeded') were rated by their students as being supportive in aspects such as 'This teacher provides sufficient time for students to ask questions' and 'This teacher answers questions carefully and thoroughly'.

The way in which you teach and treat your students has marked effects on your students' lives. Dr Butler's studies, and those of others, reveal how students read their teachers and rate them directly on approachability, fairness, and trust. How you respond to students who need help is one such critical aspect. One of the items endorsed by the students who rated their teachers positively was 'This teacher encourages students to ask for help any time, even after class'. Students strongly value teachers they can trust to assist them when they are struggling with complex ideas.

IN PERSPECTIVE: Students' expectations of their teachers

So if it is not your sparkling personality, just what is it that students expect of you? It is the ability to fulfil the role of teacher, a role that is inevitable and prescribed through the eyes of the students. There exists a well-specified adult position that involves openness and respect for others as well as upholding the agreed-upon social moral code. We now know that students want to be taught by a responsible adult who advances a constructive focus on learning, and who directly helps them improve themselves through monitoring and feedback. They prefer sensible and concise explanations about how to proceed, how to move forwards, and how to understand the tasks they are expected to be successful upon.

In one Australian study researchers surveyed 940 upper primary students about the best mathematics lessons they could recall. They found that 'In particular the students liked clear explanations, they recalled lessons that used materials that allowed connections to their lives, felt the mode of grouping to be important, and many liked to be challenged' (Sullivan, Clark & O'Shea, 2010, p. 531). One message we take from this and many other studies is that, whenever students are asked, they voice clear and well-defined notions of what they expect of their teachers.

Your students are well aware of the world beyond the classroom, and of the role played by their schooling in preparing for the future. Students value being helped to achieve independence and autonomy, and appreciate teachers who can connect the new with the familiar, can convey complex notions in simple terms, who actively recognise that students learn at different rates, and need varying levels of guidance, feedback, and instruction. Such teaching has to take place in a climate of trust, affection, and fairness. As a teacher you embody the 'just world' as an abstract, but nevertheless, realistic ideal. This is not to say that the world outside is just, but rather that your classroom represents both a place of mutual trust and a bridge to a successful future.

NEVER JUDGE A BOOK BY ITS COVER. FIRST IMPRESSIONS CAN BE MISLEADING

These two sayings convey a dose of wisdom. People often live to regret decisions made in haste, especially when they fail to access appropriate information. The trouble is, often we are rewarded when we arrive at decisions quickly. We can blink, come up with an answer, and often it is a good answer. Fast blink-type responses are sensible when judgements are based on recognition alone, or where new information does not need to be assimilated. Instances may arise when decisions based upon fast recognition can be more valid than decisions based on taking a good deal of time and thought. This is not magic, but simply that the 'thin slice' at the moment of recognition relates to earlier 'thick slice' experiences that gave you the right answer.

In this chapter we note how students appraise teachers after brief exposures of less than 10 seconds. So what is going on? Exactly what is the social brain doing? Using findings from research across several areas, we can piece together some of the story. The following events can unfold whenever we meet another person:

Within a tenth of a second. We know from laboratory studies that when exposed to brief flashes showing photographs of faces on a computer screen, people identify the gender, age, and race of the person. Clothing and general presentation may be picked up. The presence of a smile or of clear negative emotions can also be detected immediately.

Within 2 seconds. The initial response on meeting a person in the flesh, after determining generic features, is one of character assessment. Initially, this is in terms of 'Is this person a danger to me?', 'What is this person trying to do?', or 'What are his intentions?'. There is also a primitive assessment akin to 'Do I like what I am seeing?', and your attention is drawn in sharply to any aspect of the person you do not like.

Within 10 seconds. At this stage, your attitude is being shaped by how the other person is physically positioned, or moving, which are vital cues as to personality, as is the person's gait. The assessment process moves to deciding just how this individual differs from others: the key matters to resolve become, 'What character traits are there?', 'Does one trait stand out above others?', 'Do I like these traits?', and 'Am I in favour of this person?'

The next few minutes: moving toward a relationship. We maintain a high level of vigilance with the other person in focus. We check to see how first impressions are standing up. If they do, we feel validated and increase confidence in feeling we know the other person. We may shift focus to self-presentation given the possibility of a relationship with the other party. But before committing ourselves, or exposing an agenda, we try to gauge if early assessments will hold over time. We monitor just how the other party is responding to us, since this feedback is vital in deciding where to go next. One major part of the feedback process involves a hidden level of **posture matching** (or implicit mimicry) and synchronisation of gesture. If these fail to occur, the relationship is unlikely to proceed.

Perhaps we ought not to judge a book by its cover. But we cannot stop the process. The cover conveys a high level of data, with a reasonable probability of this being valid. Nevertheless, first impressions easily mislead. Many teachers report spectacular progress in students who did not shine initially. When it comes to self-presentation, competency is easily misrepresented. One of the findings from the Dunning–Kruger research (see Chapter 25) was that highly competent people may underestimate their worth. We all know of capable and hard-working individuals who present poorly in job interviews. In situations involving decisions about others, it pays to question if the slice your mind has taken really is too thin. One recent study did find that when chess players were asked to take more time before deciding on moves, the game quality of their moves increased. This effect was found in both novice and expert players. This finding fits with what is known about experts: that although experts can work fast, whenever a problem emerges, they slow down and do things carefully and accurately.

Study guide questions

1 A good deal of research, stemming back almost 100 years, went into searching for the ideal teacher personality. Why do you suppose this search largely has been unsuccessful?

2 European research into adolescent mental health has often cited schooling as a contributing factor in both physical and mental illness. Just what are our responsibilities when it comes to treating our students fairly and with basic humanistic respect?

3 What is known about young children's sense of 'right and wrong'?

4 In what specific ways are teachers (indeed, all adults) able to devalue their respect and authority in the eyes of their students?

5 Studies have shown that students are incredibly sensitive to interpersonal mannerisms. Just what mechanisms are at work in all interpersonal situations, including the classroom?

6 Can we tell if anyone is lying to us? What cues can we rely upon?

7 Students need to feel that they can trust their teachers when they need help. Just how is the help-seeking strategy different from dependency?

8 What is meant by the distinction between task-related goals and ego-based goals?

9 Overall, what are your goals with respect to maintaining a positive climate in the classroom? Can you recognise effective strategies you use as you teach? Does this chapter provide you with information that may help you to attempt to narrow the inevitable empathy gap between your students and yourself?

10 The chapter reviews findings about how dramatically fast the brain responds whenever we encounter other people. But the writers caution against using the blink response whenever serious decisions are to be made (especially about other people). Just when should blink responses be trusted, and when should they be mistrusted?

Reference notes

- Students evaluate their teachers (E. Babad, Bernieri, & Rosenthal, 1989a, b).

- Students value fairness in teachers (Peter & Dalbert, 2010; Wendorf & Alexander, 2005). Belief in a just world: unfairness and adolescent distress are linked (Dalbert & Stoeber, 2005; Peter, Kloeckner, Dalbert, & Radant, 2012). Teacher unfairness linked to adolescent medical symptoms (Hershey, 2010; Santinello, Vieno, & De Vogli, 2009).

- Children reject adults who violate the moral code. Even young children know right from wrong and can think about moral issues (Killen & Smetana, 2006; Nucci, 1984). Lying renders positive social relationships well-nigh impossible (Tyler, Feldman, & Reichert, 2006). Teacher credibility eroded through broken promises (Kidd, Palmeri, & Aslin, 2013).

- Students rate you on gestures (E. Babad, 2009; E. Babad, Avni-Babad, & Rosenthal, 2003; M. Harris & Rosenthal, 2005). Review of Babad's work is found in E. Babad, 2007.

- The blink effect is reviewed in depth in Gladwell (2006). Highly recommended.

- In an Israeli study, brief exposure to teacher produced judgements (E. Babad, 2005).

- French study in warmth (Schiaratura & Askevis-Leherpeux, 2007).

- Can teachers detect when students lie? For one well controlled study with teachers see Vrij, Akehurst, Brown, & Mann, 2006.

- There is no natural ability to tell if people are lying (Bond & DePaulo, 2008; Hartwig & Bond, 2011; Nysse-Carris, Bottoms, & Salerno, 2011). The literature basis is huge: Bond and DePaulo's paper was based on 247 experimental studies. Overall, when people declare they are not lying they are likely to be believed. Lying is a common activity in human interactions, generally successful. Although people do exhibit signs they are lying, we are generally insensitive to these. Even when we attempt to detect lies, we focus on the wrong cues. A sensible chapter on this topic is found in Wiseman, 2007.

- Truth-tellers leak much emotion when quizzed about lying (Vrij, Fisher, Mann, & Leal, 2006). Although we may control a good deal, emotional leakage is common (Gilovich & Savitsky, 1999).

- For a general review on help-seeking see Karabenick & Newman, 2010. Adolescents who seek help from their teachers obtain higher grades (Ryan & Shin, 2011).

- American study reporting question asking seen by older peers as indicating low ability (Good, Slavings, Harel, & Emerson, 1987).

- Trust in teachers relates to the meaning students place on question asking (Karabenick, 1994).

- Mastery goals in teachers linked to their student ratings on helpful support (Butler & Shibaz, 2008).

- Australian study on student views about great maths teaching (Sullivan, Clark, & O'Shea, 2010).

- Box: Just how thin is a slice? This summary stems from research cited in this book featured in Chapters 27 (on smiling), 28 (on mimicry), and 30 (on fast and slow thinking). The notion that fast decision-making can be highly valid when based on recognition is found in Gigerenzer, 2008. The study showing chess moves improved quality when given more time, even for the experts (Moxley, Ericsson, Charness, & Krampe, 2012).

5

Time as a global indicator of classroom learning

The 1970s and 1980s saw a significant amount of research on how time is used in classrooms. Many educators felt this type of research produced somewhat obvious or trivial findings. Of course students need time to learn things: what could be more obvious? On the other hand, a number of researchers took the view that time constituted a meaningful variable that tells a good deal about individual teachers' educational aims and methods. For example, David Berliner (1990, p. 30) noted that,

> The expression of educational attitudes, opinions, and beliefs – one's personal philosophy derived from normative conceptions of teaching or from experience – must result in duration of some kind in the classroom. If not, that philosophy is doomed to remain merely a verbal expression of belief, unrelated to behavior. Actions not only speak louder than words, they can be timed . . . Instructional time concepts can address issues of philosophy and quality, while simultaneously retaining their obvious simple and apparently pedestrian character.

We find the analysis of time to be meaningful, in accordance with Berliner's view. But before going further it is important to be aware of the various ways in which time was measured in the research. Table 5.1 describes four distinct, but interrelated concepts, involving definitions of time usage within the classroom.

The conceptual basis of time analysis

The scheme shown in Table 5.1 divides time into four interlinked components: it begins with time as **allocated,** which in practice reduces straight away to genuine **instructional time,** which further breaks down to **engagement**, or non-engagement, and then with **academic learning time** (or ALT) as the final

TABLE 5.1 Looking at classroom time use through four critical concepts

TIME CONCEPT	MAJOR THREATS	MAJOR FACILITATORS
Allocated time: time as programmed on timetables, documents, or curriculum plans	Interruptions, class visitors, announcements, transitions, and school-level demands such as sports days, etc.	School mandated policies, but moderated by the individual teacher's beliefs, judgements, values, and curriculum knowledge.
Instructional time: the actual time genuinely available for class instruction	Poor management. Lack of clear procedures being communicated. Teacher allowing time to be hijacked by low-priority matters.	Managerial skill and prioritisation. Ability to focus class energies on to a clear singular focus with expressed expectations and short-term goals for the lesson.
Engaged time: the time student actually pays attention to educative tasks	Students not knowing what to focus upon. Student factors such as social distractions, lack of knowledge, boredom, fatigue, and work dispositions.	Clear instructions given coupled with meaningful tasks, and with availability of monitoring, interpersonal encouragement, corrective feedback, and appropriate reinforcement.
Academic learning time: time when student is learning and responding with a high successful level evident	Despite effort, student fails to comprehend lesson structure and goals. Possible gaps in prior knowledge. Task set is too challenging, and student is unable to realign this aspect.	Individualised guidance. Encouragement aimed at enhancing pride in use of effort to achieve goals recognised as worthwhile.

component. Hence, these concepts are seen in terms of subsets, which we will illustrate with a hypothetical example. In this illustrative but realistic case, imagine taking a video of a classroom lesson, using two fixed wide-lens cameras, so as to be able to monitor the action. The teacher, Mr Berry, had programmed an hour for mathematics instruction, from 9:30 to 10:30 in the morning. But school announcements meant that the lesson started at 9:37, so 7 minutes were lost upfront. Using the video recordings, we use standard observational methods to measure the on-task engagement levels of all the students in the class. On averaging it out, using the class median score, we find that the students are engaged (time on task) for 36 of the 53 minutes. The range of engagement across the 23 students was from 21 to 49 minutes.

But to measure academic learning time we need to go one stage further. We get an experienced teacher to look at the films and judge when the individual students were involved or engaged successfully on the set tasks. That is, the teacher is asked to identify the actual moments in time when the student is not only engaged, but visibly responding successfully. Although remarkably time-consuming, making such judgement is not as difficult as it first sounds. Why? Because, substantially, this type of judgement is what experienced teachers carry out in the natural world. That is, teachers are accustomed to glancing at individual students and using cues such as concentration and facial expressions to infer that students are responding appropriately, or are having some difficulty. Now with Mr Berry's mathematics lesson, we get our experienced teacher to apply this procedure intensively and it is found that the academic learning times for individual students vary between 9 and 45 minutes, with a class median level of 27 minutes.

By reputation and direct observation, Mr Berry is a well-regarded teacher. In this illustrative lesson, the average child is rated as experiencing academic learning time for about one half of the initial allocated time. Such a finding would be interpreted positively since that constitutes 27 minutes of solid mathematics learning work going on, on average. Within one classic study, the Californian Beginning Teacher Evaluation Study (BTES), it was found that experienced teachers (working as observers) rated success levels of students in mathematics classes at around one third of the students' level of on task engagement. In short, even when the students were engaged with mathematics tasks, they were still rated as experiencing relatively low levels of academic learning time.

But in our hypothetical case, note the huge variations, with some students experiencing about one quarter of the academic learning time experienced by others within the same class. Indeed, the available research into time on task does document that such large variations are commonly found, not only within classes, but between different classes. The research into natural classroom variations has been reviewed by several key researchers. All such reviews document quite remarkable variations in time allocations and student engagement levels across different classrooms.

You will have noted how awkward and time-consuming it is to get an accurate fix on academic learning time within the classroom. In the research world we may have the luxury of recordings, and subsequent opportunity to analyse these products. In the world of the classroom, too much is occurring. It is hardly feasible, within real-time, to monitor academic learning time with accuracy.

Teachers will have the impression that certain students are working well, and others not so well. Indeed, it is known that excellent teachers do scan their classrooms on a regular basis during formal lessons. But the idea that there could be a four-fold difference in individualised time accumulations going on in your class, right under your nose, is something of which many teachers would have virtually no awareness. There is no mechanism in the mind that could enable a teacher to continuously monitor and tally individual rates of engagement. Hence, an interesting observation is that although student engagement appears highly visible on a moment-to-moment basis, the subsequent analysis of academic learning time remains a somewhat hidden aspect of classroom life.

The research basis

But why is academic learning time important? Studies conducted in the 1980s indicated that time itself does not correlate strongly with achievement outcomes. But studies did indicate that, when teachers were compared on specific curriculum topics, allocations of time to those topics can indeed vary widely. For example, in the Californian BTES study time allocated to certain arithmetic activities varied from 9 minutes to 315 minutes a year in Year 2 classes. And time allocated to reading comprehension activities varied from 10 minutes a day to 50 minutes a day in Year 5 classes. Hence, how much time is assigned to teaching specific topics can become a significant factor when it impinges directly upon the opportunities afforded to students. If students have not been taught certain topics, or have covered them in a perfunctory manner, they cannot be expected to be familiar with test items based on those topics. When researchers such as David Berliner began to ask individual teachers why they allocated greater or lesser levels of time to certain curriculum topics, many teachers indicated that such decisions reflected their personal predilections.

Similarly, on an overall basis, instructional time alone probably does not normally predict student achievement within school to any great degree. But correlations are more significant when it comes to linking achievement outcomes with engaged time and the academic learning time factor. Several studies suggested that time engagement factors become relatively more critical for low-achieving students.

One meaningful finding is that the time engagement factor, when the student is not being successful on the set task, generally fails to predict learning. Also, the BTES data indicated that when students did achieve high levels of success in mathematics, their positive attitudes towards mathematics increased. Hence, the conclusion from the BTES study was that the students' level of success became a crucial factor linked to significant gains on both achievement and positive attitudes. The study also documented how excellent teachers monitored success levels in individual students and so made adjustments in their teaching strategies accordingly.

According to the BTES researchers themselves,

> The ALT model proposes that the more time spent working with high success leads to increased achievement. However, it does not necessarily imply that all a student's time should be spent in the high success condition, nor does it imply that high success corresponds to little effort on the part of the student. In fact, high success will be attained sometimes with relatively little effort and sometimes with considerable effort. Generally, it is expected that some balance between high and medium success tasks will produce the most student learning. Low success tasks will always be detrimental to learning.
>
> (Fisher *et al.*, 1980, pp. 9–10)

Hence, a sensible descriptive model stems from this body of research. This is where academic learning time may be seen as a type of a *final common path* flowing on from teaching functions that took place earlier. The classroom is well managed, conducive to learning, and conveys an abundance of opportunities to learn. Then students engage with tasks that they are well equipped to handle. Some initial difficulty is evident before the student achieves personal success. Once an experienced teacher is able to identify that the student is clearly being successful, then this measure presages levels of achievement on subsequent assessments. Berliner (1987) has referred to such notions as a 'simple theory' of classroom learning.

Getting the simple theory into perspective

We do not treat the academic learning time model as a definitive statement of a theory of teaching and learning. It suggests, however, certain likely relationships between classroom time and student learning outcomes. Relationships between time spent in learning activities, and actual learning outcomes are never going to be simple, easy, or direct ones. It is important to recognise that such relationships will be subject to a range of moderating factors. This notion comes into sharp relief when looking at studies into how expertise is acquired. That is, it is well documented that many people can spend years performing activities reasonably successfully but without increasing their skills to expert levels.

The topic of expertise and its development is reviewed in other chapters in this book, but at this point we can note that any relationship between time spent in learning and level of expertise attained is very much bound up with the notion of **deliberate practice** (see Chapter 11). Simply spending more time on an activity will not result in skill improvement unless there is a deliberate effort made to improve performance, and the critical components are factors such as guidance, instruction, goal setting, and feedback.

Research into students' study techniques also shows no automatic relationship between time spent studying and student grades. In fact, high ability university students have been found to perform well while spending less overall time than others in their studies. Hence, although there can be a relationship between an individual's time spent studying and his or her exam performance, this will not emerge when comparing individuals of differing ability levels.

The role of time in promoting deep learning

At times it is possible to acquire surface information fairly rapidly. On the other hand, time is still needed to allow learners opportunity to think deeply about the incoming information and to find relationships between diverse ideas and experiences. Teachers frequently express the view that the curriculum they are mandated to teach is hurried and discourages in-depth studies. Should this be your view, then the finding of the following project will be of interest.

Douglas Clark and Marcia Linn (2003) reported on a study conducted in an American middle school in which the same science eighth-grade curriculum was taught in four different ways, either as a full 12-week semester topic, or in streamlined (i.e., cut down) form in either 9-week, 6-week, or 3-week versions. The same four topics were covered, but the amount of time devoted to the four units of work was dramatically reduced. Assessments took the form of both multiple choice and written tests. The results were startling. The reduced time allocations barely made any impact on the multiple choice tests. But students who had to cover the content in reduced time were unable to pass the written tests that assessed for depth in understanding. For instance, students who covered the content in three weeks scored around 25 per cent on the written sections, despite scoring 90 per cent on the multiple choice test. Students who had studied the full version scored 90 per cent on multiple choice, and 67 per cent on written sections.

What was dramatically apparent in this study was that students subjected to the abridged curricula were unable to relate ideas across the four units. The researchers noted:

> Knowledge integration takes time, energy, varied activities, and many opportunities to make connections from one topic to another. In streamlining the curriculum, we inevitably reduce opportunities for students to reflect on the connections from one topic to another. As students race through topics they have less opportunity to engage in the processes of sorting out, comparing, prioritizing, organizing, and critiquing their science ideas. These processes, essential for lifelong learning, are less practiced in the streamlined curriculum.
>
> (Clark & Linn, 2003, p. 482)

By asking students to race through mandated lessons under duress of time pressures, we run considerable risk of creating little more than isolated islands of knowledge. Isolated knowledge will be subject to rapid forgetting in the natural course of time, and is not conducive to schemata development (see Chapter 14). Should we want our students to retain meaningful information, allowing sufficient time to work on thoughtful and enriching activities, which promote knowledge, building, and consolidation, will pay dividends.

IN PERSPECTIVE: So, is this all obvious?

As we cited at the outset, we have been assailed by critics who appear to regard the empirical relationship between time and learning as 'obvious'. Of course it is necessary to spend time on a topic to enable deep learning to take place, as surely, everyone knows this?

We reply that any information presented clearly, sensibly, and which is consistent with easily understood principles will appear obvious *in hindsight*. Phenomena appear obvious once (a) they can be expressed with clarity and (b) conclusions can be accepted without needing to rearrange one's existing knowledge system too dramatically. Hence, obviousness is a clear perception one arrives at only after an event has been explained and its causal mechanisms recognised as valid.

We must be cautious not to confuse such clarity with triviality. In wider perspective, it is obvious that (a) Japan could not possibly defeat America in 1944, (b) doctors should wash their hands to prevent spread of disease between patients, (c) blood-letting would weaken sick people, (d) high levels of fishing would wipe out fish species, (e) use of pesticides would kill useful bees, and (f) carbon emissions would impact upon climatic balances.

Hindsight is such a wonderful platform. So perhaps, within the behavioural sciences, it is easy to find it obvious that (a) children from lower socioeconomic backgrounds perform less well on academic tests, (b) punitive parenting gives rise to anxious children, or (c) students who spend more time on task actually learn more.

If relationships are obvious, why would we not take them seriously? In the case of the time-on-task research, what was seldom recognised beforehand was the finding that teachers can and do vary enormously on how they allocate and employ time. Hence, students do vary on the amount of time they experience in classroom learning. In contrast to the comment that it is obvious there is a relationship between time and learning, it is possible to argue that the cumulative time factors, as described in this chapter, represent variables remarkably well hidden from view whenever one simply looks into a classroom. The impact of variations in time use on student attainment and deep processing are inherently understandable, but, as research findings, such relationships simply are not obvious.

Study guide questions

1 David Berliner makes a simple observation. That educational values and philosophies become indexed through allocations of time. How does this notion apply at both the class, and at the school level?

2 Can you relate to the notion that time allocations get eroded by external factors? Just what threats to allocated time exist in your personal context?

3 How is it possible for students to exhibit high levels of engaged time, but low levels of academic learning time? Just what might this pattern suggest?

4 The present writers suggest that academic learning time is a hidden aspect of classroom life. Why would they make such a comment about something one can so easily see? But why does 'just looking' fail to inform anyone about ALT factors at work?

5 The observational studies revealed huge variations in time measures across students, with some students showing many times more involvement in school activities. Just what are the implications of such large variations?

6 It is true that time spent on task is never a strong indicator of student learning or achievement level. At best, we might expect statistical correlations around 0.3. If so, then should we ignore time factors, or do precisely the opposite (such as work hard to ensure students do get extended practice opportunities)?

7 Now think back to the psychology of expertise. It is known that skills do not develop through simply doing or performing them over time. Instead, practice has to be deliberate. What does that imply about the use of time in learning contexts?

8 Clark and Linn's study indicated something rather important about what happens when we race through curriculum content at a high pace. What was the impact of such a treatment?

9 Is all this focus on classroom time just stating the obvious? Why do the present writers suggest such a view is mistaken?

Reference notes

■ Time management reflects values and philosophies (Berliner, 1990).

■ Reviews of time on task research (Caldwell, Huitt, & Graeber, 1982; Gettinger, 1986).

■ The Beginning Teacher Evaluation Study (BTES) (Fisher *et al.*, 1980).

■ A simple theory of classroom instruction (Berliner, 1987).

■ Capable university students study efficiently, rather than spend extended time (Plant, Ericsson, Hill, & Asberg, 2005).

■ Cut down curricula seriously disrupt deep processing (D. Clark & Linn, 2003).

■ Analysis of obviousness as an unwarranted perception, a bias of hindsight and other cognitive distortions (Yates, 2005). The feeling of obviousness provides a natural ego-serving defence mechanism.

6

The recitation method and the nature of classroom learning

One inevitable feature of classroom life is the phenomenon we refer to as the **recitation method**. This is the type of teaching that is so highly familiar to anyone who has been to school. Alternatively known as the **IRE cycle** (initiation–response–evaluation), or the **CDR method** (conventional–direct–recitation), the recitation has a long history of application. It represents traditional teaching methodology that has survived considerable criticism and attacks for over two centuries. Stanford University professor Larry Cuban (1984) noted that,

> Drawn from a large number of varied sources in diverse settings, over nearly a century, the data show striking convergence in outlining a stable core of teacher-centred instructional activities in the elementary school and, in high school classrooms, a remarkably pure and durable version of the same set of activities.
>
> (p. 238)

He called this stable core the 'grammar' of schooling.

Just why is this form of teaching so familiar and persistent? The answer lies in the predictable patterns that are set up and carried through. In IRE cycles the teacher initiates an interaction with a class, and invites some form of response, typically through presenting a question. A student responds, and the teacher evaluates the response before initiating another interaction. Lessons can be analysed in terms of cycles of structuring, soliciting, responding, and reacting. Teachers and students know how to interact with each other. After a short period of structuring, teachers emit clear signals that a sequence of questions is about to begin. Teachers display subtle ways of communicating to the class that at least some of them will be expected to respond. Student–teacher interactions proceed in an orderly fashion, and teachers are able to cover aspects they deem important. The IRE cycle (or recitation method, as we call it) represents a realistic compromise between priorities that enables a teacher to retain a level of authority and managerial control.

Criticisms of such forms of teaching are well founded and include the following:

a Observational studies that the questions asked are mainly at a low level, often calling for simplistic answers.

b Generally, only one student is active at a time: the majority of students are often powerless to do anything other than bid to answer questions they had no part in formulating.

c Education becomes a matter of receiving pre-packaged knowledge from an authority figure and demonstrating its retention.

d The nature of the conversations inherent in the recitation is predictable, task-oriented, but unstimulating. There is a topic to be covered, knowledge to be assimilated, and outcomes to be achieved. But, such business is transacted within a sterile, non-emotional, and rule-bound context.

Tensions between different teaching methods

Professor Nate Gage (2009), a pioneer researcher in the area of classroom teaching, drew attention to the long-standing tensions between two process models of teaching, which he labelled PDC and CDR. PDC is the *progressive-discovery-constructivist* approach, as formulated within the Dewey tradition, and CDR stands for the *conventional-direct-recitation* approach. Tensions between variants of these two models have been apparent over the past century. However, a large literature of observational studies has documented the sheer preponderance of the CDR approach in classrooms across the globe. Representative of such studies is the work of John Goodlad (1994, p. 230), who, in a study of over 1,017 classrooms in the United States, noted:

> In effect, then, the modal classroom configurations which we observed looked like this: the teacher explaining or lecturing to the total class or a single student, occasionally asking questions requiring factual answers; . . . students listening or appearing to listen to the teacher and occasionally responding to the teacher's questions; students working individually at their desks on reading or writing assignments; and all with little emotion, from interpersonal warmth to expressions of hostility.

In this project, Dr Goodlad reported that about 75 per cent of class time was spent on such instruction, with teachers out-talking the students by a factor of three. Students responding to teacher questions accounted for around 5 per cent of the time, and less than 1 per cent of time was associated with open questions that might ask for complex or affective responses. Indeed, the level of feedback and reinforcement observed in these classrooms was remarkably low, apparently almost non-existent in some classrooms. It is interesting to note that this figure of 75 per cent class time associated with teacher talk has been reported in many other studies since that period, and across many countries. Another commonly reported statistic is that, per day, teachers may ask well over 100 questions, as compared to 5 stemming from the students.

Despite efforts of generations of educators, reformers, and idealists, the essential features of the recitation method remain intact, and can be observed in classrooms around the world. Dr Cuban (1982, p. 28) expressed his view by noting,

> What nags at me is the puzzling durability of this teaching at all levels of schooling but most clearly and uniformly at the high school, decade after decade, in spite of changes in teacher preparation, students' knowledge and skills, and continuous reform fever to alter this form of instruction.

However, Dr Gage (2009, p. 75) reviewed the research basis of this method of teaching and concluded that the 'model embodies something profoundly fundamental in the nature of teaching'. He identified several factors that help to account for the longevity of the CDR method including (a) its traditional form and intergenerational qualities, (b) its apparent adequacy and success in building a well-educated populace within advanced Western societies, (c) the relative failure of alternative methods such as progressive education and discovery learning approaches, (d) the failure of the information technology revolution to change structural aspects of the classroom, (e) the reality of the conditions of teaching and the professional demands made upon teachers, and (f) the lack of incentives and competition to drive significant alterations in educational delivery.

Advantages and disadvantages of the recitation method

Criticisms of the recitation method, as we noted earlier, become pertinent when student engagement and active participation are acknowledged as primary goals. For example, students are often expected to participate in research projects in a small group context and then present their findings within a whole class seminar context. After many years of being exposed to teaching practices based on a recitation model, it is difficult for students to shift to any other model. The recitation method evolved in response to issues such as mass education and overcrowded classrooms, and the need to teach a set curriculum. The problem becomes one of adapting teaching methods to suit the demands of the context within which you are employed to teach.

The recitation method has several natural advantages at the professional level. The teacher remains in control of the interaction. Hence, you can progress through mandated material at virtually any pace you want to dial up. You may be able to do this due to simple realities concerning the role (or absence of) of feedback. The recitation gives you the illusion of teaching success. Your reinforcement can lie in the fact that at least some students within the class appear interested and keeping up with the agenda. This can provide you with a level of assurance. However, such a perception may be based upon illusion.

In particular there is a huge problem inherent in that students will learn little from merely listening to teachers talk. For example, studies have shown that although students can learn a great deal from analysing worked examples, adding teachers' explanations into this mix adds virtually nothing. It has also been shown that when teachers race through curriculum materials at a faster than normal pace, then deep learning is affected dramatically, whereas surface learning may be relatively unaffected.

In short, the recitation method comes with many built-in problems that involve teachers in cost–benefit dilemmas. All too often, the nature of the interaction can become that of a single teacher interacting with a relatively small subgroup of students from within the class. The issue is compounded when class participants recognise what is occurring and tacitly allow such patterns to become the norm. It is almost as though students begin to recognise just who is active within each session, and perhaps who is not.

One experience many of us recall, from when we were high school students ourselves, is developing the art of becoming invisible. We developed skills enabling us to opt out of lesson participation. It is possible to appear slightly attentive, while avoiding direct eye gaze, avoiding excessive movement, shrinking slightly into the seat rather than sitting upright, or using bluffing tactics such as pretending to be reading or writing. It is possible to sit in a classroom, away from its focal centre, cause little disturbance, and virtually never be noticed. Observational studies have suggested, this is not an uncommon experience. So often, students seem to come to school to watch teachers working.

Understanding how we process information: more problems with the recitation

One of the major principles of learning is that a learner needs to make an *active response* to the source of learning. This idea runs through all theories of learning irrespective of whether or not we use terms such as 'behaviourist', 'cognitivist', or 'constructionist'. Within the world of psychology, there is no such thing as passive learning, unless this term implies learning to do nothing, in a manner akin to learned helplessness. When we are learning from listening or watching, our minds are highly active. All such effects are mediated through our active working memories. For instance, when the mind is focused, observational learning can produce powerful effects. People will often learn more effectively from watching a model perform than from doing and performing that same action in the flesh. Although we note the learners need to be active, this does not mean being active in the physical sense of having to respond overtly.

The teacher's role, agreed upon by all parties and all theories of learning, is to invite and induce students to engage actively with learning sources. A great deal of information flows through teachers' talk. But when a teacher exposes students to high levels of their talk, the students' basis for knowing what is relevant or not can be undermined. Besides straight overload, this phenomenon is akin to the *redundancy effect* as identified by cognitive load researchers. Studies into the characteristics of effective teachers have found that they will explain material extremely well, but in brief periods of time, for instance in 5- to 7-minute bursts, whereas a novice teacher would have taken longer. In short, instructors who assume that students will learn simply by listening for long periods of time are buying into ideas inconsistent with what we know of normal human capacities, as described by information processing theories.

The available studies into paying attention and vigilance indicate that mental focus drops off after 10 minutes. Although there will be large individual differences, a sensible working hypothesis is that students at the high-school level may listen intensively for perhaps up to 10 minutes. After that, overload factors come into play, as do other aspects such as ego depletion and simple boredom. In fact, there are two major theories about **mind wandering** in the neuroscience literature. One theory reflects the notion of **ego depletion** and a failure in self-regulation (see Chapter 26). That is, one's ability to focus intensively (or to try hard) literally runs out through biological exhaustion, indexed by glucose levels available to the brain. Hence, it is necessary to conserve one's energies ready for the next trial coming up in the future. In this theory, mind wandering is an adaptive strategy for conservation of one's resources.

The second theory is called *cascading inattention*. This reflects the role of overload in preventing the mind from following the story being told. In other words, excessive input is threatening to one's clear mental organisation and gives arise to confusion. The mind is striving for simplicity, but the input implies complexity. In practice, both these theories, depletion and confusion, suggest the same: *that student attention deteriorates over the course of a lesson*. One study with university students found that by half way through lectures, 55 per cent of students will report 'yes' when asked if they are mind wandering at the time. Another study found that good students are able to regulate their attention by literally 'tuning in' and 'tuning out' throughout entire lectures.

The common-sense finding, that attention is a limited resource, is compounded by other research suggesting students (at all levels) are frequently exposed to instructional explanations they are unable to comprehend. What has been communicated to a group can be well out of sync with individual students' capacity to understand and memorise complex information relayed. Within any one class, differences in students' prior knowledge will account for large differences in their understandings of the same content. To attain high levels of understanding and mastery, instructional explanations need to be adapted to individuals' knowledge prerequisites. But this goal is unlikely to be achieved for all at the level of whole group instruction.

It has been repeatedly shown, through both classroom and laboratory studies, that students who arrive at high school with misconceptions about phenomena will not alter their misconceptions as a result of directive instruction or simply listening to 'correct' explanations. Such students are often unaccustomed to having their views of the world challenged. Such misconceptions can be altered through sensitive challenge, careful expository teaching, active discussion, and individualised tutorial guidance. But the necessary conditions for this intensive and interactive form of teaching to occur are rarely possible under general classroom conditions.

IN PERSPECTIVE: Encouraging the student voice

Attempts have been made to alter classroom procedures to encourage quality student talk and active teacher listening. For example, consider the Paideia model of teaching, which considers that there should be three major parts to learning: didactic instruction, Socratic questioning, and coached product – and each should consume about one third of classroom time. Didactic teaching is not talking but active teaching of ideas and relationships between ideas, and coached product puts an emphasis on the coached more than the product. But the Socratic questioning is the key – it entails asking students open questions (usually about higher order ideas) and then listening to them answering and asking each other relevant questions. Creating opportunities for quality student talk requires deliberate actions, learning how to ask open questions (that do not then require teacher further involvement for some time) and a subtle shift in the teacher's role away from the traditional model.

Karen Murphy and colleagues have reviewed a large body of studies on quality talk and found many approaches that promote vocabulary and understanding of the fundamental ideas of lessons, and particularly that promote higher order thinking such as comprehension, reasoning, critical thinking, and argumentation. They found reducing teacher talk and increasing student talk was not enough. That is, merely putting students into groups and encouraging them to talk was not enough. Student talk is a means not an end. Deliberate strategies are needed to structure student talk (such as Paideia and other methods outlined by Murphy) that leads to greater comprehension and learning. In surveying the literature, it was evident that particularly strong effects associated with encouraging such student talk were found in the case of below average students.

Study guide questions

1   There are several terms used to refer to the recitation method, including IRE cycles, the CDR method, or even 'traditional chalk and talk'. Why is this form of teaching still around after some 200 years of criticism and antagonism from reformers?

2   What are the justified criticisms levelled against the recitation method?

3 Roughly what percentage of class time seems to involve teacher talk? How much time seems devoted to student talk?

4 Can you list any specific advantages that the recitation affords the teacher?

5 One worthwhile research finding is that once students are working through worked examples, then additional teacher talk is virtually useless. Why would this be the case?

6 One issue to note is that our attention is limited. Just what is known about mind wandering?

7 How does the prior knowledge factor create difficulties for the effectiveness of the recitation method?

8 Can student misconceptions be addressed through lecturing or direct instruction?

9 What are some of the strategies used to try to get students to talk more and participate in higher-level activities?

Reference notes

- Professor Nate Gage of Stanford University was a most respected researcher who helped to initiate the modern era of classroom-based research (Gage, 2009).

- The continuity of the recitation method over time (Cuban, 1984).

- Problems with teacher-directed lessons (Pressley & McCormick, 1995).

- Tensions between these two models have been apparent over the past century (Cuban, 1982). For a fascinating commentary on failure of open education over past century see Chall, 2000.

- Influential American book: *A Place Called School: Prospects for the future* (Goodlad, 1994). An English study suggesting teacher dominance and student low level of responding (F. Smith, Hardman, Wall, & Mroz, 2004).

- Many studies have now shown that although students learn a great deal from analysing worked examples, adding teachers' verbal explanations into this mix adds virtually nothing (Wittwer & Renkl, 2010). Verbally based instruction is virtually useless in communicating forms of procedural knowledge. These findings are consistent with the fact that people cannot explain to others just how they can catch a ball, or ride a bicycle. Overall, procedural knowledge is immune to verbal forms of instruction.

- Students come to school to watch teachers working (Hattie, 2012).

- Effective teachers use brief instructional bursts (Brophy, 1986).

- Human vigilance studies indicate drops in attention after several minutes (Ariga & Lleras, 2011). Students may have up to 10 minutes before attention fades (K. Wilson & Korn, 2007). However Wilson and Korn note that the

10-minutes notion is too simplistic. Wide variations are evident, and many students tune in and out in cycles.

- Mind wandering as depletion in executive processing (McVay & Kane, 2010). Mind wandering as confusion (Schooler *et al.*, 2011). For a valuable paper on mind-wandering research and implications for professional practice see Smallwood, Mrazek, & Schooler, 2011.

- Students' mind wandering during university lectures (Risko, Anderson, Sarwal, Engelhardt, & Kingstone, 2012). Capable university students show cycles of 'tuning in and out' during lectures (Bunce, Flens, & Neiles, 2010).

- Instructional explanations (at all levels of group classroom teaching) frequently fail to give rise to substantial learning effects for many students (Wittwer & Renkl, 2008, 2010).

- Students' misconceptions are not altered by simply listening to correct information through direct instruction (Aydeniz & Kotowski, 2012). For a classic reading on how the mind resists new information when it already has a view in place see Chinn & Brewer, 1993.

- The Paideia method (Billings & Fitzgerald, 2002). Review on increasing student talk (Murphy, Wilkinson, Soter, Hennessey, & Alexander, 2009).

7

Teaching for automaticity in basic academic skill

You volunteer for a laboratory experiment on word recognition and are asked to stare into a computer screen, blank except for a small red cross in the centre of the screen. You note a brief flash and are asked what you saw. You find yourself saying, 'Is it carrot?' You got it right. What is surprising is that the flash was of 20 milliseconds (ms), or one fiftieth of a second. This is so brief as to be called subliminal or below the normal visual threshold. To say *carrot* took your brain several seconds after the flash to come up with the word. Genuinely, you remain uncertain as to how that word surfaced in your head. Given any normal sense of the term, you did not see the word on the screen. To see that word with genuine visual clarity would require some 60 ms exposure, or something approaching a tenth of a second.

With such ultra-brief flashes, most often, no effects at all will surface. This is especially so if the word is unfamiliar. For example, suppose the word flashed had been *cappotto* (coat in Italian). Although you do not speak Italian, you can read the word *cappotto* easily, but it takes more time than 20 ms. If this word is unknown, you read it using *phonemic analysis*. This strategy needs a good half second (500 ms) exposure on the screen, followed by several seconds of quiet subvocal rehearsal to ensure you can verbalise it to an acceptable level.

In this experiment, correctly identifying the word *carrot* after a split second reflects **automaticity**. But reading *cappotto* requires conscious effort. Through phonemic analysis, some elements will spring to mind with ease, such as the phonemes that represent chunks, such as *cap-*, *pot-*, and *to-*. These elements are familiar. Of course you can read *cappotto* accurately, but the *phonemic recoding strategy* will impose load on your brain for several seconds. While working out how to pronounce the word using your active working memory, other aspects of your mental life had to be placed on hold.

When automaticity is lacking there is reduced capacity to think and comprehend

Why are such momentary load impositions so important? Because they have the capacity to disrupt activities such as comprehension, analysis, elaboration, and deep understanding. Such effects compound quickly. A succession of unfamiliar words seriously damages understanding. You cannot comprehend a 'big picture' if your mind's energies are hijacked by low-level processing. Continuity is broken. The goal shifts from understanding the total context to understanding the immediate word before you. The trouble is that the mind knows how important words are to accurate understandings. Any failure to understand a single word threatens the entire comprehension process.

When we read, we assimilate every word, every letter, within a time frame expressed through split seconds. By way of analogy, when driving in a foreign country, you discover road signs that make little sense. But every sign could be important and critical for one's safety. You drive past them attempting to fathom just what information is being communicated. In so doing you risk losing control of the situation, breaking laws, endangering other road uses, and ending up at the wrong location. In the past, researchers had believed that reading hinged on inferring meaning from context cues, rather than being hung up upon word-by-word processing. The assumption that reading for meaning hinged upon contextual cues, to the relative disregard of individual word recognition, was undermined by a substantial number of scientific studies in the 1970s and 1980s.

Three hundred words a minute: your natural reading speed

What else do we know about efficient reading? We know that as you read the eye will focus, or fixate, briefly on virtually every word, although you skip over smaller articles such as *at* or *in*. Young children often show two fixations on each word. By the high school years the pattern is one fixation per word, virtually in the middle of each word. Fixations occur roughly four times a second, so the eyes will show a jerky jump movement, or saccade, about every 250 ms. In mature readers the saccade jumps ahead by around nine letter spaces, occasionally more, and there is a perceptual span of about 20 letter spaces maximum. This span is reduced whenever you read difficult material.

Your eyes will fixate on individual words for varying times depending on how well you know the word. In most normal reading situations it is likely to be between 60 ms and 250 ms per word. An unfamiliar word will slow you down as you fix on it for lengthy times, even several seconds if the term is unknown. We know that the average mature reader will plough through roughly 300 words per minute (wpm) when the target material is facile. If it is really light reading, we will read even faster. Reading information-laden material is likely to slow you to about 200 wpm, This reflects the need to read the same words or sentence twice, a process called the look-back or regression.

Metaphorically, reading resembles a slide show in which you see each slide for about a fifth of a second. Each slide has one single word in clear view, but with some blurred letters out on the right hand side. You allow the show to proceed, but every now and again you yell 'stop', and replay slides you could not fathom, or which fail to fit the sentence forming in your working memory.

Opinions differ widely as to the value of speed reading. Superb readers may get up to about 500 wpm. At such a pace they skim rather than read each word. After all, 500 wpm accounts for an average of 8.4 words every second. Generally, most people can improve their speed through practice and effort, and perhaps read 10 per cent faster than they habitually do. Claims made about various speed reading practices are often exaggerated and must be interpreted cautiously. In counterpoint, we note a recent movement referred to as *slow reading* that emphasises advantages of savouring text and thinking deeply about what one is reading, rather than assuming speed is the crucible of intellectual processing.

For most mature readers, about 300 wpm feels a comfortable pace. When you speak, hold a conversation, or just listen, words are likely to be paced between 150 and 200 wpm. In publishing recorded books the target pace is set at around 150 to 170 wpm. Hence, the ability to read enables a faster pace of information input than natural oral communication. But when any information flow drops below 100 wpm, problems of comprehensibility creep in. To construct meaning from connected text, the mind relies on coherent sentences falling within the working memory span. Words must come in at a pace of around two or three per second. This pace feels natural and appears consistent with the speed with which we comprehend what is being said to us, provided we know what the individual words mean.

Toward understanding children's reading problems

It is well known that reading acquisition in the young child is related strongly to oral language facility and earlier phonological skills (i.e., awareness of how to manipulate sound patterns such as in rhyme). Opportunities to discriminate sounds carefully, to practise creating sounds, and appreciating language patterns in activities such as singing and poetry, all provide valuable, rich and entertaining experiences that assist early reading acquisition between 4 and 7 years of age. But, of course, oral language skills are developing well before 4 years of age, and there is reason to believe that sound discriminations are being formed from the first months of life.

During the 1980s, several key research groups around the world were investigating children's learning difficulties and came up with remarkably similar findings. Students diagnosed as being of normal intelligence, but still showing problems in reading, proved strangely slow when asked to read isolated words. This was so even when it was established they used these same words in everyday speech. These were children who would look at a word displayed on a computer screen and take almost a second or more to read it. The fact that their reading was accurate had often been taken to assume that they genuinely could read, but needed help in comprehending text in terms of inferring the meanings and goals of the exercise. In particular, another discovery was that these such children were especially slow when reading nonsense words such as DOMIRK, taking well over a second, and often much longer, to sound out such nonsense or pseudowords.

As findings piled up, it became more and more apparent that one of the major causes of reading failure lay in the fact many children were stuck on mental processing at the level of word access. The problem lay not in comprehension, but at an earlier point, one involving the information processing system responsible for word recognition. Previously, in the era before the 1980s, researchers and educators had been misled by the observation that such students could decode individual words accurately, and clearly did have strong word knowledge.

But earlier educators simply did not have tools to uncover that the decoding process was so slow and effortful that comprehension processes were being stymied. Being able to understand and use a word in speech is not the same as reading the same word quickly within text. This position, that slow decoding hampered the capacity to comprehend meaning, became known as the *simple theory of reading*, which has gained strength and validity over the past 40 years. Put simplistically, if you cannot process whole words rapidly, at two words a second, then understanding sentences becomes impossible, even though you fully know what each word means. This theory immediately accounted for previously documented findings that students with reading difficulty would present with large discrepancies between their reading ability and their oral listening comprehension ability.

The cultural progression: from oral facility to accurately reading text

Writing in the Annual Review of Psychology, neuroscientists Elizabeth Norton and Maryanne Wolf (2012) insightfully noted that:

> Perhaps the most remarkable thing about reading is that children develop reading skills seemingly in spite of nature. Reading began so recently in the evolutionary history of our species that we have no innate biological processes devoted specifically to reading. Rather, children are born with a rich neural architecture in place to support the acquisition of oral language, which provides the pre-eminent platform for written language. Certain brain areas are activated in response to the sounds and structure of language . . . In sharp contrast, each child must develop reading skills using brain areas that have evolved for other purposes such as language, vision, and attention.
>
> (pp. 428–429)

From the early 1980s, it was becoming apparent to researchers that reading was yet another example of developing expertise. We were not born with inherent ability to read. Instead, learning to read relies on spending time acquiring necessary skills, seeing them performed by others in the social world, copying such people, and participating in the reading community. One of the major skills to learn is to process information sequentially – that is, understand the words to then intuit the meaning. This is a learned skill, but often a skill missing in students who struggle to read.

Reading represents a major cultural achievement, subject to intergenerational forces and social learning factors. In many countries literacy levels are low, and, all too often, individual coaching is non-existent. Across the globe literacy rates vary from 25 per cent to 99 per cent of a country's population. Within Western societies we hold to an expectation that every child will achieve functional literacy. This expectation was emerging in Western society during the final period of the nineteenth century, and represents a graphic example of cultural expectations and human achievements shifting over time.

The notion that all individuals within society should be literate would have been viewed as unrealistic and unachievable 200 years ago. That universal education has been able to achieve great success in such goals tells us something remarkable about three things: (a) cultural factors, (b) human plasticity, and (c) the professional skills of teachers. Attaining near-universal literacy flies in the face of aspects we overlook too readily. As the Norton and Wolf quotation above indicates, we evolved with oral language communication and social sensitivity, but literacy skills were not part of our evolutionary makeup. Our brains are set up to read vocal patterns and social cues, but not to read these strange squiggles on the pages.

However, squiggles are what you are responding to at this second. To read these printed words you had to serve an apprenticeship in decoding. In common with other aspects of expertise, every one of us quickly forgets how hard it was for such a skill to become automatic. This is of one of the themes emphasised in this book: *that achieving expertise brings with it a level of obliviousness about effort and time required to learn.* We possess no natural insight into why others fail to achieve the competence we developed successfully. Success and automaticity render us blind to difficulties experienced by the beginner.

Advancing the simple view of reading

If you read connected text (such as sentences) at any pace under 60 wpm, then understanding what you read becomes almost impossible. It is understandable, therefore, that significant numbers of young students experience reading difficulties. For many individual children, insufficient time is spent accumulating the experience necessary to develop expertise. Reading skills cannot emerge without training and encouragement from adults who exemplify extensive literacy usage in their daily lives. For many children, such facilitative experiences are lacking. Many arrive at school with a lack of automaticity within their basic sound-symbol functioning. With a minimal level of phonics training, they may be able to fully identify letters, verbalise sound symbol relationships, and read isolated words through sheer effort. But, if the pace of processing is not brought up to speed, through intensive self-directed practice, reading for understanding will remain beyond grasp.

The simple view of reading leads to the idea that if a child does not engage with reading, and fails to spend hundreds of hours actively reading for themselves, then fluency in reading for comprehension cannot develop. Inefficient and slow decoding prevents the child from being able to input written information as fast as his or her oral language skills and listening comprehension should naturally allow. This simple view, outlined originally by Philip Gough in 1972, and developed in an important paper by David LaBerge and Jay Samuels in 1974, has steadily accumulated a substantial database over four decades.

The parallels in mathematics: the importance of instant retrieval of number combinations

Two plus three equals *what*? Being able to access the word *five* within a third of a second represents knowledge that assists when you later need to respond to problems such as 'Find x in $6x - 31 = 2 + 3$'. A basic repertoire of such number facts and combinations reduces mental load. If asked to multiply 26 by 4, you instantly recall 4 times 25 is 100. So it has to be 4 more. And so on. Studies have shown that mastery of such elements can reduce memory load to almost zero. You can access the number fact that $2 + 2 = 4$, with only the slightest effort involved. So how are such basic number facts acquired in the first instance?

Some number facts are known through simplistic counting, at least for quantities fewer than five. From five and above, a cultural system is activated, which in our case employs Arabic numerals upon base 10. This code represents an incredible cultural achievement. The code becomes so natural we are unlikely to even conceive of mathematics as a cultural achievement. But you were not born knowing that one third of 12 is 4. You had to learn this little gem at some point in your early years. You did so through a combination of exposure to others, working it out for yourself, playing with concrete materials, experimenting with different forms of representation, and then rehearsing the acquired knowledge unit within your immediate memory, transferring it into long-term memory, and having it validated thousands of times.

In the early primary classroom years, teachers work hard to ensure that students acquire number facts as meaningful units, while aiming at quick and efficient retrieval as one central goal. Mnemonic devices such as the 'times tables' are valuable tools for consolidation work rather than devices for learning multiplication facts. Students who lack number sense and awareness of multiplication principles cannot learn such tables as isolated chanting devices. But after having mastered basic number facts, then students can move onto more difficult problems with the expectation of continuing success. A well-replicated finding is that students who present with difficulties in mathematics by the end of the junior primary years show deficits in their ability to access number facts with automaticity. Such deficits stymie further development in this area, often with additional adverse consequences such as students experiencing lack of confidence, lack of enjoyment, and feelings of helplessness.

There was a period in which teachers were encouraged to believe that rote learning stood in antagonism to deeper understanding. This notion is misleading since all indices of knowledge display positive associations. There is no meaningful cleft between 'mere surface knowledge' and 'deep understanding'. On the other hand, the notion of automaticity implies that when basic skills are automated, mental space becomes available for deeper levels of thinking and understanding through acquiring knowledge. Knowledge literally provides the mind with room to move, to develop, and to change. Repetition and consolidation are vehicles enabling knowledge to be stored within retrievable units, thereby accelerating mental growth through conceptual mastery and deeper understanding.

Why number facts are hard to learn

Contrary to what many adults customarily assume, acquiring these knowledge units, as basic number combinations is, by no means, a quick or simple matter. As adults, we underestimate the effort involved in initial knowledge acquisition. For young children, at some point in their development, simple arithmetic questions are difficult problems to ponder and resolve. Complexity is created because solving such problems requires the orchestration of several different knowledge sources such as (a) counting, (b) number-to-symbol correspondence, and (c) the order irrelevance principle.

At the present stage of your adult life, you can answer the question 'What is 5 plus 7?' without effort. But to the average six-year-old, this same question represents a genuinely interesting problem. Nevertheless, he or she knows how to solve it through activating appropriate knowledge sources acquired earlier. Once this 5 plus 7 problem has been resolved on many different occasions, its result can be expressed as the chunk, $5 + 7 = 12$, a unit of knowledge available for future use in activities such as understanding and problem solving.

This cognitive processing description is consistent with the finding that failure to cope with upper primary mathematics is strongly predicted by deficiencies in basic computational knowledge within the initial two years of schooling, even after controlling for factors such as intelligence, gender, adjustment, and income level. Students who display low levels of number facts at the junior primary level will proceed into the upper levels, but remain 'at risk', and are adversely affected by factors such as time pressures. To express this finding another way, when these students are expected to follow mathematics instruction quickly, or are tested under timed conditions, deficits become even more manifest as negative cascades begin to kick in.

We can also note that studies conducted under laboratory conditions show that, for both adults and children, speed of access in memory functions strongly predicts two other attributes: confidence and positive feelings. Whenever people are able to recall important information quickly there is an inherent sense in that the information is correct, together with a momentary flush of pleasure.

When automaticity is lacking, coping leads to a heavy load

The cost or consequence of failure to become fast and agile in knowledge access of number facts and word recognition is that much school learning becomes increasingly difficult as the student moves into the upper primary years. The student is forced into regarding academic demands as problems to tackle recurrently with mental techniques known under two descriptive labels (a) *means–end thinking*, and (b) *divide-and-conquer strategies*. These terms refer to the mind having to use effort to break larger tasks into smaller units that can be tackled in sequence. Divide-and-conquer is what we all do when faced with difficult and complex problems. The trouble is the sheer level of effort, or **cognitive load**, required to remain successful. Such effortful strategies involve switching between trying to work out task demands, trying to understand what the problem is, determining which operations to perform, and then trying to see if the goal is achieved.

When a child lacks knowledge access, then divide-and-conquer strategies are employed continually. But when the student has well-developed knowledge, has fast word recognition, and has mastered a large repertoire of number facts, such conscious and demanding strategies are used less often. These strategies then become valuable as System 2 backup strategies, rather than being squandered as first line defences. Metaphorically, if coping in the classroom is analogous to a battle, then it pays to keep the best troops in reserve for when they are needed to save the day.

How can automaticity be taught?

Strangely enough, we really do not have a great deal of knowledge on how to teach for automaticity. It can require a large investment in time within the school day to provide the necessary practice conditions in which students become fully automatic in basic knowledge skills. In Chapter 11 we note that experts will typically devote 3 to 4 hours a day to their craft. It could be a decade before elite-level skills are developed. In the area of reading skills, this formulation may still apply. Hence, it is inopportune to presume that the role of the early childhood teacher has to be that of the 'automaticity coach'. Automaticity is something that every child has to achieve through consistent support and application, involving all the significant adults in the child's life. It is not an attribute that can be quickly trained up, or assimilated through several short classroom lessons. Nevertheless, there are many things teachers can do to assist.

One well-researched classroom method in the literacy teaching area is referred to as **repeated reading**. More correctly, this notion represents a family of different teaching techniques where the underlying principle is that the individual student reads aloud to another person. With repetitions, reading improves dramatically on indices of fluency and prosody. Prosody refers to speech becoming more natural, animated, meaningful, and with good use of stress markers. One finding from this body of research is that word recognition improves markedly for the words read, but does not generalise to other words. For instance, repeated readings involving the word *carrot* render this word more automatic but has no effect upon recognition of *carat* or *carpet*. The impact of any form of automaticity training remains highly specific to the training materials.

The assumption is that students develop automaticity through recurring experiences within their young lives beginning with stimulation and encouragement in the home. Time spent in shared reading experiences and number games is of key importance. The opportunity to use money responsibly provides an early impetus to the mathematics area, as do experiences such as following recipes in cooking and measuring distance. The existing technology and practice of education is based on the presumption that such everyday experiences prepare the student for formal instruction. The assumption is that emergent skill development permits a coherently structured curriculum to be taught and mastered.

However, the inevitable fact is that special programs are needed whenever this assumption appears less than valid. Across the globe many remedial programs have been devised for students who fail to progress as anticipated through large group classroom teaching within the first two years of schooling. This is not the place to review such work but we can cite two such high quality programs in wide use within schools in Australia. Both aim specifically at increasing levels of automaticity, and both have been validated through positive evaluation trials. In the reading area, MULTILIT (making up lost time in literacy) was developed at Macquarie University and has had considerable success in developing slow readers from disadvantaged backgrounds into students who can cope well with fundamental literacy demands at school. In both the reading and mathematics areas, the Quicksmart program, from the University of New England (Australia), has also been thoroughly validated through follow-up research over the past decade.

Such teacher-directed programs are based on explicit instructional practices and operate through small groups where students participate with structured personal goals that involve becoming fast and efficient in retrieval times. For instance, such programs commonly use flash cards and game-like activities that encourage active participation coupled with immediate corrective feedback. A particular feature of the Quicksmart program is the use of a computer administered testing procedure that records and tracks individual response times. Students can benefit substantially from these intensive teaching programs, as has become evident from large gains on achievement tests. The evaluation studies also report on other emotional aspects, such as students no longer feeling incompetent.

An evaluation of the Quicksmart program noted its use with more than 2,000 students in 150 schools across Australia. After 30 weeks of program participation, average gains representing between two and three years progress were found on the Progressive Achievement Test in Mathematics with effect sizes commonly about 0.7, and higher in some locations. Evaluations of MULTILIT also report effect sizes of this order on a battery of measures including vocabulary, spelling accuracy, fluency in reading short texts, and reading comprehension. In the words of Dr Kevin Wheldall, 'students from socially disadvantaged backgrounds can, and do, make substantial progress when offered effective reading instruction based on the available scientific research evidence' (2009, p. 151).

IN PERSPECTIVE: Automaticity and the hidden role of time

Developing automaticity in cognitive processing represents a major goal for students as they progress through the reading and mathematics curricula in the junior primary years. Without such development, subsequent academic work becomes a matter of constantly using effortful and costly mental strategies. We want our students to be prepared to meet challenges in learning with energy in reserve, rather than being pressured to use problem-solving skills on a continual basis, at much risk of ego depletion. The paradox is that mastery of 'low level' knowledge reduces the need to keep activating 'high level' problem-solving processes when coping with more routine demands.

One underlying element, akin to 'the elephant in the room', is time and how it is deployed within the everyday life experiences of the developing individual. Scores of studies have documented remarkable differences in sheer volume of reading. For instance, one study found the content of young children's out-of-school reading varied between 16 and 1,933 words in a single week. Similar findings, showing such massive differences in both volume and time, are commonly reported. From a teacher's view, these studies make for disturbing reading.

Development requires time devoted to practicing lower order skills under conditions of relative ease, enjoyment, and strong motivation. Whatever a child spends a great deal of time doing, then skilfulness and automaticity will follow to support the fundamental cognitive demands of that very same activity. But if an activity does not take place, then development cannot proceed. This may be a simple theory of knowledge development, but it comes with profound implications.

Study guide questions

1 To be able to read a word with automaticity requires perhaps a tenth of a second. But if automaticity is not present, then just how long will you need to look at the word for?

2 If you cannot read with automaticity you will use phonemic analysis? What is this? (Sometimes this skill is called phonemic recoding.)

3 But when you have to rely on such strategies to decode, then what is occurring at the level of comprehension?

4 How fast should you read?

5 Just what are your eyes doing as you read? What is the relation between eye fixations and reading comprehension?

6 Children with reading difficulties can still read quite well, but slowly. Why is this a huge problem?

7 What is known as the simple theory of reading?

8 What is one third of 12? Just how did you discover the answer to this question? What learning processes did you need to go through in your early years?

9 In fact, acquiring basic number skills is a relatively difficult endeavour, far harder than most adults appreciate. What makes such learning so difficult?

10 Whenever automaticity is not evident, students might still proceed, but with reduced efficiency and reduced comprehension. The paradox is that they may have to use high-level mental strategies, much more so, and much earlier, than students with automaticity. Explain this phenomenon in terms of cognitive load.

11 What are some of the educational means we have for developing automaticity?

Reference notes

■ Dr Keith Rayner has devoted his career to fine-grain analysis and measurements of eye movements during reading. While such research is technical, the following two papers provide easy to read reviews (Pollatsek & Rayner, 2009; Rayner, 2001). Also an informative account found in a chapter in Samuels and Farstrup, 2011.

■ Major reviews of scientific studies in reading (Samuels & Farstrup, 2006, 2011; Stanovich, 2000). The 2006 book focuses on fluency, or speed of reading. For information more on children's reading difficulties see E. S. Norton and Wolf, 2012; Wolf, 2007.

■ The simple theory of reading, originally promoted by Gough (Gough & Tunmer, 1986; Hoover & Gough, 1990), and developed by LaBerge and

Samuels, 1974, is widely accepted. Some critics misconstrued the theory as suggesting it implies slow readers have problems simply in decoding and not in oral language. But the theory clearly recognises students as needing considerable development in language skills. No theory could possibly assume that all students are somehow 'equal' in language competency.

■ A philosophical aside is that some find 'simple' theories unacceptable because the phenomenon itself is inherently complex. But there is no inherent obstacle in analysing complex processes through clear and parsimonious explanations. This is what science does well.

■ Deficits in early number facts impact upon later mathematics progress (Gersten *et al.*, 2012; Gersten, Jordan, & Flojo, 2005). The lasting impact of early detected mathematics difficulties across the primary years (Duncan *et al.*, 2007).

■ Laboratory studies, with adults and children alike, show fast access and successful memory recall produce both confidence and positive feelings (Ackerman & Koriat, 2011; V. Thompson & Morsanyi, 2012). The Thompson article is a review drawing attention to the positive feeling of rightness that follows on from fast and fluent processing.

■ Research into repeated reading as a remedial method is reviewed in Therrien, 2004.

■ Reviews of research into necessary components in remedial reading instruction (Reynolds, Wheldall, & Madelaine, 2010, 2011). Making up lost time in literacy or MULTILIT: developed at Macquarie University, Australia (Wheldall, 2009).

■ The Quicksmart program (Bellert, 2009): developed under Dr John Pegg at the SiMEERR National Research Centre at the University of New England, Australia. Other publications and annual evaluation reports are available on their excellent website www.une.edu.au/simerr/quicksmart.

■ Massive variations in youngsters' reading volume are found (Allington, 1984). For an illuminating article indicating how reading increases students' knowledge see Cunningham and Stanovich, 2003. Major research review of effects of print exposure (i.e. amount of reading) is found in Mol and Bus, 2011.

8

The role of feedback

Imagine arriving in an unfamiliar foreign city and needing to check into your hotel. Deprived of GPS, you ask a local person on the street. Despite your bad pronunciation, this person recognises the name of the hotel and proceeds to inform you of its history, of its terrible cuisine, and tells you not to go there. But still, you plead, 'How do I find it?' The local then says to consult a street map, and tells you that his brother runs a course on navigation and direction finding. You tell him that you are not wanting to do any such course, so he asks just what sort of course are you interested in. We have a communication breakdown.

The above paragraph was intended to be humorous. But something remarkably close to this form of communication breakdown surfaces when we contrast what teachers tell us about what feedback means to them with what students say they want. When we survey teachers, the following dimensions, the ten Cs, emerge. In the teachers' view, feedback consists of:

- comments, and more instructions about how to proceed
- clarification
- criticism
- confirmation
- content development
- constructive reflection
- correction (focus on pros and cons)
- cons and pros of the work
- commentary (especially on an overall evaluation)
- criterion relative to a standard.

Teachers claim to give students high levels of feedback on their work, but students say that this is not what they experience. When we interview students on what they understand by feedback and why it is important to them, one theme emerges almost universally: *they want to know how to improve their work so that they can do better next time.* Students tend to be future-focussed, rather than dwelling on what they have done beforehand and left behind. They are aware that past products are imperfect specimens but want to move on, and are willing to learn more new stuff provided their teachers play the same game. They will continue to exert effort provided the past efforts are treated with some respect. What they do not welcome is critique, which they find unnecessary, lengthy, personal, and hurtful. Of course they expect mistakes and want mistakes corrected. But they are sensitive to the climate under which criticism is given. Often, what a teacher intends as helpful critical feedback turns to personal ego evaluation in the eyes of the receiver.

The dilemma is that students want and need information on 'where to next', but teachers often act as though that is achieved through negative feedback. Student work must be corrected, and mistakes therein can be manifest, numerous, and highly visible. But negative feedback can be problematic. Students may feel the tasks set were unreasonable. They may believe they were taught poorly, or were expected to go beyond what had been taught. They may believe that the level of effort they put in was substantial, but has gone by unrecognised.

They may feel the standard expected of them is being applied unfairly, or is differentially applied across class members. They may believe that they did a little better than their mate and that this is enough. Within the classroom, **social comparison** is rife. After all, just who is to say what is a 'good essay', and what is a 'poor essay'. Furthermore, 'we all know some teachers are unfair' is a familiar mantra. At times we have found students ignore a teacher's copious comments on written work, which they find irrelevant to their moving forward.

Besides this natural empathy gap, another hidden factor in receiving criticism concerns its volume. The principle 'bad is stronger than good' means that we mentally balance one bad event against perhaps four or five good ones. If the ratio of good to bad events drops under three we can expect trouble. Yet, when we critique our students' work, the number of negative comments can easily exceed the number of positive statements. We are not suggesting that students need a continual supply of positive affirmations (which produces its own problems), only that they will remain sensitive to the balance between positive and negative events in their lives.

Matching feedback to knowledge level

We have also noted that some instructors appear to administer feedback and marking procedures in a mechanical way, in the belief that all students are somehow 'the same'. However, it is apparent that learners need different types of feedback depending on their current skill level. Beginners need feedback based on content knowledge as they are striving to build basic knowledge and vocabulary. Hence, they need assurance and corrective feedback, often in the form of decisions such as correct versus incorrect, or right versus wrong. Intermediate learners have acquired basic concepts but need help linking ideas together, seeing relationships, and extending the basic ideas. They need assurance that they are applying the right methods and strategies or suggestions for alternative strategies (for instance, 'strong use of adjectives', 'good use of the acceleration principle', or 'a well-constructed argument, but have you thought of what this implies for the future?').

At more advanced levels, helpful feedback takes the form of supporting the self-regulated or more conceptual learner such that sincere efforts to extend and apply knowledge even further are actively recognised. In short, different types of feedback work best depending on the individual's phase of learning – corrective feedback is suited for novices, process feedback is needed as the learner becomes proficient, and elaborated conceptual feedback becomes effective with highly competent students.

Making the feedback process more effective

The vital role that feedback plays in assisting learners to improve their performances has been recognised from the beginnings of behavioural science, some 150 years ago. In the VL synthesis, feedback was associated with an effect size of 0.73 indicating it is one of the most powerful factors implicated in academic learning and resultant achievement. The not so good news is that the variability of the effectiveness of feedback is huge – certain types of feedback are more effective than others – so we need to be able to specify the forms it should take and when it is associated with strong learning gains, and when it is not.

Receiving feedback enables the learner to close a critical gap, specifically the gap between current status and a more desirable level of achievement. Feedback is not the same thing as reward or reinforcement, which are terms that refer to motivational factors. Instead, feedback refers to the process of securing information enabling change through adjustment or calibration of efforts in order to bring a person closer to a well-defined goal.

In short, receiving appropriate feedback is incredibly empowering. Why? Because it enables the individual to move forwards, to plot, plan, adjust, rethink, and thus exercise self-regulation in realistic and balanced ways. This mental processing view of feedback brings with it an important caveat. *Feedback works because the goal is known and accurately defined through realistic assessment.* This is why assessments become vital in all forms of teaching and formal instruction. Students see assignments and assessments as what the teacher actually values. The sooner the outcomes are known and articulated through objective measures or assignments, the more the student can focus on achieving them.

Assessment information is powerful if teachers and students have clear notions of what success looks like while they are engaged in the activity that leads to the assessment. Clarifying the criteria of success is not merely saying 'You must get at least a B', but showing students worked examples at various levels of success. Or in this case, going a step further, showing students worked examples of an A and a B and a discussion of how they are different.

Imagine a group of students who are about to embark on a series of lessons, and during these early experiences we pause and show them the various ways they will be successful at the end of the lessons, or tell them how they will know when they have been successful in these lessons. Now compare this with a similar class that is not told about what success looks like. The differences can be huge, and the VL synthesis has shown large effect-size differences between these two scenarios. Also, this is a relatively cheap investment, takes little time but of course it provides teachers with a challenge – that of working alongside the students to maximise the number who reach the success criteria.

The task now is to move the students from their current status to achieve these criteria of success. The purpose of feedback is to reduce the gap between current and desired states of knowing. Strangely enough, the principles are explicitly exposed in video games. These games map and monitor your current performance (where you finished the game last time), provide a challenge sufficiently above where you are now (like Goldilocks, not too hard but not too easy), and then pile in the feedback to allow you to reach the next level of success. Many of us will spend hours engaging with these games as we love the challenges involved. Imagine if there was no feedback, or no calibration of challenge – would we continue to engage in these games? Imagine if the challenge was too hard or too often too easy – would we continue to engage in these games?

For many students, classrooms can be akin to video games without the feedback, without knowing what success looks like, or knowing when you attain success in the key tasks. Further, the goals faced are either too hard or too easy. Lack of engagement is an understandable reaction. Feedback is powerful if students know (a) what success looks like, (b) appreciate it is aimed at reducing the gap between where they are and where they need to be, and (c) when it is focused on providing them information about where to next.

To praise or not to praise

Within educational circles, there has been much misinformation about the psychology of praise. To some extent this notion was mixed up with Skinnerian psychology, behavioural modification, and the notion (which is incorrect) that praise has more powerful effects than punishment. But the notion was also mixed up with the self-esteem movement. Two readily identified fallacies are that (a) people learn more when they receive praise, and (b) people need continual praise to establish and maintain feelings of self-worth. Despite thousands of projects, neither statement has any serious support. Praise makes people happier, sometimes, and in some places. It can steer you toward wanting to do certain things, or induce you to stay in the field. But it does not assist you to learn.

We know of no research finding suggesting that receiving praise itself can assist a person to learn or to increase their knowledge and understanding. Research into the classroom use of praise by teachers was reviewed by noted researcher Jere Brophy, who found that praise often is used for interpersonal reasons, or as a management strategy. But the research found that praise did not serve as viable facilitator in academic classroom learning.

Praise has been used in clinical situations, for instance in treating some types of slow learners in carefully controlled situations. One effective clinical procedure is called shaping, where small gains are encouraged through carefully timed praise. But when it comes to the general classroom, it is apparent that praise is not a strong source of reinforcement. When you praise a student in class, that class is learning that you praise a good deal, and that is what is being taught at the moment.

Praise is generally seen as a public show involving explicit terms such as 'good boy' or 'you are so clever'. We have witnessed parents and teachers attempt to operate on the principle that they have to issue praise every time the child or student does something of which they approve. Any such continuous praise violates one of the well-entrenched cannons of behavioural psychology: that intermittent and unpredictable reinforcement produces strong and persistent habits, whereas constant and predictable reinforcement leads you to stop efforts once reinforcement is no longer present. Seriously, if we want to produce people who lack persistence and self-control, who are accustomed to immediate gratification as their default position, then rewarding them on every single opportunity is one known technique.

Instead, when dealing with other people in teaching contexts, it is more responsible to increase informational feedback while going lean on praise. Students need clear indications that the worthwhile target they are harbouring is becoming real. But they do not want to waste energy being worried about their standing on your approval index. The important thing is to set a positive and friendly climate – one of mutual respect and trust. But being praised repeatedly and excessively is a recipe for suspicions such as 'What is wrong with me that teacher needs to praise me all the time?', or 'If I scratch myself, maybe she will praise that too. Big deal', or 'Why aren't you giving me honest feedback?'

When praise discourages effort

Another fascinating aspect to the story of praise surfaced through the work of Carol Dweck. In several experimental studies she found young children's persistence in problem solving can be *reduced* after being praised for being clever on earlier easier tasks. Receiving praise for being intelligent or clever has an unfortunate consequence of drawing attention to ability as a limited resource. If you then have to face a more difficult task, your ability is back on the line: quite simply, you may not have enough of it. Praising a student for possessing native ability on easier tasks may have a destructive effect on striving when the going really does get tough.

The bind is that whenever the task in front of you is seriously hard, it is important not to start thinking about your ability. It is important to keep the mind open on this score. The mental focus has to be placed upon the task rather than the ego. However, praising someone for their ability can shift the attribution process the wrong direction, paradoxically raising self-doubt.

Learners need to expect difficult tasks to be difficult. But harm is done when experiencing difficulty is wrongly interpreted. Believing one has to be successful all the time can create self-doubt leading to reduced coping efforts. A recent French study with 11-year-olds showed that the effect of failure on a difficult problem-solving task could be offset through students being helped to understand that experiencing difficulty is a perfectly normal and expected part of the learning process. Students who heard this explicit message from the experimenter performed better on tests of comprehension and memory than those who did not hear this message. These students, the ones who experienced failure they could explain, performed more strongly on the tests than other students who had succeeded on the earlier tasks when they had been set at an easier level.

Feedback in your professional world

As a professional, it is critical to *know thy impact*. It may seem ironic but the more teachers seek feedback about their own impact, the more the benefits accrue to their students. When teachers ask about who has been impacted, what they have been impacted by, and what the magnitude of impact is, then they are more likely to adapt their instructional methods and attend carefully to their students' learning progress. This is the essence of what we have called 'assessment for learning', which is better termed 'assessment for teaching'. Assessment of your students is a powerful way to learn about your impact.

The beauty of this argument is that assessment for learning is now considered to be about the interpretations that teachers make about their actions, and takes the attention away from the nature of the tests. As Michael Scriven, who introduced these terms almost 50 years ago, noted, formative and summative refer to the interpretations not the test. A test can be interpreted by the teacher as formative in that the teacher modifies what he or she needs to do next, or it can be summative in that it comes at the end of a series of lessons. The more the teacher receives feedback from student engagement, then the more likely he or she is to adapt their actions and expectations and thus students are the beneficiaries.

IN PERSPECTIVE: Ensuring feedback is effective

From the student view, receiving praise in the classroom is a social learning experience saying more about the teacher's goals than the student or attribute singled out for attention. Praise effectively informs the student of the things teachers approve. While this is an important message, it need not be repeated *ad nauseum*.

Students work out your habits, quirks, and dispositions quickly. Once that is out of the way, the class can get down to the serious business of learning without having to worry about what you will approve or disapprove of.

When praise is combined with feedback information then the latter is diluted and possibly nullified. Our claim certainly is not to never give praise; to the contrary it is welcomed by students. A modicum of praise can usefully set a pleasant climate in which to work. However, do not confuse praise with the process of providing feedback.

Instead, students are crying out for feedback that provides information they need to achieve their goals – *where to next*! They need to know how to close the gap between where they are now, and where they need to be. They are uninterested in evaluative post mortems about their past work unless there is crystal clear guidance about the next challenge and how best to get there. To be motivated is to be able to perceive how success is achievable within the short term.

One function of feedback is to assist learners discern just which goals are realistic and doable. Recall that one of the principles allied to the Willingham thesis (Chapter 1) is that we are motivated by perceivable and closable **knowledge gaps** but turned off by knowledge chasms. The feedback you offer your students provides the tools they need to be able to perceive the immediate path ahead, and so decide that it is really worth the effort. Since effort is a limited commodity, it cannot be squandered on things doomed to fail, or chasms too wide to bridge.

By way of summary, John Hattie and Mark Gan reviewed the extensive literature on the effective use of feedback principles within the process of instruction and arrived at several significant observations. Specifically:

1 It is important to focus on how feedback is received rather than how it is given.
2 Feedback becomes powerful when it renders criteria for success in achieving learning goals transparent to the learner.
3 Feedback becomes powerful when it cues a learner's attention onto the task, and effective task-related strategies, but away from self-focus.
4 Feedback needs to engage learners at, or just above, their current level of functioning.
5 Feedback should challenge the learner to invest effort in setting challenging goals.
6 The learning environment must be open to errors and to disconfirmation.
7 Peer feedback provides a valuable platform for elaborative discourse. Given opportunities, students readily learn appropriate methods and rules by which respectful peer feedback can be harnessed.
8 Feedback cues teachers to deficiencies within their instructional management and can lead to efforts to improve teaching practices.

Study guide questions

1 A type of empathy gap is apparent when teachers' and students' views on feedback are compared. What do students generally want from feedback?

2 Another gap appears in relation to how much feedback students claim they receive. What is the common finding here?

3 One finding is that feedback ought to take different forms in accord with student skill level. We can identify three such levels. Beginners need corrective feedback, but what type of feedback is of value to students at the other two levels?

4 Feedback reduces the gap between performance and desired states. Can you explain what that means? What motives are assumed by this idea?

5 How does praise differ from feedback? It is often assumed that praise is something that reinforces learning. Is this view consistent with the information given in this chapter?

6 Have you witnessed adults who seem to be praising students excessively? What observations would you make about such people? How do students react to high levels of praise?

7 Carol Dweck's studies have implicated praise as undermining effortful striving. Just how might this happen? What process is involved?

8 So what factors are important when using feedback to help students learn? Review the list from Hattie and Gan and try to see if you can add to this list.

Reference notes

■ Reviews of the literature on feedback (Hattie & Gan, 2011; Hattie & Timperley, 2007).

■ Communication breakdown: Discrepancies between teacher and student expectations (Carless, 2006; Nuthall, 2007).

■ Major analysis of role of praise in classroom life (Brophy, 1981).

■ Receiving praise can signal to the student, and to others, that the teacher sees him or her as deficient or of low ability (Graham & Barker, 1990; Meyer, 1982, 1992). Similar effects apply when an individual student gets unsolicited help from a teacher (Graham & Barker, 1990).

■ Discouraging persistence through praising young children for being clever (Dweck, 1999).

■ French study into helping 11-year-olds interpret failure as natural (Autin & Croizet, 2012).

■ General diffuse praise can reduce skilled performance through bringing attention onto the self (Baumeister, Hutton, & Cairns, 1990).

■ Formative and summative assessment: this terminology was introduced by Scriven, 1967.

9

Acquiring complex skills through social modelling and explicit teaching

How can we assist students to develop skilful learning strategies? There has been much tension in the field between the notion of the classroom teacher as an instructor, or direct change agent, and teacher as the facilitator or 'guide on the side'. One of the messages from the VL synthesis is that scores of studies support the notion of teacher as a direct change agent or activator. Table 9.1 shows some of the effect sizes evident in this area, when achievement test scores are used as the measure. The notion of teacher as a facilitator is flawed if this brings a de-emphasis upon stimulating knowledge acquisition through clear and direct instructional methods. Advances in student learning are related strongly to the nature (in terms of both quality and quantity) of the instruction that teachers provide during the course of normal lessons. But how direct should such instruction be? And what if the content to be taught involves complex cognition?

A variety of terms is often used in this area, including direct instruction, explicit teaching, active teaching, and expository teaching. This diversity of terminology is generally unhelpful. The terms do not refer to different or discrete entities. In reading the literature, we find such words are used, more or less interchangeably, to refer to moments in time when the teacher is taking a leading role in ensuring students are gaining essential knowledge and skills for the class, under the expectation that students will learn the lesson content, and so be able to acquire and demonstrate enhanced levels of knowledge and skill.

Learning complex skills: exposure is important but not enough

Explicit teaching hinges on certain foundation components. For example, the teacher assumes the role of a *coach* or *model*, consciously using the principles of observational learning in demonstrations. The central idea behind social modelling is to allow the learner an opportunity to witness the skills displayed by a

TABLE 9.1 Effect sizes on achievement for teacher as activator and teacher as facilitator

TEACHER AS ACTIVATOR	d	TEACHER AS FACILITATOR	d
Teaching students self-verbalisation	.76	Inductive teaching	.33
Teacher clarity	.75	Simulation and gaming	.32
Reciprocal teaching	.74	Inquiry-based teaching	.31
Feedback	.74	Smaller classes	.21
Metacognitive strategies	.67	Individualised instruction	.22
Direct instruction	.59	Web-based learning	.18
Mastery Learning	.57	Problem-based learning	.15
Providing worked examples	.57	Discovery method in maths instruction	.11
Providing goals	.50	Whole language	.06
Frequent/effects of testing	.46	Student control overlearning	.04
Behavioural organisers	.41		
Average activator	.61	Average facilitator	.19

competent individual. But it is vital for the model to appreciate that novice learners need considerable help. A good model does not simply reproduce the desired skill. He or she does so in a manner that witnesses can analyse, interpret, and recall. The good news is that students, sitting in classrooms, are keenly aware of when a teacher is deliberately demonstrating a skill, as distinct from merely performing it. This cueing process is called the **principle of ostension** (i.e., showing and highlighting good examples), which is one of the basic principles underpinning species evolution (see box at the end of this chapter).

Exposure to successful performances may not, within itself, constitute a viable modelling stimulus for learning. If it did, we could become musicians through attending a concert, or play excellent tennis after watching Wimbledon finals. Indeed, *negative* effects on a novice are likely if this person is expected to copy and exhibit advanced-level skills in the absence of instructional support. When distance between performers and the novice is great, the outcome is one of overload, distress, and demoralisation. When teaching, experts tend to be poor at demonstrating underlying progressive steps, such effects being well known in the literature (as reviewed in Chapter 2).

Hence, when using modelling to encourage observational learning, teachers will deliberately show progressive steps, and ensure that observers have ample opportunity to assimilate information gradually. Besides modelling, other critical instructional components involve verbal instruction, encouragement, scaffolding, and a good deal of practice under conditions where immediate corrective feedback is offered at a high level.

The essential components of highly structured lessons have been described by Barak Rosenshine (2012) in terms of lessons serving a coherent set of functions that include initial review, formal presentation, guided practice, feedback, independent practice, and follow-up review. However, in this section we will review two illustrative projects that demonstrate effective gains in student learning achieved through student participation in lessons specifically intended to teach strategic processing.

De La Paz and Felton: teaching document analysis in the high school

In the first study, Susan De La Paz and Mark Felton (2010) worked with the teachers of 10 classes at two high schools in Maryland, in the United States. The schools were described as 'average to low' in socio-economic level. Five classes were taught history in accord with their traditional methods. But another five classes, the experimental group, were taught history using an approach that focused upon a systematic analysis of how to treat source documents. All the classes had access to the same materials, but only the experimental groups were taught to analyse the available documents with the analytic schema as summarised in Table 9.2.

TABLE 9.2 Thinking with historical documents: the strategy model taught by De La Paz and Felton

STRATEGY	PROCEDURAL CONCERNS	EVALUATIVE QUESTIONS
Consider the author	What do you know about the author? When was the document written? How did the author come to know about events?	How does the author's viewpoint have an effect on his or her argument?
Understand the source	What type of document is this? Why was it written? What values does the source reflect? What assumptions underlie the argument?	What kind of world-view does the source reflect?
Critique the source	(a) Look within each source. What evidence does the author give? Are there errors? Is anything missing from the argument? (b) Look across the sources. What ideas are repeated? What are the major differences? Are their inconsistencies?	Does the evidence prove what it claims to prove?
Create a more focused understanding	Decide what is open to interpretation. Decide what is most reliable and credible.	How does each source deepen your understanding of the historical event?

This schema was taught explicitly as a means to strategically approach source documents looking for the evidence behind any claims that are made. The formal teaching did not involve merely telling the students about the schema in the table. Instead, the teachers used five period sessions to convey the schema, and directly model its use. They then allowed students opportunities to practice for themselves using the new method, using a high level of feedback. This required two weeks of concentrated direct teaching, followed by two weeks of practice in which the experimental group students were encouraged to continue using their new skills in document analysis.

The 10 classes were all then assessed on the same post-test conducted over three periods in which the students had to read documents about an incident in American history not covered earlier (the Gulf of Tonkin incident), and write an essay depicting their understanding of the incident. The essays written by the experimental group were longer, and were rated by a professional historian as showing greater historical accuracy, and as being more persuasive. Importantly, these essays were also rated as being of higher quality and stronger in their analysis and usage of appropriate source documentation.

The time teachers devoted specifically to teaching underlying skills of document analysis paid large dividends in enhancing their students' depth of understanding concerning how knowledge is generated in a realistic disciplinary context. The teachers communicated a strategic approach that was explained, articulated, modelled, and practiced over a series of lessons. The researchers noted:

> Our results suggest that students developed sophisticated task representations for writing because they experienced firsthand how reading and writing strategies converge to accomplish clearly defined goals in historical writing. In this way, the inquiry process provided focus and made the purpose of reading, pre-writing and writing strategies transparent to students.
>
> (De La Paz & Felton, 2010, p. 190)

Feldon and others: teaching principles of science at the university

In the second project, David Feldon, Briana Timmerman, Kirk Stowe, and Richard Showman (2010) addressed the issue of why university-level science courses frequently have a high attrition level, often approaching 50 per cent within some programs. They speculated that the traditional model of university teaching is at fault. They tested this idea through a controlled trial of a different teaching method based upon **cognitive task analysis** (CTA). This is where the components of a complex skill are unpacked through analysis of underlying procedures and goals.

This new term, CTA, is related to what many will know as *task analysis* as used by special education teachers. Traditionally, task analysis is a method of breaking simple tasks into step-by-step procedures. The term CTA is applied in complex learning situations that involve high levels of thinking and decision-making. Hence, CTA represents a means to overcome deficiencies often inherent in contexts, such as university studies, where people are expected to be functioning autonomously at a high level without substantive guidance.

Feldon and colleagues were able to run two versions of a biology course where 133 students participated in the topic as run by an experienced senior lecturer with publications and awards for outstanding teaching. By all standard measures, he was seen as an excellent teacher. Students viewed his lectures online. These students constituted the control group, which represented best practice as known within the university context.

Another group of 119 students participated in the same course, with videoed lectures given by the same lecturer. But for these specific students the lecturer followed a script as dictated by the principles of CTA. The topics, for both versions of the course, were concerned with the logic, philosophy, and practice of the scientific method as applied within biological science.

Just what is the difference between traditional teaching and teaching using cognitive task analysis? The CTA scripts were constructed collaboratively by a group of another three experts who focused upon procedural or 'how to do it' knowledge. As anyone who has survived a university education will know well, the traditional teaching method focuses on abstract issues, and conveying piles of information. But the CTA scripts provided more specific and detailed statements about how actual studies get carried out. Key decisions were framed as a set of step-by-step actions. In essence, CTA treatments are designed to fill in the gaps that experts leave out of their normal instructional presentations. As much as is possible, the scripts depict information through a series of *if–then procedures* that can be followed by relative novices.

Hence, instruction based upon CTA is unlike traditional university teaching. It conveys wisdom through procedures and step-by-step approaches that rarely are taught through traditional means. For example, an instruction from the CTA method noted,

> If your hypothesis does not state your expected outcomes for every condition of the experiment, then you will need to list explicitly in your lab notebook what you expected the dependent variable to do for each level of the factorial variable that you will test.

In this example, notice the use of if–then statements, which define the characteristic of CTA.

The two courses covered the same content and achieved similar overall outcomes on grade results. But there were still marked difference in students' responses across the two groups. The attrition level in the traditional group was 8 per cent, as against 1 per cent in the CTA group. Also, differences were found within the students' laboratory reports. The CTA students scored more highly on discussing data management processes, on considering viable alternative explanations, on citing experimental limitations, and on the quality of their discussion. In short, although the CTA enrichment did not impact on student achievement level, the effect was one of subtly changing the instructional agenda in the favour of the students' thinking processes. Instead of attempting to uncover the hidden aspects of expert knowledge, the students were better able to analyse the key underlying elements that determine how knowledge is generated and written-up within this complex disciplinary context.

Powerful thinking tools can be taught through instruction

We have highlighted these two projects because they illustrate ways in which explicit instruction plays a key role in conveying complex skills. In both studies, students were expected to deal with material that was inherently difficult. Too often, students are expected to cope with problems that demand high-level thinking and decision-making, but have not been given instructional opportunities to develop appropriate tools. Both studies illustrate how strategic thinking was taught explicitly through group instruction using both modelling and direct exhortation. In both cases significant gains followed from instruction targeting thinking tools students can apply to complex problems. Direct instruction in thinking in highly disciplined ways allows the mind to acquire and organise knowledge in areas that require deep understanding and complex cognition.

This view stands in contrast to the view of those who argue providing highly explicit procedural explanations can interfere with a student development of adaptive, flexible knowledge of the type that is valued in problem solving. However, in the two studies reviewed here, the explicit instructional materials provided procedural heuristics of considerable value to the students' progress within each area. Within history, it is necessary for all students to be able to critique source documents. And knowing how to apply the scientific method is an inherently powerful thinking tool.

Just how is the self an agent of knowledge building?

Here is an idea we often encounter: that people will learn better, with greater understanding, if they discover information for themselves, rather than being told this same information. Such an idea strikes a chord with many who assume it represents a truism. Often, the reasoning is that the self is an active change agent. To discover something for yourself entails deep and thoughtful processing that one is unlikely to forget. The more the self is involved, the deeper the processing. So if we can induce students to uncover or deduce knowledge for themselves, then the experience is made meaningful, memorable, and enjoyable.

Such notions remain as myths that confuse the role of the self with the notion that the mind is active as it learns. There is no contradiction between active information processing and learning from direct instruction. The idea that secure knowledge emanates automatically from personal discovery is flawed and incorrect. We certainly enjoy solving puzzles. We find enquiry is highly motivating. But there is little basis to suggest that personal discovery within itself assists a person to actually learn. In fact, additional load imposed by the need to explore and find things out can detract from our capacity to assimilate the information uncovered. This was established through the research into **cognitive load** as reviewed in Chapter 16. The discovery learning process demands a high level of non-productive mental effort, which could be more profitably directed to genuine knowledge building.

The idea that learning stems from personal discovery is further constrained by the observation that we are set up to acquire information from external sources such as social models, verbal instructions, and corrective feedback. When a knowledgeable teacher provides clear modelling, and clear direct instructional language, the conditions for strong learning are set to positive. Providing, (a) attention is captured and (b) learner capacities are not exceeded, then powerful learning can occur in the classroom. If the same teacher desists from demonstrating, or providing verbal information, then conditions for learning are lacking, and impediments to knowledge assimilation are being imposed. In the absence of directive information, and immediate corrective feedback, students are thrown back onto exercising whatever prior knowledge can be activated quickly. If you are to learn a skill, you need social models coupled with descriptive language to enable you to understand and memorise what you observe.

The fallacies and lack of research support surrounding discovery learning are reviewed in a number of publications detailed in the reference notes for this chapter. For instance, several studies have found that low ability students will prefer discovery learning lessons to direct instruction-based lessons, but learn less from them. Under conditions of low guidance, the knowledge gap between low and high ability students tends to increase. The lack of direct guidance has greater damaging effects on learning in low ability students especially when procedures are unclear, feedback is reduced, and misconceptions remain as problems to be resolved rather than errors to be corrected.

Observational learning as knowledge building

One aspect we often encounter is the metaphor that knowledge needs to be constructed within the individual mind since it cannot be transmitted into the mind. From our work in teacher education institutes we have heard novice teachers being informed that 'knowledge transmission' theories of learning are invalid, dated, and being replaced with maxims such as 'What I hear I forget, what I do I understand'. Activity thus is said to trump any form of 'passive' learning.

One variant of this idea, attributed to Confucius, reads, 'What I hear I forget, what I see I remember, what I do I understand.' Perhaps, Confucius was highlighting the primacy of observational learning over talking? Although we know that exposure to an expert is often unhelpful, there is another pertinent finding in the literature: *when observers have the opportunity to watch carefully, their learning can be greater than in people who perform the same task in the absence of a social model.* This facet hinges upon context. But it is not hard to appreciate how the keen observer can possess advantages over a peer attempting to learn purely by doing. Attention can be invested in the information conveyed without concern for either response production or coping with adversities. If there is no skill component to be developed, learning through observation provides huge benefits without cost. One example of this effect is seen in the invisible gorilla studies (see Chapter 29), since those counting ball passes become overloaded, whereas observers cannot possibly avoid seeing the beast.

The power of direct interpersonal knowledge transmission

There is another perspective we entertain seriously: *that information assimilated through personal discovery can be shallow, insecure, and incomplete.* Information communicated through instruction, interpersonal contact, direct social modelling, and verbal transmission, can be durable, more securely available, and more strongly validated, than knowledge constructed through an individual's unaided inductive processing. Socially transmitted information can be efficiently organised, with sequences arranged logically and terminology well defined.

Through listening to an excellent teacher, the critical variables are emphasised, subtle discriminations and conditional elements are identified, and the appropriate vocabulary (i.e., mental schema) is activated. Underlying elements are articulated even when they remain relatively invisible, as in the case with high-level abstract qualities. Attention is drawn to aspects that are beyond immediate view. For instance, through listening to verbal instruction you can readily learn of contingences that remain possible but are less likely to be experienced firsthand. If one is obliged to learn through personal resources, how can one ever know if the knowledge gained is adequate or complete?

Ironically, learning through individual discovery comes with two liabilities: (a) increases in cognitive load on the mind, while (b) cutting off the individual from factors that can place the knowledge building process onto secure socially shared foundations. When the learning to be achieved is complex, the need for clarity and organization in instruction assumes an even stronger role in effective knowledge transmission. In appreciating that the world is complex, our personal need is always to see and hear how other people are dealing with this same complexity, a motive referred to as **social comparison**. Rather than deny the existence of knowledge transmission, it behoves educators to appreciate the social and dynamic nature of the process.

IN PERSPECTIVE: Social transmission as an evolutionary driver

The ideas expressed in this chapter are consistent with an emerging view about human culture that places education into a central position. The acquisition of knowledge has an intrinsic social and cultural basis, with adults and teachers playing a vital role as direct communicators. This notion has been advanced recently by a number of social biologists: *that, as a species, we adapted and evolved to transfer knowledge to, and receive knowledge from, one another.* Initially, this view emerged through the analysis of tool usage in early hominids, but has been extended to human evolution in general. These notions explain why infants are attuned to attend towards, and learn from, adults from the first months of life. The principles underpinning this movement in social biology are shown in the box below. Such views account for one version of the **social brain hypothesis**.

THE SOCIAL EVOLUTIONARY PERSPECTIVE ON PEDAGOGY: MODELLING ENABLES SPECIES TO SURVIVE

'Social learning and social cognition: The case for pedagogy' is the title of a major position paper by Gergely Csibra and Gyorgy Gergely (2006). Surveying the scientific literature into infancy and early childhood, they found remarkably strong evidence for the powerful role of direct teaching from the earliest months of age. They identified a number of critical teaching principles that are intrinsic to human evolution and species survival. We list five of them here:

1   *The cooperativity principle:* There will be adults around who will transmit relevant knowledge even at some cost to themselves.

2   *The principle of ostension:* An adult signals to the child that an act is shown for the child's benefit, and not the benefit of the adult teacher.

3   *The principle of relevance:* Both child and adult teacher recognise the goal-directed nature of the learning situation, that the knowledge communicated is novel, and would not be figured out by the child unaided.

4   *The omniscience principle:* Mature members of the community store knowledge in themselves that they can manifest anytime even when they are not in any need to use the knowledge themselves.

5   *The public knowledge principle:* The knowledge transmitted is public, shared, and universal. The classic example here is language. Vocalisations and words used by one adult individual are not unique to that individual.

Dr Csibra specialises in the area of infancy and has contributed controlled laboratory studies that document how adults communicate to infants through the eyes. For instance, his team found that even by six months of age, children are sensitive to signals adults give out as to where to look, and for how long to look. Such data illustrate the *principle of ostension*, one of the key principles listed above. Even from the very earliest months, infants are locked into learning from the information adults convey. The use of eye gaze is the key communication channel opened up before language develops. If you observe parents interacting with an infant, note how eye gaze and language are totally integrated in all communications.

Other significant writers in the area of social biology and anthropology have focused upon social learning as one of the key processes driving species evolution. They have been able to map how species that learn from each other survive and adapt more readily. In nature, social learning is the rule. Literally, apes do ape. The more complex the species, the more its survival depends on its young learning through observing.

In the case of humans, this capability is developed to its highest level. We have inherited the capacity to pick up complex information by watching adult teachers who transmit relevant information carefully, deliberately, using principles such as those listed above. Such a capability has its roots in how infants respond to care-givers when only several weeks old. We are biologically hard-wired to acquire considerable knowledge through observational learning. Citations to this social biology literature are found in the reference notes.

Study guide questions

1 A wealth of data, many thousands of published studies, is being summarised in Table 9.1. Can you interpret just what these data are telling us? What overall conclusions are possible?

2 The chapter suggests there is little point in distinguishing between notions such as direct instruction, explicit teaching, and expository teaching. What is the common thread that covers such notions?

3 In relation to social modelling, just what is the principle of ostension, and how would your students know when you are using it?

4 What should a social model do in order to maximise the potential for observational learning to occur?

5 The critical functions observed in well-structured lessons have been described by Barak Rosenshine as a six-step sequence. Just what are these six essential functions to be achieved?

6 De La Paz and Felton taught a schematic approach to high school history students that resulted in students being able to analyse source documents and use them more critically. What underlying message do such findings have for instruction in higher order thinking?

7 Will people learn better if they discover information by themselves without any obvious source of instruction being evident? Is this taken as a truism?

8 In the chapter, it is suggested that discovering information all by yourself simply fails to produce deep and secure learning, especially in complex situations. What specific advantages accrue to the individual able to learn with strong social and instructional support?

9 What are the two major liabilities inherently embedded within learning through discovery?

10 The social brain hypothesis, stemming out of anthropology and biology, suggests that evolutionary species survival can hinge upon knowledge transmission through social modelling processes. Why is this the case?

11 What are the major principles involved in social learning in infancy and early childhood? Just how do adults socialise such children?

Reference notes

- The two previous *VL* sources (Hattie, 2009, 2012).
- The history of the debate between teacher-oriented instruction and student-centred approaches, such as open education, is covered in Chall, 2000.
- The argument that all learners (excluding experts) benefit from clear direct instruction (R. E. Clark, Kirschner, & Sweller, 2012).
- Domain experts make poor models in teaching (Feldon, 2007b).
- Analysis of lesson structures (Rosenshine, 2012; Rosenshine & Stevens, 1986).
- Study into teaching history using document analysis (De La Paz & Felton, 2010). Cognitive task analysis in the university course (Feldon, Timmerman, Stowe, & Showman, 2010).
- Discovery hampers student learning (P. A. Kirschner, Sweller, & Clark, 2006; Mayer, 2004). Misuse of discovery learning when instruction in complex systems is needed (R. E. Clark, Yates, Early, & Moulton, 2009).
- Review establishing failure of pure discovery in assisting knowledge acquisition, but indicating positive use of guided discovery when used in conjunction with other more effective teaching methods (Alfieri, Brooks, Aldrich, & Tenenbaum, 2011).
- Learning by viewing can be faster and be more effective than learning by doing (Stull & Mayer, 2007).

- That modelling (observational learning, or learning by viewing) alone may achieve stronger learning effects than individual exploration depends upon context. This notion comes through in the areas of anthropology and social biology. Quite literally, apes do ape. For animals to survive they closely observe and learn from others of their species. Reviews of this literature are found in Laland and Rendell, 2010; Reader and Biro, 2010. Without social learning, most animals would experience one-trial extinction.

- Social learning capabilities drive the evolution of intelligence across species and enable cultural development in humans (van Schaik & Burkart, 2011). A review of the fundamental social learning mechanisms underpinning survival across species is found in Frith & Frith, 2012.

- Box: Evolutionary perspective on principles underlying social transmission of human culture (Csibra & Gergely, 2006). Research on how infants follow adult eye gaze (Senju & Csibra, 2008).

10

Just what does expertise look like?

Experts are individuals able to perform at the very top of an identifiable skill area. For example, this could be a profession, a trade, a sport, or areas such as music and the arts. In some areas of human life, however, it is difficult to find individual experts. By definition, expertise has to represent superior performance repeated over time. Consider, for example, one well-researched area where it is difficult to identify experts – that of stock-broking or consistently picking financial stocks that are likely to rise in value. Individual brokers have good years and bad years. There is very little, if any, continuity across years, and people in this field do not perform better with experience or seniority. Several studies have shown that the average person, the 'man or woman in the street', often outperforms experienced brokers in putting together financial portfolios. However, in many areas of skilful performance, including classroom teaching, there is considerable evidence supporting the presence of expertise.

Historical background to expertise research

Research into expertise began in 1899 with studies by Bryan and Harter into Morse code operators. They studied how highly experienced operators acquired key-stroke skills in coding words and phrases. With respect to the terminology used to describe the findings, a quotation from this classic work remains highly meaningful today, after 110 years:

> The learner must come to do with one stroke of attention what now requires half a dozen, and presently, in one still more inclusive stroke, what now requires thirty-six. He must systematize the work to be done and must acquire a system of automatic habits corresponding to the system of tasks. When he has done this he is master of the situation in his field . . . Finally, his whole array of habits is swiftly obedient to serve in the solution of new problems. Automatism is not genius but it is the hands and feet of genius.
>
> (p. 375)

Beginning with this classic work, researchers then continued to study how experts operated in many different areas, such as chemistry, engineering, chess, bridge, medicine, computing, sports, music, and the arts. The world's wars gave much impetus as military instructors studied experts in aspects such as navigation, aviation, strategy deployment, and radar observation.

Over time, clear patterns began to emerge. One valuable method of study was to investigate differences between experts and other individuals who were fully competent within that same domain but not to such high levels of skilfulness. This design was often referred to as the expert–novice contrast. But 'novice' was an unfortunate term. In most such studies they were not beginners, but simply people who were not top-flight performers. In such studies it is essential for these novices to be competent individuals in order to provide the appropriate controls. For instance, specialist physicians (experts) might be compared in diagnostic skills with general practitioners (called novices). It is known that contrasting experienced but not expert teachers with expert teachers reveals many critical differences, even though the level of experience of each group may be similar (see Hattie, 2009).

The seven basic traits of expertise

In pulling together scores of studies, Glaser and Chi (1988) drew up a significant seven-point listing that has been used extensively ever since. They found that when experts are compared to novices:

- Experts excel only in their own domain.
- Experts perceive large and meaningful patterns.
- Experts can work quickly and solve problems with little error.
- Within their domain, experts possess remarkably large short-term memories.
- Experts see and represent problems at a deeper or principled level, whereas novices focus on superficial aspects.
- Experts spend relatively more time analysing problems carefully and qualitatively.
- Experts have strong skills in self-monitoring.

We need to expand in depth upon these seven key points.

Experts excel only in their own domain

The first point is that expertise is highly domain-specific. This means that experts are functioning at this elevated level only within their skill area. A brilliant teacher has no specific advantage when it comes to devising tactics for dealing with people, managing armies, or planning a holiday. Expertise hinges on knowledge the person has developed within the relevant context, rather than any general skills or ability. It has been found repeatedly that within specific areas, general ability measures, such as the IQ, fail to predict level of expertise attained.

Experts perceive large and meaningful patterns

The second point is that experts organise information incredibly efficiently. Among the major tools used are grouping or chunking strategies. In truth, the experts are limited to around the same number of chunks as novices. But what is often extraordinary is the amount of information contained within a single meaningful chunk. This has been investigated through studies into how chess players can memorise entire chess-board patterns. They are able to see patterns within the game that represent large informational chunks. This skill applies only to genuine game patterns. When randomised patterns, using the same chess pieces, are shown, then the expert's ability to use chunking is destroyed. In several studies, experts performed worse than novices at memorising such boards.

Experts can work quickly and solve problems with little error

The third point is that experts solve problems within their area quickly. This key attribute of expertise comes with one remarkable qualification. The expert is highly sensitive to the difficulty level of any given problem. Experts are fast when the going is straight-forward, but do not proceed if they sense an error is likely. Less expert people are often unafraid of making errors, and proceed with less caution. When faced with demands that exceed capacities, novices are inclined toward impulsivity. In contrast, experts are inclined towards diligence in marshalling resources, and becoming careful. You will have noticed how uninformed people are inclined to jump to conclusions, become opinionated, when more knowledgeable people shy away from such views.

Within their domain, experts possess remarkably large short-term memories

The fourth point is that experts' chunking strategies enable remarkable short-term memory effects to emerge. For example, in one study, after a year of daily sessions practicing digit spans, several individuals were able to reliably recall 70 to 80 numbers when presented as single digits. Since the natural average is around 7 to 8 digits, this training represents an effect size of 70. While such extreme effects are unlikely to be found often, it is known that once people become highly knowledgeable within a domain, their short-term memory spans appear to well exceed natural processing capacities. For example, one of us (Greg Yates) and a colleague asked an experienced gym instructor to copy a sequence of 22 physical exercise movements on video that had been put together in what was intended as a random sequence. This instructor reproduced the sequence recalling 20 movements. In contrast, a newly qualified instructor reproduced 10 movements before saying she could not recall any more. Yet on a memory test of 20 unrelated words, the novice instructor recalled 9, and the expert instructor recalled just 6.

There are many documented cases in the literature showing similar effects at the level of working memory. For example, one study found that experts in bridge could recall 10 hands (their immediate past games) with remarkable accuracy, which the researchers described as supranormal memory. Chess champions, who can play the game in blind game mode without actually seeing a board, are known to easily hold around 40 chess positions in their minds. One study found that primary-school age children who play chess frequently can recall more chess positions than adults who rarely play chess. Similarly, skilled musicians can reproduce virtually any tonal note patterns they have just heard. Experts do not deliberately set out to increase their working memory capacity. This simply comes with the territory.

Experts see and represent problems at a deeper or principled level, whereas novices focus on superficial aspects

The fifth point is that experts invariably go beyond the information given when they operate within their area. Their awareness of patterns and their extensive store of knowledge mean that they are not misled by surface features. Instead, their minds automatically shift into seeing the deeper principles that are at stake. They focus upon the underlying dynamics and can be highly sensitive to aspects that novices have trouble even apprehending. This fits with the second point above (seeing large patterns) in that experts are very quick to see connections and relationships between events that appear disjointed to other people.

Experts spend relatively more time analysing problems carefully and qualitatively

The sixth point is that when experts have a problem to solve then they use time differently from less skilful people. They need to understand all aspects of the situation. They hesitate to proceed until they understand. When situations permit, experts appear 'frozen in thought' and use time to reflect on just how the present problem relates to what has happened before. They will use recognition processes and long-term memory in locating and finding patterns.

Hence, when it comes to more difficult problems, experts give an appearance of moving slowly as they move into deep deliberation mode. One specific example of this slowing down process is seen in professional golf players. When compared with average players, they were found to take far longer to prepare themselves for a shot, a phenomenon known as the *quiet eye period*. Although first discovered in golf, it became apparent that quiet eye training can be applied to any activity involving making careful judgements.

Experts have strong skills in self-monitoring

The seventh and final point is that experts possess a keen sense of self-monitoring. They will plan a course of action involving alternative routes. They are adept at keeping track of where they are up to, and adjust strategies whenever a key sub goal does not eventuate. Experts can harbour several planned agendas, and switch between them. If one path is blocked, another is possible. In contrast, novices tend to react as though there is one single method of solving a problem. When this is blocked, they tend to abandon efforts, being unaware of back-up strategies. Hence, experts demonstrate a metacognitive attitude rarely seen in beginners.

Other attributes of experts

Since the major Glaser and Chi review, other notable attributes of expertise have been documented. Many such discoveries were made when the expert novice research design was applied in sports training areas. Researchers began to conduct fine-grain analyses using tools such as high-speed cameras to pick up aspects less visible to the naked eye. For instance, one powerful trait often seen was experts' ability to anticipate what is about to happen. This was seen when analysing how players in team sports, such as hockey and football, moved around the field. The expert players gravitated into positions in anticipation of where the play was likely to move to, a skill lacking in novice players. If you watch a Wimbledon-standard serve, using the frame-by-frame facility on your video player, you can see how the receiver initiates critical bodily adjustments, in response to the server, well before the ball hits the server's racket. In one Australian study, it was found that world class cricketers are able to anticipate the ball's path and speed with remarkable accuracy through brief exposure to the bowler's run-up and delivery actions, such as the hand orientation.

In the game of baseball, the expert hitter does not actually see the ball travelling towards him or her. The ball is coming in too fast (300 ms, or a third of a second after leaving the pitcher's hand) to permit any level of responsive behavioural control to occur. Instead, adjustments as to how to hit the ball are made by watching the pitcher and anticipating where the ball will travel. Strangely enough, these expert hitters are found to have virtually no awareness of what their eyes and brain are doing. Advice to 'watch the ball' is used to direct beginners in such sports, but, technically, this is not what happens when performing at the professional level.

We noted earlier how experts are able to hold a good deal more information within their short-term memories than novices through sophisticated chunking. In truth, their actual short-term memory capacities are more-or-less the same as novices. But what has altered dramatically is their ability to use the working memory system more effectively. Some theorists have expressed this in terms of experts using their knowledge as the primary basis for mental work, and so refer to experts as having 'long-term working memory'. This might sound like a strange use of terms, but it highlights the point that when you are an expert, your working memory system is drawing upon a high level of information directly from your long-term memory.

One critical aspect of working memory is the ability to allow items to interact and form connections with other items within the mind. To use computer jargon, such ability is akin to random access memory, or RAM. Whereas the novice tends to relate to experiences in terms of sequences and linear orderings, the experts among us are far less affected by serial orderings. In general, experts do not show the same serial position effects well known from the applied research into memory. That is, since information comes in sequences, most people will recall things that come first (**primacy**) or last (**recency**), but will forget what occurs in between (the hole-in-the-middle effect). Such effects are rarely seen when a person becomes an expert.

Another key aspect, and one we revisit several times in this book, is that the more expert a person becomes, the more difficult it can be for that person to describe what the brain is doing. Studies using high-speed cameras in sports such as professional cricket, tennis, and baseball, consistently indicate that what players say about their skills often is not what the cameras record they are doing.

The role of unconscious processing

Many of the high-level skills shown by experts have a basis in *unconscious processing*. Strangely enough, this was first described many years ago in studies of expert chicken sexers. People who have successfully learnt methods to determine sex of day old chicks (up to 1,000 chicks per hour, a valuable and lucrative skill) appeared unable to articulate just what goes on in their minds when they actually make such fast determinations. They report they 'just know'. Across different fields, many experts report on intuitive judgements, or having a sixth sense as to what is going to happen. Such feelings are not mysterious, but are the results of vast stores of knowledge being activated quickly.

In short, introspection is not to be trusted when it comes to how experts explain themselves to non-experts. Besides the problem of using words differently, very often they simply do not know how their skills operate. But lack of awareness does not stop experts having opinions on what they are doing, even though their opinions are often inaccurate.

For a simple demonstration of this lack of awareness in expertise, consider how mature readers move their eyes. Laboratory studies have shown that we look at every word in a sentence for several microseconds. As we read, we have no awareness we are doing this. But now look at someone reading. When you look closely enough, you can just make out their quick high-speed jerky eye movements (called saccades). Our perception, as we read, is different from what is actually happening. Another odd fact is that not one of us appears able to describe how we manage to catch balls, despite having caught thousands of balls over decades.

Try to consider how you can achieve any of the following skills: (a) riding your bike without falling over, (b) walking down stairs without looking at your feet, (c) changing gears in a manual car, and (d) making tiny adjustments on the steering wheel in the car to keep on the road, even when the road is a straight one. Many people today are able to type reasonably well, but cannot tell you where specific letters are found on the QWERTY keyboard. *Where is G? Where is O? How many letters sit in between S and H?* We asked these questions of several people, and not one answered them all correctly. But all then typed HOGS without the slightest hesitation. Having achieved expertise, we are unable say just how we can do such things.

IN PERSPECTIVE: The traits of expertise

Stemming back over a century, a huge database has described ways in which experts differ from people who are competent but not expert. Studies have been published in around 90 different areas, showing a remarkable convergence in basic findings. In a significant synthesis published some 25 years ago, these differences were summarised in terms of seven traits: (a) domain specificity, (b) perceptual chunking, (c) speed and accuracy, (d) working memory capacity, (e) deeper processing, (f) use of time to think hard, and (g) the ability to self-monitor progress.

Later work revealed that experts are characterised by a high level of unconscious processing. They are unable to describe what is occurring as they perform at the highest-level skills. In many areas, notably in competitive sports, experts are able to process information at high speed, in ways that defy introspective analysis, but which can be analysed through using objective recording devices such as time-lapse photography. In the following chapters we will consider how expertise develops, and then describe what is known about expertise in classroom teaching.

Study guide questions

1 If experts are those people at the very top of their field, just why cannot they be studied and analysed in certain fields? What can prevent such an analysis?

2 Although these terms seem like modern jargon, notions of 'learning curve', and 'plateaus' were being used over a century ago to describe how we learn. What is meant by a plateau in the learning curve?

3 One finding is that experts appear to store information and recall much more of a relevant experience than the average person. At times they show extraordinary levels of recall. Do they set out to develop such advanced memory skills?

4 Expert chess players will memorise chess board patterns within seconds provided what condition is present?

5 Although experts can work quickly, in fact they will often strive to slow down. What factors will drive this slowing down process?

6 It was found that in many ball games and team sports, the more experienced players did not run faster, were often slower and less agile than younger players, but still dominated ball play. How do they do this?

7 To what extent can experts really tell us what they are doing? Do they know how they can achieve such high-level performances? When are they very likely to be telling us fibs?

8 Imagine you have developed many skills to a level of automaticity, expert-like. Can you name some of these skills? Have you developed any such automated skill that makes you different from others?

Reference notes

■ Authoritative overview of this voluminous field: *Cambridge Handbook of Expertise and Expert Performance* (Ericsson, Charness, Feltovich, & Hoffman, 2006).

■ Inability to find experts at picking financial stocks (Kahneman, 2011). Laypeople shown to outperform established brokers (Gigerenzer, 2008). For a collection of essays on expertise in diverse professional fields see Ericsson, 2009.

■ Glaser and Chi, major historical review is opening chapter in *The Nature of Expertise* (Chi, Glaser, & Farr, 1988).

■ Classic studies into expert Morse operators (Bryan & Harter, 1899).

■ Expertise in chess reviewed by Gobet and Charness, Chapter 30 in the *Handbook* (Ericsson *et al.*, 2006). To see a chess grandmaster recalling chess board after 5 seconds exposure see www.youtube.com/watch?v= rWuJqCwfjjc.

■ Extraordinary memory for digits (Ericsson, Roring, & Nandagopal, 2007). Superb memory in skilled bridge champions (Engle & Bukstel, 1978). Children who play chess recall more than adults (Chi & Ceci, 1987).

■ The quiet eye period professionals often employ (Wulf, McConnel, Gartner, & Schwarz, 2002). Originally seen in professional golfers, this is a mental technique in any sport where time can be controlled. For video clip of quiet eye training in police work and gun control see www.youtube.com/watch?v= sWiGflJNFWk.

- Skilled musicians can immediately reproduce any melodic tune (Tervaniemi, Rytkönen, Schröger, Ilmoniemi, & Näätänen, 2001).

- Elite cricketers accurately predict ball trajectories from minute cues given out by bowlers (Müller, Abernethy, & Farrow, 2006). Baseball hitters cannot see the speeding ball (Takeuchi & Inomata, 2009).

- Chicken sexing as an unconscious skill (Biederman & Shiffrar, 1987). Lack of insight into how we catch balls (Reed *et al.*, 2010).

11

Just how does expertise develop?

Practice makes perfect. After being engaged in any activity for several years you become an expert in that activity. Stick at it, and you can achieve at the highest level. All it takes is practice.

Just what is the truth behind these common sayings? Well, we now know these ideas can be misleading. By itself, practice will make a skill more robust, rigid, and permanent. But that is about all. Simply spending time performing a skill you have already acquired does not automatically enhance your actual level of performance in that skill. There is little reason to assume it should. Studies into occupational skills, for example, often find virtually no relationship between measures of work performance and years on the job.

It is apparent that for many of us, length of time in employment can even occasion slight deterioration in work performance. This drop-off effect has been shown, for example, in aspects of medical diagnostics and auditing. As noted in the previous chapter, among the most thoroughly reviewed of such vocational findings is that experienced stockbrokers do not perform any better than newcomers, and performances from year to year fail to correlate. If practice automatically results in skill improvement, then such findings make little sense.

The notion that practice makes perfect is misleading, but its popularity is explained by the observation that anyone, and everyone, who does exhibit high levels of skills and expertise has got there by dint of significant effort. Often, this effort is marked in terms of thousands of hours spent honing skills. However, the practice involved is that of a special kind: **deliberate practice**. More of this later. But first, it is useful to consider how someone becomes a talented individual. Just how does expertise develop?

The Bloom report

One key project in this area was conducted by Benjamin Bloom and colleagues in the mid-1980s. They interviewed 120 individuals who, as young adults, were considered elite top-flight performers within different fields (e.g., concert pianists, mathematicians, professional artists, Olympic sports champions). Not one individual in the study had reached such high attainment in less than a dozen years, and the average was 16 years. They began practicing their craft in childhood. By adolescence they were devoting around 25 hours a week to their field. They all claimed to have had to overlearn a good deal, even after they had achieved peak levels of performance. Bloom noted how such practice enabled his high performers to develop **automaticity** in their performances.

What was ground-breaking in this study was the analysis of the formative components identified in the lives of these individuals. The following pattern appeared across all areas:

- These individuals had child-oriented parents who dedicated extensive family resources to their children, seeing this as normal.
- Their family home emphasised high achievement and striving as taken-for-granted goals.
- An intrinsic work ethic was emphasised ('Work hard and do your best' – effort mattered).
- High quality teaching was available in the skill domain from an early point, and this was often sought out by the parents.
- The child showed high levels of initial enjoyment in the domain.
- Initial success led onto higher-level coaching and dedicated classes.
- More time, effort, and money, was invested as the demands of coaches increased, and performance goals became highly individualised.
- Enhanced commitment entailed realigned priorities and sacrifices.
- Medium-level coaches deferred to master coaches as the potential of the young person was identified and became more widely known.
- Commitment became a major life decision.

Many elements of the above pattern are familiar to teachers whose students have been singled out for special training within specific talent areas. Within Bloom's analysis, it became apparent that elite-level achievement could be viewed as the product of education, or, at least, of a specific type of education with considerable encouragement and support. Many families made severe compromises and sacrifices to support developing the talents in their children, even though the high potential of these young people was often not identified clearly when they were younger children.

Although Bloom's team had deliberately attempted to interview people from within the very top performers in each field, there were no child prodigies located. Although these young gifted adults had shown early promise, they were not necessarily top performers in relation to their peers within their formative years. In one sense, they had become top performers in their respective fields by staying the distance in contrast to others who had also shown early promise, or talent indicators, but did not sustain the demands of the training routine. Gifted children do not necessarily become gifted adults, and gifted adults were not necessary gifted children.

The need for practice, but what type of practice?

In short, great accomplishment does not just happen as a product of a child's innate talent. It appears linked with years of development and steady preparation, often around two decades, and which takes place in a highly supportive context. Motivation and drive emerge as background factors linked into family goals, aspirations, and life attitudes. Nevertheless, the factors that dramatically stand out in such retrospective research are always related to hours spent practicing the skill. However, such practice is tightly structured. It is driven by a series of progressively more complex goals. It is supervised by a series of coaches or teachers who emphasise the relationship between hard work, technical perfection, and success. There exists a widely recognised rhetoric employed by coaches to help young people aspire to achieving their goals through effort, single-minded devotion, and inevitable sacrifice.

Hence, extended engagement has been identified as one of the keys. General factors, such as overall aptitude measures and IQ, have been shown to play virtually no role in predicting elite-level achievement within specific domain areas. Literature reviews report that individual development is relatively slow and graduated, even when large amounts of time are invested. There is evidence for uneven growth and periods of low growth or plateaus. But there is no serious evidence for fast or abrupt improvements in human performances in any area. Instead, performances increase steadily into adulthood, even in those individuals thought of as child prodigies.

One widely held notion is called the 10-year rule: that is, that expertise requires at least 10 years to develop. Although reasonable, this notion ought not to be held rigidly as different fields show different trends. For example, outstanding scientists and authors keep developing over 20 to 30 years. In narrowly defined skill areas, such as memory skills, peak performance seems to occur after around 2 years. In some team sports, such as football, peak levels seem to be occurring in many players after 5 or 6 years of intense training. Hence, the 10-year rule has to be interpreted as a guide only. Many researchers have expressed such a formative period as three to four hours a day over a decade, or around 10,000 hours.

Human skill levels have changed over the recent past. The Olympic swimming champions of 1908, for example, would not qualify for international competition today. Prior to 1950 it was thought physiologically impossible to run a mile in under four minutes. Today, such a feat is well respected but seen as a milestone for the budding middle-distance athlete to achieve. About the year 1900 the world record for 1,500 metres stood at 4 minutes 9 seconds. About 2000 it stood at 3 minutes 26 seconds. Advances have been noted even within the game of chess in that the top masters today make fewer errors than masters of a century ago. Many such advances in human capacities are attributable to changes in technique and training practices. Coaches develop new ways of training. High performers keep surpassing their own skill levels. In fields in which objective records are available, upward performance trends become evident across generations.

Practice as a deliberative goal-directed activity

In one classic study, Anders Ericsson and his colleagues retrospectively were able to monitor hours of practice logged by violinists undergoing training at the Music Academy of West Berlin. Although all were excellent musicians, large differences in their prior training were disclosed through studio training records. The most expert violinists had spent about 10,000 hours, whereas the least accomplished performers had logged about 5,000 hours. The records for the most accomplished students were found to match those of a group of professional symphony musicians. Such findings gave support to the concept of deliberate practice. This is an important term. This is the type of practice consciously devoted to the improvement of a skill, as distinct from the exercise of that skill.

The key idea behind deliberate practice is time devoted to training tasks that a person can identify and achieve mindfully and sequentially. Instead of being haphazard or recreational, this form of practice is highly structured. Typically, practice schedules are achieved under supervision of a teacher or coach. Performers are presented with tasks initially outside of current performance levels, but which can be mastered within hours by focusing on critical aspects and refining technique though repetition and feedback. In essence, there is always an intended cognitive or psychomotor skill targeted, and this is assessed through objective means. Immediate short-term goals and adaptive corrective feedback become major components inherent in this process.

By its nature, deliberate practice implies concentration and attention to structured goal setting. This stands in stark contrast to other types of performances that may be relatively mindless, or which otherwise involve no specific target goal related to the skill development process. For example, in one study based on how musicians responded toward singing lessons, amateur singers were found to practice for enjoyment and self-actualisation. On the other hand, the professional singers focused their attention on developing technique. Hence, the training functions, personal targets, and underlying motivations, of these two groups differed substantially, even though seemingly they were participating in the same activity.

Why practice alone can fail to improve skilfulness

The repeated finding in this area is that deliberate practice is the essential prerequisite for skill development. To spend hours performing the same activity at the same level implies repetition but possibly without much learning taking place. Upon reflection you may begin to appreciate how an individual can keep performing a skill for years, having achieved a basal level of mastery, but that is all. For example, we can think of individuals, among our friends, whose driving skills have remained abysmal for decades. In one study, Keith and Ericsson found that university students' skills in typing increased *only* when they undertook specific efforts to deliberately enhance their typing performances. Simply performing an activity, even daily, does not in itself alter one's expertise level. There simply is no reason why it should. Indeed, a curious problem emerges when we consider the role played by automaticity.

In Bloom's studies it was apparent that top-flight performers had developed their skills to the point where they could perform highly skilled routines with remarkably little conscious effort. Following on from classic studies into Morse code operators (noted in Chapter 10), Bloom referred to automaticity as the 'hands and feet of genius' (1986, p. 70). Through such an analysis, automaticity tended to become equated with high levels of skill, within the scientific literature. Furthermore, for over 50 years, researchers have documented the validity of a descriptive stage model of skill development, as shown in Table 11.1. This model makes a good deal of sense, especially since as teachers you can literally see students struggling their way through elements of these stages.

Automaticity: its upside, and downside

Although this three-level approach provides a valuable descriptive analysis, it can be misleading if it is seen to equate automaticity as the key defining feature underpinning high levels of expertise. In truth, automaticity can kick in earlier. One does not need to be an expert before one achieves automaticity. And automaticity can then serve to *prevent* further skill development. The term **arrested development** captures this phenomenon well. Development of any skill can be arrested at any point where automaticity is permitted to take firm hold.

Think about this from a broad perspective. When you acquire a skill, its development has to be arrested at some point. You cannot spend your entire life in deliberate practice activities, *ad nauseum*. There is insufficient time in the day or your life to keep yourself on skill development mode forever. Hence, automaticity, which permits a reduction in your attentional resources, can be used to allow yourself to maintain an acceptable level of skill, but without needing to try so hard anymore.

Automaticity can be seen as a neurological gift to the human race. That is, you can stay at the level attained, and do so indefinitely. Through enabling automaticity to take over, you can hold yourself at your attained level without needing to commit continuing resources. Instead of seeing automaticity simply as the underlying factor describing one's expertise, it can also be viewed as a *conservation strategy*. When your resources are stressed, or when your attention needs to focus elsewhere, then the more you can shift over to an automatic control system, your System 1, the better. Automaticity allows you to (a) relax,

TABLE 11.1 Three levels of skill development

STAGE	DESCRIPTION OF MENTAL PROCESSES	COMMON EXAMPLES
Declarative stage (or cognitive stage)	Learner uses language and words to direct action. The person often talks to oneself. (*What do I do now*? *What is required?*) Memory load is very heavy. Items are recalled one by one, as discrete elements, with little interactivity or chunking taking place.	Trying to operate an unfamiliar computer program. Trying to recall instructions you have just received about learning a new game such as bridge. Being able to read in a foreign language at only a single word at a time.
Associative stage	Actions are now linked or chained into a sequence. There is a flow to action that may begin in a staccato stop–start manner, but over trials it becomes faster and smoother. Memory load is reduced, but concentration needs to be high. This is described as shifting from declarative into procedural knowledge.	Being able to spell large words accurately. Being able to change car gears using the manual transmission. Operating the standard procedures within a familiar computer package. Singing a complete rendition of a song from memory.
Autonomous stage (enabling expert performance)	Performance is now smooth and effortless. With automaticity, actions need little conscious attention. Too much attention to automated elements can be detrimental. Memory load is low as recognition is being activated. Obstacles are unlikely to disrupt performance, but if so, capacity is available in working memory to cope. Actions are well organised, reliable, and involve large-sized chunks.	Memorising an entire chess game in 20 seconds. Ability to split attention between two tasks such as driving car and talking to friend. When observing performers in your domain you can evaluate critical aspects not seen by others, (for example, judges for Olympic diving competitions).

(b) prioritise your energies, and (c) shift your attention onto what is becoming important.

Interviews with high-performing adults such as sports people and musicians show them to be acutely aware of the problem of arrested development. Many report developing 'bad habits' that they have to overcome. Many elite performers rely on high calibre coaches to provide a continuing critique. Many such performers claim they must never stop learning. When an elite performer claims he or she is 'becoming lazy', it may not be that they are genuinely slack, but only that they are allowing automaticity to take over to an excessive level, to the detriment of further development in their art.

An apparent paradox becomes evident. Practising an activity allows you to shift control from a conscious to an automatic function, *in order to stop developing*. Automaticity allows you to peg a skill at a given level. What it takes is just enough practice, under relatively non-demanding conditions, where you are free to focus elsewhere, since it is this type of practice that makes for permanence.

This analysis points to the natural effect of undertaking practice while the mind is engaged elsewhere. The human mind is unable to genuinely focus on two activities at once, a clear finding discussed in this book in the section on multitasking (Chapter 20). If a young novice driver is driving and listening to a CD, then the driving skill is not being improved but is simply being exercised. Similarly, listening to music while studying is likely to undermine whatever benefit is hoped will follow from such study. The moment you remove your attention from a task, you can expect no meaningful learning or skill development to take place. You may still perform at a reasonable level, and you may monitor your performance intermittently. But do not fool yourself into believing that such automated performances are teaching you anything you did not know before.

So what is innate talent?

The discovery of expertise development factors has proven problematic for the notion of inherent or *innate* talent. It is not a satisfactory explanation to ascribe high performance to natural talent. Early talent indicators seldom predict development over the long term. It may be the case that recognition of innate talent is worthwhile and then deliberate practice and coaching is needed to exploit this talent. However, within any field, the top-flight performers include many late bloomers who failed to surface from early indicators. Similarly, many individuals identified with early indicators simply do not progress much beyond that point. There is danger in confusing precociousness with genuine capability. Readers wanting an excellent discussion on this issue relevant to sports training should read an article by Angela Abbott and Dave Collins writing in the *Journal of Sports Sciences* (2004). In reviewing the shaky basis for early talent indicators, they identified an alarming dilemma, namely that 'the earlier a talent identification procedure is employed, the more potentially talented individuals will be eliminated' (p. 401).

It is well documented that most students initially identified as gifted children frequently do not emerge as gifted adults. And many highly successful adults simply did not shine so brightly in their formative years. The observation that early developmental indicators fail to predict individual trajectories cannot sensibly be interpreted as loss of talent. Development is the natural outcome of many interacting factors. Aspects such as motivation, goal setting, persistence, deliberate practice, personal identifications, and knowledge building, all exert subtle but powerful effects in people's lives over time in a manner independent from tests of precocious talent taken at an early age.

IN PERSPECTIVE: Skill development and purposeful practice

Expertise hinges on extensive development, and hours spent in practice activities can approach a figure close to 10,000 hours, or about three to four hours a day over a decade. But such practice needs to be developmental, effortful, goal-structured, and actively monitored. Such a notion is embedded in the concept of deliberate practice. There are possible dangers in practising activities that lack these additional features of deliberate practice. Although automaticity was once assumed to be the hallmark of expertise, the emergence of automaticity at the individual level can itself be detrimental to further skill development. Why? Because it allows the individual to perform a skill mindlessly, with mindlessness being the natural enemy of deliberate practice.

At this point we can mention one aspect that needs to be recognised by teachers. At the level of the individual, skill development involves periods of growth followed by periods of consolidation or even lack of growth. This uneven pattern was first documented in Bryan and Harter's classic studies into Morse code experts. They introduced the term **plateau** to describe periods when little development appeared evident despite extensive practice. We find their definition of this term remains meaningful today:

A plateau in the curve means that the lower order habits are approaching their maximum development, but are not yet sufficiently automatic to leave the attention free to attack the higher order habits. The length of the plateau is a measure of the difficulty of making the lower order habits sufficiently automatic.

(1899, p. 357)

Finally, although we have emphasised the role of time in practice, we certainly do not want to give an impression that deliberative practice involves constant grind. Skill development programs often take place in short blocks of around 20 minutes of intense activity, followed by short rest periods. Hence, an athlete's three-hour training session might have cycles of intense effort and programmed rest breaks. Many elite performers are known to take short naps during training sessions. This is something we know little about, but it suggests that high performers are using short breaks to restore energy levels, and so can face their next challenge with renewed vigour.

Study guide questions

1 It is often said that practice makes perfect. How do we know this is not true, or at best a half-truth?

2 The Bloom report from 1980s pointed to a consistent pattern underpinning the development of high performers. What sequence of effects and influences was described?

3 What is meant by the '10-year rule'? How seriously should we take this rule?

4 Why do human achievements and performances (e.g., such as recorded in the *Guinness Book of Records*) keep increasing?

5 How is deliberate practice defined? How does the study of professional and amateur singers relate to this concept?

6 What are the three broad stages of skill development?

7 Automaticity is always implicated in developing expertise. But why can automaticity also stymie personal development?

8 There is much debate about the value of early talent indicators. Abbott and Collins noted that the earlier a talent identification procedure is used with children, the more likely it is to exclude potentially talented individuals. Just why are early talent indicators so unreliable? What other factors are at work?

9 The chapter suggests it is a fallacy to presume that children who show early talent but fail to develop thus constitute 'wasted talent' (as many writers used to claim). Why is such a notion often a misleading idea?

Reference notes

■ Time and experience alone do not advance skilfulness (and sometimes people get worse). Evidence reviewed by Ericsson, Chapter 38 in Ericsson *et al.*, 2006. For such studies in medicine see Ericsson, 2008.

■ Up to 2011, 50 years of research has revealed outcomes in stockbroking rely on chance (luck) not skill, see p. 200 in Kahneman, 2011. Gigerenzer (2008) has shown how simple heuristics, based on recognition, resulted in better predictions of stock market outcomes than predictions from professionals within the field.

■ Family backgrounds of top-flight professionals (Bloom, 1985, 1986).

■ Time required in developing chess masters (Ross, 2006). Berlin musicians study (Ericsson, Krampe, & Tesch-Römer, 1993).

■ Deliberate practice: in addition to Ericsson's scientific papers, highly readable accounts are provided by Foer, 2011, and especially Colvin, 2008.

■ Singers' conflicting motivations to develop professional skills or experience personal fulfilment (Grape, Sandgren, Hansson, Ericson, & Theorell, 2002). For a tribute to this dilemma, we recommend a song from noted American entertainer, Harry Chapin, accessible on YouTube: www.youtube.com/watch?v=TUCZUNevrEQwatch?v=TUCZUNevrEQ.   ·

■ Improving typing in college students (Keith & Ericsson, 2007).

- The psychological mechanisms underpinning arrested development: Chapter 38, Ericsson *et al.*, 2006.

- Dilemmas of early talent identification (Abbott & Collins, 2004). Discontinuity between giftedness indicators in children and eventual genuine achievement in adulthood (Winner, 2000). Fallacies underpinning innate talent theory are documented in the work of the late British researcher, Michael Howe (M. J. A. Howe, 1999; M. J. A. Howe, Davidson, & Sloboda, 1998).

12

Expertise in the domain of classroom teaching

The analysis of expertise stands as a major achievement within the behavioural sciences. What emerged around the time of World War II was the realisation that when humans become highly skilled, after years of constant development and learning, then a coherent set of behavioural characteristics is developed. Although each expert is a unique person, with an individual history and a bespoke profile of capabilities, it emerged that all experts, across scores of different fields, possessed traits in common. These traits were detailed in Chapters 10 and 11. We have lost count of the many different areas of expertise that have been studied. The literature is vast and held across multiple disciplines and databases, and estimates are that about 90 to 100 different areas have been studied. Classroom teaching is one of these well-studied domains.

So are there experts in the field of teaching? Do they actually exist? By definition, experts must be shown to perform at elite or high levels, on defensible and visible criteria, and do so repeatedly over extended time periods. Experts need to be defined by their performance, not reputation or years of experience. Seniority or years of experience invariably fail to predict expertise. Reputation is useful as a guide in locating possible experts. But then genuine evidence must be sought to establish expert status within the field.

Statistical analyses on student achievement data at the level of the class, however, have indicated some teachers are associated with elevated gains in levels of their students' achievement, and do so repeatedly over years. This finding has been seen consistently across nations such as Australia, New Zealand, Britain, Germany, and America. If we regard student learning gains in achievement as valid and objective criteria, there is substantial evidence that classroom teaching represents a genuine skill domain. By conservative estimates, about 20 per cent to 30 per cent of the variance in student achievement stems from teacher effects. This figure has been appreciated since the mid-1960s. In many analyses this number climbs far higher. In VL it was noted that the average teacher is associated with an impact on standardised tests each year somewhere between 0.2 and 0.4, expressed as effect sizes. But some teachers are found consistently to be associated with yearly gains of 0.5 to 0.6 and greater effect size on student attainment data.

The topic of teacher expertise has stimulated a large body of research over the past 30 years. Some of the findings are highlighted in Table 12.1 expressed in line with the known attributes of expertise stemming from cognitive psychology. You can note how researchers such as Berliner and others have been able to describe strong parallels and linkages between expertise in teaching and expertise in other fields of human achievement.

TABLE 12.1 Matching expertise factors with research findings

KNOWN EXPERTISE ATTRIBUTE	ACTUAL FINDING ABOUT EXPERT TEACHERS (ET)	RESEARCHERS
Experts excel only in own domain.	Expert teachers teach their area extremely well, but are far less skilled outside of their curriculum areas.	Berliner
Experts perceive large and meaningful patterns.	Expert teachers plan lessons as interlinked sequences with different means of achieving same goals. They concentrate on tasks relevant to goals.	Borko
Experts can work quickly and solve problems with little error.	Expert teachers explain complex ideas with astonishing clarity, using short time blocks. They use instructional methods with precision.	Leinhardt Hattie
Within their domain, experts possess remarkably large short-term memories.	Expert teachers retain a mental script of key aspects that take place during lessons, but ignore irrelevant details.	Berliner
Experts see and represent problems at a deeper or principled level.	Expert teachers recognise and interpret classroom events incredibly efficiently. Expert teachers steer activities towards classroom goals. They diagnose the need for instruction and feedback at the level of individual needs.	Berliner Hattie
Experts spend relatively more time analysing complex problems carefully and qualitatively.	Expert teachers plan for different contingencies that could happen. When learning a new topic they read and research it well before teaching. They assist students to think about a problem before providing solutions. They set worthwhile challenges, and when dealing with able students quickly shift across from surface to deep learning tasks.	Borko Hattie
Experts have very strong skills in self-monitoring.	Expert teachers able to 'stop and start' lessons most efficiently. They listen intently to (or even stare at) students to obtain feedback on their learning. They have developed unique strategies for controlling student attention. They anticipate possible problems so can respond to keep momentum flowing.	Leinhardt Borko

How can we relate to such findings?

Whenever we show findings as in Table 12.1 to our own students we are struck that some of them, people training to become teachers, appear to regard such results as somehow 'obvious'. As researchers and instructors, we feel that nothing could be farther from the truth. What is being described is a depiction of many years of professional skill enhancement, always goal driven, and typically involving a high level of **deliberate practice**. The novice teacher struggles to survive with ego and pride intact. But the level of individualised and personal teaching and adaptive instruction that takes place in the classrooms of novice (and experienced but not expert) teachers often is dramatically low. Through watching an expert, the novice can pick up a great deal, and begin to employ some of the same methods, if introduced slowly, and in such a manner as to obtain corrective feedback.

For instance, we know that one of the problems of the novice teacher is that of overestimating how much learning students attain during any one lesson period. Expert teachers are vigilant when it comes to monitoring student learning and attention. They will use a wide range of assessment tools but especially focus on genuine products such as bookwork and test scores. They keenly read individual facial expressions and are well aware that superficial aspects such as head nodding often mask genuine learning. They make constant instructional judgements to avoid overloading their students, and become highly adept at matching curriculum tasks to individual capabilities and in providing acknowledgement and feedback. They therefore are much more adept at knowing where each student should go next – this proficiency to know 'where to next' based on student prior and actual achievement is a hallmark of their expertise. These are skills that are embedded within context, and which take many years to hone. Overall, a novice can learn a good deal from merely observing how the expert operates.

One question the available research cannot answer with any certainty is *How long does it take to become an expert teacher?* David Berliner noted that the people he has been studying were developing their teaching skills over a period between 5 and 10 years. This professional development tenure is consistent with the known scientific literature that suggests that approaching 10,000 hours of structured practice is the natural prerequisite for elite level performance.

The laboratory and real life

From the earlier discussions, you will have noted that expertise studies often use the laboratory method. Expert functioning is uncovered through asking people to relate to simulated conditions. The laboratory enables a high level of control in that people are responding to the same cues (e.g., video on a computer screen). Also aspects such as response patterns and timings are measured accurately, for instance with high-speed cameras. David Berliner and his team at Arizona State University have carried out several laboratory studies with expert high school teachers. Using videotapes of classes in operation as stimuli to assimilate, they discovered that expert teachers possessed the ability to read classroom life to a remarkably high level.

In the case of experts, their perceptual and memory strategies differed from the average experienced teacher in that they focused on information about lesson structures, teacher demands and expectations, and students' work dispositions. In contrast, experienced but non-expert teachers focus attention on what they could see on the screens, without necessarily attempting to relate this information to the underlying teaching goals behind the lessons being observed. For example, the non-experts noticed superficial details such as students' clothing. Experts failed to notice such surface details. Instead, experts' attention was focused on deep structures such as timelines and the extent to which the teacher on the screen was making sensible instructional decisions.

One remarkable laboratory finding was that expert teachers, in contrast with others, were highly accurate at inferring student comprehension from non-verbal cues. This was true, however, only when they were familiar with the students seen on the films. Hence, their awareness of individual student learning was specific and depended on their relationship with that student, rather than existing in generalisable knowledge form. In short, the experts knew their students as individuals with unique quirks and expressions. They could 'read' these individual reactions quite unconsciously. Expert teachers thus become highly sensitive towards what their own students are learning and thinking.

What was strangely informative was a review of one particular laboratory experiment that failed. The Arizona team had asked expert teachers in advanced mathematics to come to the laboratory and, with half an hour preparation, begin teaching a one-off lesson to a 'class' made up of stooges recruited from the university drama department. Without the teachers' knowledge, these stooges had been instructed to misbehave on a programmed script. Through interviewing the participants of this dubious experiment afterwards, the researchers discovered the experts, in chorus, found the experience entirely unsatisfactory. They complained it was not possible to plan an impromptu lesson in a contrived laboratory period. These were people accustomed to being successful through motivating their own students to exert efforts on worthwhile tasks. Hence, asking such professionals to perform in an artificial context, before a badly behaved class, misses the point. The Arizona team realised that this procedure deprived their experts of the conditions needed to demonstrate advanced skills. This is parallel to asking a chess master to memorise random chess pieces, a task on which many such masters are found to perform poorly.

The laboratory method will yield important information when participants are given opportunities to respond to conditions that genuinely simulate circumstances existing in the real world. Analysis of the failed experiment tells us that expertise in teaching is tied to developing a relationship with a class over time, and directing that class within a goal-driven context. Issues such as behaviour management become relatively unimportant since the teacher and class share agreed-upon agendas. Hence, it behoves us to study classroom expertise both in the laboratory and in the real world of the classroom.

Observing expert teachers in action

One of us (John Hattie) participated in a large American study. The classroom skills of middle school teachers, mostly teachers of English language arts, were monitored as part of the program initiated by the National Board for Professional Teacher Standards (or NBPTS). It was possible to contrast 31 experts (those who passed NBPTS assessments) against 34 experienced but non-expert teachers (those who did not pass). A considerable body of data, including interviews, observations, student responses and work samples was collected and analysed using 22 trained raters. A number of crucial differences emerged. For one thing, the experts were adept at shifting their students' work products over from surface to deep response requirements. The students of such teachers were found to be working on tasks likely to promote deep conceptual understandings for the majority of their class time.

The overall findings were as follows:

- Expert teachers possess pedagogical content knowledge that is far more flexibly and innovatively employed in instruction.
- Expert teachers are more able to improvise and so alter instruction in response to contextual features of the classroom situation.
- Expert teachers understand at a deeper level the reasons for individual student success and failure on a given academic task.
- Expert teachers' understanding of students is such that they are more able to provide developmentally appropriate learning tasks that engage, challenge, and even intrigue students without boring or overwhelming them – they know 'where to next'.
- Expert teachers are more able to anticipate and plan for difficulties students are likely to encounter with new concepts.
- Expert teachers can more easily improvise when things do not run smoothly.
- Expert teachers are more able to generate accurate hypotheses about the causes of student success and failure.
- Expert teachers bring a distinct passion to their work (Hattie, 2009, p. 261).

The expert teachers scored more highly than the experienced teachers on a number of measured attributes. But for simplicity these attributes can be grouped in terms of three major dimensions: (a) setting goals and using challenges to bring out the best in their students' efforts, (b) monitoring student learning and using such feedback to assist their teaching decisions, and (c) drawing on strong levels of curriculum knowledge, which allows them to adapt teaching to the individual context and be able to diagnose instructional requirements quickly. From this, we have adopted the DIE model to train our student teachers. That is, to teach them the skills of *diagnosis*, *intervention*, and *evaluation* of their impact. This requires developing skills in how to diagnose based on evidence in the classroom and student work, to have multiple interventions (because if one does not work trying it again is nowhere near as powerful as trying a different intervention), evaluating the impact of their intervention on learning (in its many forms), and so the cycle continues.

To watch such expert teachers in action is to be singularly impressed with their ability in making a series of integrated decisions that juggle managerial and instructional aspects of classroom teaching in a seamless manner. Observers in these studies often comment on the orchestration and organisation of the experts' classrooms, and the virtual absence of student misbehaviour. These are rooms wherein students are too busy and goal-oriented to act out, and where misbehaviour occasions disapproval from other students.

One aspect that often surfaces when interviewing expert teachers is that they readily will talk about classroom events that could (i.e., might) happen. It is as though they are mentally prepared for possibilities, however remote. Several early studies noted that highly experienced teachers appeared to have poorly developed lesson plans, at least as furnished on paper. But what was occurring was that the more expert a teacher became, the more such plans became familiar scripts and routines in the head. However, they are not fixed scripts, but ones that permit considerable variation and improvisation. Their knowledge base is highly procedural in that many of their skills have a basis in making available a range of viable actions, rather than in believing there exists just one 'correct' way to handle any one current problem.

IN PERSPECTIVE: Expert teaching as interpersonal sensitivity

There is a considerable body of knowledge informing us that (a) not only can expert teachers be identified through valid performance indices, but also (b) that such experts share the same psychological traits that underpin expertise in other fields. In a number of places in this book we emphasise how acquiring expert knowledge within a given domain can create difficulties when that person attempts to teach such domain knowledge to a relative novice. The gap from novice to expert can become too wide for the expert to sensitively diagnose. Situations easily arise where a novice and an expert end up equally frustrated.

But we now know that classroom teaching is itself an expertise domain. There is a practice of teaching. This discovery represents a significant fact with implications for our profession. It implies that some human beings have been able to develop elevated sensitivity to the academic learning needs of the novice. Analysis of both the laboratory projects and classroom observation data informs us that expert teachers do not merely respond to arbitrary cues on call. They actively shape the classroom world and skilfully entice their students into becoming motivated learners sharing the same learning goals as the teacher. But to get to this point entails considerable knowledge and personal investment over 5 to 10 years of development. High quality teaching cannot be seen as a mechanical exercise. Instead, it hinges on developing a relationship with a group of young human beings who have come to trust and respect the goals that their teacher has for them.

One of the leading researchers noted that 'Teaching is the art of transmitting knowledge in a way that ensures the learner receives it' (Leinhardt, 1987, p. 225). We find this a remarkably profound observation. The ability to use words, demonstrations, and feedback to explain complex ideas and concepts to your fellow humans who lack initial motivation is not a skill to treat lightly. Transmitting knowledge (and understanding) does not mean just talking at people, as that is only a minor aspect of the process. Instead, this is a capacity that rests on keen levels of intelligence and interpersonal sensitivity. Many of the topics treated within this book review what research has revealed about interpersonal interactions relevant to the instructional process. Such knowledge is of value in coming to understand why it is some teachers are highly successful in inviting young people into the world of learning, reading, and liberal open-mindedness.

Study guide questions

1 Does it make sense to suggest that some classroom teachers can be labelled as experts?

2 The material listed in Table 12.1 is often labelled as 'obvious' by beginning or preservice teachers. Given your experience in the field, are those points obvious? If they are so obvious, then why are they so infrequent?

3 In reading the list of teacher expertise attributes, which are ones you can recognise in yourself, both in terms of successful strategies, but also for attributes that you need to improve upon?

4 How has the use of the laboratory method enabled expert teaching skills to be identified?

5 On the other hand, one research team found that expert teachers cannot be expected to teach impromptu lessons to students they do not know. Why not? What is missing in such situations?

6 One factor that emerges repeatedly is the notion of improvisation in teaching. What does this mean, where does it come from, and how is it achieved?

7 Another factor that emerges strongly is that expert teachers base instruction on information their students give out. Can you explain how this feedback process operates?

8 'Teaching is the art of transmitting knowledge in a way that ensures the learner receives it.' Why is it that such effective knowledge transmission hinges upon high levels of interpersonal sensitivity?

Reference notes

- Teacher effects are reviewed in Chapter 7 in VL (Hattie, 2009).

- For a historical perspective see Bloom, 1976.

- A strong statement highlighting the role of quality teaching, especially looking at data from within the Australian context (K. Rowe, 2006).

- Table 12.1 draws on findings from many studies including Berliner, 2004; Borko and Livingston, 1989; Leinhardt, 1987; Leinhardt and Greeno, 1986; Sabers, Cushing, and Berliner, 1991.

- The insights gained from a failed experiment are discussed in detail in Berliner, 2004.

- The American NBPTS study is described in Chapter 11 of VL (Hattie, 2009) and in depth in Ingvarson and Hattie, 2008.

Learning foundations

13

How knowledge is acquired

We all know learning when we see it! Or at least, many would make this claim. But we do not learn in a straightforward way – it is more staccato – we listen, we try, we concentrate, we try again, we make mistakes, we correct, and we learn together. Over the past century we have learnt a lot about learning, and this chapter looks at these findings grouped under three major topics:

a six principles of acquisition;

b six principles of memory retention; and

c five aspects of handling information overload.

After discussing each of these topics, we will briefly review the notion that we possess three types of memory systems, specifically, the iconic or sensory store, the working memory, and the long-term memory.

Six principles of acquisition

1 Learning requires time, effort, and motivation

Human learning is a slow process that can happen over months and years rather than hours or days. The necessary ingredients are (a) time, (b) goal-orientation, (c) supportive feedback, (d) accumulated successful practice, and (e) frequent review. Notions such as instant experts, superfast learning, speed-reading, and other magic-like programs, amount to faddish quackery in violation of known and validated principles of human learning. If only it was that simple.

We *appear* to learn specific small-scale behaviours, isolated bits of knowledge, or low-level objectives within only a few minutes. But impressions of quick learning are deceptive for many reasons. Unless the material is strongly meaningful, relevant and timely, it is subject to rapid and substantial forgetting. Any new learning can be readily disrupted. To become skilful in a new area takes about 50 to 100 hours of practice. Genuine expertise requires some 10,000 hours, or 8 to 10 years of consistent skill development. It is known that the average intelligent person can learn basic rules of chess within an hour, and might then play a rudimentary game. But it takes a decade to become a chess master.

2   Concentration spans are short

Most of us have a natural attention or concentration span of around 15 to 20 minutes before significant levels of **mind wandering** occur. Well-motivated learners may then refocus their mental activities back onto a task, but will still need short breaks from the task being learned in order to avoid overload effects. If you need to teach anyone some new information, you need to do it within 15 minutes, or else you will 'lose them'. Attention is easily disrupted. Paying attention to music as you try to learn something else will harm your mental focusing and disrupt your learning, a finding that stands in contrast to the fallacious Mozart effect, popularised within the media, and reviewed later in this book (Chapter 23).

3   Distributed practice is more effective than massed practice or cramming

To try to learn material within a single block of time often turns out to be less effective than if the same duration of time is broken into shorter periods spaced over several days or weeks. This distributed practice effect is especially true when developing new procedural skills. For example, if you were to learn to drive a car, you would benefit more from 6 sessions, 20 minutes each, spaced over a week, than from a single block session of 2 hours. In most human learning situations, blocks of 15 to 30 minutes are effective in cost–benefit terms. The effect of distributed practice is sometimes also called the spacing effect.

4   Prior knowledge effects are powerful

David Ausubel claimed 'that if I had to reduce all of educational psychology to just one principle, I would say this "The most important single factor influencing learning is what the learner already knows. Ascertain this and teach him accordingly."' A major determinant of knowledge acquisition will be what the mind already knows. It is far easier to build on coherently organised *existing knowledge* than it is to learn new material *de novo*. Our current knowledge and understanding is the filter (sometimes correctly, sometimes not) of new information – hence the importance of prior knowledge. New information that cannot be related to existing knowledge is quickly shed. In sheer learning power, prior knowledge effects are stronger than other variables likely to impact learning. Prior knowledge effects readily outweigh effects due to IQ or so-called 'learning styles', which have fairly weak effects on learning. When your prior knowledge is based upon misconception, however, it will create an obstacle, an effect called *interference*. Sometimes we have to start by unlearning what we already know so that correct and more powerful learning can take place.

The mind does not relate well to unstructured data. We find it extremely taxing to learn random lists or when coping with unrelated materials. We need to find the organisation, structure, and meaning in whatever we learn. *Meaningfulness*, or relatedness, stems directly from prior knowledge. We benefit enormously from being shown how to group information, how to locate patterns, how to use order, and how to schematise and summarise. Often we need to be taught a 'coat hanger' (or higher order concept) on which to hang new knowledge. In teaching situations, good teachers often provide overviews of what we are to learn, and these are referred to as **advance organisers**, which serve to activate prior knowledge and so enable us to acquire new information efficiently. If these advance organisers also demonstrate what success criteria look like at the end of learning this helps provide the coat hanger such that we can then say, 'Aha, now I know.'

5 Your mind responds well to multimedia input

From time to time, we come across theories describing 'visual learners', or 'auditory learners', or 'tactile learners', or whatever. But people are more similar than they are different in such learning styles. We cover this in depth in Chapter 19. We all are visual learners, and we all are auditory learners, not just some of us. Laboratory studies reveal that we all learn well when the inputs we experience are **multi-modal** or conveyed through different media. Our brain is set up, incredibly well, as a device that integrates information from different source inputs, especially from different modalities. Strong learning occurs when words and images are combined. Claims made such that 'some students learn from words, but others from images' are incorrect, as all students learn most effectively through linking images with words. These effects become especially strong when the words and images are made meaningful through accessing prior knowledge. Differences between students in learning are determined strongly by their prior knowledge, by the patterns they can recognise, and not by their learning style.

6 To learn, your mind has to be active

This principle is simply that learning occurs effectively once the mind responds to a meaningful experience through making a meaningful response. When the mind *actively* does something with the stimulus, it becomes memorable. Our brains are never inert when we are learning. It is possible to pay attention, to watch, and learn a good deal from many apparently 'passive' experiences (i.e., without any apparent overt responding taking place). In many classroom situations, those who observe carefully can pick up more information than someone performing a given task. This observational learning effect is especially true when there is no physical or motor skill involved. But passivity in learning situations can bring inherent dangers such as (a) not realising that you have failed to learn, (b) being distracted, or (c) falling asleep. This principle is aligned with the notion of **elaboration,** which will be discussed later in this chapter.

Six principles of memory retention

1 To recognise is easy: to recall is hard

The term *recognise* means to indicate that the material is known. This entails signalling, in a coherent way, such as ticking a box on a multiple-choice test. But to *recall* means to produce, reconstruct, or rebuild. Measures of recognition pick up partial or incomplete knowledge very easily. Recall measures are more severe and insensitive to partial knowledge. Hence, in terms of items remembered, a recall test typically yields lower scores than a recognition test. Indeed, part of the art of constructing high quality multiple-choice tests is to devise items that cannot be answered by simple, direct recognition, but which involve deeper levels of processing.

2 Information given first and information given last is often recalled more easily

As a learner, the individual deals inevitably with sequences of information. The human brain is a type of linear processor, and how you remember events is subject to what are called *serial position effects*. Obviously, some information entering the mind is more important than other information, and information that enters the mind first within a sequence is recalled more readily, and this effect is called **primacy**. In contrast, the **recency effect** occurs when the information that enters the mind last has an advantage in your learning. Put these together: when you listen to a lecture you are more likely to recall the beginning and end bits, but the middle is more readily forgotten. Recency effects can be strong immediately after a learning experience, but the primacy effect may tend to become strong remembering something that occurred a while ago. It is difficult to generalise here, however, since laboratory studies indicate some individuals tend to show strong primacy effects, whereas others will show stronger recency effects.

3 Over time, there are different rates of forgetting

With effort, it is possible to learn meaningless material. Lists of nonsense words, or columns of random numbers can be committed to memory. But retention level for this type of rote learning is dramatically low, possibly about 20 per cent can be recalled after a day. Rote acquisition results in rapid forgetting within minutes of the original learning. If such material is to stay with us, it must be constantly rehearsed or otherwise a clear pattern must be perceived – this is the difference between rote and deep memorisation. Various mnemonic devices may be activated to aid retention levels and to free working memory to attend to deeper thinking, but recall through the use of such devices should not be confused with deep learning.

The rate of forgetting will depend on the type of original learning. For example, once mastered, motor actions may be retained for a lifetime. A healthy senior citizen is able to ride a bicycle even after not riding for 50 years. Also, the retention level for vocabulary words is very high, at least within your native language. But there will be moderate levels of decay over time for most intellectual-type skills, especially if the skill hinges upon detailed knowledge of specific facts or numbers. Unfortunately, the mind will shed isolated facts very rapidly. We all have great difficulty holding onto arbitrary items such as telephone numbers, and bank account numbers, even when such things may be seen as important.

4   Memory is a highly constructive process

It is tempting to think of the memory as a 'play-back video recorder.' This metaphor is misleading. Memory is highly constructive in that it relies on the brain making sense of partial cues and imprecise information. Memory is dependent upon the focus of attention at the time of learning. But what two people focus upon, given the same experience, can be different. As Nietzsche claimed, there is no such notion as immaculate perception. Human beings are notoriously unreliable as eyewitnesses to complex events. Memory for aspects such as time estimates, vocal emphasis, specific words spoken, causal sequences, and even actor–action associations vary dramatically between witnesses. Interpretations vary in accordance with prior expectations and other sense-making strategies. The act of recall must be seen as a person's attempt to find meaningful patterns in what otherwise is chaos. Hence, our memories are subject to many different types of error such as oversimplification, abbreviation, schematizing, distortion, and intrusion. An *intrusion* is where a person recalls some aspect that was not part of the original learning experience, but which makes sense within the context of what they have remembered.

People are not aware when their memory plays tricks upon them. We fall into the trap of believing that our memories correlate perfectly with reality. Eyewitness confidence level, however, is a flawed predictor of what actually took place. Instead, such confidence reflects whether or not we as a witness are able to construct a story that makes sense. The success of the worldwide phenomenon, *The Innocence Project*, stands as testimony to tragic errors made through courts accepting eyewitness constructions. Modern DNA methods have so far been used to free more than 280 falsely accused individuals.

At times, our memory reports can be biased by factors such as stereotypes, prejudices, and faulty expectations. There can be many sources of distortion at work whenever people report on events in which they took part. It is important to realise that human interactions, especially when occurring within split seconds, are almost impossible things to recall accurately with your mind alone. Many studies have been conducted into **false memory effects**, where people report on events that did not happen. Within controlled studies, various subtle techniques have been used to implant such memories.

5   The principle of savings: what is forgotten can still help

Suppose you learnt a foreign language 20 years ago, but now appear to have forgotten it completely. Well, this is unlikely to be the full story. Studies have shown that we can learn material the second time very rapidly, even when the original learning appeared inaccessible. We know about this principle because of the huge time advantage people have whenever they relearn material. In such situations, people are unaware of the power of this effect, and may not realise that substantial savings are being made. All they know is that they seem to be 'picking it up fast'. This effect is dramatic when a person visits a country after not having spoken a specific language there for 20 years and then 'picks it up' within a week of arriving in the country. Such effects appear unconscious and can account for why you can acquire some skills very quickly.

6   Your memory is subject to interference

Interference refers to natural memory loss due to experiences either before or after the original experience. For example, if you learn a list of 20 Spanish vocabulary words and then a list of 20 French words, your recall of the Spanish words is inhibited by learning the French list. This is called **retroactive interference**. But similarly, your recall of the French list is reduced by the fact that you had earlier learnt the Spanish list, and this form of interference is called **proactive interference**. These are genuine memory effects, not merely the result of fatigue or overload.

In school situations these effects can operate in subtle ways. Although we hold that prior knowledge generally will help learning, there are times when prior knowledge can become a source of proactive interference. This occurs when your prior knowledge is faulty, or constitutes a misconception. For example, within the science curriculum words such as force, matter, vector, ratio, space, and living all have technical definitions that can be hard for students to assimilate because such words also have common-sense meanings remarkably different from their technical meanings.

Five aspects of handling information overload

At times, people find themselves in situations where they are overloaded. The efficiency and organisation of actions is threatened because there is too much going on within the mind. Overload is implicated in a host of human pathologies and miseries. This notion provides one powerful reason why people at times will act against their intentions and self-interest. For example, under provocation and stress, a teacher may strike a student despite knowing such physical gestures are illegal, ineffective, and inappropriate. The explanation for many forms of violence is that the actors were overloaded and unable to cope. In recognition of this fundamental aspect of the human condition, we can describe five key points.

1 From the learner's perspective, learning is not always a pleasant experience

Overall, learning will bring high levels of reward and personal satisfaction. But, look at this closely. Positive emotions are correlated with two things: (a) planning and goal setting in the first place and (b) achieving planned goals. For the most part the actual learning is *not* enjoyable. It is enjoyable to have skill, to display prowess, and to envisage what one can do. It is pleasurable to perform, or dream about performance benefits. However, learning can be tough. The actual process of learning, the moment when learning takes place can be stressful and loaded with emotions of uncertainty. This can quickly shift into negative feelings, once capacity is exceeded. This notion is consistent with the Willingham thesis cited in Chapter 1.

One factor implicated in this principle is that most students possess a natural tendency toward **overconfidence** in being able to learn. That is, we tend to be optimists and so believe we can perform better than we really can in most situations. Similarly, we *underestimate* the amount of time and practice it takes to master a new skill. We underestimate how much discipline and determination is needed to develop expertise. These natural tendencies are simply human default positions, neither 'good nor bad', but can be recognised by all instructors, teachers, and parents. The overconfidence effect is especially strong *before* people receive objective feedback about performances. Feedback can force a person to radically alter such assessments.

2 Learning places great stress on mental resources

A learner is vulnerable. A learner has to maintain composure in the face of often unpredictable consequences. It is necessary to mobilise high levels of effort and vigilance, and so be prepared to respond to input experiences in a variety of ways. Learners may not know how the world is going to react towards an action they have initiated. They may not know of the appropriate stimuli to devote attention to, may not know how to match the intensity of their response to the immediate input, or how to pull back if they have optimistically overstated current capabilities. In short, mental resources are stretched, and once an overload point is reached, then the ability to take on board any new information is reduced severely.

3 For all learners, it is crucial to develop coping strategies

We all develop ways of coping with overload. We can do things such as pay attention, work slowly, increase the level of practice, reread the materials, or find a good teacher. Our coping strategies need to apply to two fundamental aspects: (a) increasing our opportunities to learn, and (b) managing our emotional responses. It is necessary for every student to develop a wide range of possible coping methods. Failure to learn coping skills renders the individual passive in the face of inevitable overload experiences. Incidentally, it has been found that there is a surprisingly high level of consistency in the way individuals will respond to quite different sources of stress. These coping strategies do not seem to relate strongly to other aspects such as personality, but they are nevertheless consistent within the individual. It is thought that these individual coping styles and strategies are set by the time students go to high school.

4 Sources of overload can be identified

There is no one single cause of overload and some students will adapt to overload stress better than others. However, at the level of the individual learner, it is possible to specify that overload can be linked to *any one* of the following:

- low levels of prior knowledge;
- deficient use of mental strategies or inappropriate coping strategies;
- unrealistic expectations (e.g., overconfidence, goals set too high, or immutable);
- poor instruction, inadequate teaching, or failure to engage with learning material;
- unfavourable learning conditions (e.g., study facilities, presence of distractions);
- assessment apprehension (e.g., unfair tests, competition, emotional problems).

5 We are all subject to overload

When conditions such as those listed above are unfavourable, all of us will experience problems in learning or otherwise performing at an optimal level. There does not appear to be any natural 'alarm bell' telling us we are about to experience an overload. Instead, this is something we often discover once it is occurring. One recurring fallacy about human information processing is that the mind can learn more than one thing at a time. This trait is occasionally ascribed to young people who grew up around computers (so-called **digital natives**). There have been many studies into this effect, and we review these issues in Chapter 20 and 21. The overwhelming conclusion is that no human has yet evolved that can genuinely multitask when tasks involve active levels of conscious cognitive processing. When it concerns two deliberate acts, then *any degree of mental switching* will cost you, often dearly. Instead of being a solution to your busy life, attempting to multitask, or dividing your attention, adds to overload.

Multi-store theory

The multi-store theory suggests that the human memory system consists of at least three levels of memory, which can loosely be called banks or stores. They are the iconic store, the short-term, or working, memory, and long-term memory. These will be discussed below together with a discussion on the need for every learner to develop strategies to enable learning to occur.

Iconic memory

This form of memory is also known as sensory memory, or as ultra-short-term memory. Iconic memory relates to input experiences and perceptions within a sensory modality. Within the visual system, for example, experiments reveal that a large amount of data can be stored for around a second. In a laboratory study, for example, you might be asked to look at a screen where an image appears for one twentieth of a second. Your visual system takes it in and then has perhaps up to a second to 'read' from the image until it fades from your mind. The auditory system appears to have longer duration sensory images of possibly two or three seconds duration.

Short-term or working memory

Although researchers use different ways of assessing short-term memory, and working memory, these two terms are clearly related, and often are used interchangeably. In essence, short-term memory refers more to our basic biological capacity, and working memory refers to what the mind is doing within this capacity. Metaphorically, this is the working area or the 'workbench' of your conscious mind. But it is a system that has to stay active, lest items drop off the workbench and are lost forever. Indeed, it is a limited capacity workbench, which presents a huge bottleneck to our ability to learn.

The short-term memory system has two basic problems. First, the amount of information it easily holds is limited to only a few items at a time. Second, information is lost quickly from the system. How much information can be held, if they are to be 'worked' on? *Answer*: around four items if they are unfamiliar ones, but around eight if they are relatively familiar items such as numbers, letters or simple words.

How long does information stay within the system? *Answer*: somewhere between 5 and 20 seconds. For example, you find a telephone number in the White Pages. But someone speaks to you between your reading the number and being able to dial. This interaction destroys mental rehearsal. Your ability to get the number correct is lost after 5 seconds. And after a 20-second interruption, it has gone. To retain such information you need to rehearse in order to maintain it within an active buffer called the **articulatory loop**. Laboratory studies show that the mind uses a natural articulatory loop of 1.5 seconds. It is easy to retain as much as you can say to yourself within 1.5 seconds, and do so indefinitely. The other way to retain information is to transfer it to long-term memory.

Long-term memory

Metaphorically, the long-term memory is the archival library store where data are filed for retrieval. It is held that this system holds information in permanent storage form. Certainly, long-term memory storage will be affected dramatically by disease or brain trauma. But this system is not subject to the same decay processes that beset one's working memory efficiency. In essence, the passage of time alone does not dim this system.

There are many issues associated with storage within the long-term memory. One major issue is that the system does not possess anything like the file transfer protocol (or FTP) download capability of a computer. There is no human equivalent to transferring information from your USB to your hard drive. It can also be noted that the major cause of apparent forgetting in humans is failing to learn properly in the first place. As we noted earlier, humans tend to be overly confident in their learning ability, and will underestimate the time and effort required to achieve skills. Hence, people will often fail to pay sufficient attention to learning opportunities as they underestimate how much effort is required.

There are no known spatial or capacity limits on long-term memory. Actually, the principle of prior knowledge even suggests the opposite: the more knowledge you have the easier it is to learn even more. In the course of aging, the mind may lose certain agilities, notably those to do with fast accessing, but the volume of material stored is not affected primarily by aging itself.

The major problems of the long-term memory system hinge around three aspects: (a) the sheer difficulty of loading information into the system, (b) the need to develop efficient encoding strategies that enable inputs to be fully processed and interpreted in such a way as to relate to what the head already knows, and (c) the need to use retrieval strategies which enable ease in accessing stored memories.

Never think of your long-term memory as a passive repository. In action, it is nothing like that since this form of memory determines who you are, what you can do, and how you see your world. Every mental operation you perform hinges upon ease of access to information you acquired earlier in your life. Every time you find an experience meaningful it is because of its relationship to what is already in your head. For example, you might think of tasks being objectively 'easy', or 'hard'. This is illusory since easy and hard are defined by individual learning histories (the accessibility of information from long-term memory) and not by objective criteria. A task you find hard is easy to someone with greater knowledge in this area.

The need to develop efficient learning strategies

The multi-store theory portrays learning in terms of transfer of information across the memory banks within the mind. Whereas the iconic store appears to take in a good deal, the process of attention ensures that only a few items are transferred from the iconic store to the short-term memory. In this sense, attention operates as a filter keeping a high level of information out of consciousness.

Within the short-term memory, information may be held for brief periods, but unless immediately refreshed it fades quickly, and is lost forever. On the other hand, the learner can use strategies to move the data into long-term memory. This entails some form of active responding in that the mind has to 'do something with this stuff before it disappears'. But what? What can you do?

Within your mind you could try a bit of CRIME. These are chunking, **rehearsal**, imagery, mnemonics, and **elaboration**. *Chunking* is involved whenever the mind groups items together that did not necessarily come together in direct experience. Chunking can mean to group, sort, organise or classify. The central idea is that the mind is able to reduce mental load by arranging related items into a meaningful pattern using prior knowledge.

Rehearsal means literally to repeat oneself, to refresh the data. This can be done sub-vocally within the working memory (thus making it work). When one rehearses aloud it is called reciting. The mind is working on the notion that repetition will make the memory trace more permanent. When this practice is applied to data that cannot be linked to existing knowledge we may use the term 'rote learning'. In early childhood one basic memory strategy takes the form of *labelling* (i.e. naming whatever stimulus is present within immediate view). In later childhood, rehearsals may take the form of a list that can be quietly repeated to oneself even when objects are not in sight. By adolescence, rehearsal will take the form of a **cumulative rehearsal and fast finish**, a much more sophisticated form.

Imagery is another way to respond to an input experience. Literally, this means to 'picture it' within the mind, a skill that some people report they use very naturally. We encounter some people, for example, who claim that they even recall telephone numbers not by rehearsing them sub-vocally, but by imagining what the numbers look like written down. One of us (Greg Yates) once worked with a person who claimed to recall telephone numbers by projecting mentally the number onto a blank wall. Then by reading what was on the wall he could read them either forwards or backwards.

Mnemonics is a general word that can be used to refer to any memory device. But we often use the term to refer to temporary tricks such as using ROYGBIV for the colours of the rainbow, or Every Good Boy Deserves Fruit for the notes on the treble clef in music, or even CRIME. As a student you will know of specific mnemonics that relate to problems within your areas of knowledge. Such tricks exist, for example, for being able to memorise the value of pi, the periodic tables, the positions of planets, or the nerves of the body, and so on.

Elaboration means to process information by adding to it in meaningfully. You can use the input information as a trigger for bringing other data from long-term memory into working memory consciousness. So fusing the new with the old creates a more durable and accessible memory trace. Let us try to illustrate this: (a) you have to learn a number, 8912815, and realise that you were born in 1989, in the month of December, so you 'pretend' that it was quarter past eight in the morning. Another example, (b) you read the word Taipan in the TV program, and your mind crosses back to when you were in Queensland and the farmer told you to watch out for deadly snakes in the cane fields.

In both instances your memory for the inputs (the number and the TV program) is enhanced because your mind elaborated at the *moment of initial exposure*. Such elaborations may be either involuntary, or quite deliberately employed as a conscious learning strategy in which prior knowledge associations are used to advantage. We note that all the memory training schemes or books we have ever seen base themselves on principles of elaboration, organization and chunking.

IN PERSPECTIVE: So far, so good, but what is missing? *Answer:* our social brain

Thus ends Learning 101. This chapter offers a broad survey into factors that underpin learning. Many of these basic ideas are discussed in other chapters in this book. However, what is notably missing from this specific chapter is any sense of the social context in which we expect our students to successfully build their knowledge.

Of all the species on this planet, the one with the highest level of sensitivity towards fellow members of the same species is Homo sapiens. Our capacity to learn from social experience exceeds that of any other species. We are built to pick up subtle cues from other people and use such information to base our own actions upon. Although animals do learn a huge amount from watching fellow species members, none of the apes or monkeys possesses such acute ability to learn from observation, from social cues, and from language, as does our species. The imitative capabilities of a chimpanzee are roughly akin to that of the human child about 3 years of age. Contemporary notions concerning human brain development now highlight the role of the brain as an organ predominantly concerned with interpreting social situations. We have evolved large brains that allow us to establish and maintain social relationships and to transmit culture from one generation to the next.

We are an archetypal social animal. Such a perspective, with its implications for understanding how we learn through interpersonal contact, emerges through many of the chapters of this book. However, it is still important to consider just how the individual mind stores and organises knowledge. This becomes the topic of the next chapter.

Study guide questions

1 If we want people to focus intensively, with relatively low levels of mind wandering, learning experiences might profitably last for just how long?

2 Effects due to prior knowledge are often shown to be stronger than the effects of IQ. Can you recall any experiences with students that appear consistent with this finding? What happens when you have a student who arrives with high levels of knowledge about a topic?

3 Do some students learn better than others from images or from listening?

4 If the mind has to be active in learning, how come we learn by just observing others?

5 What types of learning are retained easily? What things are forgotten quickly?

6 The principle of savings means we often can learn things remarkably quickly. But what is actually occurring?

7 One factor implicated in overload is our natural overconfidence. This has nothing to do with self-esteem as such, but reflects a type of error people are prone to make. What experiences enable this error to be reduced?

8 Explain why learning is not always a pleasant experience.

9 The chapter lists six causes of overload. What are they?

10 Describe the strategies students are likely to use in learning situations? What is CRIME?

Reference notes

Please consult the reference notes for Chapter 14 on p. 135.

14

How knowledge is stored in the mind

What you already know determines what you can learn and how you think. Learning proceeds quietly and efficiently when what is new builds directly upon what is already secured. These ideas are among the most powerful messages emerging out of modern psychology. The effects of prior knowledge are dramatic yet well hidden from a teacher's view. In this section we review the various types of knowledge your life experiences have provided for you. These types are summarised in Table 14.1. The first five types (sensory, strings, ideas, schemata, and mental models) can be collectively referred to as *declarative knowledge*, since they relate to knowledge that could potentially be expressed through words. On the other hand, *procedural knowledge* is indexed through actions.

In this chapter we will review each of these six knowledge types, by (a) describing each one, together with (b) describing what is known about how each different type of knowledge is acquired and duly stored within the mind.

Sensory recognition knowledge: mastering sensitive discriminations

Sensory recognition knowledge refers to how our mind relates toward information within our immediate sensory experience. For instance, we all recognise elementary patterns such as square and triangle, and we have little difficulty in discriminating shapes and colours as in following instructions such as 'Watch out for the white bird with the large speckled head'. We learn to discriminate visual information that holds personal meanings such as the faces of people we know, places we frequent, or finding our bags on the airport luggage carousel. Similarly, we learn to identify sounds with great sensitivity, such as the sound a computer makes when turned on, and we are able to use sensory skills in decisions such as 'this object feels rubbery', which are readily understood by other people.

With experience we use sensory discriminations to make fine grain judgements such as detecting the trajectory of an approaching ball, determining just when the roast is adequately cooked, or how much force to use with our power tools. Given additional experience, your sensory knowledge may develop such

TABLE 14.1 Types of knowledge

KNOWLEDGE TYPE	RELATED TERMS	FUNCTIONS	EXAMPLES
Sensory recognition	Visual memory Tactile judgement Auditory discrimination	You use sensory inputs with precision and expertise in making sensitive judgements.	Knowing basic shapes, patterns, and substances. Able to judge distances. Knowing when the dough mix is the right consistency.
Strings	Serial ordering Sequences Chains Simple associations	You can access short manageable bursts of information without any specific need for elaboration.	Telephone numbers. Lines of poetry. Multiplication tables.
Ideas	Propositions Subject and predicate Object properties Facts	This allows units of information to be stored as relationships between discreet entities.	Glass is made from sand. Mary is married to Frederick with two children. The major population centre in West Australia is the beautiful city of Perth.
Schemata	Concepts Abstractions Script The big picture	Ideas are not isolated but are grouped into a higher level of organisation providing scaffolding and structure.	All countries will have a capitol, exports, money, and so on. Anything used to move things is a *vehicle*, for instance a cup is vehicle, and so is a legal contract.
Mental models	Problem solving Hypothetical thinking	Ideas and schema are used to simulate different possible versions of reality.	*What would happen if the poles melted? Suppose the cell membrane failed to block the attack?*
Procedural knowledge	Actual skills Task analysis If–then contingencies Automaticity Conditional knowledge	When a situation develops, you produce the right sequence of responses, at the right level of intensity and correct timings, in achieving a goal in real life, in real time.	Knowing how to skim read. Calculating the area of a block of land. Fixing flat tyre on your VW. Knowing how to act professionally when assailed by a rude parent.

that you may begin to see the world differently from others. For instance, your friend notices a little boat, but you perceive it as a 'well-maintained 4.7 laser sail'. Once you develop sensitive perceptions such as these you can no more turn them 'off' than you can prevent yourself from reading the letter *A*.

Conditions of acquisition. Sensory recognition skill depends upon matching gradations in sensory input with an outcome and recognising the nature of the available feedback. Paying attention to fine-grain details is paramount. This learning is typically nonverbal in the first instance. However, the person can then learn an appropriate vocabulary to describe the sensory discrimination being applied. The initial learning is fast, but times will arise when it is difficult for a person to convey to others the nature of the discrimination. Thus, having the master chef shout at you 'Mix the batter to the right consistency' is an instruction you may find distinctly unhelpful. This is why a good deal of feedback that teachers provide (seemingly valuable and sensible from their viewpoint) is not received, understood, or acted upon by the learner.

Strings: how we handle simple associations

Strings constitute a most useful aspect of your mental life. They are often known as **serial orderings**, but also as *associations*. This type of knowledge is critical to survival in our world. During your lifetime you have acquired hundreds of such strings. The ability to access the right information in the right sequence is a critical survival attribute. By way of illustration, try to identify what comes next:

A B C D _____.

We all live in a yellow _____.

He took it hook, line, and _____.

To be or not _____.

Supercalifragilistic _____.

Your telephone number is _____.

One curious aspect about the science of learning is that there is no genuinely defined phenomenon known as 'rote learning', despite popular vernacular. When this term is used it may refer to the acquisition of serial orderings. Such knowledge takes the form of a sequence easily rehearsed within a brief time frame. There is a starting point followed by a relatively short flow of information. Such information may or may not relate to any other aspect of your stored knowledge. The important aspect for you is retention of the information as a short sequence.

How we acquire strings. Strings are acquired through deliberate focus and repetition. The mind needs to be cleared. The new string entity can be rehearsed in working memory where you can deliberately vary the speed of information. For example, you get a new VISA card number and so need to say it quickly, and then slowly. Say it under your breath, then write it out. To advantage, you can use the well-known *look–say–cover–write–check* method that is often used in teaching spelling in the early years.

Ideas: knowledge as propositions

Ideas describe the next level of complexity. Ideas are conveyed through sentences that have properties such as a subject and predicate. Ideas are propositions about things, and commonly link one entity with properties. Sentences become devices that can carry many such propositions. For instance, to read 'The major population centre in West Australia is the beautiful city of Perth' is to read a single sentence conveying five separate ideas (*that West Australia must have several towns, that Perth is a city*, that *Perth has more people than any other place within West Australia*, and so on).

The notion of idea implies linkages at the level of conceptual meanings rather than simple strings. As new words are learnt, they are necessarily tied to your previous vocabulary. New words employ the same phonology and structure as old words, but permit a refinement of ideas as properties are added into your mental network. For instance, you may not have encountered the term *schema* before now. But learning this new word is not hard since it slots into the present context in a meaningful way. In essence, you are building upon your prior knowledge. You can see *schema* as a new term, yes, but it is close to the notion of *concept* already in your head.

We know that people process information at the level of ideas when they no longer recall the exact word forms used. When we relate ideas to other people we express the ideas in our own language and hence meaning takes precedence. For example, you now read that 'The largest city in Western Australia is Perth, which is a lovely city'. You may see this as the same sentence you read earlier. Only by looking back and comparing the sentences together will you see the differences.

Conditions under which we learn new ideas. Ideas are acquired though exposure to factual information. It matters little if information is given verbally or in written form, so long as attentional limits are not exceeded. But there are severe limits on how much can be assimilated, and the factor of meaningfulness looms especially large here. Much of the information cited in the previous chapter applies to this type of acquisition. New ideas are rendered meaningful once related to prior knowledge that enables a degree of elaboration to be applied to the new input sentence.

Our existing knowledge is never a passive repository. Instead, it is the means by which any new piece of information can be explained and accounted for. Any mental effort made to drive a new input more deeply into your existing mental networks will render the new information resistant to forgetting. The important motive underpinning acquiring ideas and facts is that they are easily accessed when you need them in the future. Durable and accessible ideas must be laid down carefully using deliberate focus and some level of mental effort.

The best single way to learn any new fact is to ask yourself the direct question, 'Why is this fact true?'. The important thing is to focus, and then furnish yourself with a sensible answer based on what you already know. In this way, the new idea links into the networks already inside your head. The trick is to make the links explicit, as there is a danger in any new information being treated in isolation, which creates inert knowledge, or 'islands of knowledge', rather than a richly interconnected network of meaningful associations.

Schemata: knowledge becomes organised

Schemata, or schemas, are the basic units by which we organise and structure our knowledge. Whereas ideas might be acquired somewhat randomly or accidentally, it is at the level of the **schema** that deeper meaning occurs, and the grasp of an 'overall big picture' becomes possible. Schemata provide the necessary frames we need to make sense out of ideas and facts that would otherwise exist as isolated islands of knowledge.

For instance, once a child understands that a schema for *country* exists, she can think in terms of a country having a capital city, exports, people, languages, airports, and so on. Hence, on reading 'Wellington is the capital', this information is easily filed as part of her knowledge about New Zealand. You can think of schemata as higher-level structures that enable facts, concepts, and even sequences, to become deeply meaningful. As another example, when you travel overseas there are a host of things that must take place in order to proceed. Hence, 'arranging and executing overseas travel' is an organisational schema that will apply no matter which country or mode of travel is involved. Local variations are possible (such as whether or not you need a visa), but the underlying schema is always the same. A schema for such travel can also be called a *script*, since events must occur in a specified sequence.

How we develop schemas. Schemata are not easily acquired since the level of organisation becomes more complex. Whereas concepts might be learnt fairly readily (often after three or four exposures to the same idea embedded across different contexts), schemata acquisition implies graduated refinement that can continue to develop over many years. **Schema refinement** is likely to begin with the person realising that his or her existing way of organising knowledge is not fully adequate. This process was identified originally through Piaget's notion of disequilibrium. That is, schema refinement hinges on the person contrasting successful and non-successful thinking, with a view to making subtle adjustments that can accommodate the incongruent data.

Mental models: putting schemata to work

A mental model is something that you can run entirely in your head, akin to a type of software program. Models enable you to simulate reality. This is the type of knowledge that enables you to engage in serious problem solving calling on all available schemata. For example, your home computer is not responding as it should, and so you run through a series of possible reasons. What you are doing is calling on a model of your computer system. But this model is one located inside your own mind, and it is based on your prior knowledge.

Similarly, whenever you consult a doctor he or she achieves diagnosis on the basis of mental models for illness, disease, and therapeutic treatment, learnt initially in medical school. In this case, his or her mental models call upon scores of schemata, which are in turn supported by many thousands of facts your doctor has learnt.

Models allow if–then thinking to be given free reign. For instance: *What would happen if the cost of petrol doubled overnight? Suppose air travel was made free around the world. What if people could really acquire knowledge without having to invest time in learning and studying? What if there were no dentists? What would happen if the ice caps melted?*

Mental models enable a person to engage in varieties of hypothetical or fanciful thinking. But note how the quality and success of such thinking will depend upon the schemata and ideas available to that individual. Without a rich supply of accurate data in the form of organised schemata, problem solving cannot take place. An unfortunate truth is that one's creativity can never substitute for actual knowledge when it comes to being able to run successful mental models. Although models permit hypothetical thinking, the outcomes of such processes are tied back to reality. In short, real-world problem solving is strongly dependent on two major factors: (a) the availability of accurate knowledge, and (b) the ease with which such stored knowledge can be handled within working memory. Creativity is possible when two or more knowledge sources are integrated in a manner not previously recorded.

Acquiring mental models. The conditions under which we acquire new mental models are poorly understood. However, such conditions are known to involve experiences of challenge and social cueing such as exposure to highly competent individuals who display abstract thinking. As individuals develop expertise over time (see Chapter 11), they develop a large knowledge base that enables them to activate mental models with relative ease.

As an example of such extended development, think about how the term *evolution* itself is subject to progressive refinements as a student moves through the school years. At the outset, it is possible to appreciate evolution as a simple uncluttered fact, learnt in one class at one moment in time. But with more and more knowledge entering the mind, this term takes on the properties of a concept that can be applied across different contexts. It takes three examples of the idea being seen in different contexts for the mind to begin treating evolution as a concept. Later, it will become an overarching schema used to organise a huge body of information. By the end of high school, evolution has developed to the level of a highly functional theory of living systems that provides the mind with a mental model it can employ to solve highly complex problems.

To put this another way, the basic idea of evolution, as assimilated by a bright 7-year-old, is the building block for a highly differentiated explanatory model of all life forms which the same student needs when studying Biology 101 at university. The student's notion of evolution has itself evolved through successive stages of schema refinement, to the point where complex mental simulations become possible.

Procedural knowledge: learning actions

Recently, one of us (Greg Yates) asked a group of university students if they knew how to change a flat tyre on their motor cars. Almost half the group raised an arm. When asked if anyone had ever changed a tyre, no arms were raised. You may know how to change a flat tyre in verbal terms. But if you have never done this before, you would likely injure yourself in the attempt. In general, procedural knowledge is not subject to verbal instruction, although words can cue a learner to recall procedures mastered earlier.

Procedural knowledge implies a sequence of sub goals. A task is broken down into components where each component is a distinct step to be defined and mastered. This entails a series of *if–then contingencies*. *If* the tyre is flat, *then* move vehicle to a safe area. *If* you can get to the boot (or trunk), *then* check the air pressure in the spare wheel. *If* the pressure is adequate, unbolt the spare wheel. *If* the spare wheel can be removed, *then* locate the car jack. *If* you locate the jack, *then* determine the jacking point on the chassis. And so on.

Knowledge of procedures also extends to cognitive skills, as well as physical or motor activity. For example, every student has to master key procedures in mathematics. This is the knowledge of how to achieve defined outcomes such as calculating area, working through steps in a computer program, or knowing how to determine how much stress is being placed on a critical wooden beam within a support structure.

In the early school years, knowing how to read and comprehend text implies appropriate procedural skills. For example, there are different procedures that apply when reading different types of genres, or in knowing when to read at a fast pace, and when to re-read difficult materials. Procedural knowledge allows a student to read strategically, and attune different strategies to different goals. Researchers may refer to such awareness as *conditional knowledge*, i.e., the knowledge of which procedure to apply within which context.

How procedural knowledge acquisition takes place. Procedural learning implies hands-on experience where the person responds to actual problems. It is enhanced by social interaction with others to help clarify possible problem-solving strategies. People benefit enormously from opportunities to observe social models demonstrating appropriate skills.

Procedural skills are enhanced substantially by the opportunity to study partially worked examples. Controlled studies have shown that when a learner is provided with worked examples, then providing additional verbal instructions (e.g., from a teacher) is not needed. The learner needs high levels of corrective feedback, yes, and sometimes, words help to remind a learner which procedure to use. However, when quietly working your way through procedures what you do not need is an external voice telling you what you need to do next.

In an explicit teaching situation, the detailing of lock-step production systems is often called task analysis, which can be shown as an algorithm involving a series of steps and decisions. Such tools can be partly misleading if seen to imply quick or simple decision-making. The simple truth is that procedural learning (a) is slow and (b) requires much feedback and extended practice. Once mastered, procedural knowledge becomes the basis for action and expertise, and will implicate elements of behavioural chaining and **automaticity**.

Should the procedural task be one that is essentially manageable, but in danger of overloading a person's immediate capacity, it can often be taught in reverse order (i.e., to ensure mastery of the final steps first before teaching the beginning). **Backward training** is often valuable in teaching difficult skills. Over successive trials the need for conscious guidance is reduced, the drain upon memory resources becomes lower, and the activity begins to flow readily rather than being seen as a series of separate but challenging steps.

IN PERSPECTIVE: Ways of knowing and thinking

We recognise the sheer amount of time and effort it takes for the full development of our learning facilities. Mature thinking requires decades of schemata refinement, and we never stop learning. Although we can solve simple problems as young children, the problem-solving skills of the mature adult are of an impressively different character employing complex models inside the head that define just how the world is believed to be constructed.

The present chapter reflects the analysis of knowledge emerging out of cognitive psychology. It is interesting to note how this approach differs from curriculum-based taxonomies developed in the 1950s. Within such taxonomies, knowledge was often portrayed as a basal step in a sequence that might be described as (a) knowledge, (b) comprehension, (c) application, (d) analysis, (e) synthesis, and (f) evaluation. On a logical basis, such taxonomies are useful in devising assessment items (although even this is questioned), but they do not account for how the mind actually works. It is not valid to say that somehow the mind acquires knowledge, then strives towards its comprehension, then applies it, and so on. Although the taxonomies might supply possible frameworks for instructional planning and for devising assessments, you should be aware that the mental process underpinning learning does not align with such sequences.

A more convincing taxonomy was invented by two Australians, John Biggs and Kevin Collis, which they called the SOLO (structure of observed learning outcomes) taxonomy. It posits four levels: one idea, many ideas, relate the ideas, and extend the ideas. The first two levels are about surface and the latter two about deeper knowing. This taxonomy highlights the importance of basing deeper knowing on surface information, which is often forgotten when teachers try and teach critical or enquiry learning as a generic tool. Given the premise, that you must have something to think about before you can relate, extend, critique, and enquire, it is perhaps not too surprising that enquiry and critical thinking needs to be embedded in a subject domain. It is tough to teach these thinking skills generically. Indeed, transfer of learning is one of the hardest things to accomplish.

Study guide questions

1 Deciding when the dough mix is just at the right consistency is knowledge requiring sensory recognition. Can you think of any other examples in your life where you have learnt to make sensitive assessments based directly on gradations in sensory information? How can we teach these sensory discriminations?

2 One reality of this modern world is the need to learn multiple strings of information such as your visa number, passwords, or ID numbers. Can you recall any situation where failure to recall a string has occasioned disaster in your life? What are some good ways to commit such strings to memory?

3 However, in terms of your mental organisation, Perth's standing as a beautiful city actually is *not* an information string. Instead, it is a proposition or an idea. What is the difference between a string and an idea?

4 Schemata are more abstract things than ideas. Ideas can be taught quite directly (as facts to acquire). Schemata can be taught, yes, but just why is such resultant learning so much more difficult to achieve?

5 Problem solving results from people becoming able to run strong mental models in their heads. This view says that problems are solved by activating the right knowledge, at the right time, in the right place. How does this mental model view contrast with the view that solving problems depends upon one's divergent thinking or creativity?

6 Explain just how the notion of 'evolution' could be acquired initially as an idea, but later as a schema used to organise coherent knowledge, and finally as a fully developed mental model able to be 'run' in the head. Are there any other examples you can think of in your area where simple ideas are progressively built on over many years, to create deeply elaborated models of functioning?

7 One interesting finding is that although verbal cueing certainly helps a person recall which procedure to use, in fact verbal instruction, within itself, does

not help procedural learning (and may even interfere). If that is true, then how does a person actually achieve secure procedural learning? Just what has to take place, and what helps the process?

8 Is it fair to say that knowledge is acquired, which leads to comprehension, then application, and analysis? What is wrong with such logical sequences?

Reference notes

- Research into learning has been accumulating for 150 years. These two chapters draw on this body of information, as generally found in basic textbooks in the field. However, at a more advanced level, and focusing more on learning in school, the following are high quality resources: Bruning, Schraw, and Norby, 2011; Gagne, Yekovich, and Yekovich, 1993; Pressley and McCormick, 1995.

- Quotation from David Ausubel, who was a significant figure in introducing the principles of cognitive science into educational psychology research (Ausubel, 1968, p. vi).

- The work of Dr Elizabeth Loftus on false memory effects (Bernstein & Loftus, 2009). For details on the Innocence Project: http://en.wikipedia.org/wiki/Innocence_Project.

- One version of the social brain hypothesis was advanced by British anthropologist Robin Dunbar (Dunbar, 2009, 2010). He drew attention to the role of pair bonding in brain evolution across species. However, primates specifically evolved ever-larger brains to manage their complex social systems. The typical Homo sapiens has close relationships (or 'support cliques') with about five to seven individuals, and can cope daily with perhaps up to around 40. Beyond this, our brain size enables acquaintance relationships with up to 150 individuals. Groups can work well under 150. But over this, things often come unstuck with issues of management, fractionalism, security, and moral discipline. Hence, 150 became known as Dunbar's number. High school teachers often are expected to manage student numbers well exceeding this figure.

- The notion that procedural knowledge is acquired through studying models and examples, but barely at all through verbal instruction (Wittwer & Renkl, 2010).

- The SOLO taxonomy model (Biggs & Collis, 1982).

15

Does learning need to be conscious, and what is the hidden role played by gesture?

Consider the following strange calculations. Through counting neural connections, it has been estimated that 11,000,000 signals, or units of information, could be sent to the brain from sensory receptors at any one moment in time. Such is the complexity of the visual system that the eyes alone account for around 10 of the 11 million possible units of information. To function adaptively, we can actively filter out massive amounts of potential input information, to the point where our conscious mind, or our focal attention, might zoom in (just like a camera zoom lens) to allow in about 40 units of information per second. So what happens to the other 10,999,960 informational units potentially available to the mind within such an acutely focused one-second period?

The inevitable answer is that we do not pay attention to the vast bulk of information that could be available. We are highly selective in what we focus upon. We have to be! The vast bulk of information, as apprehended by our senses, simply has no effect on our conscious mind because of this remarkable capacity for *selective attention*. With our minds we can focus on minute details, and shut out all other inputs.

While selectivity is well recognised, making such an observation itself leads onto another curious issue. *Is it the case that more input information is transferred into the brain's systems than the conscious mind itself actually knows about?* To what extent have we really shut out things that apparently are of little interest? This is not a trivial issue. *Can we learn without actually knowing that we are learning?*

There are no definitive answers to such questions. However, given the current state of knowledge, the only sensible response to such queries is, 'Yes, your brain does take in considerably more information than can be indexed by the immediate content of your conscious mind.' An experience may still affect you, and result in learning, even though you did not intend to learn, and you did not pay explicit attention to the source of the experience at the time. Broadly, such phenomena are referred to as **implicit learning**. This human capacity, to evidence learning in the absence of explicit verbal awareness, has been a topical field of research over the past two decades.

Implicit learning is everywhere

It is apparent that many basic findings about implicit learning have been known from much earlier research. For instance, in classical conditioning demonstrations, as first studied in animals and later with people, conditioned reactions are known to occur outside of personal awareness. For example, people can acquire fears, and other emotional reactions, without being able to say exactly what stimulus they have become conditioned towards.

Similarly, people, children and adults alike, may respond positively to rewards such as social attention or praise, but still be unaware how such external things are motivating their overt behaviour. In social influence situations we readily copy from other people. We take on board incidental features of a social modelling stimulus, chameleon-like, without explicitly realising how this model has influenced us. The idea that everything we do is the result of some conscious control mechanism has to be seen as a notion that contradicts much of what we know about human learning. This aspect is covered in more depth in the chapter about System 1 and System 2 functioning in Chapter 30.

In more general terms, implicit learning refers to *any* variety of learning that cannot be expressed easily in words or thoughts. For instance, implicit or tacit learning can be applied to a good deal of skill development and motor learning. Try explaining to yourself how to ride a bike: you may begin to analyse how you shift your weight to maintain a centre of gravity above the wheels but too much thinking may lead to a switch of attention and falling off the bike. Similarly, if you glance at your hands whilst driving a car in a straight line, note how your hands make tiny adjustments on the steering wheel all the time. This knowledge of fine calibration adjustment was not relevant to learning the skill in the first place. Instruction based upon such knowledge would be unhelpful.

A German researcher, Gird Gigerenzer, has described how baseball coaches can give faulty instruction about ball catching skills, being unaware of what the brain does to compute where a travelling ball will land. There is no evidence to suggest that this skill can be taught as a set of verbal codes to young children. In fact, people simply do not *know* how to catch balls, and are unaware of what their eyes, legs and hands are doing to allow this to happen. This lack of knowledge occurs despite having successfully caught balls over a lifetime. However, implicit learning extends well beyond motor skills, and can apply to how the brain processes information. Indeed, much information can be assimilated from the environment even though the individual cannot immediately describe in words what has been learnt.

Learning as an unconscious activity

Consider the following laboratory study published in the prestigious journal *Science* by Antoine Bechara and her colleagues in 1997. Adult subjects were asked to play a gambling game in which they were requested to make choices about which deck of cards to select from, while hooked up to a machine measuring skin resistance conductivity (SCR), a commonly used measure of emotional learning. Each of the card decks was associated with a combination of wins and losses, but for half the decks the odds were poor, the other half more favourable. They did not know this at the outset. The combination of wins and losses across different decks made it difficult to track the outcomes of choices as they were being made. The people were not trying to work out if there were differences in the decks, as they were not given any reason to think the decks would be different.

Nevertheless, by the end of the session, people were able to state which decks were good, and which were bad. They ended up with high levels of awareness. But the remarkable thing was that this knowledge came late in the session, only *after* their nervous systems were reacting in terms of SCRs. The emotional responses, that something was wrong, occurred outside of conscious thinking. People began to realise that certain decks were bad, *after* their nervous systems were sending signals, and they realised they were avoiding them. Emotional SCR responses were being detected after about 10 cards, behavioural choices were shifting after 50 cards, and verbal awareness kicked in at around 80 cards. The authors concluded that, 'nonconscious biases guide behaviour before conscious knowledge does. Without the help of such biases, overt knowledge may be insufficient to ensure advantageous behaviour' (p. 1293).

In other laboratory studies, people were asked to learn sequential patterns, as presented on computer screens, where the patterns were created by applying various rules. For example, suppose the following sequence occurs: **G S S Y J T H S S W J A G K S S F J T U**, and so on, for several hundred more letters.

There is an embedded pattern in which J follows S S with one letter in-between. After being exposed to this type of sequence for around 10 minutes, your mind starts to expect the J after the S S. One curious thing is that learning such recurring patterns does not depend on being able to state what they are in words. Such perceptual learning may occur without your knowing about the underlying rules, or even that they exist. This is particularly true for any spatial patterns such as being able to 'know' whereabouts on the screen a stimulus is likely to occur. Our brains are set up to learn spatial locations quickly and we do so without words or consciousness being implicated.

In these laboratory studies, people may report knowing but without knowing why. What happens is that we pass through a hunch phase in which we show signs of having acquired knowledge of an underlying rule. Such effects can be evident in actual behaviour *well before* your mind is able to put such knowledge into words. Sometimes, people fail to realise there is any pattern at all. But this lack of awareness still does not prevent them from showing improvement in anticipating what, and where, the next thing is coming in the sequence (for example, in knowing whereabouts on the screen to look for something). Indeed, by some definitions, intelligence is knowing what to do when you do not know what to do.

Implicit social learning

As another example, consider the findings from a well-controlled study by Erin Heerey and Hemma Velani (2010). Students played the rock–paper–scissors game with a computerised avatar who was so realistic that people were unaware they were playing against the computer. They played 235 games, with the level of chance of 1 in 3, or 33 per cent. However, the computer avatar was programmed to display a subtle cue (such as movement of the mouth, or eyebrows) predictive of one of the options. Thus, a specific facial cue, such as an eyebrow movement, might predict rock. Across the session, this predictive cue increased performance levels from 33 per cent to 44 per cent.

Nevertheless, the students had no conscious awareness of the link between the facial cue and their enhanced ability to predict how their opponent would behave. It is important to appreciate that the predictive cue was only one of many movement cues the avatar was programmed to exhibit. The predictive cue was embedded within a naturalistic sequence. It is apparent that we can learn to recognise and use social cues such as facial expressions in making sensible decisions, even in the absence of any explicit knowledge about actual contingencies.

Such fascinating findings give arise to questions such as *What does it mean to know something?* and *Is unconscious learning different from conscious learning?* Most researchers suggest that implicit learning does not really exist as a separate form. Instead, it is simply learning that is incomplete, or has yet to become fully conscious.

Implications of implicit learning

How should we interpret the research findings in this area? One important aspect is to appreciate that learning is not always expressed in purely verbal forms, even within areas that appear to be fundamentally cognitive or verbal in nature. Whenever recurring patterns exist in the world, the unconscious mind appears to be able to discern the pattern and anticipates the next likely steps in a sequence. The unconscious mind might be registering the pattern in the form of a correlation or likelihood of association. Not until this correlation becomes sufficiently strong does the conscious mind fix upon it, take a reading, and then articulate the relationship in words. Up to that point the relationship is under the radar. We clearly know many things we do not know we know.

Implicit learning results from regularities within the natural world. Hence, through experience, much information is taken on board without an explicit intent to learn. Spatial learning occurs in this way, such as your knowledge of the layout of a building or a city or the anticipated landing site of a ball in the air. As mentioned earlier, we actively learn from stimulus associations, and reinforcement contingencies in the absence of explicit conscious recognition. You do not need to be aware of reinforcers for them to have an impact upon you. Similarly, when we learn from social models available in our worlds, we do so automatically in the absence of any conscious plan to start copying others. Indeed, the very idea of being a 'copycat' is abhorrent to many, despite their manifest sensitivity to social influence.

Nevertheless, a moment's reflection will inform you that implicit learning mechanisms are often far from efficient. A person can spend a lifetime experiencing pain after eating bread but never make the connection that he is gluten-intolerant. People undergo tests to diagnose their allergies: yet, if implicit learning mechanisms were always effective they should be able to work out what distresses them. Given that some of the laboratory experiments into implicit learning did involve many repeated trials, it seems that waiting for explicit learning to occur from these types of experiences is likely to be uneconomical. By the time the gambler has learnt to avoid all forms of gambling, and the correlation between gambling and unhappiness has moved from implicit to explicit recognition inside his mind, the gambler could be bankrupt.

While the mechanisms underlying implicit learning effects are not well understood, one possibility is that the brain is always attuned to detecting any errors or hint of failure. Our brains react strongly and emotionally whenever things do not go well, or whenever there is even a slight threat. In the Bechara card selection situation noted above, for example, it was apparent that people were highly affected by negative information. The unconscious mind was registering which decks were the most punishing even after only 10 cards had been turned. That negative feedback information will be more powerful than affirmative information is a theme often found within modern psychology, encapsulated in the phrase 'bad is stronger than good'. We see this is also the case in terms of how we react to feedback in the classroom. Disconfirmation feedback is more likely to lead to us changing than confirmation feedback. A common finding is that in terms of psychological impacts, punishment or loss will outweigh equivalent rewards by around two or three times the objective values involved.

Gestures as a means of uncovering and using implicit knowledge

Consider the implications emerging from the following fascinating project, published by a team headed by Susan Goldin-Meadow. Theorising that a student's knowledge can take *both* implicit and explicit forms, they individually videotaped 106 junior primary school students who had been asked to explain how to work out several mathematics problems. Of the 106 students, 67 spontaneously used overt hand gestures in carrying out this task. Studying the videotapes in depth, the researchers matched the students' words to the gestures their hands were carrying out. It was found that 35 of these students communicated knowledge and strategies in their gestures that were *not found* in their words. In other words, for about a third of the students, their hands indicated a higher level of understanding than was apparent from analysis of their speech alone.

In a follow up project, students were asked to use their hands deliberately to gesticulate as they carried out their explanations on the mathematics tasks. These students displayed an enhanced awareness of strategies to use in solving the task. But this study produced an even stranger finding. Students who, as instructed, practised on the first maths task by actively and deliberately using their hands to explain themselves, went on to perform more highly on a second task that followed on immediately. The second task involved learning about rules for equivalence in equations. Since they were at the junior primary level, this task was advanced for their age.

The researchers theorised that using gestures on the first task activated a level of implicit knowledge that became available to the students when learning about equivalence. Gesture can be a means by which implicit knowledge can be (a) assessed, (b) enhanced, and (c) recruited for use in new learning situations. Knowledge that may not be fully conscious, may nevertheless be evident in some form, and duly tapped into through gestures. Metaphorically, gesture can be thought of as a way-station in the transfer from implicit to explicit thought. Before you can express things in words, you can still use your hands as expressive tools. Gestures can reveal thoughts sitting on the edge of your competence.

You can note how some people, as adults, do speak with their hands. Such individuals are often highly successful communicators. Gestures are an integral part of human communication within interpersonal situations. They are automatic and evident in all people, even in individuals born without sight. Many individuals use gestures even when speaking on the telephone. However, we have rarely appreciated the validity of the following idea: *that when students gesticulate and use their hands as they speak, their understanding of what they are saying can move to a deeper level, and their overall performance on academic tasks can be enhanced.* Of course, this does not mean we should teach children to wave their hands around. It is simply that we need to respect gesture as one possible sign of deeper thinking beginning to emerge.

Gestures as vital aids in thinking and communicating

You might wonder if asking students to gesticulate as they think or attempt to explain things can interfere with their mental processes, or otherwise cause distraction. You might ask someone to think hard. But to ask them to *think with their hands* surely is an additional demand? But the actual findings are clear.

Gesticulation assists your mental processes entirely positively. When people are asked to gesticulate as they think hard, they produce responses that are more strategic and more thoughtful. From both laboratory studies and applied research in realistic contexts, we now know that people can do this automatically, without complaint, and without duress. Using gesture as you think actually *reduces* the cognitive load on your verbal and memory systems. Your brain will work more effectively when you gesticulate as you talk, and your ability to think and solve problems can increase. Further, people report satisfaction from the experience. To gesticulate is to be human; it is communicative, socially responsive, inherently rewarding, and fun. But most importantly from our view, is that gesture is an early marker that learning is taking place. Knowledge can be expressed in gesture before it can be expressed in words.

Learning is active, and the manner in which the arms and hands move can be highly consistent with information a person is trying to learn. Our language is littered with expressions and implicit references to bodily gestures and movement. On the other hand, behavioural stillness and an overall lack of bodily movement are the well-known correlates of passivity and depression.

Children are strongly affected by adults' gestures

In one study Dr Goldin-Meadow found that children's vocabulary at 4 years of age was predicted by how much they were using gestures when they were infants at 14 months. It is known that infants will attempt to use gestures in communicating from about 10 months of age. But how parents react becomes critical. The research showed that the extent the infants used gestures at 14 months was strongly related to how their parents were using gestures in communicating with their babies. In short, clear benefits for early childhood language acquisition emerge when significant adults within the child's world actively use a repertoire of physical gestures in talking with the young child. What is remarkable about these findings is that such a powerful variable as gesture usage, so beneficial for communication and mental development, can exert its effect virtually unnoticed.

This fascinating research has direct implications for your teaching skills. There have been studies published indicating (a) students actively will use information that teachers convey through gestures, (b) that students can learn more from a lesson when a teacher explicitly uses hand gestures as a teaching strategy within the lesson presentation, and (c) young children rate a teacher as more knowledgeable when she uses her arms to point at significant details to be observed.

One recent review of the evidence showed that such gesture effects are strongest when the learning involves physical, spatial, or psychomotor components. But gestures were generally not effective in conveying abstract topics. It was found that gestures tended to be most effective when they added to the information being explained. The review found that children and students pick up a good deal of information from the manner in which adults gesticulate. Therein lies a strong lesson for the teacher: whenever you teach, your students are also watching and learning from whatever your arms, hands, and body are doing.

IN PERSPECTIVE: The hidden world of implicit learning and the role of gesture

The overall message provided by research in this area can be conveyed via seven key points:

- Our brains learn from mere exposure to recurring patterns in our environments.
- A good deal of such perceptual learning begins at an implicit or unconscious level.
- Learning often can move from an implicit to an explicit or verbal level once we notice a pattern in our own actions or emotions.
- Our unconscious mind appears especially sensitive to negative information and errors.
- Gesture plays a hidden role both in uncovering our implicit knowledge and in helping us to more fully express what we know and can communicate to others.
- Gestures play a strong role in early mental development and interpersonal learning.
- It is inevitable that students will watch your gestures, especially how you use your hands during instruction, and will use your gestures as a cue for their own knowledge building.

Study guide questions

1 One dramatic aspect of our capabilities is that we can become incredibly selective in what we attend towards. This represents the focus of the conscious mind. But does this mean that we exclude all other experiences whenever we do this?

2 What does it mean to exhibit implicit learning? If it is so implicit, how do we know about it?

3 The available research indicates we know little about how you can catch a ball. Just how do you do it? Try explaining this ball-catching skill to a robot. Just what instructions would you use?

4 In the Bechara *et al.* study about card choice, what emerged first: awareness, emotions, or behavioural choice?

5 Can we successfully acquire rules without knowing of their existence? How would we know?

6 Just what occurred in the Heerey and Velani avatar study that says a good deal about human interactions and our face-to-face dealing with other people?

7 Dr Goldin-Meadow found that asking young children to explain maths operations using hand gestures resulted in (a) improved understanding or (b) a level of mental confusion. Which?

8 Is there a relationship between gesticulation and how the mind works? Should we encourage students to think with their hands? Or should we discourage gesticulation to try to get students to think more inside their heads?

9 Should you strive to use physical gestures as you teach? Just what are your arms doing when you teach complex ideas? Try looking at a video recording of what you do as you teach.

Reference notes

■ Overviews of unconscious processing are found in several sources, especially T. D. Wilson, 2002, and Mlodinow, 2012 who gives prominence to subliminal perception. Especially valuable for reviewing unconscious heuristic processing is the noted German researcher Gigerenzer, 2008.

■ The brain is processing 11 million bits per second (Norretranders, 1998). Our attention is highly selective (Driver, 2001).

■ Implicit learning is learning without words (Seger, 1994). Although beyond the ken of this book, an accessible review of the neurological correlates of implicit learning is found in Knowlton and Foerde, 2008.

■ Unconsciously modelling incidental things (Bandura, 1986; Chartrand, Maddux, & Lakin, 2005).

■ Coach's faulty ball catching instructions (Gigerenzer, 2008, pp. 8–13). People do not know how they can catch balls (Reed et al., 2010).

■ Unconscious learning of card decks (Bechara, Damasio, Tranel, & Damasio, 1997).

■ Unconscious social sensitivity: playing rock–paper–scissors against an avatar (Heerey & Velani, 2010).

■ Bad is stronger than good: the mind relates to negative events powerfully (Baumeister et al., 2001). Neurologically, our brains remain acutely alert to any negative information, however slight (Eisenberger, Inagaki, Muscatell, Haltom, & Leary, 2011).

■ Gestures as vehicles for thinking, learning, and remembering (Cook, Yip, & Goldin-Meadow, 2010; Goldin-Meadow, Cook, & Mitchell, 2009).

■ Gestures reduce cognitive load (Goldin-Meadow & Wagner, 2005; Paas & Sweller, 2012).

- Parental usage of gestures shown to accelerate vocabulary in pre-schoolers (M. L. Rowe & Goldin-Meadow, 2009). Young children respond to teacher's pointing (Palmquist & Jaswal, 2012). Review of research into gestures in communication and teaching (Hostetter, 2011).

- A sensible coverage of issues in subliminal priming is found in Mlodinow, 2012.

16

The impact of cognitive load

One of the most important developments to emerge from research into human learning in recent years is known under the general label of **cognitive load**. This theory, often known as CLT, developed out of the broad framework we know of as information processing. The CLT research has been of special interest to educators for two principal reasons: (a) it directly addresses the problem of why learning is so inherently difficult for human beings, and (b) it specifies how teachers and instructional designers can make it relatively easier for students to learn and store new information.

The architecture of the mind

Cognitive load theory begins by specifying a number of statements referred to collectively as human **cognitive architecture**. Here are key points, as summarised by Jeroen van Merrienboer and John Sweller (2005):

- We have a limited working memory that stores around seven bits of information, but operates on only between two to four elements at a time.
- The working memory is able to deal with information for a few seconds only. All such information is lost within 20 seconds unless refreshed by rehearsal processes.
- These capacity limits apply only to new information obtained through sensory memory.
- Working memory has no known limitations when dealing with information retrieved from long-term memory.
- Hence, your long-term memory dramatically alters both the content and the characteristics of what is taking place within your working memory.
- Long-term memories exist in the form of cognitive schema that can vary in degree of complexity and automation (i.e. ease of accessibility).
- Your expertise comes from knowledge stored within schema, and *not* from ability to engage in reasoning using elements that are not coherently

stored and organised within your long-term memory. Expertise develops as learners mindfully combine simple ideas into more complex schemata, a process referred to as knowledge building.

■ The complex schemata you develop will organise your knowledge and dramatically reduce working memory load. This is because even a most complex schema can more readily be dealt with as a single element within working memory.

In essence, this approach equates mind with working memory. Indeed, this is the only type of memory that can be monitored, and everything else appears to be hidden until brought into working memory. You should see straight away that cognitive load theory provides us with a major theory about (a) how your mind gets itself organised, and (b) what it means to become skilful or knowledgeable. An expert within a field recognises complex events as single elements.

A highly experienced physician may glance at a patient's information and literally see 'Huntington's disease'. But the novice medical student struggles to apprehend a collection of diverse symptoms and needs skills to see the relationships such that a diagnosis of Huntington's is possible. To the expert, the pattern is a single meaningful chunk. To the novice, the same stimulus events present a myriad of relatively unconnected facts, which cannot all be held in working memory at once. The novice is overwhelmed since working memory capacity is exceeded. But any such memory limitations have disappeared for the expert who calls on long-term memory. When your knowledge becomes so automatic that you can access it quickly, with virtually no effort, then the working memory system is said then to be bypassed through to the **automaticity** stage – a most desirable place to be.

Coping with complexity: the notion of interacting elements

Your working memory easily becomes overwhelmed when dealing with novel or unorganised information. The essential organization in your knowledge stems from how it is stored in your long-term memory. When organization is lacking, the mind struggles since the goal is to maintain organization and reduce load. However, as any novel element enters the working memory, the number of possible **interacting elements** increases dramatically. We function well with two mental elements or items to consider. Three elements pose a problem that we can generally handle with some difficulty. We struggle to cope with any more than three elements within the same time frame.

But what is meant by interacting elements? This refers to the *relationships* between the items placed within working memory. So, if you tell a student that a battery needs a negative pole and a positive pole, but between them is an electrolyte, then we have three items but six possible ways they may interact when described as a sequence. As the number of items increases, so does the number of ways they could relate to each other. Relationships might reasonably be defined by aspects such as sequences, categories, hierarchies, specified conditions, variations in intensity, or in terms of cause and effect. In short, interacting elements create high levels of load in learning situations, even though teachers may be relatively unaware of just how quickly this load kicks in for a novice.

Many learning situations involve low levels of element interactivity. Yet other situations entail high levels of element interactivity, and this creates complexity. For example, learning to log on to a computer network involves a simple sequence with low levels of interactivity. One step follows the previous step (e.g., turn on the on-switch, go to 'My computer', etc.). But appreciating how the brakes on your car work entails knowing about the interaction between a dozen components. Although the car brakes example may appear initially as a sequence, it demands far more of the mind since the relationship between components has to be understood. In a very real sense, the whole, and knowing how the system operates, amounts to far more than its constituent parts – until it is so overlearned you can see the system as a 'single idea'.

It would be well-nigh impossible for a person who was 'non-mechanical' and unfamiliar with the car brakes operation to learn this material to mastery level within a single session or lesson. However, most adults are able to make such a lesson more meaningful by accessing existing schemata. For example, they may already know about levers, what a cylinder is, what a pipe does, what pressure is, and what friction does, and so on. To the extent a person can access such relevant knowledge, load is reduced, even though item interactivity will still remain high, since the issue is how the system works, rather than merely recalling the component items.

Sources of cognitive load

In any complex learning situation your mind can quickly become overwhelmed by the number of interactive informational units needing to be processed simultaneously for you to achieve understanding. As a learner you are strongly motivated to maintain order and may unwittingly adopt a number of strategies to reduce your mental load. However, in terms of following the theory, it is necessary to describe the two types of load that pertain to any learning task: (a) intrinsic and (b) extraneous.

Intrinsic cognitive load is fixed by the nature of the task itself. Its chief determinant is going to be a person's prior knowledge, which implies the availability of schemata at the level of the individual. Thus, learning about car brakes is inherently difficult for people who possess no technical knowledge. But the identical task can be relatively easier for people who work regularly with machinery.

Extraneous cognitive load refers to load imposed by the learning conditions and the instructional context itself, but which is nevertheless irrelevant to the desired learning outcome. Ideally, extraneous load is that which must be reduced, since it threatens a person's ability to focus upon the critical information needed to achieve mastery. Extraneous load is brought into lessons through introducing information that is not needed, or through placing unnecessary demands on the students at the time. For instance, many of us make the mistake of talking too much at students assuming we are 'motivating' them when we are merely adding to the sources of load they are experiencing.

Several studies have shown how learners may tolerate relatively high levels of extraneous load in simple learning situations. But as learning gets harder, learners benefit markedly from any condition that reduces sources of extraneous load. In short, extraneous load begins to matter when either (a) the number of interacting elements is high or (b) the individual lacks prior knowledge.

Helping students learn through reducing load

Researchers using cognitive load theory have identified a variety of instructional procedures that benefit learners through manipulations based on changing cognitive load impositions. For example, Edwina Pollock, Paul Chandler, and John Sweller (2002) worked with industrial apprentices learning to repair complex electrical circuit boards. It was found that showing the circuitry components to the apprentices beforehand considerably reduced the load imposed by the actual learning situation, which then enhanced their overall mastery (i.e. the concepts first principle, see Table 16.1). This prior exposure session was more effective than multiple lessons based upon going over the same complex tasks. The effect of this preliminary introduction to circuitry components assisted novice apprentices. But this same experience hindered other workers who were familiar with circuitry components before the training commenced.

The finding that pre-instructional experience is valuable for novices is an important finding. This is why 'flip teaching' can be successful, where students are exposed to the big ideas, the vocabulary, and worked examples such that they can begin to form a higher order idea of the things they will need to learn – prior to learning actual details and more specific information needed for mastery. For example, students may watch a video from the Khan academy, see how something works, listen to the whole piece of music, read a chapter in the text book, play around with the tools, and so on, before going into more specific aspects. This 'flip teaching' or backward design can assist learners in building relationships between the details. It is also why it is powerful for teachers to explain success criteria of a series of lessons up front.

Cognitive load theory research has been very much concerned with teaching procedures that will assist novices. But these same procedures could be far less effective, even time-wasting, when teaching knowledgeable people. This is because their memory systems are operating very differently. To help a novice focus and learn it is essential to constrain the level of information that needs to be processed through working memory. This idea becomes one of the basic

TABLE 16.1 Principles of learning described in the cognitive load research literature

PRINCIPLE	RESEARCH FINDING
Worked example	As novices, we need to see how knowledge applies to specific cases since problem solving fails to further develop our knowledge.
Multimedia	We learn better when words accompany pictures, rather than from the words alone. Our minds combine words and images efficiently.
Contiguity	Words should be placed as close to the relevant defining image as possible.
Temporal contiguity	We will learn better when words and pictures are presented simultaneously, rather than successively.
Coherence	We learn better when extraneous information is removed. In the case of novices, clarity readily outweighs elaboration. (But it is the reverse with expert learners.)
Modality	We learn better when we listen to words in combination with images, rather than having to read text while looking at the image.
Redundancy	Listening to and reading the same information is not efficient and will reduce overall learning.
Signalling	We benefit from any cues that highlight critical information.
Pacing	We benefit from being able to control the pace of incoming information.
Concepts first	We learn concepts at a basic level before applying them in any complex process.
Personalisation	You learn better when personal pronouns are used (such as in this sentence).

notions underpinning applications of load theory. Novices need to concentrate as deeply as they can on specific ideas without encumbrance from other sources.

Recognising the learner's inherent limitations is one of the key implications of cognitive load theory research. As a knowledgeable person, a teacher may underestimate load being imposed on a novice's brain, and may misread the feedback cues. For example, a learner might continue to give cues to a teacher in the form of head nods, eye gaze, or positive words such as 'uh-huh'. Such signs mean that the learner is concentrating on keeping items swirling within working memory. But teachers may often assume such signs indicate deeper understandings, and so proceed without appreciating how the novices are close to capacity point. Such a point may be reached through merely holding too many items in the mind, without an awareness of how these items are supposed to be interacting with each other.

The finding that many standard instructional procedures suit students who have prior familiarity with an area, but fail to acknowledge a novice's working memory limitations, is a theme that runs through a good deal of the work published by cognitive load theory researchers.

The problem with problem solving

Among the findings that have emerged repeatedly in the CLT research is that problem solving is *unlikely* to be an effective method to employ if you are attempting to teach a knowledge schema. You need to know the ideas well before you start to relate them or use them in a problem solving situation. Problem solving activities impose heavy load and can become a source of interference. For example, in one study, getting students to solve problems was shown to retard efficient learning of the underlying schemata in high school students learning mathematics. Even when students solve the specific given problems, they may fail to acquire the underlying principles, and so fail to generalise the experience. The effort (i.e. high load) involved in solving the problem may inhibit additional learning through depriving the student of the chance to achieve a secure level of automation. Problem solving makes heavy load demands on the mind, whereas securely consolidated learning relies on such demands being reduced, rather than increased.

Learning through solving problems becomes viable when the situation is simplistic or involves low levels of item interactivity – or when the ideas have become well understood. The paradox is that you need to learn how to solve complex problems, but what you actually learn by solving a specific problem is remarkably limited, and possibly wasteful in terms of your overall knowledge building. We ought not to pretend that problem-solving activities are a good way to help people build deep knowledge in the first place. Unfortunately, in the past, many educators have asserted that solving problems is one way to learn new material, a statement that is only valid if the material to be learnt is simplistic. So when is problem solving useful?

The power of worked examples

If giving students problems to solve straight after learning is a poor instructional method, just what do we do instead? The cognitive load theory research has fixed upon the value of *worked examples* in a number of different fields as one effective and easy-to-apply means of providing necessary guidance to beginners. This practice allows for a logical transfer process where learners shift from initially acquiring their knowledge, to seeing how this knowledge can be applied. The worked example effect now stands as one of the most robust findings from applied psychology research.

Worked examples provide a form of modelling through demonstrations of successful procedures or products. For example, they might show the working through of mathematics problems, or a step-by-step approach to researching a topic on the Internet, or perhaps a review of a case study where exemplary procedures are highlighted and shown to be effective. In many areas it is possible to show students fully worked examples, but then to introduce examples that are only partially completed. This type of worked example is generally called a *completion example*. Completion examples are where the first steps to be taken are shown, but the student then completes the sequence.

Those students asked to consolidate their learning through studying worked examples or completing partially worked examples, are more successful on later tests than students who spent the same amount of time working on unguided problem-solving activities. These effects are especially strong for novices, but as skill level increases and deep knowledge is acquired, worked examples become far less effective as they become unnecessary.

The underlying principle, consistent with the cognitive load approach, is that novices are unable, or unlikely, to apply knowledge they have just acquired. Teaching someone a new skill and then expecting that person to immediately apply it within a new and complex situation is asking too much. Even if this person can struggle through, and solve the problem, the effort involved detracts from the overall knowledge-building process and can make further generalisation less likely.

Can groups share cognitive load?

The traditional finding in this area has been that individual problem-solving activities hamper learning and schema acquisition for novices. However, a recent study by Femke Kirschner and others (2011) suggests that problem solving may become an effective teaching tool when capable students work together in well-motivated collaborative groups, rather than individually. They taught high school students complex principles of human genetics, and immediately moved them onto working either individually or in groups of three. The students also either worked on problems or were given worked examples.

Consistent with the earlier findings, it was found that problem solving generally reduced learning when students worked individually. But the same problem-solving demands actually *helped* learning when the students worked within groups of three. The explanation for this lies in the possibility that when a small group is working efficiently, its members are able to contain cognitive load through sharing the working memory functions across group members. In essence, an effective small group can become its own information processing system when it possesses all the knowledge required to solve a challenging problem, when it is working hard, and can coordinate its activities. Under such ideal teamwork conditions groups are likely to outperform individuals.

When working as individuals we are forced to struggle under conditions of heavy cognitive load, with literally no-one else to shoulder the burden. Thus, cognitive load theory suggests that collaborative work may become effective not for intrinsic 'social' reasons, but because it reduces load at the level of the working memory within the minds of the individuals concerned. Collaborative group work is not a panacea, by no means. But when group members are all pulling together, are strongly motivated, and pooling their knowledge, they can overcome some of the natural problems associated with limited working memory accessibility that prevents us, as individuals, from learning as we solve problems.

Enhancing educational materials

Over the past 20 years, cognitive load theory has generated many other research findings relevant to instruction and instructional materials, and these are covered in depth in a book length treatment by Clark, Nguyen, and Sweller (2006). Of special interest to teachers are findings related to how the mind integrates information from visual sources and from spoken words (see Table 16.1). For example, hearing words can draw a learner's attention to the critical aspects of a diagram. Reading words embedded within text is a less effective way to understand diagrams as the eyes may not locate the critical information. However, at times, diagrams can be made more effective by moving written words closer to the critical visual information being shown.

The cognitive load theory studies have also shown how novice learners suffer when excessive information is conveyed, especially through unnecessary words (which happens frequently in introducing mathematics problems). Although it is known that repetition assists learners, an often reported finding is called the redundancy principle, which says that when the same information is conveyed in different modes, such as hearing and reading at the same time, then learning will be compromised. Indeed, these studies have indicated that learners should not to be encouraged to choose which modality they would prefer to pay attention to.

It has been established though a steady stream of cognitive load theory studies that aids to learning will include (a) many signals or cues as to what to pay attention to, (b) a careful depiction and selection of the crucial words that are being used, and (c) any provisions that can reduce dependence upon memory during the initial acquisition process (e.g., such as not having to hold different sources of information in the working memory for longer than a few seconds). Principles of learning stemming from cognitive load research are shown in Table 16.1 above.

Cognitive load theory and teaching

Cognitive load theory provides the teacher with another means of attempting to view the world through the eyes of a student. The theory has produced surprising findings in showing us how novices have particular learning problems that can well be described as working memory limitations. Novices may be making all the right noises, and nodding in all the right places, but the effort involved in keeping up with an instructional sequence that is moving fast, or conveying unessential information, can still be too high to allow any lasting change in knowledge schemata to take place.

It is important to note that instruction can often be 'accepted' by a student as it is taking place even when no learning is occurring. As a teacher you can keenly observe your students paying attention. But what you are observing (or inferring) is only that individual students' brains are under load. As teachers we assume that our words are having the marked effect of bringing information into the student's working memory. But we can get this wrong, all too easily.

By way of examples, we might quiz our class by asking (a) *Is it the case that 8 multiplied by 6 has to be equivalent to 4 multiplied by 12?* Or perhaps (b) *Does the presence of alliteration in this sentence suggest a level of superficiality or perhaps irony in the author's intentions? What do you think?* Or perhaps, we relay an instruction such as, (c) *Note how the figures shown in this column must add up to the figures shown in the other five columns or else a deficit is going to occur later down the track.*

In each of these three instances we are likely to be imposing heavy mental demands on a subset of our students. For instance, in the case of (b) above, terms such as 'equivalent', 'irony', or 'deficit' could involve the working memory going through processes such as 'irony . . . yes . . . seen that before . . . it means funny . . . sort of twisted . . . unexpected . . . a bit clever'. The working memory has actively made a successful linkage, in this case by accessing a mental dictionary. But the load involved is heavy by dint of interacting elements. The successful recall requires energy that imposes load and processing time. By the time such a student has deduced the meaning of the word, the actual goal behind the teacher's question is unclear, at least to the mind of such a student. Despite the student being well-motivated and paying a sincere level of attention, working memory limitations have prevented the intended meaning from being apprehended.

IN PERSPECTIVE: The cognitive approach to understanding demands we place on learners

In short, there are many times when intended meanings appear lost in translation, but where the underlying explanation has a basis in the following idea: *one party fails to appreciate the cognitive load being imposed upon another party.* Cognitive load theory and research inform us that novices are especially vulnerable to such poorly recognised effects. The idea that novice learners reach a point of working memory overload very quickly is a basic finding supported by scores of studies conducted in the laboratory, in classrooms especially at the high school, and also in industrial training research.

Cognitive load theory represents an approach that has found wide acceptance in training facilities the world over. This is a theory that generates many useful and practical ideas about instruction that are consistent with the wisdom and experiences of many senior teachers.

Study guide questions

1 The theory of cognitive load begins with the notion that there are limitations to our short-term memories. However, there are no known limitations to

the working memory when retrieving information from long-term memory. So short-term memory and working memory are terms being used in slightly different ways. Just how does short-term memory differ from working memory?

2 What is a schema in your long-term memory? If we suggest knowledge is bundled into schemas, what does this imply?

3 Using knowledge schemas enables you to bypass cognitive demands that might otherwise load your mind excessively. How is this principle illustrated so dramatically by the example of an experienced physician 'seeing' Huntington's in front of him or her?

4 Cognitive load research says we struggle to cope with three to four items of information. But you also may have read that the short-term memory is supposed to hold about seven items. So what is the difference between 'holding' and 'coping' here?

5 Many of the curriculum tasks we expect students to master involve element interactivity. What does this idea mean? Can you think of such tasks that demand this level of mental complexity in your curriculum area? And, conversely, what sort of tasks are low in element interactivity?

6 Cognitive load theory says that many aspects of classroom instruction introduce extraneous load. Often learners can tolerate a level of extraneous load. No big deal. So, just when does it become a serious matter, and for whom?

7 Review Table 16.1, which details 11 major principles stemming from cognitive load research findings. Note that the *principle of coherence* says that novices learn from clear and direct instruction, without peripheral elaboration. Nevertheless, this finding is 'reversed' once learners become highly accomplished, or experts. Can you explain why this reversal occurs?

8 The writers suggest that teachers will easily underestimate load on a student's brain. Just how might this underestimation occur? What factors prevent a teacher appreciating what is happening?

9 What is the difference between a worked example and a completion example?

10 Load theory suggests that cooperative group work sometimes can assist students in problem solving. But it is not an automatic process. What is the key factor that underpins this effect?

11 Nevertheless, one recurring finding has been that getting students into problem-solving activities straight after teaching them something new or difficult will detract from the overall learning effect of the instructional experience. Just why would problem solving have potentially negative effects on achieving deeper understandings? What is going on (or not going on?) to produce such perversely paradoxical effects?

Reference notes

- Books on cognitive load research (R. C. Clark, Nguyen, & Sweller, 2006; Sweller, Ayres, & Kalyuga, 2011).

- Basic description of cognitive architecture (van Merriënboer & Sweller, 2005).

- Reducing load in apprentice training through prior experience (Pollock, Chandler, & Sweller, 2002).

- Instructional procedures may suit students who have prior familiarity with an area, but fail to account for novices' working memory limitations (R. E. Clark *et al.*, 2012; P. A. Kirschner *et al.*, 2006).

- Problem solving is an inefficient way to learn anything involving complexity or schema refinement (P. A. Kirschner *et al.*, 2006; Sweller, 1988). For an analysis of the failure of the problem-solving approach in teaching students with skill deficiencies see Westwood, 2011.

- Use of worked examples (Sweller, Clark, & Kirschner, 2010; Wittwer & Renkl, 2010).

- Study using collaborative group work to share memory load and solve problems (F. Kirschner, Paas, Kirschner, & Janssen, 2011).

17

Your memory and how it develops

At the risk of stating the blindingly obvious, teaching involves helping students memorise important information and understandings. This information could be ideas, relations between ideas, or strategies to make these relations – but in all cases we want the student to remember. In this chapter we will discuss some findings from a research group that has been able to relate students' learning strategies to subtle actions that their teachers may or may not be conveying. These teachers are experts in communicating subtle cues as to the need to use strategies to learn with long-term goals in mind. Before citing these studies, we will try to take you through what is known about how the memory system itself develops.

Your early memories: the role played by language

It is unusual, if not well-nigh impossible, for you to recall anything that happened to you in the first three years of your life. This phenomenon is referred to as **infantile amnesia**. It is not that you learnt nothing during those early years. A number of studies show that infants can act out actions they have seen modelled earlier by other people. It seems strangely ironic that, at this point in life, much learning is indeed taking place, but very little of what is being learnt is explicitly memorable later in life.

As a mature person, your memories of those years are largely inaccessible. You may have some vague impressions, but at that point in your life your mind was not working as it does now. You did not have a full language system you could use for interpreting events and for storage. Indeed, it has now been found that children who show advances in their early language development also show enhanced memory for real events that occurred within their early life experience.

From about 3 years of age, you develop systems of language and memory that enables you to recall specific experiences. Key events in your life now stand out. You can recall things and people you liked and disliked. Some events are especially memorable, and you have the potential to recall them in words and images. This form of memory is called **episodic memory**, since it is tied to actual events that took place within your experience, often in connection with specific people, places, or times.

Welcome to the human race. One interesting theory about animal life is that they do not possess any inherent sense of time. Apart from our species, animals live in the present, constantly, and could be 'stuck in time'. In contrast, through human thought, we have a past, a present, and a future. This comes with the territory, but note how these critical time frames become described through use of language. Being human means we have developed tools to talk about what just happened. Our predictions, plans, and intentions, are expressed in terms of what is going to happen. We have the ability to shift around in time, at least within the mind. If this sounds odd, initially, then think about the following conversation between 4-year-old Jill and her mother as both sit down to eat a piece of cake after preschool (see the box below).

A SIMPLE CONVERSATION SHOWING POSITIVE REMINISCING STYLE

Mother: What a great time we had last week at Bill's house. Didn't we, Jill? His mother had gone to such a lot of effort to put on a lovely party. All those games! Didn't you like it there?

Jill: It was alright. Bill he cried. He fell over.

Mother: Yes, Bill was hurt. But he was OK. Remember, he was happy when you gave him that present. This is good cake, isn't it? (Jill nods whilst eating). We need to think about what sort of cake we shall make for your party. Which picture is the best cake, do you think? (pointing to an open cookbook).

Jill: Not that one. Look at this one here, Mummy. Can we do this one? Bill's one was good too. Wasn't it?

At first brush, such interaction seems mundane. But what is happening deep down? Within fractions of seconds, Jill's awareness has shifted from the past, through the present, into the future, and back again. This shift is encouraged, or being mediated, through the mother's skilful use of language. Since the conversation revolves around the themes of cake and parties, there is seamless transition across time. Even at 4 years of age, Jill immediately discerns when her mother's words relate to the past, or to the present or future. This ability to use language to move around in time represents a huge intellectual achievement.

Conversations as developmental bedrock in memory acquisition

There is considerable evidence from within the child development literature that rich conversations such as this one between Jill and her mother play a dramatic role in the development of the child's memory system. In our example, the mother's words refer back to events that occurred in the past that Jill had witnessed. Note how the mother brings up the topic, so she is cueing the time shifting process central to all memory work. The two of them jointly interpret the meanings of these events that they both are recalling. They are sharing perceptions. Researchers have referred to such interactions as *reminiscing styles*. Parents who use high quality language to assist in the child's understanding of past events can be referred to as showing highly **elaborative reminiscing style**.

A key component of such conversational style is to engage the child in active responding, as distinct from merely listening to parents' words. This sharing process is referred to as **joint talk**. The child must be part of the conversation, and this participation is critical. Children whose parents habitually engage them in rich conversational interactions begin their lives with more secure intellectual advantages that include considerable vocabulary development and awareness of how sentences are sequenced in activities such as storytelling. As noted by Ornstein, Coffman, Grammer, San Souci, and McCall (2010, p. 51), 'an elaborative style in reminiscing may provide opportunities for children to practice searching and retrieving information from memory and experience in using narrative conventions to provide accounts of their experiences'.

In one especially interesting project, Boland, Haden and Ornstein (2003) staged a series of events for a group of preschool children. On a random basis, half of the mothers were trained to engage their children in interactive conversations while these events took place, so as to use language to draw the child's attention to what was occurring. Compared to children whose mothers were not trained to engage their children in concurrent conversations, these children showed far stronger recall of the events when tested later. Also, earlier studies, using a similar approach, had found that the child's recall was superior for those specific items on which mother and child had engaged in joint talk, as distinct from the mother merely mentioning the experience. When children can make sense of what they are experiencing, through conversations, they are able to attend more fully to the key features of an event, and so encode them more completely than would otherwise be the case.

So look again at that interaction between Jill and her mother. Although the mother is talking a good deal and dominating the agenda, Jill remains an active and responsive participant. In one sense, the mother's words act as instructions for Jill to focus her mind and reflect on something that occurred in the past. This may seem a strange use of the term *instruction* here, but it fits well in terms of the psychological analysis. Jill would not have thought about Bill until she was told by her mother that she had had a good time, and that Bill's mother had gone to such trouble. These are not thoughts Jill initiated or entertained herself until she heard her mother's words. It is not the case that the mother is giving any formal instructions as such. But, on the informal level, it is the case that her words provide clear instruction for Jill's mind to activate episodic memory of Bill's party.

Going to school: the child becomes the student, with profound changes in cognition

With Jill's entry into school, the nature of the demands on her memory system will undergo another remarkable change. Schooling brings with it a language system that differs from the type illustrated in the party conversation. In 1991, Stephen Ceci reviewed the child development literature from around the world concerning how children who attend school learn various cognitive skills differently from those that do not attend school. The differences were profound. He found that going to school accounts for regular advances in all cognitive functions, including intelligence or IQ test scores. Controlling carefully for age, and other factors, it was found that children who attended schools were found more likely to:

- focus their attention more efficiently;
- perform better on figure-ground perceptual problems;
- use visual depth perception cues more adroitly;
- identify abstract patterns in visual stimuli, and locate hidden figures in pictures;
- group items on a conceptual or taxonomic basis, and naturally chunk items together when memorisation is the goal;
- develop strategies for memorisation, such as rehearsal, recoding, and recitation;
- use words spontaneously to help them describe and solve problems;
- display superior memory performances;
- be advantaged by up to 6 IQ points per year higher when contrasted against peers not at school.

In his literature review, based on studies going back into the 1920s, Ceci found that such marked differences (i.e., between children who attended school and those that did not) were stronger in the case of school-type tasks, rather than in terms of native capacity measures such as Piagetian measures of cognitive development. Going to school dramatically alters the way students organise their perceptions, language skills, and knowledge storage systems. Sometimes this difference between the earlier home and school phases is called code switching – and this requires a skill in making this switch – once again favouring the well-prepared.

Jill adapts well to her role as student

So Jill is now at school. Instead of the gentle one-on-one conversations she enjoyed with her mother, she now has to sit and pay attention to a single adult who is talking with a group of similar-aged students. But her teacher is conveying verbal information that the teacher expects will be remembered by every student in the classroom. The demands placed on Jill have become very different from her home socialisation base. She has, however, arrived well prepared. She is accustomed to listening to adults and taking in their words. She is accustomed to having the adult's words direct her attention and thought processes. That is, she is accustomed to taking instructions from the adult voice. But a good deal of additional development in her memory system still must occur.

What is known is that during these early years at school, the memory strategies available to the mind go through predictable stages of development. For example, we ask students to recall a list of objects such as 'apple, pen, car, tree' by presenting the list one at a time on flashcards. The Year 1 child simply labels whatever card is in view at the time. But a Year 4 child will build up a *rehearsal frame* such that she keeps all the items in her head, and recites the list when items are no longer visible. A Year 7 child will try to build up more than one rehearsal frame in the head, so as to increase the number of items that might be held in working memory.

Similarly, older primary age students cleverly will use *chunking* and grouping strategies. Younger students generally tend not to use grouping spontaneously. However, they generally can do this when prompted to do so under explicit instruction, or when their attention is explicitly drawn to how similar objects can be easily linked together.

Developmental researchers have established clear linkages between students' age and their changing organisational and rehearsal strategies. With increasing age, children will use their long-term memory system more effectively when they attempt to memorise any new information. So instead of treating incoming information as a stream of novel items, they will begin to link items together because of their stored knowledge of prior linkages.

There is a major advance once they begin to use the strategy of **elaboration**. This means to relate a new item to an already known piece of knowledge, or otherwise add to the stimulus by making an association with it. For example, a child spies a new car in the street and says, 'Look Mum, that's the one that runs on electricity'. The child's comment adds to **encoding** of the experience, making the event memorable. In such similar ways, the increasing knowledge base of the older child enables and enhances memory skills. Hence, the growing knowledge base becomes a highly strategic resource for older students. One reason why older children can remember more resides simply in that they know more.

But child development does not occur in a vacuum. As we noted earlier, parental conversational style is known to play a vital role in early memory development. Researchers have speculated about the possible role that teachers might play in assisting students develop *mnemonic skills*. The term mnemonics is a general term that can apply to any action that a person does to help the memorisation process. Mnemonics can include acronyms (*ROY G BIV* for the colours of the rainbow), phrases (*Super Man Helps Every One* or *HOMES* for the Great Lakes in North America), and rhyming (*In 1492, Columbus sailed the ocean blue*). Rehearsal, organisation, elaboration, imagery, and knowledge activation, are also all mnemonics, within the broadest sense of the term. More generally, however, we use the term to refer to whenever a person makes a deliberate conscious attempt to place information in the long-term memory.

Hence, repeating something over to yourself is to use *recitation* as a mnemonic device based upon the verbal rehearsal process. Trying to recall your password by linking it to the town you were born in is a mnemonic device based on *elaboration*. Trying to recall someone's name by linking it to a mental picture (such as Mr Bookman stepping into a library) is to recruit *imagery* as a mnemonic device (a Bactrian camel's back is shaped like the letter B, a Dromedary's back is shaped like the letter D). Every individual person has a range of mnemonic tools available, with recitation being the most common everyday practice as used automatically by virtually all adults. Whenever you ask people to remember something, the first thing they will try is to recite it over. We use the term recitation to refer to saying things aloud, whereas rehearsal refers to the process the mind is doing.

Classroom-based research: do teachers teach memory skills?

Moely and Hart (1992) investigated ways in which teachers might attempt to communicate mnemonics skills in their normal classroom teaching. Their early research was based on observations of 69 primary-level teachers. Using interval time sampling procedures it was found that instruction in memorisation strategies occurred 2 per cent of the time. Indeed, 10 per cent of teachers apparently never offered any direct suggestions about such strategies. A paradox seems apparent in that although teachers make it plain that they expect students to accurately remember information, there is surprisingly little instruction taking place about how to remember. Students might be told to remember, but appear to receive almost no guidance in how to remember.

The later work of Peter Ornstein and his research group, with first grade teachers, puts a slightly different perspective on such issues (Ornstein *et al.*, 2010). Using a fine grain classification scheme for observations their research indicated that around 50 per cent of classroom observations did implicate some level of, or demand for, memory work, even though the level of direct instruction in memory strategies was low, at about 5 per cent of the time.

What was seen in both the Moely and Ornstein projects was that individual teachers showed remarkably large natural variations in the extent to which they would cue their students in memory strategies. For example, Ornstein's group found teachers varied in the level of cueing memory strategies between 1 and 14 per cent of the observations carried out during actual teaching (e.g., 'If it does not make sense go back and re-read it carefully'). Similarly, teachers were found to vary between 1 and 10 per cent in levels of metacognitive questioning (e.g., 'What are some strategies you could use to figure it out?').

Using several such different measures, they were able to identify high mnemonic teachers and low mnemonic teachers. High mnemonic teachers

(HMT) were characterised as using high levels of memory-relevant language, such as directly cueing learning good methods and asking students why a particular method might be effective. The low mnemonic teachers (LMT) focused less on mental strategies, tended to ask basic questions rather than use processes-oriented prompts, and spent less time on metacognitive activities such as understanding why a particular method is valuable. So the research question became, would students who are taught by HMT teachers (who explicitly emphasise mnemonic efforts as they carry out the business of teaching Year 1 classes) display any measurable learning advantages across the course of their year?

Do some teachers teach memory skills better than others?

The answer, as emerging straight from research findings, appears a clear 'yes'. The researchers followed the students closely over a two-year period. Although the students taught by LMT and HMT teachers initially had similar scores on tests of memory and grouping, they began to diverge over the course of the first school year. Effects were still found when these same students were at the second year level. In particular, the students exposed to HMTs began to use organisational strategies on the memory tests that were given periodically. The advantages were seen in use of grouping methods and use of semantic categories. For example, on one such assessment, the children were given two minutes to attempt to memorise an interesting assortment of objects. The HMT students spent more time in active memory efforts, and displayed higher levels of item clustering. The differences between the groups were still evident on a word-sorting task when administered at the Year 2 level, and also on two out of three tests of study skills administered when the same students were followed up in Year 4.

Of especial note in these studies was the finding that the effects of learning from the HMTs were especially apparent in the case of students who began school with low scores on a test of basic skills. In essence, such children 'caught up' with their more advantaged peers in terms of displaying memory skills. When the high ability students were taught by LMTs they did not differ substantially from such students taught by high mnemonic teachers. In order words, an interaction between student entry skills and teacher quality was evident, with exposure to teachers who actively convey mnemonic skills being especially important in the case of the less capable students.

IN PERSPECTIVE: How memory skills are taught

We now know that the memory-rich dialogues taking place in the classrooms of certain teachers have enduring benefits for their students, which may show up years after they have left those teachers. From these studies, it becomes apparent that there is something special about the way in which young students are introduced into the 'academic world' by certain high mnemonic teachers who are able to coach students in memorisation techniques embedded subtly but directly within their normal instructional practices.

Such teachers appear successful in helping their students appreciate ways in which the human mind has to develop its knowledge base through personal mnemonic efforts. This is a difficult lesson to learn. Whatever assistance is available to the young individual mind in its early years appears to advantage subsequent development. Although the early parent-to-child dialogue differs in nature from later teacher-to-student interaction, the themes of mnemonic assistance, adult-initiated cueing, and rich language usage, appear to play significant roles across each socialisation context, providing advantages to some young people more than others. The quality of the verbal and social environment we provide for our young people is directly implicated in providing them with tools for coping with the inherent demands placed upon their memory capabilities.

One final point is that whenever we think of our memory, we are inclined to treat it as an objective or mechanical device that has set capacity limits. We all know our memory is not perfect. But, for the most part, it seems adequate enough, since its failures must reflect normal human life, no more, no less. But the research cited in this section, the work of child psychology researchers such as Dr Ornstein, tells us memory skills are being modelled, prompted, encouraged, and reinforced by significant adults within a child's world. The manner in which we talk to students can serve to either encourage or discourage their efforts to further develop their memory competencies. Such social learning effects are evident both at home and in school.

Study guide questions

1 Although animals appear stuck in time, we humans possess the ability to think about the past, the present and the future. But could we do this without words? What do you think? Is how you think about this *now* the same as you thought about this issue *before* you read the chapter?

2 Many conversations can appear mundane, but in fact contain detailed instructions about what to think about. Why is this critical in helping young children develop notions of time? Just what is a 'time shift' within normal conversational speech?

3 Parents are said to stimulate the child's memory system through using an elaborative reminiscing style. How would you know instances of this style when you see them in real life?

4 Allied to this notion is the idea of joint talk. Just what does this idea refer to?

5   In research from around the globe, many profound differences have been found between children who do, and those who do not, attend school. What are the major findings, as reviewed by Dr Stephen Ceci?

6   Explain how parental conversational styles can serve to either assist or handicap students' response to initial schooling.

7   Developing one's memory is seen as one type of skill. What such memory skills (or mnemonic skills) can we identify?

8   Initial studies seemed to indicate that teachers expected students to remember things, but seldom taught any memory skills directly. With later work, however, it did seem to be the case that some teachers did naturally cue mental strategies as they interacted with their classes. What sort of things did such high mnemonic teachers emphasise?

9   What sort of benefits have been shown to accrue to young students exposed to such high mnemonic teachers?

10 Do you have students in your classes who seem to have poor memory skills? Has anyone ever tried to teach them how to remember important things?

Reference notes

- Infantile amnesia as a phenomenon (M. L. Howe & Courage, 1993).
- Early language development linked with memory for life events (Haden *et al.*, 2011).
- Animals appear stuck in time (Roberts, 2002).
- High quality parenting and elaborative reminiscing style: conversations with adults that bridge time develop the child's memory system (Fivush, Haden, & Reese, 2006; Haden, Ornstein, Rudek, & Cameron, 2009; Hedrick, Haden, & Ornstein, 2009). When mothers discuss events, their young children recall more (Boland, Haden, & Ornstein, 2003).
- Major review of how schooling affects children's mental development (Ceci, 1991).
- Massive advances in reading and maths skills as child encounters schooling (Fitzpatrick, Grissmer, & Hastedt, 2011).
- Development of memory strategies across the school years (Bjorklund, 2012).
- How teachers teach memory strategies (Moely & Hart, 1992; Ornstein, Coffman, Grammer, San Souci, & McCall, 2010).
- Recommended website featuring Professor Ornstein's remarkable research work: http://childrensmemoryproject.org.

18

Mnemonics as sport, art, and instructional tools

In 2005, a young journalist, Joshua Foer, was assigned to cover the United States Memory Championships. Memory championships are competitions, akin to sports tournaments, where participants compete against each other on tasks such as memorising lists of digits, packs of cards, or lists of words, or attaching names onto photographs of faces. They are genuine tournaments where mental performance levels are actively stretched to the limits of human capability. Around the world, they are held in 30 countries and attract several thousand participants every year. The organising panels refer to this as a mind sport, and the competitors refer to themselves as *mental athletes* or MAs for short. Besides annual championships, every four years a separate championship event, the Memoriad, akin to the Olympic Games, is staged.

Greatly impressed with performances he had witnessed, and being told by the athletes that 'anyone can do what they do', Foer accepted an invitation to compete in the American championship the following year, an exercise in what he described as participatory journalism. He returned in 2006 and duly won the event. It had taken a year of training under the supervision of Edward Cooke, a British expert in the art of memory. After representing America in the 2006 World Memory Championship, and finishing thirteenth overall, Foer left the sport but wrote an inherently memorable book about his experiences, *Moonwalking with Einstein: The art and science of remembering everything* (2011). We strongly recommend this as an intelligently written, and remarkably balanced, account in which the art of mnemonics is reviewed within its historical context.

Before and after his intensive training year, Foer allowed himself to be tested in the psychology laboratory at Florida State University, under direction of Dr Anders Ericsson whose work is prominent in the research field of human expertise. Indeed, Ericsson's research informs much of Foer's eventual commentary on his experiences, and figures strongly in the sections on expertise found in this book (Chapters 10, 11, and 12).

It can be recognised that, for the most part, memory competitions are based upon the immediate recall of randomly presented information that generally will need to be forgotten as soon as it is brought back. Any retained information is likely to become a source of interference for any future such attempts. This type of quick in-and-out feat involves a very different skill from activities such as memorising the value of pi, which represents a mathematical constant. Incidentally, the record for recalling pi stands at 67,890 decimal places, held by a Chinese gentleman called Chao Lu. After years in preparation, it took him 24 hours to recite this number of digits.

The mental training program

The training program Foer undertook was based upon mentally developing and using personally relevant locations such as houses, buildings, or walks through familiar streets. These are used as *memory pegs*. Information entering the mind can be associated with specific locations. Foer was encouraged by Cooke to deeply imagine the sensory sensations associated with those locations. This is referred to as the **method of loci**. Foer refers to his technique as developing **memory palaces**. Under Cooke's guidance, Foer developed many different such palaces and was able to use them to encode words and similar lists. Thus, as information enters the mind, there are places in which items can be dropped, or otherwise forced into an interaction with objects already present within the palaces.

When it came to attempting to memorise numbers he used the Major system in which digits are converted into phonetic sounds which can then be converted into words using a modicum of personal creativity. The scheme is given in Table 18.1.

Notice how the system is essentially arbitrary. There are more complex schemes as developed by the mental athletes. However, the Major system can be used within an hour of training. Hence, 37 might be encoded as *MG*, the car one of us owned BC (before children). At base, this system describes only consonants, so you are free to insert vowels to achieve meaning. Hence, within your mind, 61 could become *SHoT*, 62 could become *SHiN*, 101 could become *DuST*, and 3001 could become *MoSSaD*.

At times your creativity needs to be stretched. For example, we had trouble with 2012, which is *NSTN*, so we decided this was a fictitious radio station. The theory is that in the long run, it becomes easy to use the mnemonic. At the outset, the load is heavy, or in common parlance, involves a 'learning curve'

TABLE 18.1 The Major system for memorisation

0	1	2	3	4	5	6	7	8	9
S	T or D	N	M	R	L	Sh or Ch	K or G	F or V	P or B

investment. But over trials, the user gains enhanced capacity to store items such as unrelated numbers using the phonetic consonants as anchors, upon which a meaningful image can then be projected.

The world of championship mnemonics is a rich world of constant development and upgrades. The more serious participants are involved in the constant attempt to invent new and more complex mental schemes. The goal is to outperform one's competitors who could still be using outmoded methods. As in all fields where human performances are being stretched, records are regularly broken. In 1991 the leading mnemonist MAs were able to memorise a pack of cards in around 2 minutes. Twenty years later, the world record stood at 22 seconds (as can be seen on YouTube).

Just envisage this. An individual takes 22 seconds to scan a pack of playing cards, and then is able to accurately recall the sequence of all 52 cards. Such feats are 'mind blowing'. We were able to locate some similar examples and demonstrations on YouTube. Readers who are interested in the type of task, or in further testing out their own memory skills, can visit the Memoriad website. One notable feature of this website is the free availability of computer software enabling you to test and practise such achievements for yourself. That is, once you feel able to memorise an entire pack of cards, you can practise and time yourself using online tools.

Should we train our memories?

But do we need to develop such powerful mnemonic skills? We live in a world of immediately available external memory aids. Computers, telephones, reference manuals, books, and the Internet are tools quickly accessed. We rarely need to memorise information in the sense of consciously sitting down to memorise large banks of data. We seldom bother to memorise even key aspects such as our passport numbers, tax file numbers, bank account details, or our friends' birthdays. If information is important, it is written down and stored. We scratch notes on calendars. We put up post-it notes to remind ourselves. When we shop for groceries, we take a list. We have learnt that the effective way to get through life is *not* to depend on our memories alone. We have become familiar with the idea that our memories are unreliable, fallible, and can become a source of bias. Instead, we know that external devices, paper, photographs, recordings, and hard drives provide us with reliable tools.

As you learn more skills within a domain, your ability to store more within your working memory increases. Your short-term memory itself, or the raw capacity, is not increased. But what has happened is that your ability to process large and meaningful patterns means your working memory becomes highly effective. Often such effects can be dramatic, and can be surprising even to the individual concerned. The champion chess player did not set out with the goal of memorising entire game plans. But as expertise increased, then so did this capacity. However, the advanced skills of the mnemonist MAs are of a different order. In his or her case, memorisation itself has become the goal. Hence, the material that this skill is being demonstrated upon is irrelevant.

For example, one of the skills often sampled in the memory championships is the ability to recall lists of binary digits, with strings such as 00101110010010, and so on for pages. These strings involve presentations that are generated randomly, without pretence that they might represent anything meaningful. The trick is to (a) get the information in as fast as possible, then (b) dump it out, and then (c) forget it as soon as is possible. The memory athlete may want to reuse the same pegs (memory palaces) in another task. One aspect described by Foer is that MAs typically will not practise their skills a week before major competitions since they must 'clean out' the memory palaces for use on the day.

For certain individuals, a practical benefit of advanced mnemonic skills lies in the ability to track card patterns in gambling games such as blackjack. Through monitoring cards as they emerge from the dealer, a blackjack player can anticipate whether choosing another card will increase or decrease the odds. Card counting strategies have been depicted in several feature films including *Rainman*, *21*, and *The Last Casino*. Such films are based on elements of truth and actual incidents. Casinos will ban players they perceive as using such memory tricks. A mnemonic-based card counting system as shown by the English magician, Derren Brown, is readily seen on YouTube. Brown is naturally banned from casinos. Although such methods clearly can work – by shifting odds in the players' direction – to hone skills to this level requires several hundred hours, and such training needs to be done under pressure.

Getting a balanced perspective

So is it worth the effort striving to develop such mnemonic skills if not planning a casino junket? Although the mnemonist MAs are people who are generally well-educated individuals, it is not the case that their memory skills place them in the forefront of human achievement. Many of them appear to see themselves as ordinary people, doing ordinary jobs, but have developed an extraordinary skill through dint of hard work, structured goal setting, and **deliberate practice**. To such people, memorisation just happens to be their sport, and something they find personally rewarding.

One aspect that clamours for explanation is why intelligent people would devote hundreds of hours to honing an inherently unavailing skill. One observation, as backed by Foer's account, is that many such individuals are motivated strongly by competition. But in addition, some of them appear to subscribe to beliefs such as the following: (a) that our modern education system fails to teach people to memorise, (b) that memorisation is a lost art, an essential human attribute as developed and practised by the ancient Greek civilisation, but which now needs to be reclaimed, (c) that mental performances such as committing lists of random words to memory provide an index of higher order human capacity, and (d) such mnemonic skills are of wide applicability in human society and life in general.

When placed against reality, however, none of these four beliefs stack up well. Being able to recite pi to 1,000 places does not make you a mathematician, any more than memorising random binary strings makes you a computer programmer. Being able to activate excellent memory tricks itself does not add to your understanding of the material you are memorising. Memorising lists of words cannot add to the mental schemata that enable you to read and learn with any greater level of comprehension. The mnemonist uses available schemata to help him or her to memorise, but such brief split second usage does not develop the mental schemata in any meaningful way.

It is apparent that ancient Greek orators used mnemonics to track the points they would wish to make. Developing such mnemonics was important since they lacked the means to write on tools such as notepads. Paper and pens had yet to be invented. It remains a strange argument that the value of one tool stems from its use prior to the development of other tools. Passing on knowledge through oral traditions becomes less laudable if more effective communication vehicles have become available. As a culture, we have learnt (a) how huge levels of information can be relayed through external storage devices and (b) how fallible the individual mind is when it comes to holding arbitrary pieces of information such as numbers. We are aware of how our memories often will differ from objective records.

Overall, attempting to achieve, with the human mind, what a small digital computer can achieve without a mind, represents an uncertain exercise. Nevertheless, there can be a strong case made for incorporating mnemonic devices and instruction directly into the content of the curriculum that you are responsible for teaching. This theme emerges in the work of Peter Ornstein, cited in Chapter 17, and we need to consider just how students can benefit from being taught memory strategies they would not otherwise employ.

Should we be teaching mnemonics?

Clear and usable techniques for memorisation can and should be actively taught in classroom situations. The most basic reason is that they represent genuine skills that can be applied when situations arise. Teachers expect their students to have the ability to memorise important information, but we are often guilty of not embedding mnemonic instruction into our teaching when this can be achieved with minimal cost. Whenever memory load is high, then students benefit from being shown memory aids, and being encouraged to develop their own deliberate strategies.

There is nothing wrong in stressing that memorisation and understanding go hand in hand. At times, memorisation assists understanding. Other times, it is the reverse. There is nothing inherently mysterious in appreciating that our minds work in this way, and in training situations, learners benefit enormously from being shown specific ways to memorise information that would otherwise be difficult to learn.

TABLE 18.2 A pegword mnemonic scheme for memorisation

1	is a bun	2	is a shoe	3	is a tree	4	is a door	5	is a beehive
6	is sticks	7	is heaven	8	is gate	9	is wine	10	is a hen
11	is cricket	12	is a dozen	13	is hurting	14	is courting	15	is lifting
16	is licking	17	is beckoning	18	is waiting	19	is pining	20	is two hens

We can promote the idea that simple and deliberate memory tricks can be cultivated as possible mental tools. The following is one such **pegword** mnemonic scheme that we have used in university classes to demonstrate a fast way to learn any listing of up to 20 unrelated items, such as a shopping list (Table 18.2). The items have to be meaningful ones, already in your mind. The trick is to create associations between these to-be-learnt items, and the pegs, as shown in the table above.

Our experience is that within an hour, adult students easily learn and apply this method with success. Such systems work through allowing a meaningful input item to interact with its available peg. The pegs are there permanently, so recalling the peg brings back with it the memorised item. This scheme allows for a level of random access memory in that it allows people to access, for example, the fourteenth item (associated with *courting*). This stands in contrast with any situation where your recall is based on earlier sequential input through natural recitation. Try asking someone what is the fourteenth letter in the alphabet, and note how the random access principle cannot be applied to this type of learning, which is of course a serial string (see Chapter 14).

We have found that primary age children can cope with the first 10 items in this type of pegword system, but older students can learn all 20 pegs. To begin with, it requires concentration, imagination, and practice. The pegs can then be used as one type of memory palace. We are familiar with teachers who have taught remedial students the first 10 items, up to *hen*, in the specific aim of establishing for the student that they are 'not dumb after all', and can succeed, and have good memories whenever they use a good strategy.

The range of content-related mnemonics

Further, many excellent teachers employ local mnemonics in the form of *acrostics* and *acronyms* (see the box below). The term acronym is used when an abbreviation comes to stand as a word in its own right (such as NATO, COBOL, or GIF, which means 'graphic interchange format'). The term acrostic tends to be used when a word can stand as a memory aid to help cue a procedure. For example, we watched one experienced teacher instructing her students to 'Call in the COPS' when encouraging them to review their own written products. Calling in the COPS refers to capitals, organisation, punctuation, and spelling. There are many variations on such themes. In learning to spell difficult words, there are many examples of rich local mnemonics, such as *Rhythm Helps Your Two Hips Move*, or *A Red Indian Thought He Might Eat Toffee In Church*. These are examples of what are called *first letter mnemonics*. Incidentally, if you count the number of letters in the sentence following, then behold, the value of pi: *How I wish I could calculate pi easily*.

Keywords for studying mnemonics

- *Pegword* schemes such as 'one is to bun, two is to . . . etc.', as described in the text.
- *Story chaining*: invent a short story to link together disparate items.
- *Method of loci*: using images of physical locations enabling you to position items along an imaginary walk.
- *Acrostics*: using a word to instate a listing. For example, *COPS* means capitols, organization, punctuation, and spelling. *ROYGBIV* stands for the colour spectrum. Here is one for medical emergencies. If you encounter someone who has just suffered a severe blow to the head, or a possible stroke, then you must get them to *START*. This stands for the patient to *Smile* and *Talk* to you, *Arm Raise* (both arms to above shoulder height), and finally ask them to poke out their *Tongue*. If the injured person cannot do all of these, then call for immediate assistance.
- *Acronyms*: where a new word replaces a needlessly long string, e.g., *NAPLAN* for National Assessment Program Literacy and Numeracy, and *JPEG*, which stands for Joint Photographic Experts Group (which created the image compression standard).
- *First letter cues*: recalling a short poem cues important details. E.g., 'Rhythm helps your two hips move'.
- *Specific word associations* employ linguistic elaboration tactics. For example, spelling school *principal* since she is my pal, whereas the alternative spelling must be a *principle* of a different order, and not my pal at all. Or think of *potassium* as ordering 'one tea with two sugars, please'.

Students in the medical faculty commonly use mnemonics to commit large chunks of information to memory. For example, if such a student in training has to deal with a patient in a coma, then recalling COMA MIDAS could help to prompt recall of appropriate procedures. The primary elements brought to mind are CO_2, overdose, metabolic, and apoplexy (stroke) to form COMA. Other important conditions to test for are meningitis, intoxication, diabetes, air flow, and subdural haemorrhage, hence MIDAS. The medical world has developed an extensive set of such mnemonics of tremendous value in training the noviciate, and these can be found on several websites.

Specialist mnemonics have been developed for specific purposes. In learning new vocabulary items, or in acquiring foreign language words, one especially effective method lies in the use of the keyword technique. The *keyword mnemonic* strategy is based upon linking new words to meanings already in the long-term memory. The trick is to find memorable linkages. Here are some examples:

1 Ranidae is the scientific name for a type of frog found in the far north of Australia. A science teacher can associate ranidae with 'rainy day' and instruct students to imagine a frog sitting on a lily pad in a Queensland rain forest.

2 *Crinia signifera* is the common frog found in many Australian cities that sings with a cricket-like chirp that goes on and on and on. This incessant chirping makes you 'cringe significantly forever'.

3 The scientific term for the common lawn weed soursobs is *oxalis*. Think of an 'ox' grazing on soursobs in your lawn.

4 Mela is Italian for apple. How many apples will make an entire meal?

5 *Flughafen* is the German word for airport. It is a 'haven for flight'.

It is important to note that such keyword methods work when the unfamiliar term is studied and assimilated well to begin with. The keyword mnemonic is not primarily a tool for the initial word acquisition as such. Instead, it becomes an aid for remembering what this unfamiliar term hints at within your own language. Thus, the next time you see *flughafen*, your mind responds with 'haven for flight', which then triggers 'airport'. For this sort of retention, keyword methods are highly effective when introduced straight after your initial exposure to the unfamiliar term. That is, it is helpful to stare at the unfamiliar word, pronounce it slowly and correctly at least three times, and only then think of a keyword, or otherwise ask a teacher for one. Hence, teachers are able to provide students with mnemonic linkages that enable an unfamiliar item suddenly to 'make sense', rather than remaining as a word to be learnt by blunt rehearsal alone.

Mnemonics at the whole-class level

There have been several attempts to investigate if young students can benefit from explicit training in mnemonic skills. The results are variable. The typical finding is that children show clear improvements on the tasks used within training, but generalisation of effects is less likely. In 2010, Helen St Clair-Thompson and a team from the University of Hull reported an interesting study in which, from each of five schools, one class used a computer training program called Memory Booster, and another comparable class did not. The program taught strategies such as rehearsal, imagery, and story linking and involved six to eight hours of training in an enjoyable adventure game context. About 100 children were in each group. The students were junior primary level (around

7 years of age), and the treatment effects were monitored over 5 months. Some gains were evident on aspects of memory improvement such as being able to listen to, and understand instructions. Gains on measures of school attainment did not differ between the two groups. The researchers interpreted their findings in the following way:

> computerised memory strategy training can improve children's performance on tasks of working memory and performance in the classroom. However, strategy training does not result in improvements on standardised ability measures which do not require the use of memory strategies.
>
> (2010, p. 215)

The bottom line seems to be memory skills help to learn lower-level surface knowledge but not necessarily the deeper aspects (relating and extending this knowledge). But, of course, we need to know this surface knowledge before we relate and extend it!

IN PERSPECTIVE: The limits of mnemonics

Artificial mnemonic devices are seldom used by individuals once they become skilful. A skilled interpreter has no use for contrived keywords. An experienced emergency physician does not stare at a comatose patient recalling first letter mnemonics. This is not how the skilled mind can possibly operate. High-level discriminations and recognition processes have become dominant and memory access is automatically facile and efficient. However, when the novice physician began training the memory load was high. There was a need to seek out any available learning aid, just anything that would help restore that vital information back into the puny and overloaded working memory system.

During contextual training experiences, mnemonics are things that excellent teachers are able to communicate quickly and meaningfully to novices. Useful mnemonics are embedded within context, rather than being seen as generic tools for assimilating lists of meaningless information. Indeed, those generic mnemonic tools, as practised by Foer, are of little practical value. Some memory athletes claim to be able to 'ace' formal examinations, but such data are seriously lacking. The memory athletes are simply not using their skills for knowledge building as we recognise the process within educational institutes.

Foer ended his book describing how, after a night celebrating with friends his achievements as a champion mnemonist, he took the subway home having forgotten he had driven a car to the venue. When it comes to everyday living, even memory champions evidence minor memory lapses.

Study guide questions

1 Just what are the goals of the mental athletes (or MAs)? Do their goals differ from our goals within education?

2 Can you explain why anyone would attempt feats such as to memorise pi to 1,000 places?

3 Numbers can be tricky to recall, so many MAs use variations on the Major system. What does this achieve?

4 Would you really enjoy having a photographic memory? When would you use it? When would it be a curse?

5 Exponents of mnemonic arts often assail educators for failing to teach memory techniques. They claim memorisation is akin to a lost art. How would you respond to such charges?

6 It is apparent that teachers often do convey memory techniques, but within what specific context does this appear to occur?

7 Besides the examples of mnemonics given in the text, what specific tools do you employ as you teach within your area?

8 Although there clearly can be much value in directly teaching memory skills to young students, is this likely to produce marked gains in terms of their scholastic attainments?

Reference notes

■ Highly informative book, *Moonwalking with Einstein: The art and science of remembering everything* (Foer, 2011).

■ International memory tournaments: see www.memoriad.com.

■ Research into extraordinary memory effects (Hu & Ericsson, 2012).

■ For information on Chau Lu see the above citation, but also www.pi-world-ranking-list.com/lists/details/luchao.html.

■ The topic of mnemonics in general is handled well in most introductory textbooks within psychology and educational psychology.

■ The University of Hull study into training primary school children on Memory Booster (St Clair-Thompson, Stevens, Hunt, & Bolder, 2010).

■ Accomplished British magician, Derren Brown, can be seen in various YouTube clips, including: www.youtube.com/watch?v=eqiiYYmJNKQ.

19

Analysing your students' style of learning

In September 2012 we conducted an Internet search on 'learning style assessment'. Within moments Google located 10 websites offering to either (a) diagnose our personal learning styles online or (b) display the questionnaire instruments used to do this. An inspection of those questionnaires located revealed all were based on what researchers refer to as the VAK model. This model says that human beings, as individuals, naturally fit into one of three categories, associated with the input sensory systems that we use to process information: visual learners (V), auditory learners (A), and kinaesthetic learners (K) (or VAK, for short). It is said that most of us are visual learners and will benefit from instruction which features visual elements, imagery, or spatial relationships, at least when shown in visual form. Auditory learners benefit from hearing words and learn effectively through language and building vocabulary. Kinaesthetic learners learn from movement, from action, from doing things with their hands, and tactile resources in general.

These ideas are familiar to all educators. Variations upon the VAK theme have been around within educational thought for 50 years. But this model is only one of about 20 different learning styles that have been seriously proposed. One British review team located 71 different varieties of learning style assessment described in the literature (Coffield, Mosely, Hall, & Ecclestone, 2004). However, in considering the various learning styles posited, we reach a clear conclusion: *that there is not any recognised evidence suggesting that knowing or diagnosing learning styles will help you to teach your students any better than not knowing their learning style.*

This is not a conclusion arrived at lightly. Although there is some evidence to suggest that learning styles can influence other aspects of how we might behave, there is not any serious evidence indicating that learning styles genuinely can predict learning in any meaningful manner. As a field of research, learning styles is essentially a non-productive area when it comes to attempting to analyse the processes that underpin learning. We certainly want to be clear: learning styles are not the same as developing various learning strategies. Learning style refers to the claim that we have preferred sensory systems or mental patterns for processing information, and that these attributes will differentiate individuals.

Learning style theories hold that individuals are different. While this is a simple and blatant truism, such theories then posit specific dimensions along which people spread out. Thus, there could be a visual-to-verbal dimension, with some students being rated as more visual, others more verbal, and others could be sitting around the middle. Another popular approach has been to posit the existence of different categories of learners. For example, in one scheme, students can be described as being either activists, reflectors, theorists, or pragmatists. Many such category-based schemes have been suggested. Each tends to have its own assessment devices that can be used to allocate individuals into the postulated categories. For instance, within North America, one popular model, promoted by Dunn and colleagues, draws attention to five major dimensions: (a) preference for the type of environment in which the individual learns, (b) preferences in relation to motivation, (c) preference for working in groups or alone, (d) preference for input modality and time of day, and (e) preferences associated with global or analytic processing. These broad groupings gives rise to 20 different measurement questionnaires, which are readily procurable.

A brief topical history: why did this field develop?

Before going further into the research findings, we digress to tell the story of how this field emerged, starting with the Great War (or World War I). When the United States entered the conflict in 1917, it faced a problem. Over 1.5 million men were drafted to serve the military. Such logistical problems had never existed on this scale before. They came out of the cities, and off the fields, but there were no recognised criteria by which a modern army could be created. Within months, these men had to change from experiencing a peaceful urban or agrarian existence to becoming components of an effective fighting force. The matter was compounded by modern technologies with the machinery of war becoming more precise and expensive than before. The problem was one of locating sound ways of matching individuals to appropriate military training roles. Into this agenda, the general ability test was recruited.

A young psychologist, Arthur Otis, was commissioned to devise an ability test that could assist the military in classifying its recruits. The Army Alpha test was devised within a short six-week period using the multiple-choice format. It could be scored easily, and most importantly, could be administered within a mass group situation such as in local halls. Within two years, almost 2 million recruits sat the Otis test, earning a grading between A and E, which determined their placement within the military machine.

Due to the success of this enterprise, the group ability test morphed into different forms throughout the 1920s and 1930s. Within this era, the notion of the intelligence quotient or IQ, as developed earlier in relation to special educational placements, took hold of popular imagination. Testing was developed for use by business corporations, vocational guidance, and educational institutions. A widely held assumption was that human ability is constrained by inherent intelligence. Tests such as the Otis, and its derivatives, could be used to index an individual's IQ rating, and such an IQ could determine an individual's potential. Hence, just as with the military experience, significant decisions involving responsibilities, work allocation, training opportunities, vocational placement, and scholarship opportunities, could be made using these new 'scientific' measures.

But during the 1930s it began to be recognised that general ability tests were less useful when it came to certain specialist placements. This came to a head in the aviation field. It became plain that IQ tests were less useful in attempting to select trainee pilots. Hence, aviation professionals began to devise a series of unique testing instruments that reflected spatial skills, perceptual orientation tasks, and decision-making. Among the battery of such tests developed were instruments some of which were later developed for general use and became labelled as tests of 'perceptual or cognitive style'.

The idea behind **cognitive style** was that people would differ in the manner in which they would normally focus on stimulus information. For example, some people would tend to fixate on clearly defined aspects of their perceptual field, and be able to make clear-cut decisions based on isolating a crucial stimulus. Such individuals can be called *field independent*. But other people may focus instead on the whole picture, and by taking in more, they respond well to impressions or to global features. These people are said to be *field dependent*. It was found that pilots need to be field independent in their perceptual processing to control an aircraft. Being able to tell the vertical from the horizontal, under stress, trumps having a high IQ once behind a joystick.

After World War II, a popular thesis was that the human capacities and dispositions ought to be described in terms of (a) general ability traits such as the IQ, (b) differential ability traits, such as mathematics, but also by (c) relatively non-intellectual attributes such as cognitive styles. These styles were to be seen as describing ways in which different individuals would approach learning tasks, bringing to bear different perceptual and mental stratagems in a manner independent of ability factors. Around this same period, the VAK model began to be toted as a possible explanation of why certain students had problems in school situations despite presenting with adequate intelligence. Suppose your dominant style of learning is through pictures, but you are expected to learn from words and text in books. If so, the claim was that a mismatch would occur between your natural style of processing information and the context within which you found yourself embedded.

But what was happening was a remarkable confusion between notions of ability and style. If people have different abilities, it does not imply that strengths in one area are matched by weakness in another. But that was the underlying assumption when theorists began to posit the existence of styles. As far as scientific psychology, in Britain and the United States, was concerned, variations on the VAK model were tested during the immediate post–World War II period and found to possess no validity. When it comes to understanding how normal and intact human beings learn and process information, it is simply untrue to suggest that people are different in the apparent and manifest strengths of their input modality systems. In other words, it is nonsense to hold the idea that some of your students can be classified as visual learners whereas others, within the same class, are auditory learners. There simply is no known validity to making any such classifications on the basis of either neurology or genuine behavioural performance. But such realities did not stop the VAK notion taking off in another direction.

Styles as preferences

What then occurred throughout the post-war period and later, was a remarkable proliferation of theorists developing notions of learning style in different ways. Lacking the technology to develop behavioural tests, they often used survey methods to tap people's verbal responses. Questionnaires were trialled in which people would be asked about their *preferences* when it came to learning difficult things. For example, people might be asked if they generally want to think a good deal, or if they want to engage in action. Do they prefer to read about an issue, or proceed anyway? Do they focus on the big picture, or do they concentrate on small-scale building blocks? Do they exhibit convergent or divergent thinking patterns? And so on.

It was found that questionnaire instruments could be developed that enabled people to rate themselves on various dimensions, including ones based upon the VAK model. For example, if you ask someone 'Do you prefer to learn from images or from reading?', then people are able to answer this and similar questions. Hence, in the period from the 1960s on, the term 'style' shifted from being seen as a behavioural attribute into the realm of questionnaire assessment. Many of these questionnaires can be located in any Internet search today. As we noted earlier, many such instruments are freely available, but many others are held under degrees of protection and copyright. To this day, diagnosing learning styles using such tools still represents a significant commercial trade.

But there is an interesting issue here. The observation that people can make clear preferences tells us only that people think they can make clear preferences. Questionnaires ask for blanket judgements about generalised notions. You typically are not permitted to give conditional answers or respond by noting 'Well, it all depends'.

Among the worst are questionnaire items that expect you to supply your own context. For instance, suppose you are asked if you would agree with the statement, 'When circumstances are appropriate, I think quickly and try to take action as soon as possible'. Or how about, 'I need to watch a speaker's facial expressions and body language to understand what he or she means'. These items are taken from inventories available on the Internet. Should any human being disagree with the first notion, we would presume a misreading of the words rather than diagnose stylistic preferences within learning dispositions. Similarly, how a person responds to the second notion depends on how the word *need* is to be understood at that moment. It certainly helps to observe a person's body language as they speak, but if that statement is totally true for you, then you could never hold a telephone conversation.

Another way of expressing this idea is to note that the items used in the questionnaire instruments to index learning styles involve little genuine choice since common sense would suggest there ought not to be much variance among people. When such variance occurs (that is, people responding differently), it is related to interpretations of word meanings and to blatant misunderstandings. To state the matter bluntly, learning style inventories tap self-reports but fail to possess any acceptable validity for diagnosing beyond what can be observed on the surface.

The nature of individual differences

A teacher does not need such inventories to identify individual differences in students' natural dispositions. Some of your students are more intellectual, some are more anxious, some react quickly, and others plan more carefully. Some tackle new areas with confidence, but others appear less optimistic. But do not think that modern psychology offers you scientific tools to uncover subtle differences between your students' learning dispositions such that you can group them into a few style categories. And be wary, and distrustful, of any theory-based scheme that informs you there are different types of students sitting in your class that need to be taught in different ways.

An old joke within personality psychology is that there are two types of people in this world. There is the type that believes there are two types, and the type that does not believe this. Another such old joke is that although we may use some information to classify individuals for statistical purposes, the students just do not arrive at school with labels on their foreheads. One strange aspect of the learning styles literature is that many theorists were inclined to advance two ideas: (a) that students are unique individuals, and (b) we can classify them into groups, categories, or styles. One moment's reflection may suggest a remarkable inconsistency, or logical absurdity, between these two fundamentals.

More than one hundred years of research goes into the following idea: *once we get beyond basic notions such as gender and demographic traits such as race, religion and socioeconomic status, it becomes relatively difficult to pigeonhole any one individual.* But learning style research typically ignores such aspects and suggests that enduring and profound human differences are easily detected through asking people, adults and children alike, to make a series of choices on brief questionnaires employing superficial items.

The problem of the match

From time to time we come across an even more insidious idea. This is that your students suffer from the mismatch between three aspects (a) their personal learning styles, (b) the nature of the instruction they are getting, and (c) your personal teaching style. For example, you may be a teacher who exemplifies an auditory learning and teaching style. This suits the 30 per cent of your students who are also auditory learners, since they are happy to listen to you droning on. But the other 70 per cent are experiencing a mismatch. However, the teacher in the room next door is using pictures and imagery, and so is teaching to the strengths of her visual learners. The third teacher ensures her students are given opportunities to develop through physical activity and action such as using role plays. Of course, all students benefit from instruction that encompasses analysing images, hearing words, and acting out key aspects. But this is not what is being suggested by the match hypothesis.

The problem here reflects what researchers call the **aptitude–treatment interaction**. This is the theory that different treatments could suit different types of people. We know from well-controlled research that such aptitude–treatment interactions are readily found in two known areas: (a) anxiety and (b) knowledge-level effects. Anxious students respond well to strong guidance, direct supervision, and a restriction on choices. But non-anxious people respond well to almost the opposite conditions. It is also well established that in acquiring knowledge, beginners benefit from clear step-by-step instructions and an absence of problem-solving tasks. On the other hand, highly knowledge-able learners may benefit from working on problems to solve and are held back by step-by-step instructions.

But beyond such findings, aptitude–treatment interactions are very difficult to locate, or at least they are not well replicated through serious research. It is a reflection on the quality of the research reported into learning styles that such aptitude–treatment interactions have never been validated. One argument is that they have not yet been thoroughly investigated. But in contradiction to this, one reviewer was able to locate over 1,900 articles in the area of learning styles. Despite apparent popularity, the basic ideas behind the match hypothesis simply have not been validated, and we urge caution in accepting or advancing any such ideas. This is an area in which the claims made race well ahead of secure data. So what do the major research reviewers conclude?

Significant reviews of the empirical research literature

In this area, we have the benefit of several key literature reviews from several research teams. In 1987, Kavale and Forness reviewed 39 studies into matching instruction with modality preference (i.e., the VAK model), and found no significant effects on learning. In 1999, Steven Stahl, a key researcher in children's reading, also reviewed the available studies and noted, 'The reason researchers roll their eyes at learning styles is the utter failure to find that assessing children's learning styles and matching to instructional methods has any effect on their learning' (1999, p. 1).

In 2004, Professor Frank Coffield, of the London Institute of Education, and his colleagues published a major review closely examining the fundamental validity behind claims made in the learning styles literature. In a year-long project, they carefully examined the published empirical studies and noted a remarkable lack of independent research. Often, studies supporting learning styles were conducted by individuals promoting their own theories and specific products. When independently conducted research was examined, the data failed to validate any of the major notions concerning learning styles.

The language used in the Coffield report is notable. For example, several learning styles schemes are described as 'highly questionable' (p. 25), 'theoretically and psychometrically flawed' (p. 19), and 'not suitable for the assessment of individuals' (p. 19). They noted, 'We therefore advise against pedagogical intervention based solely on any of the learning style instruments' (p. 140), and, 'Some of the best known and widely used instruments have such serious weaknesses (e.g., low reliability, poor validity and negligible impact on pedagogy) that we recommend that their use in research and in practice should be discontinued' (p. 138).

Coffield et al. characterised the field as one of 'theoretical incoherence and conceptual confusion' (p. 135), as well as 'labelling, vested interests and over-blown claims' (p. 137). In a later newspaper report, Dr Coffield was quoted as saying, 'We do students a serious disservice by implying they have only one learning style, rather than a flexible repertoire from which to choose, depending on the context' (*The Telegraph*, 29 July 2007). In that same news item, the brain scientist Baroness Susan Greenfield is quoted as stating that 'the method of classifying pupils on the basis of learning styles is a waste of valuable time and resources'.

While this debate was unfolding within Britain, the American Association for Psychological Science commissioned four leading cognitive psychologists to review the evidence behind learning style claims being aired in the public domain. Their specific brief was to evaluate the style matching hypothesis. Their report was then published in the *Psychological Science in Public Interest* (Pashler, McDaniel, Rohrer, & Bjork, 2008). As with the British report, the American report was highly critical of claims made within the area and noted that

there is no adequate evidence base to justify incorporating learning styles assessments into general educational practice. Thus, limited education resources would better be devoted to adopting other educational practices that have strong evidence base, of which there are an increasing number.

(p. 105)

In particular, the American review highlighted the fact that the matching hypothesis (that different students respond differently to different teaching practices), has received only negative support from the published research. The theory that learners will learn best when their preferences are taken into account also received no serious support from the available literature on human learning. Overall, the report was highly critical of the industry that has developed based on marketing learning style products.

In 2010, a group of researchers, led by Professor Scott Lilienfeld of Emory University, published a remarkable compilation book entitled *Fifty Great Myths of Popular Psychology: Shattering widespread misconceptions about human behavior*. The entire book is compelling reading as it reviews genuine evidence associated with effects generally assumed to be true. The notion that students learn best when teaching styles are matched to their learning styles is detailed as Myth No. 18. The authors concluded that this idea constitutes 'an urban legend of educational psychology' (p. 96).

An Australian report was highly critical of the manner in which learning styles have been used as diagnostic tools within certain schools. There has been a tendency for students with academic difficulties to be labelled as tactile/kinaesthetic learners leading to inappropriate instructional methods, time wasting, and stereotyping. This report concludes that 'Rather than being a harmless fad, learning styles theory perpetuates the very stereotyping and harmful teaching practices that it is said to combat' (Scott, 2010, p. 5).

In addition to these major reports, we located many other writers who have examined aspects of the data and who came away less than impressed. It is never possible to assert the null hypothesis and say something akin to *learning styles just do not exist*. Indeed, it is very clear that once we define learning styles in terms of the learner's own stated preferences, then they do exist. But there is a huge issue in attempting to lay claim that such learning styles have anything to do with how we actually do learn. That is the stumbling block.

IN PERSPECTIVE: Getting to the truth behind claims

The area of learning styles is a confused and not a happy one. Claims are often made that well exceed any known basis in reality (see Table 19.1). Knowing a student's learning style on the basis of the self-report questionnaires fails to provide insight into how that student genuinely learns. Measures of learning style run risk of focusing attention upon the wrong variables.

Claims that there can be a mismatch between your teaching style and the style of learning an individual student supposedly exhibits are highly dubious. Certainly, it is possible for clashes to occur between teacher and student. Certainly, it is possible for a teacher to exhibit deficient teaching methods. But to try to account for such clashes and deficiencies as being the product of interaction between student learning style and an individual teacher's teaching styles is erroneous and misleading. Should a teacher present with a problematic teaching style, then the 'mismatch' is likely to be not with just some of the students, but with all of them. The notion that one style of instruction can advantage one type of student, but disadvantage another type of student, remains unsupported by any known evidence and is simply wrong.

TABLE 19.1 Learning styles and rhetoric: the truth behind four big ideas

Idea 1: Students are unique human beings, different from each other. Since one size does not fit all, teachers need to be sensitive to such individual differences.	True: This truism is recognised by all educators. No two people have ever been found to be the same. For instance, differences in learners stem dramatically from the level of knowledge that they bring into any learning situation.
Idea 2: Learners indicate viable preferences about how they feel most able to learn. When given choices people are able to inform us about how they want to learn and study.	True: But the trouble is that preferences appear unrelated to genuine learning in real situations. What individuals say about how they learn does not actually predict how they learn any more than statements that are valid for virtually everyone.
Idea 3: An individual learner learns more effectively when the instructor's teaching style matches the learning style of that student. Hence, the way you teach could benefit some, but disadvantage others.	False: This theory lacks supportive data. This big idea predicts an interaction effect between teaching methods and different groups of students which has never been demonstrated to exist, and is counter-indicated by scores of studies into effective teaching strategies that show main effects (that work with all rather than just some) to be powerful.
Idea 4: Different students need to be taught in different ways. At some level, instruction has to be individualised.	Partially true: But the devil is in the detail. It is a truism that people are different (Idea 1). But the accommodations you plan for such learner differences must relate to how your students actually learn in realistic contexts, using genuinely individualised feedback, rather than postulated traits whose existence is unproven.

Study guide questions

1 In trawling the Internet, Hattie and Yates found several examples of question-naires claiming to tap into 'Learning style', which seemed slightly different but still were based upon the old VAK model. What does this model assume?

2 People are different, therefore we should analyse their learning style. Just what is faulty about such logic?

3 Explain how the notion of styles partly emerged out of (a) the apparent failure of IQ testing in pilot training, and (b) the belief that questionnaires could be used to diagnose profound differences in mental organization.

4 Why should responses to such learning style questionnaires be totally mistrusted? What really drives the way people respond to such questions?

5 How meaningful is it to rate someone in terms of the 'type' of person they represent? How many such 'types' are supposed to exist? What does the science of personality now tell us about such human types?

6 Are you a visual learner? If so, does this mean that your teaching style will favour the visual learners in your classroom?

7 There has been one major problem associated with the research literature into aptitude–treatment interactions. What is this problem?

8 Learning styles research has gone on for more than 50 years and generated around 1,900 research articles. What is the overall finding?

9 It is not possible to ever say 'learning styles do not exist', as people can express clear preferences on the inventories. But just what is the relationship between what people say on those questionnaires and how they genuinely learn?

Reference notes

■ One British review team located 71 varieties of learning style assessments (Coffield, Mosely, Hall, & Ecclestone, 2004).

■ One popular model of learning styles (Dunn, 1984).

■ How people decode questions within questionnaires (Schwarz, 1999; Shulruf, Hattie, & Dixon, 2008).

■ Individual human beings do not fit meaningfully into psychologically described categories, or 'types' of people (Cervone, 2005).

■ Aptitude treatment interaction research history (Corno, 2008).

■ Significant literature reviews undermining credibility for learning styles as a determinant of learning (Coffield *et al.*, 2004; Kavale & Forness, 1987; Lilienfeld, Lynn, Ruscio, & Beyerstein, 2010; Pashler, McDaniel, Rohrer, & Bjork, 2008; Scott, 2010; Stahl, 1999).

- Coffield on learning styles as a disservice to students (also quotes Baroness Greenfield): *The Telegraph*, 29 July 2007: see www.telegraph.co.uk/news/uknews/1558822/professor-pans-learning-style-teaching-method.html (accessed 20 May 2013).

- See Yates, 2000 on the sheer practical impossibility of matching students' learning styles with instructional procedures.

20

Multitasking

A widely held fallacy

Have you admired those people who can talk on the phone, clean their nails, read the paper, and eat a sandwich all at the same time? With demands placed upon us, coping through handling multiple problems simultaneously, or *multitasking*, appears as an attractive approach to efficient time management. The term began life in describing early computer operating systems, but is now widely used. In some quarters, the term appears as a pointer for a type of life style. We recently noted a brand of bread being advertised as promising energy for 'multitasking individuals', and an employer wanting to recruit a purchasing officer able to cope with a 'multitasking environment'.

But, can we really multitask? We could accomplish so much more if we could do more than one thing at the same time. Many activities in our lives seem to involve multiple goals with overlapping activities. We drive a car while holding a conversation. We cook a meal while reading a good book. We chew gum and hold a conversation. We may do our best thinking while doing the gardening.

Our children study while listening to music. Many students declare they can do their homework while interacting with Facebook. Several studies have surveyed school students who claim to be multitasking successfully. For example, in a large American survey, Ulla Foehr found that 64 per cent of students at primary school age claimed they multitask when using computers. When she asked a subgroup of students to keep a diary, she found that 50 per cent of the time spent doing homework on the computer was also spent using the computer for other purposes. It is not uncommon for students to be characterised as **digital natives**, having grown up in the computer age and so have developed skills that permit multitasking as a natural extension of human capacity.

What about learning? Can we really overlap our activities such that we might *learn* two things at once? After sifting through the available research evidence, we can only give a clear negative to such a question.

What is multitasking?

The term multitasking can be applied to any of the following: (a) the brain accomplishing two or more activities simultaneously, (b) accomplishing multiple goals within a single time period through switching between tasks, (c) focusing on one primary goal, but periodically allowing other tasks or secondary goals to assume priority, or (d) consciously dividing your time attending to several essentially non-demanding tasks, such as monitoring email, watching the oven, and listening to a radio program.

This first notion (that the brain may genuinely be able to do two things at once) is widely recognised to possess no serious validity. In studies of simultaneous processing, as studied in psychological laboratories, it is apparent that such a capacity lies beyond any effective human functioning. When two signals come in at once, your attention will be drawn to one of them. Whenever people claim that they can multitask, they refer to a feeling of being able to *switch across* activities efficiently. People may achieve more than one goal within acceptably brief time periods, and so experience the feeling they have accomplished this through multitasking processes within their minds.

A further notion, commonly overlooked in claiming effective multitasking, is that some goals and tasks will involve *learning and thinking*, whereas other tasks involve *performing* an act already well learned. This distinction is highly important. The effect of distractions and any additional demands is far greater upon learning new material, than upon using what is already in the head. Although it may be possible to tolerate some level of overlap when practising well-learnt activities, attempting to learn different things at once is a straight invitation for mental disaster, politely referred to in the literature as *interference*. If you try to learn two different things within 10 to 15 minutes of each other, the brain gets them mixed up, and confusion results. Such interference effects have been firmly documented in the research into memory, from its early beginnings over 150 years ago.

But a more contemporary model for human thinking is the digital computer. We are often informed that computers handle information by multitasking. But this is hardly the case. The computer's CPU is governed by time sampling protocols in which it handles tasks by *switching* between them in terms of microseconds. Computers are designed this way, with the CPU checking on demands made upon it several hundred times a second. Handling multiple demands creates virtually no loss of efficiency, so long as the computer's memory capacities are not exceeded. The computer CPU is designed, from ground up, to operate within a time-sharing system. This is why your home PC effortlessly handles multiple devices such as USBs, disk drives, printers, and so on.

As a metaphor for the mind, the computer is highly inappropriate. The human brain is quite unlike any known computer. We do not possess any facility that resembles the computer's ability to time-share. We do not have a CPU waiting to process data queues. To put it bluntly: when it comes to actual learning situations, *multitasking does not exist*. Students ought to be discouraged from believing they have the capacity to do two things at once, if one such activity involves any form of learning. If attention is split, learning cannot occur. Students ought not to be encouraged to believe they can study efficiently and interact with instruments such as MySpace or Facebook within the same time period.

The more a person overlaps activities during intended learning sessions, the more interference occurs, and it brings a huge toll.

The hidden but high cost of mental switching

As far as laboratory studies can inform us, any level of switching between demanding tasks produces lapses in performances, otherwise known as 'switching costs'. Several studies have suggested that younger people and females are relatively less disrupted than older people and males. But overall, the hope that human brains can switch between activities that call for serious concentration or learning, gets no support from the available evidence. People who expect to multitask across activities typically show reduced overall effectiveness. The laboratory tests also reveal how people remain unaware their performances are deteriorating under multiple demands.

Switching between demanding activities is associated with some level of cost, relative to not switching. But here the killer: when you switch between uncompleted activities, there is no automatic way of detecting how much your overall performance is being disrupted. One study found that the very people who believed they could multitask well were the worst performers on the laboratory tests. They were poorly organised and were failing to use their memories efficiently. People who claimed to multitask were unrealistic and overconfident about their actual capabilities. Those who switch between uncompleted activities too rapidly are displaying a form of impulsiveness coupled with poor levels of metacognitive discrimination in being unable to discern their overall drop in efficiency.

Applied research in the 1950s found that when a typist is asked to answer a company's telephones, his or her overall typing capacity drops substantially, with the cost being far more than duration of the phone calls. If it is not a simple routine matter, then the average time taken responding to an e-mail in a work situation is approaching 15 minutes. Even when employees appear to be coping well with overlapping duties, it is apparent they report heightened levels of stress and frustration due to task switching. More recently, it has been shown that merely attending to incoming social media messages has serious effects on students' reading performances.

Switching costs are also apparent in studies into how people cope with television news programs that use the headline banner at the bottom of the screen, sometimes called 'crawlers'. We really cannot attend to both the main story and a separate item on the crawler line at the same time. Although we may attempt to monitor both a crawler and the main story, we end up remembering less overall. Ironically, although more information is coming in, attention is split, and less overall is retained in memory.

There is a historical angle to the concept of switching costs. The notion first emerged in that, during the course of World War II, developments in the warplane occurred rapidly. Over a short period of time, cognitive demands on pilots escalated in accord with enhanced performance of the airplane and remarkable advances in technology. One unfortunate consequence was that pilot error became a commonly logged cause of accidents. Since that period, huge strides have been made within engineering psychology and aviation design to build aircraft control systems consistent with human capacities and limitations.

What about driving the car?

Instances of apparent multitasking in human functioning are explained in several interesting ways. For instance, we can drive a car and engage in other meaningful activities, such as conversing, at the same time. This is possible through **automaticity**. Metaphorically, you allow your automatic pilot to take over control of the car. Conscious mental activity is not needed as this pilot knows which pedal is the brake, and so on. Your eyes focus on the road without your having to exert voluntary activity.

Experienced drivers glance into the rear vision mirror every few seconds, and yet do this without thinking. The mechanical act of driving is fully automated, a stage achieved through hundreds of hours of successful practice. Ironically, at this point you have forgotten how hard it was to hold a conversation and drive the car when you first were learning. Indeed, one of the major themes running through cognitive psychology is that automated cognitive processes require fewer resources than non-automated processes.

Nevertheless, achieving automation does not imply that driving is unaffected by whatever else is going on within your nervous system. Holding a conversation, listening to the radio, or talking upon a mobile phone, are events known to drain attention away from driving. If this is multitasking, then it is achieved at major cost. Your eyes are less focused on the other cars on the road, your reaction times are slower, and your ability to brake efficiently is seriously impaired. Talking on the phone while driving has been shown to be associated with many aspects of poor driving such as lane violation, failing to stop in time, running the red light, and slower reactions to changing traffic conditions. Laboratory studies, with computerised driving simulators, indicate that you fail to detect about one half of the road information in front of you when using your mobile. In one large American study, it was found that only 3 per cent of people show relatively unimpaired driving skills while talking on the phone.

This body of research, conducted both on the road itself and on laboratory simulators, has found that people are unaware their driving skills are being impaired in such ways. Participants are often alarmed when shown objective data indicating performance drop-off. The performance reduction from using a mobile while driving has been found to be equivalent to the effect of an alcohol intoxication level of around 0.08 per cent blood alcohol level. Many accidents, involving motorists and pedestrians alike, are attributed to phone usage. If the brain could genuinely multitask, then banning phones from drivers would not have been necessary.

Whenever you are under stress when driving, such as in an unfamiliar city, then the best strategy is to (a) turn off the CD player, (b) stop talking, and (c) focus upon the driving. If you need to use a GPS, then stop driving as it requires around 55 seconds to set the device. Glances away from the road for longer than two seconds can result in catastrophe. Pulling over may save your life.

The following Internet resource is well worth a visit: the American government has a website targeting young people with information about the dangers of driving and using devices such as mobile phones (see reference notes for this chapter). It is estimated that 90 per cent of young drivers carry a mobile phone switched on and within hand's reach. Observational studies report around 10 per cent of drivers continue to drive while on the phone. The website highlights some of the cognitive research as cited in this chapter. We feel this site ought to be compulsory viewing for all drivers, young and old.

Within Australia, one of the largest insurance companies regularly commissions surveys that disclose alarmingly high rates of phone usage and texting being reported by drivers. The Centre for Accident Research and Road Safety, based at the Queensland University of Technology, has an informative website conveying downloadable pamphlets based upon solid research that can be distributed to young drivers.

Multitasking and studying: the problem of sustaining attention

Anything that saps attention is potentially a negative factor in learning and studying. It should come as little surprise to learn of surveys indicating that students who obtain low grades often appear to be spending excessive time on social network pages as they study. The laboratory studies with adults indicated that multitasking affects deep learning more dramatically than simple learning, and this is an important factor to emphasise when advising students, and helping them to identify the myths that abound in this area.

Similarly, listening to music is another potentially unhelpful factor. The available research into music is unclear as gentle or unobtrusive background music may be harmless or may even help. But as the music becomes loud and dominant it quickly reduces learning performances. Listening to music quickly saps the learner's attention. Music becomes an issue once the learner starts to listen to it, rather than focus on other material.

Occasionally, you will encounter successful high achieving students who openly claim to study while listening to music. On closer interrogation we find that some individuals become accustomed to having music as a background factor. The music is there, but they are not actually listening or paying attention to it. In other words, such a student is using a strategy of *selective attention*, rather than multitasking as such. It is ironical to realise that studying with music can only be successful when the student is not paying attention to it, but using it as a type of ambient white noise.

So should teachers ever suggest such a strategy as a means to study? We would not encourage this strategy because the available studies suggest that the more one listens to music, the less attentional capacity there is available for other mental activity. Nevertheless, when activities are not demanding, people will often allow music into their environment as a background factor, in part to reduce boredom, in part to create mood. For example, while exercising, or taking the bus, or painting the roof, music creates a positive context that allows another activity to flow easily, more enjoyably, over several hours. But plainly, these are not learning situations. Music can turn a boring repetitive task into a pleasant experience, and young people readily appreciate this reality. Modern technologies enable anyone to introduce music into their mental worlds at the turn of a switch.

In terms of being able to focus, study, and learn, the recommended context has to be that of *quietness and lack of external stimulation*. In all libraries we know of, the only sound allowable is the quiet hum of the air conditioner. Steps are taken to reduce all other noise. Studying requires clear mental focus. The student who needs to study in a home situation may be faced with problems of simply containing and controlling his or her learning environment. And so, being able to shut out the rest of the world by wearing headphones and playing background music might (*just might*) be a strategy developed by an individual to procure an acceptable level of mental focus. Nevertheless, this is not a recommended strategy, and we would not suggest you recommend it to any student, especially the student who presents with study deficiencies.

Can multitasking ever be helpful? Yes, to relieve boredom

In seeming contradiction to all we have said so far, a minor level of multitasking may genuinely help you to perform well in some situations. However, this is easily explained. When someone is asked to attend to an easy task, but one involving constant attention over time, then fatigue effects kick in after several minutes. This is inevitable. Performances tend to drop away over time. Whereas cognitive researchers refer to this as **vigilance decrement**, laypeople use terms such as tiredness, or loss of concentration. Whenever there is a boring or repetitive task to be completed, then performance drops after relatively short periods such as 10 to 15 minutes. People may strive to maintain high levels of concentration, and still perform reasonably well, but not as effectively as when they were fresh and eager.

In such boring vigilance situations, the decrement effect itself can be reduced (but not eliminated) if the person has to occasionally switch onto another task, make a simple response, and then switch back onto the main task. Superficially, this looks like a form of multitasking. However, this is not multitasking in any meaningful sense, and learning is not taking place. Multitasking on boring non-demanding activities will help you remain aroused and alert when your brain is working at low capacity, and just wants to close down, or retire itself to sleep. This arousal function can serve to restore some of the energy lost over time. For instance, listening to lively music may assist you to remain alert on long, boring drives.

IN PERSPECTIVE: What teachers should know and respect

Multitasking is what computers do. When it comes to acquiring new knowledge, however, humans cannot multitask, not in any genuine manner. A deeper analysis suggests that even when we appear to do more than one activity at once, we are overlapping well-practised skills and switching between them. We can do this provided that their task structures do not demand either (a) continuous vigilance or (b) assimilation of any new information.

Many activities in your life can appear to look like multitasking. However, this impression is superficial and sustained by the fact that many activities are non-demanding, and relatively automated. When people appear to be multitasking, they are overlapping two or more tasks but still remaining within capacity limits. Multitasking cannot increase your capacity, even when you are fully alert and strongly motivated. Under any level of stress, task switching will itself drain capacity, resulting in reduced overall effectiveness.

Perversely, whenever we try to multitask, we cannot recognise the attached switching costs. The human brain seems designed not to multitask, at least not with any precision or accountability, and the irony is that the act of multitasking deprives you of the conscious mechanism, or the metacognition, that could be employed to index the disruption to your performance. Researchers refer to such effects as *hidden costs*; that is, costs one cannot see or monitor. Although not serious for the most part, provided task demands remain low, such costs disrupt and destroy the ability to process new information or to construct any new knowledge.

Overall, the message is that multitasking is the wrong option anytime you expect to learn, acquire knowledge, or think deeply. Should you need to react with diligence and sensitivity, attempting to multitask will guarantee inferior performance at some point. Under a multitasking regime, your ability to apply your intelligence, and allow metacognition to drive careful decision-making, become first-line casualties.

Study guide questions

1 Is multitasking something that is expected of us all today? Is it a new mantra? Have you seen or heard people claiming they need to multitask?

2 There seem to be four ways in which this term multitasking gets used. What are these?

3 What is the distinction between learning and performing a skill? Which of these is disrupted easily?

4 The notion of switching costs looms very heavily in this area. Just what is a switching cost?

5 Surely people are aware of switching costs? Are they not obvious? If not, why not?

6 It is often assumed people can drive cars and do things such as hold a conversation at the same time. So why is it illegal to use mobile phones as you drive?

7 In terms of effect on performance, mobile phone usage has been shown to be equivalent to drunk driving at what blood alcohol level?

8 Many students claim to study with music playing or social media open. Should we accept such practices as simply the natural order of students today, who have to develop 'multitasking skills'?

9 Sometimes multitasking can help with overall performances. Just when can this happen?

10 What is the most appropriate advice we can offer students about multitasking? Indeed, why is any notion of 'multitasking skill' an inherently flawed notion unto itself?

Reference notes

- Majority of students claim they multitask while studying (Foehr, 2006).
- Distinction between learning new information versus retrieving old information (Naveh-Benjamin, Craik, Perretta, & Tonev, 2000).
- Switching costs: adults who multitask a good deal have trouble concentrating, resisting distractions, and remembering (Ophir, Nass, & Wagner, 2009). People attempting to learn whilst multitasking fail to generalise learning to new situations (Foerde, Knowlton, & Poldrack, 2006).
- Heavy switching costs in a work situation (Mark, Gudith, & Klocke, 2008).
- Text crawlers overload memory for TV news (Bergen, Grimes, & Potter, 2005).
- Attending to emails and social messages disrupts concentration in reading (Bowman, Levine, Waite, & Gendron, 2010).
- Human factors in aviation is a huge topic, but for a readable account of its history, from an American perspective see Roscoe, 1997.
- Effects of driving under the influence of distraction: phone use and alcohol (Strayer, Drews, & Crouch, 2006; Strayer & Watson, 2012). The 2006 article conveys the research equating phone usage to blood alcohol of 0.08.

- The frequency of people whose driving is unaffected by phone is 3 per cent of the population (Watson & Strayer, 2010).

- American government website detailing research about dangers of driving and phone use: www.distraction.gov.

- Excellent brochures available online from Centre for Accident Research and Road Safety (QUT): www.carrsq.qut.edu.au.

- Listening to loud music can disrupt attention and studying (W. F. Thompson, Schellenberg, & Letnic, 2012).

- Students who multitasked in class had reduced grades (Ellis, Daniels, & Jauregui, 2010). Reduced grades correlates with Internet social media usage (Junco & Cotten, 2012).

- Multitasking can help break boredom and prevent fatigue (Ariga & Lleras, 2011).

21

Your students are digital natives. Or are they?

An especially interesting notion lies in the theory of **digital natives**, proposed a decade ago by several writers. But it was Marc Prensky who made a deep impression on contemporary educational thought with statements such as 'today's students think and process information fundamentally differently from their predecessors' (2001, p. 1). This effect is attributed to their having grown up in the context of the digital age with access to computers and the raft of other electronic devices. According to Prensky, 'Our students, as digital natives, will continue to evolve and change so rapidly that we won't be able to keep up' (2006, p. 9), together with, 'Our young people generally have a much better idea of what the future is bringing than we do' (2006, p. 10).

These comments were advanced in a leading professional educational journal, aimed at a wide teacher–professional readership. As such they 'hit a nerve', and the reverberations continue to this day. The direct implication is that teachers, as **digital immigrants**, are generally unprepared for the wave of computer-savvy students who can do things that their teachers just cannot. The implicit presumption was that, given technological advances are occurring with such speed and facility, digital immigrants ought not be in the position to hold back the digital natives.

The need for computer literacy

Sensible ideas are evident in Prensky's argument. For example, when discussing the need for computers and other electronic tools in education he notes, 'Educating or evaluating students without these tools makes no more sense to them than educating or evaluating a plumber without his or her wrench' (2006, p. 12). Every teacher experiences the realisation that many of his or her students are more skilled in using certain programs on the computer. Once students spend time using certain programs, then they will appear skilful in using those tools. One theme we emphasise throughout this book is that whenever an individual spends time in **deliberate practice** activities (see Chapter 11), the knowledge base allied to that activity expands to allow the person to develop expertise.

It is also salutary to appreciate that surveys indicate the average American child is spending more time watching television or interacting with electronic media (about 50 hours a week) than he or she spends in the classroom. Recent surveys are showing that more than 70 per cent of students routinely use social networking, and that the average student is on the Internet for around an hour a day. Many commentators note such trends have been increasing steadily over the past decade. The notions that students are increasingly computer savvy, and likely to be accessing social media as they study, appear to be worldwide phenomena.

On the other hand, digital native theory is considerably overstated. Prenksy suggests that the natives are different from earlier generations in how their minds work. He declares, 'In fact they are so different from us that we can no longer use either our twentieth century knowledge or training as a guide to what is best for them educationally' (2006, p. 9). Such natives have been characterised as learning at high speed, and being able to make divergent connections to navigate a complex field quickly. For instance, they will rapidly learn complex topics, such as algebra, when presented deeply embedded within game-like contexts.

There is a clear 'gee-whiz' factor to all this. We have seen newspaper reports wherein various educators and senior administrators are quoted as saying that today's students are now accustomed to learning from multiple screens at the same time, that they live in an electronic world, and so are disadvantaged if their teachers fail to adjust their teaching practices to these new world realities. In short, the digital native is a new type of animal whose needs will be respected only through somewhat radical changes in how we structure our educational practices, curricula, and institutional provisions such as online study opportunities.

Can human nature change?

The central problem with digital native theory is that it is advanced in the absence of any known database. Students appear to have characteristics attributed towards them that they just do not possess. The notion that exposure to certain types of experience will alter the nature of human information processing is almost impossible to investigate. In its raw form, digital native theory has to be seen as considerably overstated and basically incorrect. Human capacities are not as flexible or tied to experiences as this theory might suggest.

What is evident to us when we read in this area is confusion between two things: (a) your students' familiarity with using and operating modern technology, its devices, and powerful software tools, and (b) descriptions of natural human capacity. The notion that experience with the electronic world advances natural cognitive capacity is a seriously flawed thesis. It would appear only sensible to avoid making significant decisions or judgements on the basis of untested notions.

In short, we remain sceptical of the majority of claims concerning the advantages of being born within the digital age.

We remain sympathetic to the view that interacting with ICT resources *does not* automatically facilitate either (a) deep and meaningful mental processing, or (b) alterations in the child's information processing. Indeed it may require additional skills, such as the proficiency to evaluate the quality of surface information that dominates the web. Skills such as becoming highly familiar with the digital world, being adept on mobile phones, being able to perform Internet searches, and being able to use clever graphics packages, ought not be confused with actual advances in knowledge acquisition, genuine understanding of complex ideas, and becoming aware of deeper understandings.

When it comes to human learning, there simply is no new magic. The advantages of the digital revolution when expressed in terms of what students learn have been overly promoted. As educators over the past 40 years now, the current writers have heard about a forthcoming revolution in teaching attributable to computer-assisted learning. Computers certainly have proven themselves as valuable resources, but there is no revolution.

Computer access promotes opportunities to learn, but does not create learning through any novel or intrinsic mechanisms. The brain does not come with any specific programmes that enable information to leap off the screen into the head. Being able to use sophisticated tools to create impressive products cannot be equated with depth of knowledge and understanding. Similarly, being able to use Wikipedia to locate isolated facts (such as the dates of the Boer War) signifies mastery of another valuable resource, but in merely the same way that all encyclopaedias and dictionaries are valuable learning tools.

Toward evaluating the role of computers in teaching

So, are computers contributing to student learning in this modern world? We have experienced various forms of computer-assisted education over the past 30 years. Has it all been worth the effort? In VL, John Hattie was able to locate and review the remarkable number of 81 meta-analyses published in this area. The impact of computers upon student achievement was found to be generally positive with an overall effect size of 0.37 – which is about an average influence on learning. Effects were reported at all levels of schooling, and all ability levels. All curriculum areas seemed to evidence benefit, although the lowest effects were noted in mathematics teaching. And this effect size has not changed over the last 30 years.

Several important generalisations were warranted including (a) effects were stronger when computers were used to supplement traditional teaching, rather than being seen as its alternative, (b) effects were stronger when teachers received higher levels of training in the use of computers, (c) effects were strong when computers offered students opportunities to extend their learning practice periods or take advantage of tutorial assistance, (d) there were clear advantages in the students assuming control over the learning situation in aspects such as pacing and mastering new material, (e) students were able to use computers most effectively when working in pairs, (f) computers have the ability to provide highly adaptive feedback to the learner, and (g) students learn more when they work in pairs when using technology.

What became apparent, through a careful reading of the extensive research literature, was the realisation that such positive effects are achieved through applications of the same principles of learning that apply in all others areas of human learning. This point has also been made repeatedly by Professor Richard Mayer, one of the leading exponents of multimedia and ICT instruction. The computer platform can bring with it significant advances such as individual diagnostics, step-by-step presentations, attractive and motivating visuals, the ability to monitor responses immediately, and provide valuable feedback. All this can be carried out with the machine's infinite patience. But it is still the same clunky brain that has to make strong efforts to learn. As implied earlier, we have yet to see any examples of information leaping off a computer screen into a student's head. It is too easy to confuse information access with genuine knowledge acquisition.

And here is one hidden aspect, rarely recognised in the digital natives literature: it is critical to realise that the computer is not 'the teacher'. But what it can do is to allow a human teacher or teachers to design and deliver instruction to other humans through a different medium, and in a different manner. Well-designed instructional packages are likely to have been developed by a team of experienced teachers who continue to develop such products over time. Nevertheless, underlying principles of presentation, instruction, practice, knowledge acquisition, feedback and application do not vary between traditional instructional contexts and any new world of computer-assisted instruction.

IN PERSPECTIVE: Evolution trumps revolution

After more than 30 years of educational computing in the schools, we concur with digital native ideas in that every child in our schools today needs to become computer literate to participate fully in contemporary life and society. These are inherently valuable skills. Students must be able to access and appraise knowledge sources efficiently. Most importantly, they must be taught not to confuse obtaining information mindlessly with genuine knowledge building and achieving depth of understanding. They need to be discouraged from the 'cut and paste' approach to information gathering that became possible through Internet searching. We note that, within the school context, computers can be programmed to deliver high quality instructional opportunities, which are best seen as resources able to be used by knowledgeable and well-trained classroom teachers.

However, we find little evidence or justification for two notions, as advanced in some quarters. Namely that (a) computers can replace or displace outmoded teachers and (b) students can function and learn at ever-increasing levels of depth and sophistication due to their recently developed electronically enhanced cognitive resources. We find such notions unrealistic, unattainable, and fundamentally incorrect.

Study guide questions

1 The digital native theory does embody some sensible notions. What are these?

2 But the same theory also embraces several unrealistic or overly optimistic notions. What are some of these overblown ideas?

3 It is noted 'that experience with the electronic world advances cognitive capacity is a seriously flawed thesis.' Have you ever encountered this flawed thesis before?

4 In general terms the literature shows mildly positive impacts associated with computer-assisted learning. What factors seem to be implicated in moderating such positive effects?

5 However, what is a balanced perspective educators can take in relation to digital native theory?

Reference notes

- The terms digital natives and immigrants stem from articles and book by Prensky (2001, 2006, 2010).

- Children spend considerable time on the Internet (Foehr, 2006).

- Notion that experience with the electronic world advances natural cognitive capacity is a seriously flawed thesis (Bennett, Maton, & Kervin, 2008).

- For a synthesis of ICT impact on achievement from Visible Learning, see Hattie, 2009, pp. 220–227.

- Instruction through ICT and non-ICT still involves the same learning demands upon the learner (Mayer, 2003).

22

Is the Internet turning us into shallow thinkers?

In the past 20 years classroom teachers have had to mount concerted battles against a phenomenon created by the information superhighway. This is the 'cut and paste' approach to student assignment construction. When students are skilled in Internet searching and using electronic tools, they possess the ability to create products to a remarkably high level of presentation. Certain routines and formulas allow a student to take text and images from any available source and repackage these, as though they duly represent the individual's own work (as do many academics when preparing their PowerPoint presentations). There are distinct fine-grain skills inherent in cutting, pasting, editing, and presenting. But the problem exists in that individuals may begin to use such skills to present products that mask deficiencies in their mastery of appropriate subject content.

Every teacher will encounter situations where impressive and substantial pieces of work can be produced and presented by students, amid creeping doubts as to exactly what was the individual student's own contribution. Students, and indeed, sometimes their teachers, may remain insensitive to issues such as copying and copyright. One standard joke in this area is that to copy from one source is 'plagiarism'. But to copy from ten is 'research'. The problem of illegitimate copying is taken seriously in many institutions even to the extent of using electronic programs (such as Turnitin) that locate Internet text sources that closely resemble a submitted sample of text.

The alarmist view

Is the Internet encouraging us to think and behave in shallow ways? It can be noted that ever since the development of the Internet, significant individuals have written strongly against the possible effect of modern technologies. In 1994, the American writer, Sven Birkerts was unimpressed with the notion that technologies could replace books as a source of knowledge and wisdom. He speculated that such alternatives might yield 'an expansion of the short-term memory banks and a correlative atrophying of long-term memory' (p. 139).

In an important book published in 2007, Maryanne Wolf expressed serious doubts about e-reading, especially with young children or any students experiencing learning difficulties. What was notable in Dr Wolf's case is that she is a well-respected researcher in the area of children's reading, with considerable professional expertise in helping students overcome reading difficulties through well-validated programs. She felt that children who use the Internet could become 'mere decoders of information who have neither the time nor motivation to think beneath or beyond their Googled universes'. She also noted that 'immediacy and volume of information should not be confused with true knowledge' (reported in *The New York Times*, 6 September, 2007). These are powerful notions.

In Dr Wolf's words:

> I have no doubt that the new mediums will accomplish many of the goals we have for the reading brain, particularly the motivation to learn to decode, read and experience the knowledge that is available. As a cognitive neuroscientist, however, I believe we need rigorous research about whether the reading circuit of our youngest members will be short-circuited, figuratively and physiologically. For my greatest concern is that the young brain will never have the time (in milliseconds or in hours or in years) to learn to go deeper into the text after the first decoding, but rather will be pulled by the medium to ever more distracting information, sidebars, and now, perhaps, videos.
>
> (Reported in *The New York Times*, 14 October 2009)

Writing in a key professional journal, *Educational Leadership*, she states this position even more directly:

> the digital culture's reinforcement of rapid attentional shifts and multiple sources of distraction can short circuit the development of the slower, more cognitively demanding comprehension processes that go into the formation of deep reading and deep thinking. If such a truncated development occurs, we may be spawning a culture so inured to sound bites and thought bites that it fosters neither critical analysis nor contemplative processes in its members.
>
> (Wolf & Barzillai, 2009, p. 36)

In 2008 Nicholas Carr published an article provocatively entitled 'Is Google making us stupid', and then followed this in 2010 with the book *The Shallows: What the Internet is doing to our brains*. The underlying message was that heavy Internet usage can have detrimental effects upon our minds, diminishing our capacities for concentration and deep thinking. We may become expert in information gathering, editing, and scanning. But if so, our strategic reading behaviours take the form of skimming, rather than genuinely being able to assimilate knowledge deeply. That is, the Internet encourages us to think of knowledge acquisition in terms of assemblages of information garnered from several minutes' intensive Internet searching. Knowledge building takes the form of a superficial 'cut and paste'.

Does human nature really change?

It is fascinating to note how the idea the 'Internet encourages shallow thinking' stands in marked contrast to the idea that access to IT produces highly capable digital natives. But both views flounder on the same point: the notion that Internet usage itself will occasion alterations or deterioration in cognitive capacities has no genuine support from within the known research literature. As in the case of digital native theory, it is likely that the fundamental hypothesis (that Internet usage reduces human cognitive capabilities) is untestable, at least within the immediate future. It is apparent that key individuals express strong views on such issues. But there really exists no clear way in which such views can be tested against reality.

We feel that a balanced perspective on these issues is most likely expressed in the following way: *that human capabilities are not as malleable as certain theories imply*. We are talking about our inherent native capabilities and human limitations here, rather than what the species can do with these capabilities. Christopher Chabris and Daniel Simons, two leading neuropsychologists, well known for the invisible gorilla studies (see Chapter 29), were asked to comment on this issue and stated it this way:

> The basic plan of the brain's wiring is determined by genetic programs and biochemical interactions that do most of their work long before a child discovers Facebook and Twitter. There is simply no experimental evidence to show that living with new technologies fundamentally changes brain organization in a way that affects one's ability to focus.
>
> (Reported in *Los Angeles Times*, 25 July 2010)

Our perspective is consistent with this quotation from Chabris and Simons. A balanced perspective has to recognise that the mode of an information input is not especially important in determining human understanding. We build understandings from combining what we can see with what we can read. We rely on having opportunities to learn and using words in the right place. It would be deemed non-sensical to try to conduct a controlled study to find out if reading the printed page resulted in more, or less, comprehension than reading the same page on a computer screen. The powerful variables determining comprehension are known and are concerned with the accessibility of words and propositional knowledge. Aspects such as font type, size, and italics basically are irrelevant to comprehension *provided* the text is genuinely legible, the reader is focused and comfortable, and has adequate vision for the task (but see reference notes for this chapter for additional comments on this point).

The Internet as a source of information

Although human dispositions cannot alter, we are all witness to the remarkable spread of the Internet as a source of information. Although in a different vein, we note that leaders within the medical profession have expressed much concern about a phenomenon identified within their field as the FUTON bias. This is the tendency to use only information, research, and reports that are quickly downloadable. As an acronym, FUTON stands for *Full Text On the Net*. Also, an influential American writer and poet, Professor Kenneth Goldsmith published a provocative essay in 2005 entitled 'If it doesn't exist on the Internet, it doesn't exist'. Citations to this essay, and also the FUTON bias, are found (through website links, of course) in the reference notes.

Finally, of ourselves, we remain in possible danger of a form of FUTON bias in that tools such as Google and Wikipedia have become essential tools in our lives as resources of general knowledge. For instance of late, (a) we see a gifted actor on TV, and seek out her life story, (b) we feel the need to verify what our doctor tells us about osteoarthritis, and (c) we need to find out what type of fertiliser to use on fruit trees. Within seconds we access information we feel we need. In short, it makes no sense to dispute the following notion: that the majority of the population can, with ease, use the Internet to access valuable information which enriches their lives profoundly. This capability represents a major cultural achievement of our era.

IN PERSPECTIVE: The essential continuity of human nature

What we find today is a situation where our society and its educational systems are adapting to the new technologies in an evolutionary, and not a revolutionary, manner. Teachers have been at the forefront of this movement and have been responsible for making intelligent and sensitive adaptations. We are learning how to balance the benefit of the old with the new. And we are doing so with the same old brain that has tottered along for some million odd years. The media we exploit may alter. But this is the surface feature. The ways we think, feel, and learn, owe far more to the basic language, interpersonal behaviours, and essential culture, we encounter within our infancy and preschool years, than they do to any recent technological development.

Whenever we are challenged about such partisan views in our classes, we suggest that our students might look toward the works of William Shakespeare. The words are an impediment, but only at the level of surface or vocabulary usage. The plots, intrigues, propositions, and sentiments are universally human. Indeed, it is a comforting thought to appreciate that the writings of an English playwright, who lived 400 years ago, are able to be made more vivid, accessible, and meaningful to students today through the responsible classroom use of modern computer capabilities.

Study guide questions

1 The advent of the electronic revolution and Internet in particular has not always met with approval from significant educators. Can you outline the critical or alarmist view here?

2 Maryanne Wolf has noted how students with learning disabilities can present with problems associated with reading digital media. How does she explain the nature of the problems she has identified?

3 So which is true? Digital media enhances student capabilities, or digital media dulls student thinking? What sort of evidence might apply to such an issue?

4 Is it possible for experience with the electronic media to actually alter human brain organisation? Does the ready availability of the Information Superhighway alter the way we can think and feel?

Reference notes

- An alarmist view that technologies may undermine human mental efficiency (Birkerts, 1994, p.139).

- E-reading may discourage thoughtful reading and deep comprehension (Wolf, 2007; Wolf & Barzillai, 2009). These essays provide a general perspective, but with a special focus upon the poor reader.

- Quotations from respected reading researcher, Dr Maryanne Wolf, taken from *The New York Times*, 6 September 2007, and 14 October 2009, accessed via http://roomfordebate.blogs.nytimes.com/2009/10/14/does-the-brain-like-e-books/ (accessed 20 May 2013).

- Basically, font type is irrelevant to comprehension: on the surface this contradicts findings we cite in Chapter 30, to the effect that difficult-to-read font pre-empts impulsivity in jumping to wrong conclusions. But the underlying factor is prior knowledge or familiarity. When font is familiar, one reads fast, when it is not, one reads slowly.

- Internet as the 'shallows' (Carr, 2010).

- Within the medical literature, the 'Full text only' or FUTON bias is described in http://en.wikipedia.org/wiki/FUTON_bias. We note the irony in that tools such as Wikipedia provide the means by which FUTON operates.

- Dr Goldsmith's essay ('If it's not on the Internet, it doesn't exist'): http://epc.buffalo.edu/authors/goldsmith/if_it_doesnt_exist.html (accessed 20 May 2013).

23

How music impacts on learning

Making and listening to music is one of the most pervasive aspects of human life. Music infuses our world, providing us with rich and emotional experiences. From the earliest days of our life, our attention is drawn to our parents' singing, which provides comfort and assurance. The maternal lullaby is a near universal feature of human cultural life. Research has consistently shown infants and toddlers are drawn to the melodic properties of the voice. The brain and auditory system are set up to attend closely to human singing, and it is now believed this predisposition plays a role in infant–parent bonding.

A visit to any child-care centre reveals that singing and making musical sounds form a significant part of the day. Many of us spend a proportion of our earnings on musical entertainment. Music infuses the media since virtually every television program has signature tunes. Musical edits feature in drama productions although you have little awareness of how your emotions are being manipulated. Try to imagine what films such as *Chariots of Fire*, *Rocky*, *Out of Africa*, or *Dances with Wolves* would be without their rich musical scores. The core value of music lies in emotional expressions of human activity, representing one of our most significant cultural inventions.

So what can cognitive research tell us about the relation between musical activity and human learning? When it comes to thinking about the role of music in the classroom, three lines of research are pertinent, which we will review through addressing the following questions:

1 What is the effect of background music?
2 Does listening to music affect our brains? Can it help us learn or perform better?
3 Does music instruction have any benefits for student learning in non-musical areas?

What is the effect of background music?

It has been established that background music can influence people's movements, such as how fast they walk, or their general tempo. Nevertheless, there appears to be no overall relationship between the presence of background music and actual learning when people are engaged on non-musical tasks. People do not learn any better or worse because of the gentle music playing quietly in the background. At times, however, music can become intrusive and detract from learning. If the situation is one demanding attention, or there is a test or examination to be undertaken, it would be unwise to introduce music into the situation. When you need to focus hard, music can become both an irritant and a source of distraction. On the other hand, music can be used to alter mood states, especially when used as a device for calming and relaxation. Listening to such music can induce positive emotions and make a situation more conducive for many individuals.

Some children will benefit from applications of music therapy, especially when asked to persevere on tasks that might otherwise be seen as demanding. For example, in one study, singing familiar songs was shown to help young students become more creative in their artwork. More out of curiosity, we note one study that found people's driving performances improved when they were allowed to listen to their preferred music CDs. In addition, there are a substantial number of studies indicating positive benefits for music in medical settings. For instance, one review concluded that patients receiving music therapy after invasive surgery evidenced lower anxiety, and required lower levels of analgesic medication.

Can listening to certain types of music, such as Mozart, alter our brains to help us perform better?

One issue that has attracted attention in recent years became known as the *Mozart effect*. It was claimed that listening to a part of Mozart's piano sonata K.448 for 10 minutes would improve people's performances on aspects of the IQ test, specifically spatial reasoning. This was first claimed in an article in the prestigious journal *Nature* in 1993. But claims got out of hand with publicists asserting such treatment would boost IQ scores by some eight to nine points. Commercial products were licensed and marketed under the banner 'Mozart Effect' and the term was copyrighted by an enterprising businessman. Extraordinary claims about its beneficial effect on the mental well-being of infants, pre-schoolers, school children, and college students were advanced. The development of the Internet provided a huge boost to the popularity of this effect. The finding seemed to tap straight into deeply seated cultural ideas about the value of music, now given an apparent scientific basis.

The claims advanced sometimes took on a comical twist such as suggesting that babies who hear Cosi Fan Tutte in gestation could emerge from the womb smarter than their peers. Beneficial effects were attributed to many forms of classical music. Listening to such music was said to 'resonate' within the brain, as though to activate dormant neurons that could then yield an extra IQ boost. Students were recommended to listen to Baroque music before proceeding into study, to enable their minds to become more receptive. This was a means to open up their untapped potential. Fuelled by such claims, in 1998, three American states mandated that classical music be played to young children in their local educational institutions. At that time there was much debate as to which types of music might trigger the Mozart effect and which might not. In truth, there was no substantive effect.

Descriptions and analyses of how the myth of the Mozart effect developed are covered in depth in two sources, Bangerter and Heath (2004), and Lilienfeld, Lynn, Ruscio, and Beyerstein (2010). Bangerter and Heath found that 80 per cent of Americans were familiar with the effect, and in another survey at that time it was found that three-quarters of university students believed the Mozart effect was a validated phenomenon. Later, in 2010, Chabris and Simons asked 1,500 Americans, a community sample, if 'Listening to music by Mozart will increase your intelligence'. They found 40 per cent said it would.

The reality is that the Mozart effect remains well researched but unproven. Several key literature reviews have been published, reviewing scores of published studies, with data from several thousand research participants. These data establish that listening to classical music may help to keep you alert and awake, but will not boost your intelligence. Researchers now see the Mozart effect as an artefact of what is called arousal. Anything that prevents you from drifting off can assist in keeping you motivated. Intrinsically, the validity of the Mozart effect has nothing to do with listening to music. Lilienfeld *et al.* suggest a similar effect is achieved through drinking a cup of coffee. In reviewing the various myths that pervade popular psychology they labelled the Mozart effect as popular myth No. 6.

Does music instruction have any benefits for student learning in non-musical areas?

This third issue is one that has intrigued many writers over the past century. Since instruction in music involves high levels of commitment, practice and goal setting, all taking place under highly disciplined conditions, then does this type of instruction provide a learner with generalised intellectual benefits? Music lessons take place in the context of a formal curriculum with graded exercises, precisely defined goals, subtle discriminations, continuous feedback, and excellent exemplars. Feedback is both external, and self-administrated in that students are able to appraise their level of progress for themselves quickly and easily.

This issue is especially interesting in that, unlike the Mozart effect (which makes an appeal to extraordinary neurological mechanisms), the idea that music lessons may assist academic learning could be based on sound psychological principles. This could be an issue of what is called far transfer. That is, attributes such as effort exertion, self-control, precise matching, metacognitive monitoring, studying worked examples, and other mental strategies could underpin skill development in both music and other skill areas. No one would suggest that learning music is a method for remedial education. But the idea that disciplined practice in music may have additional spin-offs in non-musical areas remains a serious hypothesis.

It has been found repeatedly that students who practise music a good deal tend to perform well in school and have higher IQs. However, it has also been found that the more intelligent a child, the more likely he or she is to receive music lessons. In the context of the available studies, such links are well-nigh impossible to untangle since many variables are implicated such as family background, wealth, and availability of music tutors. Nevertheless, there is some evidence that participation in music training can have benefits beyond learning music. In one recent Canadian study, 4- to 6-year-old children participated in a 20-day computerised program for music listening, pitch, and melody. Compared to others, these students showed significant gains on two intellectual tests, a vocabulary test and a measure of inhibitory control.

Although controversial, the idea that music training has cognitive benefits for students is gathering supportive evidence. For example, one researcher, Sylvain Moreno, has been able to demonstrate links between children's experiences in music, their auditory skills, and making fine-grain discriminations in second language learning.

IN PERSPECTIVE: Weighing the evidence

Music is a fundamental part of our world. Whether or not we so choose, its presence makes an impact on how we think and feel. It is used in many forms of gatherings, ceremonies, and *rites de passage*. The background music we hear has been shown to influence how we move. It can make us walk faster or slower, or help us ponder choices in the shopping mall. When you feel sick or are recovering from medical interventions, your choice of music can help ameliorate your condition. It may even help you to drive long distances through increasing your arousal level.

But music has no special impact on learning capability. When we are really making an effort to learn, the presence of music is more likely to be distracting. The notion that certain types of Baroque music will stimulate the mind, or unlock unused potential, turns out to be an irresponsible overstatement based on misrepresenting an experimental report that could not be replicated.

On the other hand, a number of studies point to possible beneficial effects that may accrue when young children undertake structured music lessons and practice. The database is slim, and the effects may not be strong. However, the notion that the formal learning of musical conventions can assist the young mind in thinking and learning beyond the music curriculum represents an intriging idea that invites further research.

Although some theorists have speculated that music practice could assist mental development directly, it may be that its effect could extend moreso to notions of self-control and willpower. Music practice often has a student practising a highly structured activity when he or she might otherwise be engaged in pleasurable but less productive leisure activities. Hence, if there are any developmental spin-offs, they may lie in connection with personal control and self-discipline, coupled with the feeling of contingency between effort and achievement. Indeed, these are difficult traits for many students to absorb.

Study guide questions

1 How do we know that sensitivity to sounds and music is central to our human existence?

2 Listening to beautiful music, such as Mozart K448, can have beneficial effects on many aspects of human adjustment and fulfilment. Can it help with our learning and intelligence?

3 Just what is the central assumption underpinning the Mozart effect? What mechanisms were said to exist? Just why do you suppose so many people were taken in by this theory?

4 Should we introduce music into our schools? When can music help?

5 It is possible that training in music may have a beneficial impact upon mental skills even outside the music field. If so, what aspects of music education could be important? Could the impact represent both direct and indirect effects?

6 It has been shown that students who study and practice music a good deal tend to do well in school. But why is such a finding very difficult to interpret?

Reference notes

■ Infants and toddlers are drawn to the melodic properties of the voice (Trehub, 2001).

■ The effects of background music are reviewed in Črnčec, Wilson, and Prior, 2006. Literature review concerning the role of music in alterring human feelings and behaviour (Kämpfe, Sedlmeier, & Renkewitz, 2011).

■ Music can be played to have a calming effect in classrooms (Hallam, Price, & Katsarou, 2002). Singing familiar songs implicated in helping students become creative in artwork (Schellenberg, Nakata, Hunter, & Tamoto, 2007).

■ Intrusive music has negative effects on reading comprehension and deliberate memorisation when people need to focus (W. F. Thompson et al., 2012).

- Beneficial effects on driving when listening to chosen music (van der Zwaag *et al.*, 2011).

- Music therapy helps patient recovery (Rudin, Kiss, Wetz, & Sottile, 2007).

- Analyses of the myths concerning the Mozart effect (Bangerter & Heath, 2004; Chabris & Simons, 2010; Lilienfeld *et al.*, 2010). Review of scientific literature debunking the Mozart effect (Pietschnig, Voracek, & Formann, 2010).

- Internet sources for the Mozart effect: http://mozarteffect.com and www. howtolearn.com/products/mozart-effect.

- The above two websites promote ideas at variance with the known data. However, the following three sites provide sensible commentary: http://en. wikipedia.org/wiki/Mozart_effect; www.psychologytoday.com/blog/your-musical-self/201005/the-mozart-effect-doesnt-work; www.skepdic.com/mozart. html.

- Students who practice a good deal of music have higher IQs, but students with higher IQs are more likely to participate in music instruction and practice (Schellenberg, 2011).

- Young children participated in a 20-day program for music (Moreno *et al.*, 2011). Links between music training and second language discriminations (Moreno, 2009).

Know thyself

24

Confidence and its three hidden levels

It would be silly to ask if a machine can perform its operations confidently. But when it comes to human activity, *confidence* is a term we all use freely. We admire television personalities for their confident manner. We discover, after we have been doing a job for a while, that we become far more confident. At times, we lack confidence, and try to prevent others from sensing this reality. Other times, we may even advertise low confidence, perhaps as a means of social reassurance, team building, or personal defensiveness. Confidence is both something we feel, on the inside, and something we display to others. Within any social situation, confidence is something that we quickly sense within other people.

In the classroom, students exhibit confidence, or perhaps display its absence. When a student answers a question, we infer a level of confidence from vocal expression and behavioural signs such as latency or speed of response. Although being knowledgeable, clever, and correct are correlated with confidence, there are many times when an individual will display **overconfidence**. Several studies have shown that boys, more so than girls, tend to report higher levels of academic confidence than would be justified objectively. For example, on multiple choice tests, girls often are found able to judge when they are incorrect. On the other hand, boys tend to be relatively confident even on those items they are getting wrong. Whenever it comes to deciding whether or not to enter competitions, boys are more inclined to push themselves forward than girls. The underlying factor has been found to be confidence, with higher levels in boys, even when ability differences are negligible.

As teachers, often we evaluate students on the level of confidence they exhibit. When diagnosing what our students know, we are tuned to pick up information from voice and behaviour. We use this as feedback to tell us how to proceed. Even when a student is answering probes apparently correctly, we want that student also to show strong confidence before we proceed into more complex territory. The student must get it right, must know he or she is getting it right, and must able to apply and extend this knowledge. Since the process of knowledge building is inherently cumulative, we need to hear confidence in the student's voice to be assured that strong foundations are in place. Parroting back superficial, low-level answers, in the absence of confidence, implies a need for more time investing in revision and consolidation work.

But aside from our own perception, we have almost no secure index of what it means to be confident. The term is confusing in that we use the same word to refer to different phenomena in slightly different ways. Within the history of motivational psychology, we readily identify three distinct ways, or levels, in which confidence has been investigated. The three levels of confidence are the (a) global level of **self-esteem**, (b) domain level of **perceived competency**, and (c) task-related level, often called **self-efficacy**.

Global personality confidence: your self-esteem

Our global self-esteem involves beliefs about our own self-worth. This is one part of our overall personality. There are several well-respected questionnaires researchers use to tap into global self-esteem. The questions used are ones that are deliberately abstract and holistic such as, 'I take a positive view of myself', and, 'On the whole, I am satisfied with myself'. Some items are expressed negatively, such as, 'I feel I do not have much to be proud of'. It is important to note how such statements avoid referring to context. Instead, they are written to be as general as possible, to tap into higher-level feelings that people harbour about their personal worth across situations.

Research into self-esteem has been both prolific and fruitful over the past 50 years, and a number of findings are evident. People with high scores on these general self-esteem measures also report being happy and productive, which is perhaps not surprising given that they can see ample evidence as to why they should 'back themselves' in their self-beliefs. These are individuals who expect to succeed and are accustomed to success as a natural default condition in terms of their expectations about themselves. Correlational studies show links from self-esteem to many positive traits such as school achievement, sociability (i.e., being liked by others and having friends), reduced anxiety, robust mental health, and positive social attitudes. These correlations are not always statistically strong, but they are often found. Overall, having high levels of self-esteem has to be seen as a strong sign that the individual enjoys life, is achieving goals, is actively pursuing worthwhile activities, and is seen by others as being a successful human being.

So is self-esteem then the logical target of educational endeavours? Is it our professional role to develop our students' self-esteem and promote such a trait wherever possible? Such ideas represent theories widely popular from the 1960s through to the present day. The idea is that self-esteem is the central part of the personality, the important core that requires nurturance. If we can develop positive self-regard in our students, other positive outcomes such as motivation, social responsibility, and achievement, will follow. In the 1970s, one version of the theory had it that raising self-esteem through programs within schools would alleviate societal problems such as teenage pregnancies, crime, drug abuse, and poverty. In essence, every social problem can be ascribed to people's lack of self-regard. The theory is interesting, optimistic, challenging, but wrong.

Cracks in self-esteem theory

The trouble with such an approach has been that of ugly data. From the 1970s on, studies began to show that self-esteem increase is the natural outcome of successful life adjustment, rather than being its root cause. For example, in schools, when students achieve well, increases in self-esteem will tend to follow, rather than precede the gains in learning. In a significant review, a group headed by Professor Roy Baumeister writing in the journal *Psychological Science in the Public Interest* in 2003, exposed the myths that underpin self-esteem theory. They surveyed a wide body of data and arrived at the remarkable conclusion that

> most of the evidence suggests that self-esteem has no impact on subsequent academic achievement. The few studies suggesting any positive causal impact of self-esteem generally found only tiny effects. Some findings even point (again weakly) in the opposite direction, suggesting that high or artificially boosted self-esteem may detract from subsequent performance.
>
> (pp. 13–14)

Another issue is that remarkably few individuals can be located who genuinely present with objectively low self-esteem within the general population. When you carefully examine what people say on the survey instruments, it is difficult to locate individuals who score under the half-way mark. Within normal, or non-clinical, populations, there appears not to be any serious problem as to lack of self-esteem. We note there is a body of research as reviewed by Jean Twenge, suggesting that narcissistic tendencies (being in love with oneself) have been steadily increasing over the past 25 years, along with both desirable and undesirable correlates. Our language embodies many words suggesting negative aspects related to such elevated self-esteem, for example, smug, conceited, arrogant, and boastful.

But more sobering has been the uncovering of the dark side to elevated self-esteem. Researchers have documented that many aspects of social pathology such as crime, delinquency, amoral conduct, inconsiderate behaviour, aggression, narcissism, lack of inhibition, sexual experimentation, and social prejudice, have at times been found to link up with elevated levels of self-esteem. Of course such things are not the result of high esteem but when in potential conflict with others on this planet, those with high self-esteem typically are less afraid of acting in self-interest.

As an example of this type of research, consider the *in-group bias effect*, which is the tendency to act more favourably towards people close to you, such as immediate family and friends, as against the interests of anyone not close to you. Such biases have been found in the case of people with high self-esteem. The hope, as expressed by early theories of self-esteem, was that positive regard for the self would translate across into enhanced social responsibility. This hope has been destroyed by the accumulated findings. As a target for community and educational reform, individual self-esteem is an unlikely and uncertain candidate since people with high self-esteem appear more likely to act out of self-interest than those with a lower sense of self-importance.

Confidence through your perceived competencies

The second major way we normally use the term confidence concerns what you feel you are 'good at'. You can mentally divide your skills into different areas. Are you good at maths? How are you at tennis, or chess, or driving, or swimming? Would you feel comfortable about having to socialise with strangers, or being asked to take a senior position in your school? At this level we are still talking about large areas of functioning, or what researchers refer to as 'domains'. Thus, there is the mathematics domain, the verbal domain, the various sports domains, but also broad areas such as the interpersonal domain, or the domain associated with your employment.

We can back ourselves in many ways. Criminals pride themselves on their ability to pick locks, evade detection, and have loyal bonds to mates; water polo goalies back themselves on egg beating high out of the water, flexibility of upper body, and anticipation of where other players are. Such people can have high self-esteem but this does not, for example, translate into higher academic achievement. Only when one backs oneself as a learner or high achiever would you expect self-esteem to be related to achievement.

In the research studies, **perceived competencies** are measured by asking people to respond to questionnaires concerning how good, competent, or clever they feel about themselves and their skill in area X, and area Y, and so on. Just because you are good at X does not imply you are good at Y. Particularly when children move into adolescence they tend to move from 'being good at everything' to backing themselves in fewer domains. Each individual will have a profile of competencies. For example, one might feel oneself to be good at tennis and mathematics, but not good at basketball, or at talking to strangers.

One curious aspect of perceived competencies is that often they do not line up well against actual indices of the same competencies. We have natural tendencies to see ourselves as better than others will rate us. This inflation effect is especially strong in the absence of any genuine feedback data about just how good we are. If there is a shadow of doubt about what feedback implies, our egos can inflate to fill such gaps quickly and with conviction. This issue is discussed in depth in the next chapter describing **self-enhancement** effects.

What is the relationship between your global self-esteem, and your perceived competencies? It depends on how valuable a skill is seen to be within your social world. For example, we both can get through life reasonably well feeling useless at tennis; one of us feels he is good at cricket, and has spent many years taking responsibility for coaching and umpiring players; and both of us feel we are 'okay at writing', largely because of the world we inhabit professionally.

Suppose you feel that you are 'not good at academics', but were born into a high-achieving academic family. Your self-esteem may suffer because of a mismatch between the values in your natural family and your perception of your competencies. On the other hand, your academically successful sibling was exposed to a social world highly conducive to his or her positive self-image.

Your overall self-esteem cannot necessarily provide you with domain-related confidence. Having overall high self-esteem is irrelevant to how confident you feel about painting your house. However, it is the case that, as students succeed in school, they naturally develop an overall *academic self-concept* as school can be such an important part of their whole life. We want our students to have confidence, pride, and expectations of success as learners, so developing academic self-concept is crucially important. This aggregate about how they feel about competency in school is implicated in making students more motivated and attentive, which leads to higher levels of achievement in school subjects. It is this gained sense of self that can provide buffers and coping strategies that permit even more learning (especially in the face of failure to learn, difficulties in immediate understanding). When students can say, with evidence, 'I am a learner', it is more likely they will invest in learning, and get pleasure from learning. It is indeed a virtuous cycle.

The third level: self-efficacy on the task

Efficacy is an old English word meaning to achieve an effect, or to accomplish. It was reintroduced into common language in the early 1970s through spectacular research published by Albert Bandura of Stanford University. Self-efficacy is indicated by one's confidence level about being successful on the next task on your life agenda. Hence, this level is not so much domain-related as it is task-related. Instead of being something you can carry around with you (such as your esteem and perceived competencies), your efficacy is confidence for succeeding on the very task you can see there in front of you.

Hence, this aspect of confidence is an actual judgment, made in real time, rather than a feeling about what type of person you think you are. Also note how this form of confidence is not about your being 'good at' anything. Instead, it is your expectancy that you will cope well with the task you can see, in the here-and-now, or within the immediate future.

Your efficacy is going to be informed by your competencies, certainly. But it is still something quite different. We might feel we are 'good at athletics', but when it comes to running 100 metres in under 12 seconds, we lack any level of self-efficacy or confidence to meet this expectation. We know we are likely to fail, irrespective of effort. Self-efficacy is tied to actual contexts and realistic goals. Hence, being unable to achieve one specific goal at one specific time is unlikely to affect your esteem or competencies unless a catastrophic interpretation is being placed upon the failure.

To exert effort in life implies (a) weighing up the task as being worthwhile for you and then (b) deciding '*Yes, I can do that*'. You cannot make such judgements in the abstract. Instead, efficacy hinges on a careful analysis of the situation, and generating a realistic assessment. Note how this implies genuine sensitivity to the context of the problem. One's chronic self-views, such as elevated self-esteem and perceived competencies, run the huge risk of creating misleading assessments should the task be too difficult. There is little point in beginning an important task when failure is the inevitable outcome.

Rather than involving knowledge of *how* to do something, self-efficacy implies deciding whether one *can* do something. But researchers have documented that actual ability and self-efficacy beliefs are far from being perfectly aligned. Among individuals of similar ability levels there are still large differences found within their efficacy or confidence assessments. Some individuals appear to hold themselves back from challenges, perhaps underestimating their capabilities. Others will push themselves forward, in a manner that suggests they overestimate their actual competencies.

Distinguishing genuine self-efficacy from grandiose self-affirmations

Grandiose statements such as *I can do everything*, or *No such word as can't*, are not genuine markers for, and should not be confused with, self-efficacy. The essence of efficacy is that it is genuinely task-related, and so it becomes almost the opposite of many such global notions. Ideas such as *I can do anything* may be vacuous or silly, depending on context. Nevertheless, a level of **self-affirmation** can often help people sustain persistence over time, through inducing them to stay focused, rather than accept defeat after a minor failure. We will discuss this aspect in the next section.

The common procedure used in the research into self-efficacy is not the questionnaire, but involves presenting a task in terms of progressively increasing difficulty levels. The person is then asked if he or she could be successful, or not, at each level. With this test format, it is found that people will make personal efficacy assessments within a second or so of appraising the demands of the task. Typically, the response is either, *Yes, I can do that*, or *I don't think I can do that*.

The efficacy assessment is the first thing your mind does whenever it sees a task that will need your attention and participation. Making a positive efficacy assessment then enables four immediate outcomes: (a) a willingness to undertake the task even when known to be difficult, (b) mobilisation of available effortful resources to match the perceived difficulty level, (c) a willingness to increase effortful resources in response to setbacks, and (d) the person's attentional focus shifts onto the demands of the task rather than dwelling on personal or emotional reactions.

Although a blatant cliché, the phrase *When the going gets tough, the tough get going*, or *I think I can, I think I can, I know I can*, conveys much of the essence of self-efficacy. This is how the concept of challenge enters into situation – most of us welcome challenges provided we have a reasonable level of self-efficacy that we can meet them, and then we can invest in the task of meeting the challenge. There is a kind of Goldilocks principle at work – the challenge cannot be too easy but it cannot be completely out of our reach.

The psychology of striving with confidence

So where does your self-efficacy come from? At base it is unrelated to your self-esteem, although it relates to your perceived competencies when the task falls within a relevant domain. But the one dominant factor that drives your self-efficacy is your *memory*. To feel confident about the next task, you must be able to activate *knowledge* about similar tasks you were successful on in the past. You are not recalling your success, however, as much as you are remembering the underlying knowledge schemata that enabled you to be successful. So the critical memory is not 'I did well in the past', but, 'This task means using knowledge I can access quickly'. **Ease of access** to knowledge is the one key element in self-efficacy, which is why it takes a second or so for the mind to arrive at a judgement.

Very often your knowledge can be activated through observing and identifying with other people. In early work in the 1980s, Albert Bandura and his research group found young students could gain a sense of self-efficacy through observing peers work on difficult problems. Exposure to a successful model is an excellent way to encourage a person to believe he or she can be successful as well. But there needs to be in place a good reason why the model is appropriate to the individual. Exposure to a high-performing model becomes discouraging if the difference in skill (e.g. novice vs expert level) is made salient. Again the Goldilocks principle needs to be at work – not too easy and not too hard. Models can influence you because they are like you, not because of the differences that can be seen to exist.

Studies have also found it is possible to boost a child's self-efficacy through some types of verbal exhortation. But there is a trick here. Simply telling a student *'You can do it'* is not an appropriate message if it conflicts with what this young person is telling him or herself. Such messages only work once they convey meaningful information such as 'I know you can do these problems as they are just like the ones you did last week, but a bit harder, that's all'. Encouragement works, not so much through persuasion, as it does though jogging the right memories at the right time. If you have been successful in the past, there is every reason to assume it will continue.

Consider statements such as 'I believe in you and expect big of you', and 'I know you are a worthwhile person who can succeed at anything you try'. Unfortunately, these ideas sometimes can be rooted more in emotional blackmail than in genuine encouragement. If a person harbours self-doubts, then such messages may add to the mental confusion experienced, but without offering constructive resolution. The trouble is that strong self-efficacy has to be based on accessing and activating the fundamental knowledge needed to be successful.

Nevertheless, there is still room in the mind for a degree of **self-affirmation**. This is where the encouragement stems not from outsiders, but from yourself, as first person. Ideas such as 'I can do this' or 'I am a competent and worthwhile person', or 'I should not accept defeat', or 'I have succeeded in other things in life', will play a role in keeping a person motivated and striving to move forwards. When you experience difficulties, quietly rehearsing self-affirmations can serve to help you regroup and recalibrate your efforts. But, once again, it is vital that affirmations have a basis in reality, indexed by genuine past accomplishments being recalled. Obviously, there is a fine line between making realistic self-affirmations and grandiose ideas such as 'I can do anything'. The critical element is whether or not the affirming idea has a genuine basis in your memory.

Calibrating our strivings

Our ability to calibrate or estimate the difficulty of a task, the amount of investment we need to make, and our probability of success is critical to making decisions to learn. If we underestimate the difficulty, investment, or probability we are likely to give up and say we cannot do it – and if we overestimate we are likely to say it was too easy, and can lose the excitement of being challenged. We know from a synthesis of more than 900 meta-analyses that student self-expectations, or the degree to which they estimate their results from a task are among the most powerful influences in schooling. If we calibrate our success on an up-coming test to be about the same as the time before we may not invest extra learning – thus one of the major roles of teachers is to help students exceed their expectations! Too often students (like us all) set safe targets when we face tests of our ability, and teachers are needed to provide us with evidence, support and encouragement that we can exceed our expectations.

When we calibrate our possible performance we are setting a gap between where we think we are now and where we expect or want to be. In too many classroom situations, learners have little or no knowledge of the standards or success criteria of lessons and thus default to calibrating their performances to their current levels. This is why success criteria or worked examples can assist in recalibrating current conceptions of proficiency. We certainly do not want students saying 'this is just too hard' or 'I can't do this', as then any new learning will be seen to merely confirm these efficacy beliefs. Instead we want a virtuous cycle of learning – where the calibration of success is sufficiently above their current level of achievement, and thence they are likely to invest in learning, strategise, seek help and persist in learning to attain the goal, and thus gain the evidence that their efficacy beliefs about themselves were correct.

There are many ways we can teach students to improve their calibrations and efficacy of learning judgments. We can focus the learners' attention on valid cues when judging learning – showing them what supports their beliefs and what does not; we can provide learners with worked examples so they know what success looks like both in terms of illustrating the gap between where they are and where they need to be, and so they know 'when they get there'; we can be clear about their current knowledge (inaccurate understanding of current knowledge can be a barrier as much as not knowing that one's current knowledge is inaccurate or only partially correct); we can assist the students through the power of diagnosis of current learning and appropriate feedback to reduce the gap between this current and desired learning; and we can reteach if the information is still not learned.

The value of overconfidence

So should adaptive self-efficacy always match actual ability or capacity? Well, no! Self-appraisals need not be accurate to be highly motivating. Research into aspirational levels suggests it can be totally healthy to have a slightly exaggerated view of one's ability. This becomes especially true if one can pull back without excessive penalty. A degree of overconfidence is a normal aspect of human behaviour that will motivate a person to improve skill level up to match self-beliefs. For example, the student who believes she is 'good at maths' may seek out additional maths work, and persist doggedly on difficult problems, in order to achieve a higher level of understanding.

On the other side of this coin, under-confidence is linked with poor motivation. Self-efficacy is quickly implicated in vicious cycle effects. Low efficacy leads to insufficient effort, leading to poor performance, less mastery learning, which then reinforces the original efficacy perception. Breaking free of such circles, or self-traps, involves more than a few minutes of kindly advice or office-type counselling. Within classroom contexts, low efficacy can often have a basis in skill deficits or genuine knowledge gaps. Hence, addressing such deficits, through direct instruction and structured practice, is a viable means of enhancing efficacy. It is important to recall the findings we cited in connection with self-esteem research: that increases in general esteem follow on from success in school, but do not predict such success.

IN PERSPECTIVE: Educational implications

So what are the educational implications of this analysis? First, positive esteem and pride in oneself are commodities that can follow from being successful at learning. But one's esteem has to have a secure basis in reality. High self-esteem can be an indication of social and scholastic success, but raising self-esteem cannot necessarily raise school achievement. It is helpful to think of self-esteem metaphorically as a petrol gauge in a car. The gauge tells you the car will go far. But if the gauge is at a low point, it is little use moving the hands of the dial to make the car go any further.

Second, the crucial factor underlying confidence is the self-efficacy response, which in turn, hinges upon accessing awareness that the tasks you face in life are inherently doable. But the structure of knowledge within the world is complex. The curriculum we expect students to master is large, extensive, and based upon multiple and cumulative elements. As students, we each begin the journey with initial optimism. However, as the gradient of difficulty changes so does the basis of our confidence. Being able to perceive the links between what you did in the past, successfully, and where the journey is going today, is the only known path to maintaining confidence-based motivation and coping.

There can be two cycles of effect relating to confidence and the self. The vicious cycle involves convincing oneself that one cannot succeed on a task or challenge and thus not investing effort, not listening to instruction, and not receiving feedback, thus leading to evidence that one was right – one cannot succeed. The virtuous cycle involves convincing oneself that one might succeed on a task or challenge and thus invest effort, listen and even seek instruction, welcome errors as opportunities to learn, and receive feedback, thus leading to evidence that one was right. The way out of the vicious cycle is to keep demonstrating the value of investment, listening, seeking and receiving the power of feedback, and then providing evidence of the effects of these instructional cues to assist in moving to 'I think I can, I think I can, . . . I now know I can, I now know I can'.

In short, teachers play a vital role in helping their students achieve confidence in their ability to cope with the pressures of the modern school curriculum. In the following box we summarise a number of excellent teaching tactics implicated in stimulating and maintaining confidence in young learners.

HELPING YOUR STUDENTS DEVELOP THEIR ACADEMIC CONFIDENCE

The two major ways we influence students' confidence are through teaching and motivating.

First: use active teaching strategies

1 Use 'can do' language abundantly (i.e., everyone will learn, we expect this).
2 Use active direct teaching methods in short bursts, ensure that skills are beautifully taught with clarity, good methodologies, use of prior knowledge, well-mapped metaphors, and so on.

3 Ensure all students engage with materials. Ensure movement from 'easy' to 'harder'. Try to program scaffolds (e.g., hints, cues, prompts, additional research resources, or peers that help), so that all learners feel able to move forwards in your classroom.

Second: use active motivational strategies

4 Help students 'own' products of their academic work (e.g., projects, essays, maths working, maps, and so on). Ensure that everyone has products of which they can be proud.

5 Rather than focus on ability, subtly attribute success to effort. Convey the message that effort is cyclical, or comes in bursts. (I.e., effort is temporary, but infinitely renewable.)

6 Emphasise how current challenges actually do relate to past problems. Goals set today are building on the past. There are always common elements, prior knowledge, underlying schemata, and learning is always cumulative, ('I know you can do these because you did similar problems last week. These are a bit harder. Ok, but look, it's the same principle').

7 Ensure high levels of feedback serving a corrective function. Be careful not to overdo generalised praise ('You are such a wonderful person'). Any such praise has to be tied to reality, justified by the context, and appreciated by the recipient. In general, praise is an ineffective motivator.

8 Recognise the individuality of your students. Know them as real people with personal lives. They have likes, goals, values, jobs, and family responsibilities. Learn how to sit down next to individuals, to talk and listen. Make written notes, a file, of what you know of their likes and values. Such knowledge is invaluable in adjusting teaching in individual feedback and remedial work.

9 Directly teach healthy attributions. Do not get sucked into negative attributions or discussions about things such as 'I can't do maths', or 'I am useless'. Recognise that helplessness is often manipulative and produced in defence of self-worth. The problem for teachers is to avoid reinforcing self-defeating cognitions. If a student's learning failure has to be explained then teachers can cite one of the following diverse attributions: (a) lack of input (not paying attention, student missed lesson, concept just not taught well); (b) lack of practice (moving into harder materials too soon); (c) a gap in knowledge or 'buggy algorithms'; (d) lack of effort, possibly due to student getting life priorities unbalanced; (e) goals way too high, without short-term goals in place, hence a bridge too far.

10 One underlying principle to communicate is that ability simply is not fixed. Ability is the natural result of applied effort. Learning takes time, often far longer than

we expect. And so a sound strategy is to reset goals and expectations to realistic levels.

11 Actively discourage social comparisons, but, instead, emphasise goals in terms of personal progressions that take place over time.

Study guide questions

1 Why do most measures of overall self-esteem avoid asking questions about specific contexts or experiences?

2 List the positive attributes known to be associated with high levels of self-esteem.

3 High self-esteem can at times be associated with negative attributes. What are these negative attributes?

4 Is self-esteem enhancement an appropriate educational goal?

5 What is the relationship between self-esteem and one's perceived competencies? When do they converge? When are they likely to be quite unrelated?

6 Being able to activate self-efficacy is very different from one's self-esteem. What is the major decision involved when making self-efficacy judgements?

7 Once you make a self-efficacy judgement, four outcomes or consequences can immediately follow. What are they?

8 Sometimes encouragement can be used to assist students' self-efficacy. But if so, what crucial ingredient, or underlying message, must such encouragement convey?

9 Personal encouragement can stem from self-affirmation. How does self-affirmation differ from grandiose notions such as 'I can do anything'?

10 What are the well-established methods that teachers use to encourage confidence in students as learners?

Reference notes

■ Boys overconfident on tests (Lundeberg, Fox, & Punccohar, 1994).

■ Being under-confident, females avoid competition relative to males (Niederle & Vesterlund, 2011).

■ Self-esteem reflects positive life factors, but does not predict positive change (Baumeister, Campbell, Krueger, & Vohs, 2003; Emler, 2001; Leary & Guadagno, 2011).

- The dark antisocial side of high self-esteem (Baumeister, Smart, & Boden, 1996). In-group bias found in high self-esteem people (Aberson, Healy, & Romero, 2000; Jelić, 2009).

- Academic self-concept promotes school success (Marsh & O'Mara, 2008).

- Self-efficacy research (Bandura, 1977; Bandura & Schunk, 1981).

- Using exhortation to encourage effortful responding (Usher & Pajares, 2009).

- Self-affirmation (P. R. Harris, 2011; Schmeichel & Vohs, 2009).

- At times, overconfidence can be motivating (Johnson & Fowler, 2011; S. E. Taylor & Brown, 1988; S. E. Taylor, Lerner, Sherman, Sage, & McDowell, 2003).

25

Self-enhancement and the dumb-and-dumber effect

A key aspect to one's fulfilment is self-presentation. People who show outward signs of confidence are rated favourably by other people. What is 'on show' is dramatically important in life. For instance, it has been found that being seen as confident renders you more likely to be chosen as a leader, more likely to obtain a job, more likely to attract a romantic partner, more likely to have your advice taken seriously, and more likely to be viewed as trustworthy. Whenever you need to report or give evidence, then the level of confidence you are perceived to exhibit becomes a key determinant of how much weight people place upon your testimony. The extent to which people can effectively enhance their self-confidence increases the chance they will be able to influence other people, or be chosen for important roles. Whenever people are together, those who can appear to possess confidence, those who present well, quickly discover they enjoy a raft of social advantages.

People know that they are good

Considering the important role of self-presentation in life, it should come as little surprise to learn that several decades of research has uncovered considerable evidence for the phenomenon of **self-enhancement**. This refers to the individual's tendency to portray personal attributes in a positive light. In some of the classic work, it was found that about 80 per cent of people see themselves as excellent automobile drivers. Similar findings abound in all fields in which this aspect of self-regard has been investigated. For instance, in one study, 94 per cent of university lecturers saw themselves as above average in their work. Have you ever met a teacher who says 'I am a below average teacher'?

In one high school study, 60 per cent of the students declared they were in the top 10 per cent of people in terms of social skills. One leading researcher expressed such findings sardonically, 'On average, people think of themselves as anything but average. The average person claims to be more disciplined, idealistic, socially skilled, a better driver, good at leadership, and healthier than the average person. Mathematically, this cannot be right' (Dunning, 2006, p. 601).

In some studies people were asked if they were biased, and how biased they might be when compared to others. This is an inherently negative trait, so people do not lay claim to any such biases. They note that it is other people who are biased. People are biased to think that other people are biased. But such attributes, clearly visible in others, cannot apply to oneself . . . of course not!

Whenever the trait is a negative one, the self-enhancement process works in reverse. Negative traits are associated with other people, not oneself. When it comes to many negative aspects such as having or causing accidents, getting into disputes, or contracting diseases, people rate themselves as less likely to experience such things than the average person.

Why do we self-enhance?

When self-enhancement findings began to emerge in the social science literature, it was initially felt the effect could be a form of boasting, manipulative false-representation, or outright lying. A series of studies, however, showed that enhancement appears to be robust and genuine. When people are induced to answer honestly, where there is no reason to lie, or when unpleasant consequences could follow on from providing inaccurate self-assessments, then self-enhancement effects still remain. People really do believe they are better than others. At best, the follow-up studies show that we possess vague notions of what it means to be average. People have great difficulty in benchmarking the notion of 'average'. But whatever this average is, we all know that we are a great deal better.

Another key idea tested is that self-enhancement is a form of deception, even one of self-deception. This idea, however, is debatable. Studies have indicated that it is *not the case* that people quietly weigh up their 'true worth', and then discreetly add something extra. Deception would imply that the person *really knows* where he or she stands, and then reports something different. Nevertheless, the research suggests this explanation fails to account for why people think and feel so positively about themselves in the first place. When people rate or praise themselves, even in front of others, they commonly believe they are stating the truth as would be seen by any fair umpire.

Many people, including children, will afford themselves any opportunity to talk-up, exaggerate or boast, for example, by inflating achievements, whenever they sense an admiring audience. In such instances, the person is well aware truth is being twisted. But the chance of being unmasked is minimal. Many people are obsessed with attempting to impress others, and this is one of the defining aspects of narcissism. Even if this idea is too extreme for most of us, it is still true that we strive to leave other people with a positive impression about ourselves.

In general, people will admit to being close to average, but only on traits that do not matter. Take for instance, the ability to balance a pencil on its end. Being average on such tricks is immaterial, and we are happy to say we are average on these skills. But whenever the trait is seen as desirable, then the majority of people, worldwide, adults and children alike, lay claim to possessing this trait as their personal default condition. This tendency to claim positive attributes becomes especially strong when the trait in question is seen as being fixed, rather than being something inherently changeable.

We can accept the credit because we have earned it

How do we justify such feelings? Universal ownership of desirable traits is made possible through two intersecting factors: (a) ambiguity of our daily language, coupled with (b) the richness of our life experiences. Within our minds, language is the vehicle we use in our own reflections. *What does it mean to be an honest person?* Are you able to find evidence in your long-term memory that you have been, and will continue to be, an honest person? What other memories can you quickly activate? *Are you truthful? Can you be relied upon? Do you possess self-control?* The answers to self-relevant questions are not illusive.

And what of your professional qualities? *Are you an excellent teacher?* Does your memory allow you to locate evidence that you have performed with high professional standards? You have given superb lessons, well received, and which resulted in students learning a good deal. You can recall how your students expressed their warmth and gratitude for how you had assisted them. You did well because you are an excellent teacher. In retrospect, there are many instances when you acted in accord with high standards of professionalism. Not only are you an honest person with integrity, you are also a valued member of your professional fraternity.

In short, whenever a desirable attribute is cited, it is not difficult to access memories of incidents that fit the bill. Valid and indisputable evidence can be located. Within cognitive psychology terminology, we describe such memories as being **available** quickly, and so possess **ease of access**. These are important notions since these cognitive factors are implicated forcefully in how we construct our self-images. *Who are we? What attributes do we possess? Just how do we differ from other people? Are we good?* The sheer diversity and breadth of information locked away in the depth of your long-term memory provides rich personal data. Locating information in support of positive qualities is seldom problematic.

The possibility of self-assessment

Taking such ideas seriously leads to another key question: *To what extent is genuine self-insight possible?* Such an odd question! The individual's basic assumption has to be that he or she is in possession of unimpeachable self-knowledge. As Socrates advised: know thyself. You have been observing yourself for years. You must be a superb judge of your own character and competencies.

The data from numerous studies reveal that, when compared with objective indices, self-assessments are not only (a) poor, but (b) frequently turn out to be less accurate than assessments made by other people. Paradoxically, once you become familiar with another person, you are often able to predict his or her actions with a higher level of accuracy than that person can. The notion behind this statement has been supported in several remarkable studies by David Dunning of Cornell University. For instance, in one study, students' dormitory peers were better able to predict just who would do volunteer work in the future than were the individuals themselves. In other work, it was found that people are more accurate in predicting IQs and other test scores in other people, than they were in predicting their own scores.

Just what is going on here? In studies that examine the relationships between objective performances, self-assessments, and assessments made by other people, the assessments made by others align with objective performance measures more closely than self-assessments align with actual performance. For example, in university courses, students are able to predict other students' grades with some precision, much better than they can predict their own. Graduate students can predict how long their peers need to complete studies, but dramatically underestimate how long it takes themselves. Similar effects have been shown to occur in industry, office work, military training, and medical practice. This is not a mysterious process once it is appreciated that people are simply not very good in assessing their own actions and performance levels – primarily because we overestimate in our favour.

People approach the notion of self-assessment from a baseline of natural self-enhancement. On the other hand, observers can arrive at reasonably accurate predictions of how others are likely to behave, since they do not begin with this inflated default condition. It sounds strange, but if you do want an accurate prediction of how you might perform in a new situation, you may get one from someone who knows you. This insight, that others may know you better than yourself, is what research in social science has been consistently suggesting for several decades.

Our self-assessments go off track all too easily. The accuracy of self-assessment seems to hinge deeply upon whether or not accurate *feedback* is available within any given skill area. A major literature review found that within the area of athletics, where feedback is common, performance measures correlated with self-knowledge at 0.47, which is considered strong, very high indeed. For social skills the correlation was much lower at 0.17. This is a huge difference.

For managerial competence the correlation shows a zero relation. We repeat this interesting finding: that people who manage others in workplace situations appear, as a group, incapable of accurate self-assessment as to how well they function as managers. This issue, surely one of major concern in running a modern and just society, is reviewed in depth in a literature review paper written in 2004 by David Dunning, Chip Heath, and Jerry Suls, in the key journal *Psychological Science in the Public Interest*.

To sum up then, studies published over the past 50 years indicate that self-assessments and objective performance indices are, at best, poorly aligned. In many studies, they show almost no meaningful relationship. It is only in fields in which accurate and objective feedback is readily available (such as competitive chess and athletics) that self-assessments then begin to converge on, and then can reflect, more objective data.

The impact of chronic self-views on self-assessments

Your self-assessments are linked intimately to what you believe about yourself. Hence, given the absence of other data, it is natural for such assessments to reflect your overarching views, which are informed by the self-enhancement tendency we spoke of earlier. To put this more deeply, your self-image takes the form of things you know about yourself, in terms of three major areas: competency, morality, and lovability. You are a good person, who is inherently capable, and to know you is to love you.

These key ideas have three distinct psychological properties: these ideas are (a) chronic or enduring, (b) sacrosanct or unassailable, and (c) inherently positive. Whatever you are, you always secure in the knowledge that you are inherently a good person. Irrespective of circumstances, you will not change deep-down. No matter what happens around you, or what you are forced to do – you always will be you.

To gain insight into the centrality of our chronic self-images, it will help to read the description of personality as shown in the box below. This cleverly written material has been used in research over the past 60 years. The traditional finding in this area is around 80 to 90 per cent of people shown this paragraph, under guise of individualised assessment, will rate the material as valid and insightful for themselves, as unique individuals. When asked to rate how accurate people find this assessment, on a 5-point scale, the average rating score generally is just over 4 out of 5. The finding is called the **Barnum effect** (since one-size-fits-all), or sometimes the **Forer effect** after the researcher who created the script below in 1949.

THE BARNUM PERSONALITY PROFILE

You have a great need for other people to like and admire you. You have a tendency to be critical of yourself. You have a great deal of unused capacity which you have not turned to your advantage. While you have some personality weaknesses, you are generally able to compensate for them. Disciplined and self-controlled outside, you tend to be worrisome and insecure inside. At times you have serious doubts as to whether you have made the right decision or done the right thing. You prefer a certain amount of change and variety and become dissatisfied when hemmed in by restrictions and limitations. You pride yourself as an independent thinker and do not accept others' statements without satisfactory proof. You have found it unwise to be too frank in revealing yourself to others. At times you are extroverted, affable, sociable, while at other times you are introverted, wary, reserved. Some of your aspirations tend to be pretty unrealistic. Security is one of your major goals in life.

Note the use of statements that both push and pull. They will advance an idea, then retract the very same idea. The bases are covered, and all bets are hedged. You have capacity, but it is unused. You have aspirations, but they may not be realistic. You are both extroverted and introverted. You are an independent person, but you value social approval. It is not possible to disagree with such ideas. Although the self is a private entity, such descriptions are perceived to lift the lid. They do so because it is the very same lid for all of us.

Dumb-and-dumber effect

In the absence of feedback information, a person has little solid basis upon which to base self-knowledge. This natural tendency comes to a head in the following way to produce an interesting effect that is vital for teachers to appreciate. That is, *people who lack competence do not have any intrinsic basis for knowing how incompetent they are.* By default, incompetent people still feel they are comfortably above average. This effect is referred to as the *Dunning–Kruger effect*, after the two American researchers who first documented the finding through controlled research. More colloquially, it is called the *dumb-and-dumber effect*.

In one study, Dr Dunning and his group asked university students to estimate their scores on an important test upon leaving the examination room. For analysis purposes, they grouped students according to quartile groups, that is the bottom 25 per cent, two middle groups, and the top 25 per cent. The top students, as a group, scored more highly than they themselves had anticipated. Out of 40 points for this examination, these top students scored an average of 35, but had estimated their scores at 33. The bottom 25 per cent of students scored an average of 22 points, but estimated they had achieved 30 correct. The bottom students, sitting on average percentile ranks averaging around 12 per cent (by definition) assumed that they were well above average at the 60th percentile. In contrast, the top 25 per cent thought they were around the 77th percentile, when their actual level was a percentile rank of 87 (by definition).

To put this finding another way: students at the bottom of the class had no awareness that they were below average, and overestimated their test performance by some 20 per cent. They achieved 55 per cent but, at the moment

QUOTATIONS CONSISTENT WITH THE DUNNING–KRUGER EFFECT

Like a flawed painting, our self-image suffers from poor perspective: we consistently overestimate our skills and overlook our flaws.

Dunning, Heath, & Suls (American social researchers)

One of the painful things about our time is that those who feel certainty are stupid, and those with any imagination and understanding are filled with doubt and indecision.

Bertrand Russell (British philosopher,1872–1970)

Ninety per cent of the world's woes come from people not knowing themselves, their abilities, their frailties, and even their real virtues. Most of us go almost all the way through life as complete strangers to ourselves.

Sydney J Harris (American writer, 1917–1986)

There are three things extremely hard: steel, a diamond, and to know oneself.

Benjamin Franklin (American polymath, 1706–1790)

Real knowledge is to know the extent of one's ignorance.

Confucius (Chinese philosopher, 551–479 BC)

I am not ashamed to confess I am ignorant of what I do not know.

Cicero (Roman orator, 106–43 BC)

To be conscious of one's ignorance is a great step forward.

Benjamin Disraeli (British statesman, 1804–1881)

To admit ignorance is to exhibit wisdom.

Ashley Montague (British anthropologist, 1905–1999)

All you need in life is ignorance and confidence, then success is sure.

Mark Twain (American author, 1835–1910)

The way of the foolish man seems right to him; but the wise man gives ear to suggestions.

Proverbs 12: 15

Paradoxically, it is easier to construct a coherent story when there are fewer pieces to fit into the puzzle. Our comforting conviction that the world makes sense rests on a secure foundation: our almost unlimited ability to ignore our ignorance.

Daniel Kahneman (American psychologist, 2011, p. 201)

the test finished, had thought their test scores would be posted at 75 per cent. It was also found that even those students who had failed the test still left the room believing they were comfortably above average.

On the other hand, the top students were inclined to slightly underestimate their final scores. They failed to realise just how good they were, relative to their classmates. Other studies have shown that top performers often underestimate their achievement level whenever they find a task is easy for them. In such instances, they assume it was easy for others as well. This is a natural effect of your achieving a high skill level (see sections on expertise). As you become skilful, your perception changes, and you cannot appreciate how inherently difficult a task is for others. This factor, in turn, becomes another explanation for why experts in a field often experience trouble teaching beginners.

Swimming out of one's depth

The finding that incompetent people cannot gauge their incompetence, has been replicated a dozen times since the classic studies were reported by Dunning and Kruger in 1999. But, the effect is not specifically tied to incompetent people. Instead, it may be a more general outcome whenever attempting tasks excessively difficult for yourself. If you are out of your depth, then you do not realise how far you have strayed. Once out of your depth, you have no idea where the bottom is, but you can still tread water, albeit in a panic-laden state.

Here is the scenario, as it gets played out: tackling a truly difficult task produces excessive **cognitive load** that overwhelms your thinking, but also destroys your judgement. Nevertheless, you assume that you really are OK. Considering how tricky the assignment is, then you would not expect yourself to be getting it all perfect. However, you can still feel confident that you are doing okay – at least as okay as anyone within the same position. Even the occasional modest success sustains the illusion of basic competency. You know you are not perfect. But your chronic self-view also tells you that you are not stupid.

The overall explanation for the effect is that people who lack skills of production also lack skills of recognition. We can see this, for example, in children with poor written language skills. They are unable not only to write well-formed sentences, but are not in any position to judge the quality of their attempts or the attempts of other people. Such students do not set out to produce grammatically poor sentences. But lack of knowledge prevents them from making the appropriate metacognitive discriminations needed to distinguish adequate from inadequate products. Those who perform poorly cannot become good judges, since a judge needs to base his or her decisions on a secure knowledge base.

The key role memory plays in the dumb-and-dumber effect

One speculation is that it may be virtually impossible for individuals to think they are below average on a performance, a test, or an otherwise important attribute, largely because they have no memory content that clearly will signal 'failure'. The issue is one of memory **access** and **availability** which are constant themes with cognitive psychology.

Whenever a student completes a test or examination, and then reflects back on how he or she performed, there are three distinct data sources available, located through a gentle interrogation of the memory base. In turn, these memory sources can then drive three types of feelings. They are:

(a) the feeling that some test items were answered strongly, with deep, thoughtful answers, deserving of high credit (feeling type A),

(b) the feeling that some test items were answered superficially, but nevertheless some credit is deserved and must be given, out of fairness (feeling type B),

(c) an awareness that some items were not answered successfully, as they were not genuinely attempted (feeling type C).

Personal reflections of one's test performance are based directly on weightings given to the first two types of feelings. A balance can be located between these two possible anchor points. Since perfection cannot be expected, the low ability individual moves toward the ideas reflecting the second feeling type, that is type B. This means placing trust in the generosity of the marking system being used by the test administrator. The goal is not to demonstrate mastery, but to be 'good enough' to scrape through sufficient percentage points.

Since this is a benign and just world, credit will be given for any words dumped on that test page. Further, the mind recalls that it took much effort to write (i.e., 'cook up') those words on the day. Thus, you will pass that test because the world you know is inherently fair.

But the existence of the third type of feeling, type C, is one that is hard for anyone completing a formal test to get a fix upon. The problem concerns what a philosopher would call 'errors of omission'. The light is dim here. You cannot know what you cannot know. Lack of knowledge cuts you off from accurate assessments, and so getting such issues into perspective is impossible.

Within recent experience as university teachers, we had seen extreme reactions such as (a) a student crying having 'messed up' her exam as she did not know some questions, but on marking her paper, we found she had 88 per cent against the class average of 63 per cent; (b) being rung by one student saying he did not know the answers to 'a couple' of the final exam items. In fact, he had completed only quarter of the paper. In both cases, we had the impression that the students had no insight into how their actual performances measured up.

The idea behind the errors of omission problem is that one cannot account for what one does not know. As an amusing illustration, consider the following: *How many uses for WD-40 oil can you think of?* WD-40 is a commercial product, sold in spray cans, and universally available in retail stores. Many people might suggest 10 or 20 different uses. But the manufacturer's website details 2,000 uses. Being able to name 20 out of 2,000 might be seen as a 'good' or a 'bad' score, depending entirely on one's perspective and basis in knowledge. If you live in a world that expects you to know all about the value of WD-40, then a score of 20 can hardly be seen as a passing grade. But lack of knowledge itself prevents you from knowing just how poor this score of 20 stacks up.

Overall, is elevated self-image good or bad?

The body of studies into the universal phenomenon of self-enhancement needs to be taken seriously. It implies something is odd with self-assessment. The self has a fundamental problem in that its view is pre-configured. We come with built-in blind spots. There is no special entity called 'self-insight' which has any greater validity than assessments rooted in the realities acknowledged by other people.

This is a disturbing insight in that it casts doubt upon the first person (the 'me' or 'I' component), and that person's ability to advance propositions that would be endorsed by another. Beware the perpendicular pronoun. The first person holds a great deal of information, but the balance and sampling of perceptions is unique to that individual. Discrepancies between self-views and others' views of the self are inevitable, and provide one potential obstacle to many forms of social relationships.

We also note the existence of yet another effect as described in the social psychology literature. The **spotlight effect** is the feeling that oneself is, or should be, the centre of attention. An adolescent may walk into a room assuming all eyes are on him. It takes years for him to find out that others do not care. Egocentric biasing is also reflected in the way people rate their own contributions in group work situations. A group might collaborate and achieve a jointly shared goal. But when its individual members are asked to rate their own and others' contributions, huge discrepancies are found. People rate their own contribution considerably more highly than do the others.

That self-assessments are naturally elevated is not in itself a bad thing. In one sense, they reflect a level of health and happiness that is motivating, optimistic, and serves as a buffer against the inherent insanity, nastiness and loneliness of the world. There are good reasons to presume that individuals, your students included, should think well of themselves, should believe they are worthy human beings. They should hold self-images that they are benign, moral, honest and kind in disposition, and capable of good careful thinking and sensible decision-making.

One of the traits of depressed people is that they tend not to self-enhance. Imagine walking down the main street, for example, and seeing the evidence that no one will talk to you, recognise you, or have any interaction – the world is indeed a lonely place. The self-enhancing person would explain the same experience as 'they just do not know me and are courteous in not getting in my way'. This realism is often why counselling depressed people can be so difficult – they locate sources of evidence for their depression and often fail to self-enhance.

The self-image and social relationships

Self-images need to be positive, but holier-than-thou perspective is a gravely unsound strategy, one destined for social disaster. Huge problems emerge when your self-image begins to diverge from the perception and attitudes of key people within your world. While we may harbour a level of personal and private narcissism, it is an unattractive trait observed in someone else. As a teacher, this is one hard lesson you have to help individual students to recognise, in the goal of social integration and life skills.

To describe people in terms of 'loving themselves' is not a reference to their self-esteem, happiness level, or their disposition to share their good nature. Instead, it is seen as an impediment to maintaining a positive relationship. One interesting finding from personality psychology is that people who present with high scores on the Narcissistic Personality Inventory exhibit a revealing social pattern. They will make friends quickly, but have trouble keeping them for long. It has also been found they are well aware of this problem in life, but often are not motivated to change. They are accustomed to dealing with the world in terms of their own inherent superiority. In this sense, high self-esteem, accompanied with narcissism, becomes a personality liability, at least as far as the rest of the world is concerned.

Major issues surface when one individual's inherent sense of being good, virtuous, and above average in all things, is observed to define an individual's personality. You may feel somehow 'better' than others, but you cannot expect others to take kindly to any such notion. Learning to fit in with others means learning not to start telling them they are any less virtuous or competent than yourself. Instead, it entails learning to show deference and respect for them, and humility toward yourself. It will assist your social adjustment considerably when you sync your actions, gestures, and words to the models you can see and value around you (see Chapter 28 on being a social chameleon).

IN PERSPECTIVE: Helping students 'get real'

As a teacher and mentor, it is helpful to understand the research findings cited earlier, namely that unchecked self-judgements will sit closer to worthless than they do to perfection. The common finding is that what people think they know about certain topics, frequently will fall short, when matched against reality criteria. In the absence of objective data, the individual student's self-knowledge, as expressed verbally to you, must be seen as an unreliable data source upon which to base educational guidance.

Aside from narcissism, there are no intrinsic problems in harbouring elevated self-views. However, issues will arise whenever students' hopes and aspirations are defined in terms of the relatively unobtainable. When self-images are defined in terms of beating others, failure is guaranteed at some point. Competitiveness and **ego orientation** motivate people when they expect to succeed. But when frequency of available rewards is low, disappointment is inevitable for many. At this point recalibration of goals becomes psychologically necessary.

Recalibration of aspirations must entail slight adjustments to be made in relation to self-image. There is every reason to believe that behavioural motivation is strong when aspirations race slightly ahead of actual current abilities. It is perfectly healthy to advance expectations and goals that take you just beyond your comfort zone. But the question is one of sensible judgement and calibration. Just how far can you go? One does not need to win a gold medal, as getting to the Olympics is a remarkable achievement.

Finding one's place in life constitutes the most daunting enterprise every one of your students has to undertake. Helping an individual to understand the importance of valid feedback information in calibrating aspirational goals will play an important role in both (a) constraining the effect of natural self-enhancement and (b) preserving the integrity of the individual's feeling of self-worth. In the absence of apprehending appropriate feedback, the individual's aspirations and conscious simulations of reality will be given over solely to natural egotism, and this is not a secure basis for life fulfilment in any modern society.

ARE EGOS INFLATING OVER TIME?

Have you ever felt we could be living in the age of the Me generation, or Gen-Me? Has this emphasis on self-esteem and individualism gone too far? Is self-centredness the new norm? Are our young people becoming less caring, more egotistical, more expecting, more demanding, and more narcissistically self-loving? Within the United States, a remarkable debate has sprung up around such questions. Here are two informative titles we recommend:

Generation Me: Why today's young Americans are more confident, assertive, entitled, and more miserable than ever before, by Jean Twenge of San Diego State University (2007).

The Narcissism Epidemic: Living in the age of entitlement, by Jean Twenge and Keith Campbell, published in 2009.

The books are well-researched and disturbing to read as they examine trends within American society suggesting increasing levels of egotism and narcissism, as well as decreases in traits such as empathy and respect for authority. The books review the data in terms of psychometric questionnaire findings, and relate such findings to societal factors as well as to changing expectations of what it means to live a successful life.

Dr Twenge and her group (2008) reviewed data from 85 surveys published between 1979 and 2006, in which 16,000 university students had completed the Narcissistic Personality Inventory. This questionnaire gives people 40 possible chances to select a narcissistic response when asked to choose ways to describe oneself. Scores rose progressively over the 27-year period, indexing an effect size of .33, or around a 14 per cent increase in mean scores over time. The increase appeared stronger for females to the point where they caught up with the male level over the time period. Similarly, another research group, headed by Sarah Konrath of Michigan University, has documented decreases in empathy over time (Konrath *et al.*, 2011). Especially disturbing is her finding that over time, young people were indicating a reduced willingness to attempt to see others' perspectives.

There is an opposing view: that such psychometric data trends reflect more what educated young people (university students) say about themselves, rather than index genuine changes in human dispositions. When it comes to commenting on social trends, there is the ever-present problem of overstatement and oversimplification. We can have perceptions stemming from our own window on the world. But the extent to which such perceptions represent general trends, or shifts in human dispositions, always needs to be questioned. We note there is a respected view that modern societies are more democratic, moral, and far less brutal, than societies throughout history (e g. Pinker, 2011).

However, if you are querying if young people today are cultivating attitudes somewhat different from your own generation, then these two well-researched American books listed above will prove of great interest. Even if you are sceptical of societal shifts, the second book listed above, by Twenge and Campbell, provides a readable review of the research into egotistical narcissism and its destructive impact. The narcissist takes the self-enhancement process to an extreme level, to the detriment of others who share his or her world.

Study guide questions

1 Although notions such as vanity and narcissism have been around for a long time, the notion that we all routinely engage in self-enhancement would have been seen as absurd a generation ago. What are some of the basic findings in this area that apply to people just like us?

2 Is self-enhancement just a form of boasting, exaggeration, or simply lying?

3 Why do we tend to self-enhance more so when the trait in question is a fixed one such as basic honesty?

4 We can self-enhance because we always can locate good evidence. How do we do this? Where does this evidence come from?

5 It turns out that often we can predict other people's actions better than our own. Just why is this?

6 To what extent should we trust what people say about themselves?

7 It is likely to be the case that sometimes you are sociable, but other times you are more introverted? How does that make you different from other people?

8 Is it possible that you fail to appreciate just how incompetent you really are? Can you describe what is known about the Dunning–Kruger effect?

9 How does the Dunning-Kruger effect fit with the notion that you are basically clever, a good person, you will not change deep down, and you are fundamentally likable.

10 Explain how a degree of self-enhancement and overconfidence often can be useful to an individual's adjustment.

11 But also account for the problems associated with self-centred narcissism. Are egos inflating over time?

Reference notes

- We all feel we are above average drivers, great at dealing with people, superb teachers and lecturers, socially skilled, and unbiased (Dunning, 2006; Dunning, Heath, & Suls, 2004).

- We also know that we are unbiased (Ehrlinger, Gilovich, & Ross, 2005), we own positive traits whenever ambiguity allows, and especially when the envisaged trait is a fixed characteristic (Dunning, 1995; Ehrlinger & Dunning, 2003).

- Self-enhancement is a genuine process, sincere, not faked (Williams & Gilovich, 2008).

- Self-views are dramatically flawed (Dunning, Johnson, Ehrlinger, & Kruger, 2003; Mabe & West, 1982). This finding is analysed in relation to professional training programs by Eva & Regehr, 2008.

- The Barnum Effect: The universal personality profile (Furnham & Schofield, 1987).

- Dumb and dumber as an effect in the classroom (Ehrlinger, Johnson, Banner, Dunning, & Kruger, 2008).

- Incompetent people have little awareness of what they lack (Caputo & Dunning, 2005).

- Adolescent spotlight effect (Gilovich & Savitsky, 1999).

- Positive effects of inflated self-views (S. E. Taylor & Brown, 1988).

- Narcissism and short-term friendships (Carlson, Vazire, & Oltmanns, 2011).

- Increases in narcissism over decades (Twenge, Konrath, Foster, Campbell, & Bushman, 2008), whereas empathy appears to be decreasing (Konrath, O'Brien, & Hsing, 2011).

- Narcissism epidemic (Twenge, 2006; Twenge & Campbell, 2009).

- But another view says human conduct and morality have risen over time, when seen in historical perspective (Pinker, 2011).

26

Achieving self-control

Terms such as self-control, **impulse control**, and willpower have figured a good deal in recent scientific descriptions of human development, in large part stimulated by a surprising set of findings about how children learn to resist temptation. In the early 1970s Professor Walter Mischel, heading a team at Stanford University in California, conducted a series of projects in which preschool children were assessed on their ability to delay gratification. This test involved waiting, in a room, for 15 minutes to obtain a desirable reward, for example, two marshmallows. Children were free to terminate the waiting period at any point and accept a lesser value reward, possibly just one marshmallow.

If the rewards were left in full view in the room, most of the children were unable to wait. Any strategy that diverted attention away from the rewards was found to work. But any focus upon the available rewards was destructive. For example, even if the marshmallow was removed out of sight, the children were relatively unable to wait if they had been instructed to think about eating the lovely marshmallow as they waited.

The Mischel studies reduced core issues of human self-regulation and impulse control to the level of a 4-year-old child. Repeatedly, it was established that the ability to delay gratification was determined by the focus of attention in the face of temptation. The testing rooms were deliberately bland thus providing little in the way of anything to look at. Under these conditions, the more the child focuses on reward and pleasure, the less resistance can be mobilised, the harder it is to contain impulses, and the more the child is driven to accept a short-term resolution.

If willpower is a personal resource, then it is eroded and defeated by the combination of two powerful factors: (a) strong stimulus cues offering immediate pleasure and (b) a train of thought upon the immediate benefits of such indulgence. When thinking is directed to pleasure, then one's cognition is said to be 'hot'. But one of the most dramatic findings from this research was that young children, when given clear direct instructions, could learn techniques that enable them to 'cool down' such cognition, and so avoid the consequences of giving into temptation.

Why the Stanford findings produced a shift in self-control theory

These laboratory findings, as they emerged in the 1970s, stood in conflict with then current theorising. It had long been held that gratification delay relies on a person anticipating the benefits of exerting self-control. By focusing on the value of making clear and sensible choices, and forming expectations of attaining the most worthwhile outcomes, it was believed that people would resist temptations. Through determination, faith, and stoical character strength, they should stifle short-term needs, and achieve long-term goals. The situational dynamics are clear, are rationally defined, and so it was believed that the essential thing was for the mind to become acquainted with such realities.

Within economics such a notion was called *utility theory*, whereas within psychology, similar ideas were called *expectancies*. Similar positions had been taken by significant writers in psychology, psychiatry, economics, and philosophy alike. This type of reasoning has been shown to apply successfully to how people make choices (i.e., good intentions) about future concerns, such as planning for retirement, decisions about vocational training, selecting health plans, and making sensible long-term consumer spending decisions.

However, the findings published by Mischel's team turned such long-held beliefs on their heads. They had found, across 12 experiments, that children who focused on the enjoyment of eating the more valuable rewards, the lovely marshmallows, were unable to sustain delay orientation. Instead, these children wanted and needed gratification in the present: and this was being offered by the less valuable reward. The Stanford team was able to show that certain variables that can determine whether or not children would *choose* to delay gratification (i.e., thinking about the benefits of such choice) could work against self-interest in the long run. A paradox became apparent.

Mischel's findings told us something profound about human nature. The earlier theorising had ignored a critical aspect of the story. Self-control is not only a matter of making sensible choices in the first instance, but hinges on capacity to sustain goal-directed action over time. When thinking about the benefits of achieving a long-term goal, we need sustenance over the long haul. Paradoxically, such sustenance can take the form of actions that make the long-term goal less likely. Thinking about delayed gratifications can create an urge, a hot urge that finds relief in gratifications more attainable. If there is a nasty secret to self-control, it is that it becomes less likely when dwelling excessively upon its anticipated benefits.

Life's indulgences and temptations will create many a problem for individuals striving to attain long-term goals. Many goals are in natural conflict. We live within a society that requires continual efforts in the direction of personal discipline. Much social pathology has, at its core, a breakdown in personal self-control. If this is a free world, then one is granted freedom to act in self-defeating ways. For instance, everyone is responsible for their own budget. We strive for individuals to save money, but people are presented with opportunities to gamble and destroy a lifetime's earnings in a matter of minutes. We can contract to purchase cars, houses, and holidays we cannot possibly afford. We can indulge habits such as smoking, drinking, and sloth, and resist those who attempt to restrict such pleasures. We experience a barrage of advertising material providing misinformation about (a) the value of the service offered, (b) the contingencies we have to live by, and (c) the realities of the social order. According to Dr John Bridges, insightfully writing in 1587, 'a foole and his money is soone parted'.

It should come as little surprise to learn that, within the social sciences, one major theory of crime is that it can represent failure of an individual to develop robust delay capacity skills during early years, surfacing in self-control problems in later life.

On one level it is possible to say that all adults inherently possess ability to control their impulses. However, the societal problem is that many people attain adulthood with impulse control strategies either (a) insecurely learned, (b) relatively unpractised, (c) unavailable when needed, or (d) easily depleted. Even worse, such strategies may be actively devalued by an individual's immediate family or social reference group. For example, it is known that a level of adolescent delinquency is linked to efforts to establish reputations in the context of peer relationships. This form of acting out is unlikely to occur beyond adolescence. Nevertheless, all adults quickly learn that self-control is an aspect of character difficult to attain. Even once achieved, it can break down easily.

So just what are the secrets behind successful self-control?

Self-control as a developmental trait

The laboratory studies reported by Walter Mischel, 40 years ago, were conducted to investigate mental strategies young children can learn to activate in gratification delay. However, a curious thing happened. He noted that within each group, some children were more able to delay gratification than others. This was apparent even after accounting for the fact that different children participated under different conditions of the experiments.

Put simply, the researchers were able to establish that gratification delay at 4 years of age represented a personal trait. It was apparent that some children (i.e., the high delayers), when confronted with the experimental test, worked out how to deflect their attention away from the rewards, without need for explicit instructions as to how to handle the problem. Low-delay children could delay, yes, but only when given explicit instructions about what to think about as they waited.

The next stage of the research was to monitor the life progress of the research participants over time. Over 500 children had participated in the studies as 4-year-olds, and the research group, now located in Ohio, was able to follow up a large number of them as they moved through adolescence into adulthood. It was found that low-delay individuals reported behavioural problems more frequently. They obtained lower SAT scores, which is the recognised index of high school achievement within the United States. They struggled in stressful situations, admitted they had trouble paying attention, and found it difficult to maintain friendships. In the absence of explicit instructions about how to handle life's complex demands, people who had trouble delaying as 4-year-olds were making less successful adjustments within the adult world. These effects were found to exist independently of intelligence and school grades.

In recent work, it was found that even at age 40, people who had shown low-delay functioning as children, still evidenced some problems in laboratory tests of inhibitory control (i.e., when to push, or not to push a button, under precise testing conditions). Some 60 of the original group participated in a project using the brain scanner, the fMRI machine. Neurological evidence was found for the 'hot' and 'cold' theory. Under some conditions, the high-delay people showed strong activity in the prefrontal lobe areas associated with mental control, the area immediately above and behind your eyes. Under the same conditions, the low-delay people tended to show arousal associated with mid-brain activity. The implication is that high-delay individuals have the advantage of possessing brains that allow control processes to operate with ease, while low-delay individuals have brains that produce strong arousal from within the mid-brain area, but are less able to activate the cooling down processes afforded by frontal cortex activity.

However, direct correlations between neurology and behaviour are always uncertain, difficult to document, and they remain difficult to interpret. Although delaying gratification appears to be an enduring personality trait, showing much consistency over the life span, it is premature to suggest that it is the product of biological tendencies or otherwise of differences at the level of brain organization. In many cases, when brain scans reveal differences across individuals, effects can be ascribed to experiences and extensive training. A lifetime's successful practice results in changes in brain organization. Issues such as cause and effect become impossible to disentangle.

Further evidence for the continuity of self-control over the life span

In Dunedin, New Zealand, a remarkable multidisciplinary study into human development began in 1972. More than 1,000 people participated in this project, from their birth through to the present day, with individuals presently in their forties. As a joint medical and social science project, a large number of research publications have been generated. But of considerable interest is the finding that patterns of pathological gambling in adulthood are evident in people rated by trained observers as under-controlling at 3 years of age. Under-controlling 3-year-olds were identified from observations made during a 90-minute testing session. These children were defined as the lowest 10 per cent (98 individuals) on the assessment. This group evidenced problem gambling at a level of 28 per cent some 30 years later, with the level shooting up to 40 per cent of the males in this group. These levels were about twice the rate of problem gambling reported by others in the study.

In another report from the Dunedin project, remarkably strong linkages were found between indices of self-control during childhood and subsequent outcomes during adulthood. The researchers used 9 measures of self-control, obtained when the children were between 3 and 11 years, to categorize the sample into 5 different levels, from 1 (low self-control) to 5 (high self-control), with 200 in each group. The findings were astonishing, as the 5 levels produced what they called gradients. This refers to linear (straight line) relationships between the five groupings and adulthood outcomes. For instance, 24 per cent of the 1,000 had a criminal record, but frequencies of criminal convictions across the five levels, from low to high self-control, were 42, 26, 23, 15, and 12 per cent. For levels of school leaving without educational qualifications the figures were 42, 21, 19, 8, and 4 per cent.

Similar gradient effects were evident for other significant life factors such as unplanned pregnancy or parenthood (from 14 to 3 per cent), smoking (from 48 to 20 per cent), and having status as a single parent (from 58 to 26 per cent). Gradients in the other direction were found for positive outcomes such as income, wealth, home ownership, and financial planning. Similarly positive gradients were found for a variety of health outcomes such as weight control, cardiovascular function, metabolic health, dental care and maintenance, and the absence of drug abuse.

These relationships were shown to occur independently from both IQ and original social class (SES). In many cases relationships from childhood self-control to adult outcomes were stronger than relationships with IQ, but especially so in the area of personal financial management. If you want to predict which children will become both wealthy and healthy in their adulthood, their ability to exercise self-control appears the most powerful predictive factor we know about. It is not mere whimsy to appreciate that your ability to resist eating a marshmallow, as a preschooler, strongly predicts how many teeth you retain in old age, but this is not a result of the sugar in that particular marshmallow.

Self-control as a trait in adulthood

Other recent projects have shown clear relationships between self-control as reported on personality scales and a variety of significant outcomes. For example, people who score highly on the self-control scale report more successful social relationships in general, and more satisfying marriages in particular. One secret of a successful marriage appears to be that at least one partner is high on the self-control scale. High self-control individuals appear to get on well with other people, are socially skilled, and are able to show restraint and understanding when dealing with others. Such people enjoy more academic success, and are seen as valued work mates. Self-control predicts persistence, striving, and willingness to allocate time to worthy goals. On the negative side, it has been shown that low self-control is associated with substance abuse, criminality, impulse buying, and procrastination.

The evidence is more mixed when it comes to three aspects: (a) overall happiness level, (b) overall adjustment, and (c) dietary or weight control. In these areas, the available studies have yielded variable findings. It now seems that trait self-control has little to do with dietary control. However, it has been found that it becomes difficult to control one's diet when one is tired or ego depleted (as described in the next section).

One significant observation is that the character trait we call self-control manifests itself strongly in any situation involving social interaction and interpersonal assessment. It was found that high self-control people respond to interpersonal issues through a process of accommodation in which they strive to understand other people. They tend to take more time when dealing with other people. When they judge a situation as appropriate, they are prepared to show empathy, and become willing to forgive transgressions in others. In contrast, those who lack self-control tend to handle interpersonal matters with tactics such as immediacy, forcefulness, and possible aggression.

THE EFFECT OF DIFFICULT PEOPLE: DEPLETION THROUGH HIGH MAINTENANCE SOCIAL INTERACTION

The theory of ego depletion is one you can relate to in your everyday world. However, certain findings are of great interest to teachers. In one study, Michael Zyphur and colleagues had college students spend a few minutes with a peer (a confederate) in either (a) a pleasant friendly interaction or (b) a curt unfriendly interaction, and then asked them to work on difficult problems. Compared to the other group, people exposed to the unfriendly confederate worked on the problems for only a short time before stopping, and helped themselves to more candy sweets left in the room. One of the costs of dealing with unfriendly people is the need to 'be good to oneself' immediately afterwards.

Much human activity involves coordinating your actions with another person. But collaboration does not always work. Your actions and theirs may not mesh smoothly. Having to deal with a high maintenance person results in high levels of ego depletion. In laboratory studies, Eli Finkel and colleagues showed that the ego depletion effects kick in under three minutes, and resulted in people showing less persistence in problem solving, picking easy tasks rather than difficult ones, spending less effort on a maze puzzle, and exerting less effort on a test of physical fitness.

Teachers and counsellors know that dealing with certain individuals is 'draining', a valid observation since 'draining' and 'depletion' are virtually indistinguishable. The notion that every class you deal with contains certain high maintenance students is proverbial, but describing their impact on you as ego depletion is possibly a new idea. Once in this depleted state, induced by a high maintenance person, then it is likely your own self-control will be affected adversely, as the need to 'be good to oneself' is then activated.

Of special interest in this work is the experimental methodology used to create high maintenance interactions. Two procedures proved effective: (a) having to listen to a person whining, complaining, and showing unhappiness, and (b) having a bossy interaction partner provide you with instructions that are unclear and being changed from moment to moment. Unclear instructions that you attempt to follow, but then are rescinded unpredictably, will 'drive you crazy', and result in rapid onset ego depletion. As professionals who deal with people for hours every day, these two conditions will hit a nerve with all teachers.

Self-control as a personal capacity: the role of ego depletion

A further breakthrough in the analysis of human self-control occurred in the late 1990s when Professor Roy Baumeister and his team, then at Case Western University, began publishing a series of remarkable laboratory studies into the effects of short intensive periods of mental work. Having to focus one's full attention on a demanding task for several minutes produces **ego depletion**. This accounts for a subtle type of exhaustion based on mental fatigue that is distinct from physical fatigue, or one's mood, or overall feeling state.

After perhaps seven or eight minutes of intense mental work the mind is said to be in a state of depletion. While not surprising, what made this research significant was the finding that once depleted, people evidenced dramatic reductions in energy, effort, persistence, and self-control. People were unaware that performance on subsequent tasks was being impaired. Nevertheless, across different studies, the effect was shown to apply to several score of tests having the common theme of impulse control. If an easy option is available, then ego-depleted people will take that route.

For example, across different studies, (a) deliberately trying to avoid thinking of a white bear for five minutes made people less likely to control their alcohol intake when about to face a driving test, (b) attempting to control facial expressions while watching a sad film resulted in people making relatively poor decisions on a planning task, (c) people required to give a short talk showed less persistence on problem solving tasks, (d) people asked to resist eating tempting food were found to be more aggressive after experiencing a minor criticism, (e) people asked to work hard on a letter identification task indicated negative evaluations of other people, (f) people induced to pay concentrated attention to a six-minute silent film then showed increased willingness to pay higher prices for products, and (g) young children induced to count activities appearing and disappearing on a computer screensaver for five minutes then selected to work on easy mathematics problems on the computer whereas their classmates selected difficult problems to work upon.

The common thread behind these, and many other studies, is that we have a temporary store of ego strength, a capacity we call upon when engaged in activities that require us to apply self-control. Whenever we need to try hard, to think, plan, make choices, or exert ourselves, we call upon this personal reserve of strength. We need energy to override impulses. But what if this energy has just been used, however slightly, by earlier demands on our reserves? Unconsciously, we eke out and conserve mental resources. Hence, whenever a second task is laid on us, we have less capacity. We had to use some level of capacity in dealing with the first task. While laboratory studies have shown such task sequences take a toll on coping abilities, in our heads we appear to be unaware how we have been affected. In effect, we need to 'be good to ourselves'. We have less in reserve, and are less willing to undertake any new enterprise, at least until reserves are restored again.

How depletion effects can wreck your life

Laboratory studies found depleted people would quickly use aggression in response to minor frustrations, a finding of acute relevance to classroom management. Also disturbing for teachers is the finding that ego-depleted individuals appear more willing to turn to dishonesty. One particular project involved university students being asked to complete and then score two academic tasks. The initial task was made easy for half the students, but difficult for the rest. Students who completed the difficult task then rewarded themselves on the second task with extra points (exchangeable for money) they had not earned. In other words, those depleted after the first task then cheated on the second task, taking double what they had genuinely earned.

Within the wider world, ego depletion effects have profound consequences. One project found that when depleted, adult individuals, of both genders, were less able to resist attractive members of the opposite sex in a manner that could undermine their existing relationships. In an analysis of parole sentence practices in Israeli courts, a significant factor determining outcome across 1,100 cases was found to be time of day. Benign decisions were occurring early in the morning or straight after meal breaks. Severe decisions were meted out the longer the case followed a meal break. The probability of a benign decision varied from 65 per cent to zero depending on the time of day the case was heard. When human systems are overloaded, individuals become depleted, actions alter accordingly, although people fail to notice such shifts. In the Israeli study, the determining factor of time of day was unknown to the courts' participants.

Depletion effects are less evident when people are given short breaks. For example, five minutes between tasks is often enough for the mind to regroup. At times, depletion effects can be averted by inducing people to keep trying harder. This clearly works, but only up to a point at which they become even more severely depleted. One significant discovery was that depletion effects are considerably reduced through consuming high-energy foods. Close linkages between ego depletion effects and blood sugar glucose have been documented. However, it is not the case that your students will suddenly increase in impulse control through eating sugary food. It is simply that self-control failures and withdrawal of effort in general, become almost inevitable when blood sugar levels are at a low point. Thus, dieting can be described as the 'perfect storm': it becomes difficult to resist temptation when your body is crying out for the food needed to assist in applying one's self-control.

Self-control breaks down when people are emotionally stressed. Under stress, the mind fixes upon short-term needs. Anything that offers immediate comfort becomes more attractive since an upset individual needs to feel better immediately. Long-term goals are placed 'on hold' while short term priorities are addressed. Hence, depletion can wreak havoc upon strategies formulated when the individual was in his or her more energised or non-depleted state.

There are documented linkages between ego depletion effects and problems in deep thinking. As described in Chapter 30, our mind possesses two systems of action. System 1 is fast and automated. System 2 is slow and deliberate. It has been shown that System 2 is subject to ego depletion. Our ability to think deeply is disrupted by activities that stress us even for relatively short durations. On the other hand, laboratory studies indicate that System 1 remains unaffected by similar brief ego depletion experiences.

Let us take stock: when depleted you are deprived of your thinking brain and your impulsive System 1 biases take over without permission. This brings a halt upon your natural tendency to monitor yourself carefully. Your ability to resist gratifications is reduced. Your needs revert to finding comfort through whatever resources are available in the present. Despite being in a stable relationship, you can find yourself less able to resist attractive members of the opposite sex who just may offer an alternative. You are inclined towards helping yourself to higher levels of monetary reward than your objective performance justified. These notions are all accounted for in validated research findings. It is not hard to see a pattern to such findings: *depletion can wreak havoc.*

Learning to use your self-control capacity: the shift from reactive to proactive mode

One may suppose people who rate highly on the trait of self-control are able to use their self-control capacity with abundance. We can expect such individuals to report successfully exercising self-control within daily life. From surveys, however, a strangely different picture emerges. When Roy Baumeister and his colleagues began investigating how people use willpower within their lives, one curious finding was that self-control surfaced through people *avoiding* having to deal with situations likely to require impulse control.

It turns out that it is people low on trait self-control who front up to situations that require serious levels of energy and willpower. However, an alternative strategy in life is to be proactive and not expose oneself to a situation that might result in depletion or possible self-control failure. People low on trait self-control are the same people who need to use high levels of willpower. They seem less able to plan routines that would enable them to avoid meeting life problems head-on. For instance, students who procrastinate or neglect their studies need to exert high levels of control to cram the day before an important examination. A safer strategy would be to set aside routines as governed by habits, times, and places. People who rate high in trait self-control are found to plan ahead and take steps to avoid need for extraordinary exertions.

Surveys showed that people report two types of self-control on a daily basis: (a) reacting and responding to situations as they arise and (b) proactively arranging life to avert the need to keep reacting to predictable threats. People rating low on the self-control trait may become experts in reactive methods, and accustomed to last minute brinkmanship. People rating high on trait self-control strive toward proactive tactics. Such survey findings with adults are consistent with lessons we can take from Professor Mischel's earlier research. The pre-schooler is able to wait through learning to deflect his or her mind from thinking about tempting delights. Similarly, adults with high self-control deal with the various temptations of the world by ensuring that enticements are not sitting under their noses and hence will not require massive dollops of willpower to be applied repeatedly.

A new approach to willpower

The discovery and analysis of self-control and ego depletion seriously shook the thinking of social science researchers across the globe. The issue was that self-control had hardly figured within traditional theories of personality development. For instance, psychologists were accustomed to assessing children and adults alike in terms of fixed traits such as IQ, natural capabilities, and easily described personality traits such as introversion, sociability, and openness.

But the literature on self-control, as stimulated by ideas derived from cognitive psychology, began pointing in a different direction. It is now often reported that self-control is as important, and sometimes more important, than IQ in predicting outcomes. It has become apparent in recent years, that many 'common sense' notions of character, willpower, personal discipline, and sheer 'guts', possess more validity than was recognised traditionally within modern psychology. People from the Victorian era of modern history emphasised inner character strengths as keys to living a successful life. It took science some 150 years to validate such notions.

What has emerged over recent years is a conception of the individual placing self-control, determination and willpower, at the core. But there is a twist: the ability to use self-control is not an inherently individualistic matter. It is neither stoicism nor moral rectitude. Instead, it is a matter of social development and learning. This invokes what we call the individual's *social learning history*.

People do well in life, make sensible choices, control their impulses, delay gratification, and are careful with expenditures because their formative years provided them with a series of graded experiences in which discriminations between good and poor indulgences became well defined and often explicit. For example, it will not hurt to take one night off studying to watch a movie, but the university student who does this three times every week is likely to fail. This student needs mechanisms in his head that, through time management, allow short-term actions and long-term goals to align.

How we learn to resist temptation through social learning

How does an individual learn to control impulses? We can identify several promising leads from the literature. One of the most powerful explanations resides in the concept of *social modelling*. The self is not alone: other people exert strong effects. However, it is known that children and adolescents are selective about who they will use as models. Often, there needs to be a viable basis for the relationship, or what psychologists often refer to as *identification*.

When children have people in their lives they can identify with, they become more likely to copy the characteristics they see modelled. Models depict valued life goals as well as sound reasons for striving to achieve such goals. Skills and strategies implicating impulse control can be taught to children, both directly and indirectly, through modelling. Exerting effort, making sensible choices, exercising restraint, and delaying gratification, are all activities that children can witness and assimilate when displayed by the significant adults within their worlds.

Social models that young people observe provide valuable information as to natural relationships between effort and outcomes. Models will provide information about specific short-term steps to take (the how to do it knowledge), as well as essential information about the likelihood of certain outcomes. Observing a strong and resilient model allows a young person to build up realistic expectations. Seeing a model undertaking a lengthy apprenticeship, and persevere under conditions of hardship, informs young observers of the need to expect similar realities and so not to expect immediate gratifications to arrive after minimal effort.

On the other side of the equation, a large body of social and psychiatric research, especially with the older adolescent, indicates that gambling habits, substance abuse patterns, interpersonal dysfunction, and criminal activities are modelled and transmitted through family experiences. Intergenerational transmission (where a disposition is seen across both children and parents) is a solidly supported finding validated through scores of research projects. Social modelling represents one of its major vehicles.

How we learn to resist temptation though mental cooling strategies and if–then plans

Another key aspect of self-control development was highlighted through Mischel's work. He identified mental deflection strategies that can be readily taught and assimilated by people of any age. We possess a mind that enables us to translate our sensory experiences into thoughts. One of the most effective methods taught to the children in the 1970s Stanford studies was for them to pretend the marshmallows were like 'fluffy little clouds', and 'round and white just like the moon'. By transforming a threatening stimulus into a pleasant distraction, its effect through stimulating hot cognition is undermined and destroyed.

The underlying principles are of **distraction** and **deflection**. These dual techniques represent realistic ways by which anyone can control their thoughts. Whenever you harbour unwanted thoughts, unfortunately, you cannot dismiss them voluntarily. This is well known. But what you can do is gently regulate them through consciously programming distractions for yourself. One such deflection strategy is to use what you can see in front of you to make it suggest something quite different within your mind.

In Dr Mischel's theorising, the effect of such deflection methods is that of allowing a person to move thinking from hot to cool mode. The problem of self-control is one of shutting down the potency of situational cues through engaging cool information processing. Mental cooling strategies prevent a person from sabotaging his or her long-term interests in the face of threats. In later work, Dr Mischel was able to show how cooling strategies assisted people suffering other life problems such as handling aggression and social rejection. Furthermore, other studies have indicated that many mothers are adept at using deflection methods when interacting with young children in ways that assist their children to develop self-control.

A further method shown to assist children resist temptation involves the direct teaching of **if–then plans**, otherwise known as **implementation intentions**. This refers to specific statements that can be rehearsed in the mind as self-instructions. Here are four examples of such plans, (a) *If Peter offers me a cigarette I will say 'no thank you'*, (b) *When the waiter asks for my order I say 'salad'*, (c) *When my flatmates invite me to the movies I will say I am studying*, and (d) *If that student is rude I will stare him down saying nothing*. The effect of forming such clear plans has been shown to be remarkably effective, with effect sizes on performance measures around 0.6 and greater in many studies. German psychologists Peter Gollwitzer and Gabrielle Oettingen have published widely on the impact of if–then plans, and citations to their research are found in the reference notes for this chapter.

IN PERSPECTIVE: Self-control has effects beyond the self

The message you can to communicate to your students is that self-control is a natural skill, a product of socialisation, which enables them to bridge time whenever there is a preferred, but deferred, goal at stake.

Here is the message: *You do not need to respond to the first impulse you experience, especially if such an action will deprive you of greater happiness in the long run. It is important to carefully identify just what will help achieve your goals, and what will not. When temptations are placed in your path, you can resist them, but this effort in itself will begin to deplete your capacities, and it becomes more difficult for you to maintain the same level of resistance for long periods.*

The world's temptations are best handled by (a) first resisting them and (b) learning how to defuse them, or turn them off altogether. Mental strategies enabling this to happen are available, are well known, and can be assimilated and perfected by young people often with help from older and wiser models. Nevertheless, these are difficult lessons for many young people. Their attention must be drawn to realistic models whose actions and life experiences can be examined in depth.

An important note, but one of strong perspective, is that the image of a person with self-control standing as an individual resolute against hostile forces is not one finding support in the existing scientific literature. Instead, what has emerged is a conception of self-control locked directly into social sensitivity. People who score highly on self-control tests are people holding down social relationships that they strongly defend to maintain long-term benefits. They are more likely to identify with successful models, and use emulation as a personal guide. They hesitate to respond impulsively, but take other people's views into account before settling. They adjust to their social world through listening and accommodating, rather than forging their own agendas through force or aggression. These are serious scientific findings.

Humans are by nature social animals. Being able to (a) assess the social order, (b) identify with it, and (c) work towards its maintenance, are aspects consistent with notions of personal self-management. Given this perspective, one of the core empirical findings, emerging from Dr Mischel's longitudinal research, from the New Zealand data, and also from Dr Baumeister's studies, begins to make much sense: *that individuals able to exercise self-control are the same individuals who establish, maintain, and protect significant long-term relationships with others.* Consistent with this notion are findings from criminology indicating that deviant activity in young adults shows significant reduction after forming stable relationships such as marriage.

In sum, people high in self-control are far from stoical or solitary figures in an unfeeling world. Instead, they are part of the social group, responding with sensitivity and empathy towards those who share their world. This scientific view, voiced by writers such as Roy Baumeister and John Tierney (2011), is that self-control, as both a personal trait and a temporary capacity, enables individuals to move beyond self-interest and serve wider interests of other people as well as their own needs. We all possess an inevitable self-serving bias, but our capacity for self-control enables us to override this at crunch times, in the interests of a greater good. Such an idea is not as paradoxical as it first seems.

Study guide questions

1 In the 1970s, it was discovered that young children could delay gratification provided they did not pay attention to what they were waiting for. Why did such findings change the way all previous theories talked about self-control?

2 When faced with a dilemma, what are the two main factors known to destroy one's impulse control? They apply to both children and adults alike.

3 The research implies that self-control is a collection of skills learnt in early life, which we may refer to as will-power. In broad societal terms, what are the likely effects of failure to develop such skills?

4 So what actual findings are reported in the literature? The writers noted that 'your ability to resist eating a marshmallow, as a preschooler, strongly predicts how many teeth you retain in old age'. Was this intended as a joke?

5 In the chapter, it was noted a finding from the psychotherapy field that 'One secret of a successful marriage appears to be that at least one partner is high on the self-control scale'. Just why would this be so?

6 People who score high on the self-control scale are also found to exhibit a particular style of interpersonal behaviour. How does this style differ from people that are low on self-control?

7 Just what is ego depletion? One strange aspect of this research was that depletion effects could kick in fairly quickly. Just how quickly?

8 How can depletion effects literally wreck your life? (As they have done so for many.)

9 It has been found that adults high in self-control actually use less will-power to get them through each day. This is because they habitually use what types of strategies in everyday life?

10 What are the major known ways than can help people achieve better impulse control? What does it mean to shift thinking from hot to cold mode? And just what is an if–then plan?

11 Do you have to cope with difficult people? If so, can you identify effects of such ego depleting experiences upon yourself?

Reference notes

- Walter Mischel's ground-breaking studies into delay of gratification (Eigsti *et al.*, 2006; Mischel, 2012; Mischel *et al.*, 2011).
- Theory of crime (Engel, 2012; Gottfredson & Hirschi, 1990; Hirschi, 2004).
- Adolescent delinquency linked to efforts to establish reputations (Carroll, Houghton, Durkin, & Hattie, 2009).

- Dunedin Multidisciplinary Health and Development Study. Infant status predicts gambling at age 32 (Slutske, Moffitt, Poulton, & Caspi, 2012): self-control and outcome gradients (Moffitt *et al.*, 2011). Details of this major on-going medical study are available on website: http://dunedinstudy.otago.ac.nz.

- Research using the Trait Self-Control Scale (de Ridder, Lensvelt-Mulders, Finkenauer, Stok, & Baumeister, 2012; Tangney, Baumeister, & Boone, 2004). Self-control in marriage (Vohs, Finkenauer, & Baumeister, 2011). Self-control in interpersonal life (Fitzsimons & Finkel, 2011; Luchies, Finkel, & Fitzsimons, 2011). Associations between interpersonal relationships and self-control also were found in the Dunedin studies (see above note).

- Ego depletion studies (Alquist & Baumeister, 2012; DeWall, Baumeister, Gailliot, & Maner, 2008; Mead, Baumeister, Gino, Schweitzer, & Ariely, 2009; Price & Yates, 2010; Schmeichel, Vohs, & Baumeister, 2003; Vohs, Baumeister, & Schmeichel, 2012). The study linking depletion with dishonesty was Mead *et al.* The Vohs *et al.* study showed cumulative effects of several depletion experiences, to point where people almost run out of energy, and crash even harder.

- Depleted people easily provoked into aggression (Stucke & Baumeister, 2006). People in relationships less likely to resist attractive opposite sex member when depleted (Ritter, Karremans, & van Schie, 2010). Judicial decisions turning harsh (Danziger, Levav, & Avnaim-Pesso, 2011).

- Self-control breaks down when people are stressed (Gailliot & Tice, 2007).

- Studies with adults reporting self-control in everyday life (Hofmann, Baumeister, Förster, & Vohs, 2012; Hofmann, Vohs, & Baumeister, 2012).

- Adolescent gambling and other social deviance transmitted through family modelling (Burton & Meezan, 2004; Delfabbro & Thrupp, 2003; Wilber & Potenza, 2006). Fathers' history of antisocial activity (deviant modelling) when children are young predicts antisocial conduct in teenagers and poor adult outcomes (Dishion, Owen, & Bullock, 2004).

- Intergenerational transmission is supported by a multitude of findings going back to the 1920s. But one recent Dutch project is of interest. They found correlations between behavioural conduct symptoms in childhood, and parallel symptoms seen in the children of these same people as parents 24 years later (van Meurs, Reef, Verhulst, & van der Ende, 2009).

- Mothers use deflection methods in handling young children. Such methods are linked with their children showing greater self-control (Putnam, Spritz, & Stifter, 2002).

- Developing if–then plans (Gawrilow, Gollwitzer, & Oettingen, 2011; Gollwitzer & Oettingen, 2012).

- Forming stable relationships (e.g., marriage) reduces crime (Forrest & Hay, 2011).

- Willpower as a core aspect of our personality (Baumeister & Tierney, 2011; Mischel, 2012).

- Box: The ego-draining (depletion) effect of high maintenance individuals (Finkel *et al.*, 2006; Zyphur, Warren, Landis, & Thoresen, 2007).

27

Neuroscience of the smile

A fundamental tool in teaching

Smiling is infectious. Seeing your kin, friend, or colleague burst into a wide, open smile means that you are highly likely to smile and experience positive feelings. The smile works its magic, and the relationships you have with people become that much richer and more rewarding. In this section we will cite research findings that lead to the conclusion that the smile is one of the most powerful tools to use in interpersonal teaching situations.

Putting the smile onto a solid research basis

The research literature into the human smile has revealed many strange things. Here are just some such findings. People that smile are more likely to be successful at hitchhiking, receive more tips when serving in the hospitality trade, and are seen as more generous and likable than other people. Fashion models who smile generate higher ratings for the clothes they model. People who smile are more likely to be seen as attractive, to make friends, and to be regarded as someone others would like to befriend. They tend to be treated with leniency when they break rules or violate social conventions. If they are doctors, they are less likely to get sued for medical malpractice.

Smiling can be recognised from over a 100 metres away, and appears to be the most easily identified emotional cue over such distances. On average, females are more likely to smile than males. There is strong evidence for intergenerational transmission in that children's smiling in the classroom has been linked to levels of smiling and warmth evident in the child's home, and the child's patterns of smiling tend to match that of his or her parents in a manner consistent with social modelling theory. There is some evidence indicating that children who smile a good deal are more socially competent than others.

In an online shopping context, consumers were found to increase their trust in human-like avatars when these images were programmed to show gentle smiles in the course of a sales pitch. One study found that participants in a virtual reality environment approached the simulated people quite differently depending on the type of smile seen on the target figures. In a more realistic vein, several studies have shown that ratings of smiling taken from pictures in college yearbooks predicted later life outcomes such as being married, having successful marriages, being less likely to divorce, as well as overall enhanced well-being. It has been found that people who smile a good deal tend to live longer lives.

Research into priming effects has documented that a split second's exposure to a smiling face can gently alter people's minds with attitudes to neutral objects becoming more positive, as well as other people being rated more favourably. Plainly, as far as being successful in life is concerned, this ability to display your face with a quick and sincere smile, at the appropriate moment, appears to be a remarkably powerful facility.

The power of 43 little muscles

The human face is a strangely mobile entity. It is served by 43 muscles, all being involved in facial expressions, with the majority of these also involved in creating the large repertoire of activities recognised as smiling. However, there are three key muscles to know about. The major muscle implicated is the *zygotmaticus major*, which pulls back the corners of the mouth. The *orbicularis oculi* muscles around the eyes may also contract, and in many people can produce the crows' feet effect, a minor level of wrinkling to the side of the eye. The third major muscle is the *corrugator*, which is implicated in furrowing the brow above the eyes.

These muscles operate not to move you, but to move other people. The 43 muscles can move to form literally thousands of possible configurations. However, there are 12 basic facial patterns instantly recognised by others. You may have never set eyes on someone before, but a split second's exposure to her face reveals the type of mood or emotion she is experiencing. For instance, brow furrowing suggests negativity, which, when combined with a downturned mouth, displays anger and frustration.

Consider this: some of the most dramatic photographs ever taken involve emotionally provocative images of people's faces. With the advent of the camera 180 years ago, facial expressions that occur in split seconds could become frozen in time. One heart-wrenching episode, recognised as one of the most provocative examples of modern photo-journalism, is found in the story of the 'Afghan girl' as published on the cover of *National Geographic* in June 1985. The power of this image, the emotions it conveyed, made an impact upon millions of people.

Observational systems for classifying facial expressions have been developed for research purposes, but are complex and cannot be used by untrained people. When it comes to describing different possible types of smiles, the listing is arbitrary, but here are some of the terms used: the social smile, the sneering smile, the mocking smile, the sad smile, the happy smile, the coy smile, the apologetic smile, the nervous smile, the glowing smile, and the angry smile. The key thing to note is that in each case there is a pattern that is able to be recognised by another person, and this perception holds significant implications for the nature of any subsequent social interaction.

What does the smile show?

Most obviously, smiling is a personal response that you display in response to experiencing pleasure or happiness. On the other hand, smiling can and does frequently show on the faces of people experiencing acute negative emotions such as embarrassment, anxiety, and disappointment. One of us witnessed a school principal fall from a stage during an important assembly. He was badly bruised. After taking a few moments to regroup, he stood up before the assembly smiling broadly, to rapturous applause. Smiling through pain represented an important act of social cohesion at that moment.

Smiling is a fundamental social signal that occurs in the company of other people. As the previous paragraph implies, the human smile will convey multiple meanings, rather than any one simple message. It conveys messages about the importance of the interaction, the nature of the relationship between various parties, and the goal to be achieved at that moment.

Strangely enough, evidence suggests that people rarely smile when by themselves (although we will revisit this idea later this chapter). Even when people receive positive news, or win a computer game, or receive a prize in the mail, they do not smile if no one else is within sight. In a classic piece of social psychological research, Kraut and Johnson (1979) reported that people in bowling alleys seldom smile after learning they have achieved a winning score. But they burst into a huge smile when they turn to share this information with their team. Smiling is less of a private response, but more of a public display intended to establish and affirm important social connections.

The idea that the smile is a basic social signal, well-nigh universal to the human species, can be tested on the personal level. Try smiling at strangers in the street. This study was done in one American city in 1991, with the finding that about half the adult population smile back, with men and women about the same level. Responsive people smile back in a fast, automatic, contagion-like manner. Such interactions occur within a half second, which implies that conscious thought is not involved. What is remarkable about such interactions is the absence of an agenda, other than recognition that the other person is someone worth smiling at: another human being trying to go through life with a sense of decency.

Obviously, you must judge moments and times when this activity would be inappropriate, such as when others would perceive you as harbouring an agenda. It is worthy of note that this American study clearly showed a strong contagion effect for smiling, but within the same study, the contagion effect was not found for frowning.

Smiling as natural language

Should you feel comfortable in carrying out such personal exercises, you might attempt to validate a curious but important phenomenon: that this reciprocal mirror smiling response appears to occur irrespective of age, gender, social background, or cultural group. Another finding is intriguing: people report it far easier to smile at a person directly in front of them than to smile without another person being present. It can be quite difficult for many people to even raise a clear smile when there is no other person to beam at directly.

Here is yet another odd finding from laboratory research: people smile more at a stranger, and then will converse with this person more easily, if that person is similar to another person they know and like. That is, people will smile at someone who simply reminds them of another person. Hence, many researchers regard the smile as an indicator of our hard-wiring, a product of how our species evolved. Our brains are biologically set up to receive and produce social signals with the level of control far more unconscious than conscious.

There is also a meaningful literature indicating that human positivity, with smiling playing a pivotal role, works through **three degrees of social separation**. If you smile at someone, they are more likely to smile at another person. The effect appears to be washed out at the third level (i.e., the fourth person). The theory of three degrees of separation is now thought to apply to many aspects of social life in relation to both positive and negative outcomes.

Although smiling is a basic social signal, differing cultural conventions apply across different societies. For example, some societies enforce rules about who can smile at whom. At times, the hand has to be used to cover a smiling face. Certain types of smiles are interpreted as conveying an insult, personal contempt, or generally a mistrustful relationship. For example, Russian people quickly regard a lingering smile as implying insincerity. Indeed, within Russia, people will generally smile at other people only once they know them. In some countries, smiling at strangers is literally frowned upon. Hence, we recommend you do not conduct the personal experiment suggested above in such countries. One American researcher noted higher levels of Duchenne smiles in English people, when contrasted against his native country. So what is the **Duchenne smile**?

The perception of sincerity

An interesting discovery was made 150 years ago by French scientist, Guillame Duchenne. Through using photography, he was able to discern a difference in facial muscles when a person was smiling in response to a genuine pleasurable event, as distinct from smiling for more contrived purposes. When you examine video footage, especially frame-by-frame slow motion, examples of Duchenne smiles can be discriminated from other types of smiles. The non-Duchenne smile is centred around movements in the lower face or mouth area, with very little movement above the cheek level. On the other hand, the genuine Duchenne smile produces greater movement across the whole face, the cheeks may move up slightly, and the muscles to the side of the eyes contract slightly, sometimes giving the eyes a 'squishy' look.

The sight of 'crow's feet', or crinkling, to the side of each eye is a strong sign of a clear and genuine smile taking place. It is thought that this smile pattern cannot be produced voluntarily. Another potential bodily cue is that the genuine open smile is likely to be performed with shoulders back and head upright. On the other hand, a tilted head may suggest a less than sincere smile. Plainly, it is unwise to read too much into ambiguous body language cues. But it is well documented that human beings do form judgements about other people using such subtle and barely perceivable cues.

Despite many studies into these effects, it remains unclear whether or not people, in everyday life, can accurately discriminate a contrived smile from the full Duchenne. From laboratory studies it is known that some individuals quickly will spot the difference when they are asked to discriminate, and are shown crystal clear examples of each, for example, on video. But the research indicates that possibly only a minority of the population, somewhere about 10 per cent, may do this naturally. Within the everyday world, people who exhibit non-Duchenne smiles do so without being seen as 'fake', for the majority of the time.

Overall, it is simplistic and just wrong to think that non-Duchenne smiles are insincere or fake. Many people do not show the full Duchenne features even when genuinely relating to others in a positive way. Also, a high percentage of genuine social smiles do occur at a low intensity level, and thus will not show Duchenne features.

However, we all spot fake smiles under more blatant conditions such as when they appear to (a) begin too quickly or eagerly, (b) stay fixed on the face for too long, (c) be disproportionate to the experience, or (d) be selfishly motivated or manipulative. One vital cue we use to infer insincerity is when a person holds an intense or wide smile for too long, perhaps more than two seconds at a stretch. It is necessary to feel empathy for contestants on various reality television shows when winners are announced, but with the losers still seen on full camera. They all need to smile. You can watch out for differences in involuntary facial movement across winners and losers. The fake smile has been called the Pan Am smile, after the American airline, and more recently, the Botox smile, after the beauty product.

Genuine smiles in human interactions often tend to be brief, sometimes just a fraction of a second. Some people appear to exhibit a smile that may fade in and out, over several seconds, rather than be held rigidly fixed. As noted earlier, it is not sensible to think that all smiles can be seen as either as genuine or not. Very often these types seem to merge. Even trained observers are likely to disagree on whether or not a specific smile shows the full Duchenne features. On the other hand, when negative emotions are present, terms such as the grimacing, sneering, or frowning smile, can be more easily defined and agreed upon.

Although it is hard for most people to discriminate the Duchenne smile from a more staged social smile, any smile associated with the negative emotions tends to be recognised immediately even by young children. There is some suggestive evidence that young children are more likely to rate wide-mouthed non-Duchenne smiles as being genuine ones. That is, they may be fooled more readily by blatantly fake smiling. But such effects are not strong, and overall, the clear finding has been that adults and children alike score remarkably similarly in laboratory tests involving judgements of the human face and sensitivity to its changing expressions.

The role of low-level facial cues as signs of comprehension

Earlier we had noted that smiling, more readily than other emotional states, is easily seen at a distance of 100 metres. This finding applies to wide open-mouthed smiling. However, another significant discovery about the smile is that it is correlated with comprehension and understanding. Although, we had noted earlier that smiling generally will not occur when people are by themselves, this notion appears untrue once we broaden notions of smiling to include even slight movements of the *zygotmaticus major* muscle around the mouth.

Of course this hinges on just what we mean by smiling. But it is possible to take a broad view to include any movement around the mouth suggesting benign positivity. It is now thought that such gentle, low-level smiling is triggered whenever people feel comfortable in understanding something. This activity appears to occur most clearly when the mind is puzzled, but then something 'clicks', and all is well again. For instance, carefully controlled laboratory studies have shown that people show gentle low-level smiles when they recognise familiar objects, when they hear information they understand, or appreciate that a task is easy. Sometimes such smiles are barely visible, but are easily detected with slow motion films or physiological measures of facial muscle activity. It has also been found that people smile gently when they see smiling faces on television, or even in still photographs.

Although such low-level facial activity is unconscious, it still may be picked up by another human being, albeit unconsciously. Effectively, the turn of phrase 'She showed a flicker of recognition' is based on soundly validated phenomena. The face will register the extent to which a person understands his or her current predicament. The gentle low-level smile, indexed by a brief, almost imperceptible, movement of the muscles around the mouth, provides an external cue that the brain comprehends whatever task is immediately pressing.

These findings suggest that teachers are likely to use low-level smiling as feedback cues implicated in interpersonal interactions. The processes involved are likely to be unconscious, but potent. Your students' faces put out vital cues about their level of understanding. As you teach, it is not always clear just why you make certain moves, why you repeat certain instructions, or why you vary the pace of your speech. The body of research into smiling suggests that you are locked into using your students' facial cues and smiling displays, since these provide essential sources of feedback data you require to move forwards. This idea is consistent with the studies cited earlier concerning teacher expertise, especially David Berliner's finding that expert teachers acutely read their students' body language.

Smiling as a necessary component of your professional persona

So how does this large body of research inform the teacher? One important message is that students inevitably read your smiling behaviour. They will observe how you smile and use this as an index to tell them what mood you are in, what sort of person you are, and the likely reaction you might have to them today. Your smile will enable them to rate you on approachability. There will be contagion effects in that when you smile at a student, he or she is likely to smile back, and also at his or her classmates. Your disposition to smile at your students will constitute one of the most important aspects about you that they will remember over time.

Following from our reading of the social research, we suggest that genuine smiling is among the most powerful tools a teacher can use to advantage. This idea becomes especially salient when it comes to dealing with an individual student. You can smile at the student to signify that you respect him or her as another human being. Ideally, your genuine smile is accompanied with a quick verbal affirmation such as, 'Chris, thank you for coming today'.

Taking a second to establish the climate of the interaction through basic social rituals will pay enormous dividends. Both parties feel more at ease, and the genuine purpose of the meeting can proceed with less call for either party to activate psychological needs such as denial or defensiveness. In short, quick and brief smiling enables you to proceed into meaningful human interactions in an efficient manner signalling to the other party your intention that the communication channel is established as an open two-way process.

The research informs us that genuine smiling is likely to be brief, natural, and unforced. Smiling that occurs too frequently, is badly timed, goes on for too long, or involves obvious deliberation, runs risk of being perceived in a negative frame. Aspects that may assist or detract from natural positivity are described in Table 27.1. Smiling is not the content of the interaction between people. Instead, it remains an aid enabling you to set the *climate and context* of an interaction in a manner that other individuals are likely to recognise.

Failure to smile, or failure to acknowledge the other person's smile, will itself signal a powerful message, albeit that of a negative, possibly punitive, climate. It is well appreciated that teachers often need to suppress displays of displeasure and disgust when dealing with severe misconduct. Similarly, times arise when suppression of your naturally warm smile will represent the appropriate professional response. Laughing and smiling about student misdeeds is best reserved for the staffroom.

TABLE 27.1 Smiling and gesture: distinguishing positive and not so positive interpersonal cues

SOURCE OF CUE	POSITIVITY ENHANCED	POSITIVITY DECREASED
Timing of smile	Brief, less than half second, or even shorter.	Lengthy, over a second.
Facial muscles movement	Facial movement widespread. Muscles around eyes may contract slightly.	Facial movement more restricted to mouth.
Flexible nature	Smile seems mobile, changing, and the smile may even 'flicker' on and off in some people.	Smile appears rigid as though being held consciously fixed.
Eye-gaze pattern	Eye gaze is dancing around the person being smiled at, but direct gaze is often brief, virtually split seconds.	Eye gaze fixates the target person for too long, too direct. This makes the action appear deliberate or calculating.
Head angle Shoulders	Head upright, slight nodding. Shoulders held either back or leaning forward.	Head slightly tilted. Shoulders slumped, possibly one higher than the other in accord with head tilt.
Arms, hands and palms	Open expansive arm gestures, showing palms upwards, suggestive of general encouragement.	Gestures are less expansive, with palms turned down as though to place control over the interaction.

Note: There is danger in overreacting to any one cue in isolation. It is the pattern that conveys the message, not any one single attribute.

Beyond the smile: how we read other people

Although we are focusing on the smile as a universal social cue, the smile is simply one factor implicated in the wider process of interpersonal communication. For instance, we will read body language and facial expressions in other people. Impressions gained are key determinants of how we go about engaging with them, or perhaps attempting to avoid such interactions. The human brain is hard-wired to instantly apprehend emotional states in other people. As noted earlier, some cultural differences are found, but they tend to be variations in the manner of expression. The notion that humans everywhere share a common basis in being able to recognise emotions in others embodies considerable truth.

There appear to be three distinct types of information we use whenever we encounter another person. They account for judgements concerning (a) temporary mood, (b) stable personality, and (c) familiarity. In the first place, we infer a person's mood or emotional state. Within a second of meeting another person your brain will infer how this person is feeling and experiencing the world at that actual moment in time. This impression is strengthened dramatically once the person moves or speaks, and several studies suggest that their tone of voice conveys such messages very powerfully. Evidence from laboratory studies suggests that whenever you meet someone your brain has to figure out just what state (e.g., emotions and motives) they are in, which takes around two seconds.

There is solid evidence that people automatically infer personality traits in other people on the basis of how they look. This process also proceeds quickly, without any actual evidence. We are talking here of more enduring attributes, as distinct from momentary states. For example, someone with a wide jaw is seen as an inherently strong individual. A large forehead can be seen as signalling intelligence. Our brains appear to rate faces on several dimensions but most notably upon aggressiveness, trustworthiness, dominance, and friendliness.

It was discovered in the 1990s that the process of inferring personality from faces is totally automatic. Under laboratory conditions, such judgements have been shown to occur after seeing faces on computer screens for 100 milliseconds. In one study, it was shown that people will assess political candidates on their competence merely from looking at photographs. That people are inclined toward making significant judgements about other people on the basis of minimal information has been studied extensively in the laboratory and is referred to as the **spontaneous trait inference** effect.

The third data source relates to the faces of people we know and interact with on a regular basis. Through exposure to people over time, you form valid impressions of their unique character. For instance, you learn who you can trust, and who is aggressive. Above all, you discover that your initial inferences, those first impressions, were in need of revision. It is not that your implicit view of certain facial features has changed; merely that knowledge of a specific individual now overrides these fast and automatic responses.

What is now known to happen is that you learn to associate a specific person's behavioural cues with a specific intention that you believe they are harbouring. In other words, you begin to read the other person's normal motive patterns. Thus, once you get to know someone, you interpret their faces, movement patterns, and gestures with accuracy, since you know implicitly what they are striving to achieve.

This type of learning is implicit in that you do not know exactly what cues you are responding towards, although you are being successful at 'reading' the other person. However, the enormous benefit to you is that, through associating with the other person, you become able to anticipate how that individual will react to new situations. Your ability to anticipate the behaviour of the individuals around you is one of the keys to successful life adjustment.

Recognising people's individuality means reclassifying them

Another subtle shift will take place in your mind when you begin to see another person as having experiences, goals, and expectations unique and personal to that individual. When you first meet people, adults or children, there is a strong tendency to see them as being similar to other people. This individual in front of you seems typical of a group of people with the same traits, same goals, same values, and so on. The mind plays tricks in that you will assume that all people with a specific trait are thereby similar or stereotyped. This tendency makes it very easy to classify people, or otherwise to see an individual simply as one member of a group.

However, as you become more familiar with an individual, this type of biased trait-like thinking becomes impossible. Instead, you discover that individuals never fit into neat categories. The dramatic theme of beginning to recognise the human qualities of people previously marginalised is often found in literature and films. However, a remarkably similar process actually occurs in our everyday interactions, which helps to explain just why this theme is such a powerful one. Once you become truly familiar with someone, and recognise his or her unique pattern of smiling, you can no longer apply a stereotype to that person since you now know it cannot possibly fit.

IN PERSPECTIVE: The value of the smile

Marianne LaFrance, a leading figure in research into the effects of smiling, summarised the findings thus:

> Human smiles are designed to captivate. We see smiles, distinguish those that are genuine from those that are not, and move toward the former and away from the latter. All this happens in a split second and typically out of conscious awareness. This, then, is a key fact about smiles. They are consequential – they affect what others feel and do. Far from being merely a nice gesture or a great asset, a credible smile is a force to be reckoned with. Smiles are not merely consequential: they are indispensable to physical health, well-being, and social viability.
>
> (2011, p. 53)

It is possible to reflect on how this research knowledge applies to the classroom context. We have emphasised how interpersonal judgements are fast, automatic and inevitable. We now know that whenever you deal with your students part of your brain is apprehending what motives they are harbouring. You judge students, and they judge you. How you look has some initial bearing on how you are perceived but this can alter. Your face, your voice, and expressive gestures are all tools in that you are able to communicate a positive view of the world (see Table 27.1, above).

Your smile can be used to reinforce a world-view that stresses shared humanistic values bolstered by common interpersonal decencies such as respect and polite-ness. In effect, you invite your students to share your view of the world and in so doing you are providing a strong model for implicit emulation. As their teacher you are an inevitable coach in interpersonal mannerisms. Hence, a deep understanding of how these social processes operate will prove of inherent value in your professional work. Students clearly will evaluate their teachers on their smiles, and the research indicates that teachers' liking for their students is linked to whether or not students exhibit responsive smiling.

To close this section, by way of dramatic effect, we want to revisit one of the findings, as cited in the opening paragraphs, concerning the power of smiling in making people attractive. One study, conducted in a singles bar, found that when a woman quickly smiled at a man the probability of the person smiled at making an approach increased from a baseline of 20 per cent to a remarkable 60 per cent!

Study guide questions

1 People who smile have been shown to secure many advantages in social situations, relative to those who do not smile. What are some of these known research findings? Can you think of situations where your smile has proved a great asset?

2 There are 12 basic facial patterns, and the smile is one of these. Name the three major muscles implicated in the smile.

3 The smile means far more than simple pleasure or happiness. In fact, people are unlikely to display the smile if they are by themselves, even when receiving wonderful news. What does this tell us about the role of smiling in social life?

4 What happens when you smile at another person, for no apparent reason?

5 There are two findings: (a) smiling is a universal social signal with responsiveness built into the nervous system and (b) smiling takes different forms across cultures. Are these ideas in conflict?

6 At times, it is said that Duchenne smiles are genuine, and non-Duchenne smiles are not. However this notion is neither sensible nor valid. Why not?

7 Studies have compared how young children, older children, and adults react to the smiling face. Are there any known differences in such reactions?

8 What is meant by a 'low-level smile' (i.e., barely visible), and how is this wrapped up with comprehension processes?

9 Whenever you meet someone, your brain has to infer instantly what sort of person you are dealing with. There are four known dimensions people have been found to use, totally automatically. What are they?

10 As you become familiar with someone, there is a shift in how you see this person, from trait-like classifications to just what?

11 Overall, can you describe the body language cues that signal positive social interactions?

Reference notes

- Marianne LaFrance's book, *Lip Service*, provides an accessible overview of studies into human smiling (LaFrance, 2011).

- Smiling enhances hitchhiking (Gueguen & Fischer-Lokou, 2004), tips (Rind & Bordia, 1996), being likable and attractive (Krumhuber, Manstead, & Kappas, 2007; Walsh & Hewitt, 1985), leniency for offenders (LaFrance & Hecht, 1995), and reduced levels of litigation in medical negligence (Hickson *et al.*, 2002). The models' attractive smile impacts product evaluation (Peace, Miles, & Johnston, 2006).

- Smiles are easily recognised at a distance (F. W. Smith & Schyns, 2009). Females smile more than males (LaFrance, Hecht, & Paluck, 2003).

- Smiling at school linked with the child's home life (Oveis, Gruber, Keltner, Stamper, & Boyce, 2009). Children who smile are socially competent (Y. E. Babad *et al.*, 1983).

- Smiling avatar rated as more trustworthy (Siu Man & Hui, 2010). Smiles in a virtual reality situation (Miles, 2009). Adolescent and college smiling predicts life course outcomes (Harker & Keltner, 2001; Hertenstein, Hansel, Butts, & Hile, 2009), and longevity (Abel & Kruger, 2010).

- Brief smiling primes people to respond positively (Anderson, Siegel, White, & Barrett, 2012).

- The power of the face: the story of the Afghan girl: http://en.wikipedia.org/wiki/File:Sharbat_Gula_on_National_Geographic_cover.jpg.

- Smiling in the bowling alley (Kraut & Johnson, 1979). Smiling at people in the street (Hinsz & Tomhave, 1991). Three degrees of social separation (Fowler & Christakis, 2010). We smile at people who remind us of other people we like (Berk & Andersen, 2000).

- Children and adult appear similar in how they judge smiles (Thibault, Gosselin, Brunel, & Hess, 2009).

- A low-level smile signals comprehension (Musch & Klauer, 2003; Winkielman & Cacioppo, 2001).

- Automated processes activated whenever we meet someone (Van Overwalle, Van Duynslaeger, Coomans, & Timmermans, 2012).

- The phenomenon of spontaneous trait inference in interpersonal judgement (Uleman, Saribay, & Gonzalez, 2008). On basis of photographs, attractive politicians seen as more competent (Surawski & Ossoff, 2006).

- Major review about how we form impressions and what goes on in our minds as we meet people (Uleman & Saribay, 2012).

- We make judgements about people's intentions within a second of initial meeting (Van Overwalle *et al.*, 2012).

- Study conducted in a singles bar (Walsh & Hewitt, 1985).

28

The surprising advantages of being a social chameleon

Whenever human beings meet and begin to interact many curious things take place. The phenomenon of basic interpersonal interaction involves sets of rules and rituals. We had to learn these as a key aspect of growing up and getting on with other people. It behoves us all, but especially anyone who makes his or her living as a teacher, to observe these patterns with care.

One fundamental fact of life is that people who fail to observe the rules render us uncomfortable. They become difficult for us to appreciate, or even interact with. Violations of social conventions define a common topic for literature and drama. For instance, at the time of writing we note the popularity of two television series, *Doc Martin* from England and *The Big Bang Theory* from the United States. The underlying themes depict antics of individuals with defective interpersonal repertoires. In these programs, humour is created through the insensitivity of such individuals to commonly accepted rules of social interaction. This is no different in class and staff rooms.

Measuring interpersonal reactions

We pose the simple question: *What has social science discovered about the dynamics of human social interactions?* Researchers have used several techniques to advantage such as systematic observation, the high-speed camera, and the electromyograph (or EMG), which is a device measuring slight muscle activation. For example, the EMG can be used to detect facial expressions. You cannot help it, but your facial muscles function as a type of read-out system for aspects of emotional expression. From such methods researchers have uncovered a good deal more about human behaviour than people are normally aware of. When it comes to being aware of how we negotiate the tricky task of getting on with other people, we are truly strangers unto ourselves.

Suppose two individuals in Western societies meet face-to-face. In all probability, they are careful not to hold mutual eye gaze for more than brief periods, perhaps around a half second. Eye gaze is important, but it is a dangerous tool. Long fixations can be used only for specific purposes such as power displays or sexual intent. Instead of long fixations, a remarkable dance of eye movements occurs. The eyes of each person scan the other, especially the other person's arms and hands, and lower face. The eyes dart from face to upper body, to the hands, back to the face, and so on. When interacting with someone, it is necessary to monitor their face every few seconds. But this is a quick glance, often under a half second, which provides the essential feedback. Holding a fixation for longer than a second typically signals something unusual, rather than routine business.

On one level, the interaction constitutes a verbal interchange. An important flow of information is occurring at the conscious level and this aspect is captured by the audio recorder. But a good deal more is going on. At an unspoken level many of the significant dimensions of the interchange are taking place. How can we know what is happening if it is unconscious? Well, it relates to factors such as cueing, timing, synchronicity, and gesture. Our brains apprehend these facets and use them to attach meanings onto the nature of the interaction. In interactions, all parties are processing information with dramatic speed. In normal human conversation, the gaps between two individuals naturally taking turns in speaking typically are in the order of a tenth of a second, and it is common for one person to begin speaking before another person has finished. Timing is a critical dynamic in all interpersonal interactions.

The importance of timing

Try watching two people walking together, for example, down a corridor. When relationships are positive and friendly, there is a visible synchrony at work. The two move in step with each other. But the parties themselves have no awareness of what they are doing. One or other adjusts body posture and timing to mesh in with the partner. It is easy for a third party to observe their movements and sense that there is some level of harmony. You can watch a group of people and work out just who is friendly with whom, without needing to hear verbal dialogue. This notion of bodily synchronism applies widely in all relationships. For instance, it applies to how parents interact with their children. As a teacher, you can watch how your student walks across the yard with a parent. Whether or not the relationship is harmonious is suggested by their movement patterns.

Whenever two people are together, but their movements are out of sync, observers immediately detect 'something is wrong' even though these witnesses remain unaware of just what they are reacting towards. It might seem ludicrous to hold a thought such as, 'They do not get on as Janet did not move her arm at the right time'. However, that is akin to what your brain is registering and telling you about Sally's relationship with the other person. If they are not in time, they are not in tune.

These perceptions are so strong that researchers can replicate the effect with stick figures on the computer screen. When such stick figures move in unison, people infer the presence of a positive relationship between them, and will say, quite spontaneously, that the figures form an 'entity' or a group working together. This ability to see individual people as units of a social group is built-in as an aspect of human perception. We can speculate that evolution has programmed us to read human relationships through sensing the correlations and timings of bodily gestures in other people. As a social animal we acquired, perhaps early in our species' evolutionary history, a deep sense of who is like us, who will work in with us, who is working in sync with whom, and who is a threat.

Posture matching

One well-documented finding is that whenever two or more individuals meet, a degree of **posture matching** often will occur. If you need a graphic image of posture matching, think of how a military squad is trained to behave on the parade ground. Every soldier moves in perfect match with the others. While this is the extreme case, something not unlike this occurs in social life. Researchers discovered posture matching in the 1950s using the new technology of slow motion films to analyse interpersonal conduct when people work together productively. Posture matching refers to the level of consistency between group participants in aspects such as arm waving, posture angles, standing, leaning, facial movements, and a good deal more. When groups are working well, their members appear to converge in their actions such that they lean into each other, move in unison, spread their arms more widely, and mutually nod at each other. It is possible to note high levels of contagion in the group, most notably with aspects such as smiling, laughing, frowning, and yawning. Such findings gave rise to advancing *body language* as one of the subtle keys to effective communication, and this became a popular theory by the 1970s.

It turned out the saying 'yawning is contagious' was fully validated. It was found that even reading about people yawning was enough to start college students off yawning themselves. It has been shown that children from 4 years of age will yawn after seeing someone else yawn. But yawning is only one of many such mimicked actions in normal social interactions. A close inspection of video-taped interactions showed that as groups developed better rapport and sense of collaboration, the levels of posture matching would increase. At the time of this early research it was assumed that posture mirroring was occurring because people were learning to work together, and so liked each other. If you liked someone, then you would match your body posture to resemble him or her. Incidentally, posture matching crosses gender distinctions. If someone is going to trigger your yawning, it matters not if that person is male or female.

Later studies, however, revealed that the effect works also in reverse mode. That is, unconscious posture matching can come first, and emotional aspects such as feelings of liking, mutual attractiveness, and rapport, may follow. Think about this: it is easy to begin interacting with someone you did not especially like. But after a few seconds of posture matching, you could begin to change your mind.

On the other hand, if posture matching failed to take place, there is a sense of unfriendliness, and a lingering feeling of disjunction. Posture matching allows people to feel a degree of human contact and empathy during the course of social interaction. However, the research also says that when there is a good clear reason to dislike someone, then a few minutes spent matching posture with this person certainly will not alter anything. The chameleon effect (see below) is known to occur even when people dislike each other.

The social chameleon in all of us

Many studies have been published into what is called the **chameleon effect**. This refers to the fact that when people are in close proximity, a level of mimicry occurs; even though none of the parties may be aware this is taking place. For example, if you are working alongside someone who occasionally taps his foot, or uses large arm gestures, or touches his nose with his finger, or rocks in his chair, tugs his ear, or pats his leg, then, behold, within minutes, you tend to mimic such gestures, automatically and unconsciously. This form of natural mimicry has early roots as it is known that babies mimic tongue thrusts and facial expressions from around one month of age, and other body movements from around one year. In many social situations people tend to take on board many of the behaviours exhibited by the people immediately around them.

The chameleon effect is one type of posture matching. The term matching is used more when people mirror each other while interacting. The chameleon effect does not necessarily rely on talking or interacting with another person, and the copying does not necessarily occur immediately. For example, it can occur after the other person has left the vicinity.

Dr Tanya Chartrand has conducted many laboratory studies into such effects using adults and college students. As part of the debriefing process, once a project is over, she asks her participants if they were aware that they were mimicking the behaviour of the other person in the room, who was her confederate (i.e., someone paid to act out a role, such as to deliberately tap his foot). Of several hundred people tested, not one suspected that the confederate's pre-arranged gestures were influencing how they acted. Their conscious minds were focused on the given task, which could be sorting through photographs. However, the foot-tapping, and other imitated gestures, were totally unconscious.

Significantly, the quality of the relationship relates to the level of mimicry. People who cooperate, and get on well, will show a high level of this behavioural mirroring. It has been found that when people attempt to make friends, then they mimic the other person strongly. Nevertheless, Dr Chartrand's studies also found that this type of mimicry still will take place even when there is little genuine basis for the relationship, with the other person merely being in the same room at the time. In fact, mimicry is so automatic that it normally increases when people are placed under conditions of cognitive load.

Building relationships

This type of social mimicry, or chameleon behaviour, is highly adaptive since it is one basis for building a positive relationship. Through detailed analysis of film recordings, the effect is seen not only in superficial gestures such as foot-tapping, but has been shown to occur in speech and vocal behaviour. Without realising what is going on, people adjust their voice, such as in speed, tempo, and stress patterns, to more closely match the characteristics of the person with whom they are associating. In the case of the voice, these are likely to be gentle shifts, but nevertheless, it is apparent that the form of your voice (in pitch, tempo, or stress patterns) tends to alter slightly depending on how you perceive other people, and the type of relationship you have with them. Most importantly, your voice shifts in the direction to match the other person more closely.

Studies have also shown that when people interact, then within a few minutes they tend to show convergence in their use of sentence structures, vocabulary, and vocal stress patterns. If you are in the immediate presence of another person, supposedly in some form of interaction, and this behavioural convergence does not take place, or if the other person does not mimic you, then you will experience a feeling of dissatisfaction or rejection. Your unconscious mind is signalling a message akin to 'this relationship is going nowhere'.

Mimicry is a key part of your social repertoire. It is a strategy you use to allow yourself to slot comfortably into social situations. It is easy to fit in when your actions closely match the actions of people around you. Dr Chartrand has also established that we tend to mimic people at a higher level after receiving unfriendly treatment from another person. That is, after having an unfriendly interaction with one individual, people then increase the level of mimicry when meeting another person soon after. Being rebuffed in one possible relationship encourages people to increase efforts to ensure the next relationship is a more positive one. In a further study, she also found that when people are induced to feel that they are somehow different from other people, this information also produces increased levels of social mimicry.

One direct implication of this research into automatic mimicry is that we harbour unspoken goals to socialise and get on well with others. Events that threaten these goals result in subtle adjustments in how we relate to others. Although we could find only research with adults on this specific point, it is reasonable to assume that such findings apply also to children and young students sitting in classrooms. Indeed, one argument is that children are more likely than adults to exhibit patterns that suggest inherent social dependency on available models in the social world.

Is chameleon-like behaviour built into us?

Why do we become such chameleons? One immediate answer lies in the fact that it is rewarding and highly successful. Yes, but there are other strange findings in the literature indicating that chameleon-like mimicry occurs even when people are exposed to a robot's face, or other non-human facial representations. We also mimic facial expressions we see on television. When we watch television, our faces are often active in subtle but predictable ways.

If able to do so discretely, try to monitor the faces of other people as they watch television. When people are watching intensively, there is a degree of subtle bodily and facial movement, which frequently matches the emotions they are witnessing. When you see someone smile, you also smile. When the figure on the screen experiences pain, it shows on your face and your entire body tenses slightly. If someone nods, then you tend to also nod, ever so slightly, as you watch.

Chameleon-like functions are bound up with how we understand other people and their emotions, even when there is no actual interaction possible. Researchers have found that it becomes a strangely difficult task to watch TV with a passive or poker face. People report such an experience as unnatural and unpleasant. For instance, one commonly used laboratory task used to get people to exercise self-control is to ask them to watch comedy films without showing any outward emotion. Professional card players attest to the fact that disguising their emotions in a card game does not occur naturally. It requires years of stealthy development.

Studies with the EMG show also that facial mimicry can even occur when people are asked to look at still photographs of other people. Whenever people recognise emotions in other people, they tend to replicate some aspects of the same emotion within their own bodies. Although it sounds strange, it is a serious finding that the face tends to mimic what we can see in the face of another person, even in response to a still photograph. To understand other people entails empathising with their experience, and this is detected through fine-grain measurement techniques.

For example, in one laboratory study conducted in the early 1970s people were connected up to an EMG reading muscle activation levels. When watching someone lifting a weight, the muscles in their arms showed activation, and when watching someone speak, the muscles around the mouth were activated. At the time when first known, this type of finding was extremely difficult to interpret. There was simply no known theory that could explain what was happening. But we now believe that the underlying process is one of *mirror neurons* being activated.

Your mind as a mirror

An interesting perspective on teacher skills and traits has emerged in recent years out of contemporary neuroscience. *Mirror neuron theory* suggests that whenever humans interact within the same physical space, the brain of the individual who is observing will neurologically 'mirror' the person they are watching. The mirror neuron system was discovered through a strangely unexpected event seen in a laboratory context in the early 1990s. Researchers, studying brain activity in monkeys that had to remove objects from a box, noticed that brain activation was occurring even when the monkeys were watching the experimenters handle the objects. In terms of what was known about the brain at the time, these effects ought not to have been happening.

A good deal of research into this effect then followed to the point where a general conclusion appears possible: *the same cortical circuits that are implicated in executing an action respond also when observing someone else executing that action.* Although research with human beings cannot be carried out with the same level of precision possible with animal subjects, many studies using magnetic imaging techniques show critical areas of the brain are highly active when people watch and interpret other human beings.

Researchers within this field are beginning to speculate that such mirror-like mechanisms would enable a species to develop a highly adaptive repertoire of cooperative social skills. There is much speculation that this is how the human mind has evolved. An efficient mirror neuron system in place allowed members of the species to interact and cooperate successfully. The system is activated through observing physical movement and monitoring all social activities taking place within the perceptual field. Although we can only deal with speculations about evolution, nevertheless, the neurological basis for social learning theory and the notion of the social brain is now substantial.

As an example of the strange and curious effects being discovered in this area, consider the following: when people look at artwork that depicts apparent brush strokes, then areas of the brain associated with moving the arms and hands become active. Upon looking at a painting with obvious brush marks on it, people understand what they see by activating parts of the brain that would be active if they were doing the same painting. Seeing brushstrokes, your mind mirrors how they were created, enabling you to mentally imitate the action involved.

What your mirror neurons can do for you

The implications of the mirror system have yet to be explored. However, the evidence suggests that, within any teaching situation, your interpersonal gestures and bodily movements assume enormous importance in the brains of your students (i.e., physiologically). What has been established through the laboratory studies is that the use of physical gesture, hand movement, and facial expression all contribute strongly to the mental activity people will experience as they watch another person behave.

In recent years, researchers have begun to speculate that your mirror neuron system allows you to infer another person's immediate intentions. When you look at another person, your brain informs you what that person is intending to do at that second. You may not be able to gauge other people with total accuracy, of course. But nevertheless, you are going to make clear and inevitable judgments, which is the result of your mirror neuron cells firing as they would if you were doing what that other person is apparently doing.

What became apparent from this research is that the mirror neuron system is directly telling you how to *understand* other people. You can no more ignore this than you can prevent yourself from reading the word 'monkey' in text. The theory suggests that physical bodily gestures serve as vehicles that do not merely assist information flow, but are intrinsic to the information being communicated. Such gestures provide the basic structure and grammar for any message a speaker is attempting to communicate.

Another notable aspect that has emerged from recent speculations in this area concerns the observation that language contains many words that have a basis in physical or gestural moves. We often use terms such as 'on the other hand', or 'let me shoulder that burden for you'. The theory suggests such expressions are not accidental, but reflect how the brain's mirror system evolved to allow us to understand other people by observing their gestures closely.

IN PERSPECTIVE: Developing your social skills in teaching

The information reviewed in this chapter stems mainly from studies in social psychology, but it can apply directly to teaching in any context that implies interpersonal interaction and dealing successfully with people. For instance, the research into chameleon behaviour conveys immediate implications for how you can establish and maintain strong social relationships. Whenever people are important to you, you mimic them, and are highly sensitive to their movements. Matching another person's gestures may seem strangely facile, yet it is highly effective. To enhance your overall impact as a classroom teacher, you must take such body language ideas seriously. Strive to use your arms, hands, face, and body as fundamental components of your essential communication repertoire. Make sure your body language is open and expansive as you teach. And remember to smile. You can do this in full knowledge that such gesturing is consistent with findings from modern neuroscience. And it is these gestures that will define the personality by which your students will evaluate you. In turn, the feedback they give you will make your smile even more genuine.

Study guide questions

1 We are strangers unto ourselves. Why is it that this idea resonates so deeply with researchers in the area of interpersonal behaviour?

2 When two people walk down a corridor, just what is likely to happen? And what does a casual observer infer by just watching them walk?

3 Analyses from slow motion filming methods in the 1950s gave rise to the notion of posture matching within productive social groups. Just what was noticed about such groups?

4 The chameleon effect can be said to be one type of posture matching. When is this specific term likely to be used? How would you define the chameleon effect?

5 This tendency to be influenced by, and mimic, the people around you is known to increase under certain conditions. What are these?

6 It sounds bizarre to suggest we mimic from the television screen. But what happens when we deliberately try to watch television with a total poker face? (Please try this. People can do it, but report it strangely demanding and unnatural.)

7 A discovery from the 1990s is that of our mirror neuron system. This has been hailed as a major discovery since it suggests a neurological basis for all forms of social learning. What is going on in your head as you watch another person do something with their arms?

8 Just why is it that you ought to cultivate the art of copying people's actions? Just who should you copy? What benefits does this produce in your favour? How can you use this skill in the classroom?

Reference notes

- When stick figures move in unison (Lakens, 2010).
- When gestures are synchronised between people, we sense positive relationships (Bernieri, 1988; Grahe & Bernieri, 1999; Maurer & Tindall, 1983).
- Posture matching (LaFrance, 1985, 2011; LaFrance & Broadbent, 1976).
- Contagious yawning in children (Helt, Eigsti, Snyder, & Fein, 2010).
- Behavioural contagion within groups (Provine, 2000, 2005).
- Chameleon effect (Bargh & Chartrand, 1999; Chartrand & Bargh, 1999; Chartrand et al., 2005; Cheng & Chartrand, 2003).
- Actor Alan Alda visits Dr Chartrand's research facility and gets mimicked: www.youtube.com/watch?v=7BKwBsPlR04.
- Mimicry increases after a bad experience (Lakin, Chartrand, & Arkin, 2008).
- People mimic robots (Jones & Scmidlin, 2011).
- Unconsciously, we mimic faces on television and photographs (Dimberg, Andréasson, & Thunberg, 2011; Dimberg, Thunberg, & Grunedal, 2002; Neal & Chartrand, 2011; Stel & Vonk, 2009).
- The brain reacts neurologically to understand brush strokes in artwork (J. E. T. Taylor, Witt, & Grimaldi, 2012).

- EMG studies from the 1970s (Berger & Hadley, 1975; Berger, Irwin, & Frommer, 1970).
- Mirror neuron theory described in depth (Iacoboni, 2008).
- Implications of mirror theory for social learning (Paas & Sweller, 2012; van Gog, Paas, Marcus, Ayres, & Sweller, 2009).

29

Invisible gorillas, inattentional blindness, and paying attention

The saga associated with **inattentional blindness** (or IB) research involves the modern flight simulator as used in pilot training. In simulators, trainees are subjected to unpredictable events such as engine misfire, instrument failure, or sudden changes in weather. Today's pilots undergo the most rigorous training of any professional group, with this being directly tied to the emergence of the knowledge base referred to as human factors research. The aviation industry represents the most successful example of how basic research into human capacity has been used to solve applied problems. The development of the modern flight simulator represents an achievement that would have been inconceivable at the outset of controlled flight 120 years ago.

With the advent of sophisticated computer-generated displays, a curious phenomenon was noted, somewhat disturbingly. When another plane was positioned stationary on the runway, in full view from the simulator cockpit, an alarming high percentage of pilots would still attempt to land their craft. Although the industry cannot acknowledge such data, apparently some 30 per cent of trainee pilots did not see the runway blockage until too late. Furthermore, this phenomenon was not unique to trainees as it was noted also with experienced pilots, 25 per cent in one study. Pilots pay close attention to aspects such as airspeed, height, drift, engine power, through an array of critical instruments. Paying attention to this complex world, they may glance at the runway, but apparently fail to see what is there, right before their eyes.

A type of blindness?

This notion of perceptual blindness is by no means specific to pilots. Generations of road accident investigations have noted that many car drivers report not seeing the other vehicle involved in a collision. Traditionally, carelessness and recklessness were blamed. But researchers began to wonder if other factors could be implicated. Cyclists and motorcyclists in particular appear to become all too easy victims of this apparent inattention on the road. This phenomenon became to be known as a form of blindness, albeit temporary blindness created by problems of attention when a person is under stress. Attention is being paid to one source, or to immediately pressing demands, but not to what is right there before the eyes.

We operate on the natural assumption that what is in front of your face must automatically draw in your attention. This is the default position. Researchers within the field of visual perception began with this assumption, which was not seriously questioned until the early 1970s. However, it turns out that this assumption is incorrect under certain conditions. Some early studies had reported strange findings such as when people are fully engrossed in stressful tasks (such as trying to 'add 1' when undergoing a digit span test), they become momentarily blind to what is sitting right there in front of them, for half a second or so. Although poorly understood, such a phenomenon had been known in the laboratory since before the 1960s, although it was not generally referred to as inattentional blindness until the late 1990s.

The Chabris and Simons study: the classic paper

Although it had been known that people under stress can miss seeing something that quickly flashes in front of them, it was assumed such effects were not common, and of short duration, possibly split seconds. This notion was considerably revised with the publication of the invisible gorilla studies. In a paper that became an immediate classic, Christopher Chabris and Daniel Simons (1999) reported asking college students to watch a brief video and count the number of times a basketball was passed between certain people on the film. At the 10-second mark, an actor dressed in a gorilla suit, entered the frame from the right, walked across the screen view, through the group of people, turned and thumped his chest before walking off to the left.

The gorilla was on screen for 9 of the 30 seconds. Remarkably, only 42 per cent of the participants reported seeing it. Since then the film, and versions of it, has been shown in thousands of locations to many thousands of individuals. The results have consistently proved robust across locations and different groups of individuals. If people are simply asked to look at the film, then 100 per cent of witnesses will see the gorilla. However, when viewers mentally count the ball passes, about one half of the audience (50 to 60 per cent) fail to perceive the gorilla. The effect has also been shown to occur with children. The films, and others which can be used to show the same effect, are widely available on resources such as YouTube.

What is now known about IB from the research?

The IB effect has been thoroughly investigated over the past decade. A number of critical findings have been made. It is now known that it makes no sense at all to presume that the world is divided into people who show IB effects and those that do not. How people respond on one IB test fails to predict how they fare on a different version of the same test. It is known that there is no significant practice effect. The effect is greater when the central task (i.e., counting) is more demanding, and this factor is known as cognitive load. Indeed, handling high levels of load is the most powerful explanation for why IB effects occur. As your mind focuses on one central task, there is insufficient attention left for other aspects in your world.

For instance, our novice pilot, attempting to land in the simulator, is experiencing extreme load, monitoring several sources of vital information at once. His or her mind is literally taken over by the demands of the situation. To land an airplane represents one of the most demanding tasks any human can undertake. The number of variables that come into play during a landing, but which could demand sensitive adjustments, exceeds natural human processing levels. After several hundred landings the experience may become procedural. But to the novice, the mental load is immense, the most mindful experience that he or she has ever experienced.

In laboratory studies, the ball counting task can be made more complex by asking people to count aerial passes and bouncing passes separately. Making the task more complex increases load, which requires people to devote even more attention. Under this additional demand, even fewer perceptual resources are available to see the gorilla when it strides on unannounced. For example, in one study, enhanced load increased the percentage of people who displayed IB effects up to 81 per cent.

Why training cannot reduce IB

What else do we now know about IB? It is apparent that even when people do spot the gorilla, their performance on the counting task is not necessarily as disrupted as we might presume. This is somewhat surprising but it suggests an impressive mental agility such as, 'There is a funny gorilla, but it is counting I have to do. So keep up with that, and do not look at that stupid gorilla'. That is, just seeing the gorilla for a split second does not necessarily destroy the on-going goal of counting.

It is known that the effect cannot be predicted from any global measure such as gender, intelligence, or personality. Also, it appears to be unteachable. Training people to improve attentional abilities in general will not enhance their ability to detect unexpected events in this type of experiment. When you think carefully about it, there is little reason why training should have any effect, since IB occurs when the mind is occupied with another demanding task. In the case of the pilot training, the crucial aspect is one of adding 'check the runway is clear' into the necessary checklist. This is far more sensible than instructing the young pilot to 'watch out for anything unexpected'.

In other words, one way to prevent IB is to prepare the individual for the possibility of an unusual, but possible, occurrence. Of course you will not find the IB effect in the gorilla test if the person knows about it in advance. It would be pointless to ask someone to watch 'the invisible gorilla video' having just cued them as to the content and purpose of the demonstration. When people are told in advance about the film, and then watch, the universal comment is that they cannot believe others could possibly miss seeing such a huge animal walk across the screen.

In other research it has been shown, somewhat surprisingly, that the IB effect appears to be basically unrelated to the person's eye movements. Since the gorilla actually crosses the visual field, surely those that report seeing him spend more time looking at him directly, rather than focusing on the ball passes? But several studies found this factor did not discriminate those who saw the gorilla from those that did not. The eye movement studies suggested that most people actually will look directly at the gorilla for around one second on average. In other words, the gorilla lies in direct focal vision for a second, but despite this apparent opportunity, many such people still fail to report seeing him.

In one remarkable study, researchers did uncover the fact that IB is considerably increased when a person has consumed alcohol. Volunteers whose blood alcohol level was measured at 0.04 per cent dropped their hit level down to 18 per cent gorilla sightings, when the expected level (sober) performance is around the 50 per cent point. By most accepted world standards, 0.04 does not represent a high level of intoxication, and in many countries it may still be under the legal limit for road usage. This research paper was meaningfully titled 'Blind drunk'.

IB as a natural human condition: the first casualty of overload

The significance of the IB effect lies in appreciating how events can occur in the world, yet apparently, not reach the conscious mind. One recurring finding in these studies lies in the fact that the individuals who report seeing the gorilla also report no understanding as to how their peers could have failed to see it. After all, they all had the same experience. This is a very important observation. It implies we have little natural sympathy for those who fail to share our perceptions. And worse, we may infer lack of capability in such individuals.

Why do people not see what is right there in front of them? Are they incompetent? Is the trainee pilot negligent for attempting a simulated landing on a blocked runway? Well, he or she would be negligent after having one such previous experience, since the pilot must be trained to expect the possible. But the pilot's base problem was in being engrossed in the critical task of keeping the craft trim and in safe flying condition. By trying hard, and being under conditions of full mental load, then one's ability to take in unanticipated events is diminished dramatically. Yet, the individual whose brain is not under load will clearly see everything going on within the field. But such a smug observer possesses no special insight as to why the other person fails to respond in the same way he or she does.

In one study, people who were more expert in basketball were more likely to see the gorilla than those that knew little about basketball. This could be simply because such experts are accustomed to monitoring an entire court. It could be that counting ball passes imposed less cognitive load on their minds. Either way, it seems that experts in a field are going to be less likely to suffer IB effects. This idea is consistent with the notion that expertise brings with it the ability to work efficiently but still use less brainpower to achieve similar performance goals when compared to others. If an expert's performance is inherently less effortful, there is greater spare capacity, more in reserve, to serve as resources available to cope with the unexpected.

There is one final research finding in this area of special relevance to teachers or anyone whose job involves communication through speech. Although we may think of IB more in the visual modality, a similar effect is known to apply to audition. When concentrating on one specific sound input, it is possible to become deaf to other sounds. In an English study, Polly Dalton and Nick Fraenkel found such inattentional deafness in the majority of the adults they tested. Whilst listening intensively for a female voice over a period of a minute, they failed to notice a male voice even though the male voice had lasted 19 seconds, in the middle of the period, and was heard clearly by those not listening so intensively to the female voice.

Hence, someone can be told something quite clearly. But when the mind is elsewhere and the working memory is fully loaded, then this input message may be filtered out so adroitly that it may as well never have occurred. Perhaps teachers have long known of such realities? Students do not always hear what they are told. But the research suggests that such effects appear less the result of lack of attention, but more the result of attention being focused strongly elsewhere.

Implications for instruction and management

IB is not just a silly example of human foibles. For one thing, it is a trait taken advantage of by professional magicians who skilfully exploit IB tendencies with attention misdirection techniques. Awareness of the IB phenomenon has resulted in reassessments being made in many fields. For example, in relation to the phenomena of bank crashes, the global financial crisis, and other worldwide financial disasters, two researchers commented,

> The history of accounting fraud is replete with examples of inattentional blindness, causing people to overlook significant red flags. This lack of attention has also been said to characterize the actions of US regulatory agencies tasked with dealing with alleged Ponzi schemes.
>
> (Kleinman & Anandarajan, 2011, p. 38)

Knowing about this effect, and appreciating it as a natural trait, can make you a more sensitive teacher. How? Through a deeper understanding of how attention works. You can recognise how students under stress fail to apprehend events that to you are obvious. Attention is a limited resource. The IB research has thrown into sharp relief the fact that our attention is not necessarily governed by what lies within immediate experience. We are born with an ability to focus on tasks and goals that totally take over our minds for short periods. Whilst such mindfulness is occurring, we may miss an unexpected event directly before our eyes, even when such an event would otherwise be viewed as important or dangerous.

On the mundane domestic level, we surely all have had experiences not unlike the following. After watching the nightly television news, your spouse enters the room, asking what the weather information was for the next day. Although watching, you were not taking it in. Sorry, you never heard the appropriate information, even though you were staring intently at the screen throughout. You were attending to the presenter's clothes, and that is what you can recall well. Your spouse then reminds you that she had said at breakfast she would go out shopping that evening. But you were reading the paper at the time, and although grunting acknowledgement, nothing entered memory. So you had made plans having 'forgotten' the obligation you had entered. If there is negligence in such interactions, it lies in failing to activate appropriate attention at a critical time: the time when learning had to occur. Attention is not in itself such an automatic process as you might presume. To make it work, it has to be activated, and if not, the opportunity to learn slips past.

When the world is complex, however, the novice learner does not always know exactly what cue is the appropriate one to attend towards. We can listen to a lecture that stimulates many strong ideas in our brains. But since the information is so rich it overwhelms us. By thinking and dwelling on one key aspect, we fail to hear about another key aspect communicated a few seconds later. Hence, we become blind to the lecturer's point B because we had had our mind taken over attending fully to point A.

Consider whether or not such effects could occur within your classroom. Do your students always pay full attention? You can see how the problem of attention has several dimensions. On one level we speculate that at all times a student is paying attention to something. But attention to what? Since schooling is a group activity, some part of everyone's attention is on the other people in the room. We speculate that mental life is defined by focal attention and peripheral attention. Your focal attention is what you allow to currently drive the other parts of your brain. So by focusing on one object or input, you allow your mind to be momentarily taken over by its importance. Past memories relevant to this input may be triggered. But such memories may be quite irrelevant to whatever else is occurring. While dwelling on some pleasant thought, other sensory experiences, anything on the periphery, will slip past unnoticed.

In many instructional contexts, students' minds are overloaded. They can miss identifying and picking up details we see as significant. We may emphasise certain aspects in our teaching and instruction, but students still fail to grasp the essential points. Many factors come into play, but the IB effect provides another possible explanation as to why an individual student has failed to respond to information that was right there before his or her eyes.

IN PERSPECTIVE: Understanding IB at work in the classroom

It is important to appreciate how attention works, and how it involves limits. When people in the classic IB experiment are asked to count ball passes, their working memories are occupied fully. Information is being both (a) held over time and (b) combined with an input experience that is relatively complex and dynamic. When you access the Internet and view the gorilla film, then you can appreciate that it was *not a simple matter* to count the passes with the action on the screen involving two teams, and two moving balls. You have to decide if a movement really represented a pass or not. The act of paying attention might seem easy. However, seeing, witnessing, judging, and responding appropriately, are complex psychological activities. Knowing about the extent of IB effect makes you acutely aware of our natural human limitations and how they can affect people within learning situations.

All teachers need to appreciate issues concerning the act of paying attention. If alpha and beta are two distinct inputs within your field of attention, the more you attend to alpha, the less mental space you have available for beta. As the need for coping with alpha increases the load within working memory, then opportunity for beta to make an impression drops away. The research tells us it can drop away completely. Under high cognitive load, input beta may as well not exist. Within the human brain, the process of paying attention works to prevent such mental multitasking, a topic discussed in Chapter 20.

Similar principles have been shown to work on the level of voluntary self-control. People learn to employ techniques of **deflection** or **distraction** to prevent themselves dwelling on stimuli or events they would rather not focus upon. Such self-applied deflection methods have even been found in studies with young children (see Chapter 26). If you can focus on something else, then your problem is out of mind, and does not exist. This coping principle applies across a broad range of human dispositions, and is seen in instances of both adaptive and maladaptive behaviour.

Study guide questions

1 Have you ever experienced an accident where you simply did not see something that you 'should have' seen? Given hindsight, was it carelessness? Could IB have contributed?

2 The original theory was that inattentional lapses of focus in attention might occur for a second or so. But why did this theory have to be revised totally after the gorilla studies were published?

3 IB is found in about half the population. Is this true?

4 What happens to IB effects as we increase the cognitive load on people?

5 Those who see the gorilla universally cannot believe that others would miss it. What does this fact tell us about the assumptions we all make about human perception?

6 At the outset it was assumed that people might fail to see the gorilla if their eyes did not fix upon him. Was this theory supported or not?

7 An English study noted that similar effects are also found in listening. When listening intensively for a female voice, people failed to hear the male voice, and later denied it had happened. Just what are the implications of such a finding for classroom practice?

8 These IB studies tell us much about our ability to attend to one thing. We know that humans can be selective in what they attend towards. This has been known for centuries. So, can you reflect upon just why these more recent IB findings are so dramatic or spectacular? What implications do they have for instructors?

Reference notes

- Highly recommended book, *The Invisible Gorilla* (Chabris & Simons, 2010).
- The 1999 classic study into IB (Simons & Chabris, 1999). Further information, and videos, are available on their websites www.theinvisiblegorilla.com and www.dansimons.com.
- Professor Simons also has his own YouTube site: www.youtube.com/user/profsimons.
- Enhanced load got IB up to 81 per cent (Beanland & Pammer, 2010).
- Cognitive load increases the IB effect (Lavie, 2010).
- Spotting gorilla does not normally disrupt performance (Bressan & Pizzighello, 2008).
- The eyes focus on gorilla, but still IB occurs (Beanland & Pammer, 2010).
- Being only slightly intoxicated seriously increases the IB effect (Clifasefi, Takarangi, & Bergman, 2006). Basketball experts did better at seeing gorilla on court (Memmert, 2006).
- IB-like effects found in audition: inattentional deafness (Dalton & Fraenkel, 2012).
- Professional magicians exploit IB and use misdirection (Macknik, Martinez-Conde, & Blakeslee, 2010).

- IB effect linked with failure to react in financial auditing situations such as banking and company disasters (Kleinman & Anandarajan, 2011).

- Strategic management of attention is a fundamental component of self-control from a young age (Mischel, 2012).

30

Thinking fast and thinking slow

Your debt to the inner robot

An idea being taken seriously in neuroscience is that we have two functioning minds, the mind you know well, and another mind you know about only indirectly. You know about the second mind because of what it does for you. This mind looks after your interests and gets you through the immediate present. One mind is conscious, but the other is unconscious. One is alert and aware. The other is a robot. Thankfully, this is your friendly and benign servant, your *inner robot.*

It seems oddly contradictory to suggest we harbour a mind that is unconscious. This hinges more on a definition of the term 'mind' rather than upon any debate about how we function, physiologically and psychologically. Alternatively, we could suggest there is one mind with two distinct systems of working. There is a fast response system whose operation is indexed through actual behavioural measurements. And then there is a slow thinking system indexed though verbal expression and conscious awareness.

Within cognitive psychology, they are referred to as System 1 and System 2. Although the dual systems work with each other, and function within the same neurology, the fast System 1 accounts for handling and responding to a great deal more information than is apprehended by the conscious mind. Despite working in intimate collaboration, however, moments occasionally arise when the operation of the two systems appears somewhat divergent, and we will discuss this situation next before moving onto the key issues.

Can your two minds be in conflict?

Studies in the field of social psychology reveal that we can hold *both* explicit and implicit attitudes, which are not always the same. An implicit attitude is an unspoken tendency to react in a certain way. Such an attitude may, or may not, be reflected in what the same person states in words. Many studies indicate that stereotypes, as well as other unfortunate tendencies, such as racial prejudice, can occur on the implicit level. Researchers have used several tools, but especially the Implicit Association Test, to reveal such hidden attitudes.

Simulated versions of the Implicit Association Test are available on the Internet, and you can undertake these online. They test for efficiency in the ease by which you can respond when asked to link target stimuli (such as faces of young and old people) with evaluative terms such as *good* or *bad*. For instance, if you can link *old* with *bad* more quickly than you can link *young* with *bad*, it suggests a pre-existing association in your mind, namely that *old* is implicitly linked with *bad* already deep within the brain's networks. These tests have been used to show that people can have difficulty associating certain targets with *good*, but might easily link the same targets with *bad*.

Researchers caution it is possible to over-interpret such findings. Devices such as the Implicit Association Test may give false readings. Hence, there has been much debate as to what such findings really imply. However, from a scientific view, the existence of dual attitudes, one verbal, the other behavioural, is not in doubt. This basic notion is supported by a wide range of findings going back to the 1930s. How we react in words is not always correlated with how our bodies are reacting. The problem is more to do with knowing how to tap into and recognise such unspoken attitudes. One interesting finding has been that implicit attitudes often appear resistant to change. New experiences might quickly change spoken attitudes, but may leave implicit attitudes unaffected.

At times, the existence of unspoken attitudes comes as a surprise to the individual concerned. For instance, you believe you treat all your students the same. But a recording can show your tone of voice is one of encouragement to well-behaved students, but one of shades of curt coolness when dealing with others. Or you might use wait time when interacting with some students, but appear impatient with others. Differential treatment of students in the classroom is, in one sense, inevitable. But research from the 1980s indicated that teachers are almost totally unaware of just how the phenomenon operates, and of the biases they display. Similarly, in other areas of research such as factory or office management, it was found that supervisors had virtually no insight into how they treated their people differently. Differential treatment is, of course, the basis for the self-fulfilling prophecy (or Pygmalion) effect.

Origins of dual systems theory

The notion that the mind functions with two operating systems is thought to stem from writings of an American psychologist William James (brother of novelist Henry). Writing over 120 years ago, he distinguished associative thinking from deep reflective thought. Associative thinking is essentially the bridge from the past to the present. It is reproductive, and linked to images and experiences. On the other hand, reflective thinking allows us to go beyond experience, to envisage the future, to make plans to alter the world, and so engage in thinking that does not parallel one's immediate experiences.

Similar ideas are reflected in modern cognitive theories about how the mind operates. The fast or associative system, known as System 1, is the system that learns in accord with the principles of classical and operant conditioning. Such learning can often occur outside of conscious awareness. You will acquire conditioned reactions, such as attitudes, emotions, and simple responses, through associations occurring naturally within your experience. These reactions represent the type of learning well described by behavioural theories. The principles of behavioural learning were worked out by the 1930s and can be expressed in terms of conditioned associations, stimulus cueing, and reinforcement contingencies. These principles constitute powerful explanations of why people behave in certain ways at certain times. It is worth noting that such associative learning is basically unrelated to differences in intelligence and thinking capacity.

However, the second system, referred to as System 2, reflects the more conscious aspects of our thinking mind. System 2 comes into play when System 1 is not functioning well. For instance, an error is suspected. Life has been moving along fairly easily, but a problem is becoming visible. Anxiety will rise, triggering more alarm bells. Resources need to be marshalled. One powerful means of error correction has to involve activation of one's deep knowledge. But this entails a level of inhibition, or slowing down. Whereas System 1 is fast, and responds with immediacy, System 2 entails using time and thought to effect, enabling you to 'Stop, look, listen, focus'. At such points in time, it is critical for System 1 to be taken offline. System 2 is brought online until the problem is resolved. Only then can System 1 be let loose again.

AN EXAMPLE OF SYSTEM 1: DRIVING YOUR CAR

Despite decades of development, it has as yet proven impractical to devise a robot computer system able to drive a car safely through normal city traffic. Yet this is a skill expected of almost everyone today. Computers have been able to control vehicles in settings such as the desert and open roads. But the task of safely controlling a vehicle in the complex urban environment remains an elusive step beyond today's computers. How can that be?

It has been estimated that driving is not a single skill but one involving about 1,500 components or subskills. The sheer number of routines, and finely calibrated adjustments to be mastered, is voluminous. But the real complexity inherent in this is to bring the subskills under the control of the visual system. We are born with eyes that can select their focus from about 10 million signals potentially available to the brain at any one time. Although there are many species, notably birds, possessing superior vision, we have yet to devise machines to match our natural human system in terms of fast and efficient visual pattern recognition.

There is another critical factor holding back the full emergence of the computer-controlled automobile. As we drive through urban streets our brain is not merely controlling the machine. We are monitoring the social world around us, especially what other cars and people are doing now that will predict what they will do in a second's time. *Is that car going to move into my lane? Has that pedestrian seen me? What is that child on the bike likely to do next? Is that other driver waving me on?* Such questions require immediate answers. There is no room for reflection or conscious decision-making. Instead, you find yourself attending to whatever you can see of the other driver and making assessments of what that other person might do. You will make lightning fast inferences from signs such as head angles, facial expressions, and the dispositions of any other vehicle in view. Getting a computer to read such subtle social cues at speed appears impossible at the moment. But this is just what your System 1 is doing quietly, efficiently, and reliably.

Information within this box stems from Tom Vanderbilt's (2008) book *Traffic: Why we drive the way we do and what it says about us.* He surveyed the extensive research body into the psychology and engineering of car travel. While a serious scientific book, it is written with much humour. For instance, the first four chapters are entitled (a) how traffic messes with our heads, (b) why you are not as good a driver as you think you are, (c) how our eyes and mind betray us on the road, and (d) why ants do not get into traffic jams and humans do.

Evidence for the two mental systems

How do we know such systems exist? One source of evidence is neurological. Activating System 2 brings with it clear changes in bodily movements. Initially, you slow down. An upright angle of your head, coupled with a change in facial expression, will suggest to others that you are paying attention. At this point, your heart rate increases by up to seven more beats per minute. Muscles in your face and lower arms will tension slightly, and there is an overall increase in the electrical resistance of your skin, for example on your forearm.

Another subtle effect is that the pupils in your eyes will dilate slightly (increase in size). This dilation is then a second-by-second indicator of how much mental effort you are exerting. We said dilate slightly, but in fact when under extreme conditions of mental stress the dilation is roughly 50 per cent greater than the resting state. Indeed, once a person's pupils begin to shrink back, it is a sign that System 2 has stopped trying to exert itself. This is one possible outward cue that the person has effectively 'given up' and could be feeling helpless.

As well as these physiological cues, there is direct evidence from the way we behave whenever we attempt to solve problems. By way of illustration, try answering the following three questions:

1 Divide 20 by one half.
2 A cricket bat costs $100 more than the ball, and together they cost $110. How much does the ball cost?
3 A group of people are called folk. A funny story is a joke. What is the white of an egg called?

If you said 10 to the first question, then your System 1 was highly active. It responded quickly, and you possibly felt a degree of confidence. If so, your confidence was sorely misplaced. In a recent lecture, we asked this of 120 people in the room, all intelligent people. Only 4 responded with the correct figure of 40. Given this feedback (amid gasps of disbelief and displeasure), all were then able to self-correct by drawing on their knowledge. This ability to self-correct is a key aspect of System 2. In this instance, all these bright people needed was feedback that they had 'got it wrong'.

In the case of question 2, the manner in which the question is presented will invite people to subtract incorrectly. The mind (per System 1) tends to assume the bat cost $100, when in fact it is $105. To get these problems correct, people need to slow down, appreciate complexities, evaluate context and available feedback, and activate corrective thought processes. This is System 2 in its override operation.

The egg problem (question 3) is a natural example of **priming**. *Folk* and *joke* hit the mind and allow *yolk* to emerge initially unchallenged. This is the principle of **ease of access**, as the automatic system relies upon fast processing. We have played with this one a good deal, and find that most people will self-correct within several seconds. The common reaction is, 'Yolk . . . no hang on . . . That is silly . . . It's the white'. In such cases System 1 is responding quickly but it also raises anxiety as to a possible problem. There is a 'niggling doubt'. However, the problem, once defined, poses no serious worries to System 2, other than a cost of several seconds before override kicks in.

At this stage, you will be able to recognise that the two systems dramatically differ in what they do for you. Table 30.1 further attempts to provide show how the two systems function side-by-side but with differing achievements. Take note of the final point: that one system gives you confidence or self-efficacy. But with what might seem a cruel joke, the other system threatens to deprive you of that very same commodity. Such is human nature.

A very strange finding: can hard-to-read font help you to think?

Suppose the material you need to read is poorly presented, is in difficult font, or is generally hard to read. You cannot read this quickly. Experiencing this

TABLE 30.1 What the two systems each do well

ACTIONS THAT SYSTEM 1 HANDLES WITH EASE	ACTIONS THAT DEPEND ON SYSTEM 2
You scan the classroom broadly and globally.	You focus your attention on a key attribute such as the boy with scowl on his face.
You detect hostility in a student's voice.	You realise how this student has a right to be angry, and empathise with his situation.
You cannot help but react with dismay and disgust when informed of a student's past history and police record.	You begin planning how this student can be helped to develop more appropriate modes of functioning.
You expect that students from certain backgrounds will have behavioural problems.	Through careful observation you now realise that individuals can never be pigeonholed.
You respond with generalised views and attitudes, pre-judge a situation, or allocate people into groups with definable traits.	You devote time to finding valid data that you then can appraise in the light of humanistic principles such as fairness.
Having practised thousands of times, you race over the hurdles almost effortlessly. The race just 'flows'.	Under high tension, you brace yourself for the starter's gun before the hurdles race begins. You focus hard, and stop yourself jumping the gun.
You hear a sound far away.	You scan your memory hard and try to think what that sound could be.
You skim through a contract quickly knowing you will sign it.	You read every clause carefully questioning what the words mean.
You buy a car because it is cheap and looks good.	You compare several cars, read the reviews, test drive them, list the good and bad points of each.
Overall, System 1 provides you with confidence since you know you are right.	This system keeps you on edge and vigilant in case of a future threat, however remote. Besides, you may not be as good as you first thought.

problem means extra forces must be applied, and your mind activates System 2. Moments can arise when this slowing down effect can work in your favour. Laboratory experiments show that when printed material is made difficult to read, people read more carefully, and will process the extracted information with greater deliberation. The classic demonstration of this effect concerns the type of problems we looked at earlier (e.g., 'Divide 20 by one half'). When such problems are given to people in written font that discourages quick reading, then they answer more such problems correct. Another demonstration of this effect is shown the box below.

DEMONSTRATION OF THE EFFECTS OF PRINT

Hyunjin Song and Norbet Schwarz (2009) asked students to read and answer the following:

How many animals of each kind did Moses take with him on the ark?

They found 40 per cent answered incorrectly, since Moses was not on the ark. However the error rate dropped to 6 per cent in another group when switched from Arial font to Brush Script MT:

How many animals of each kind did Moses take with him on the ark?

Of course such findings do not justify making font difficult. Overall, reading comprehension is not being enhanced, and the experience of reading difficult font is painfully slow. When we read fast, we naturally employ System 1. However, there are times when we want students to slow down and think deeply. Anything that accomplishes this goal helps the mind activate System 2. Fast reading promotes comprehension through efficient inference processes. But slow reading may discourage jumping to faulty conclusions.

There is yet another strange finding in this research area: we improve our success in problem solving when we deliberately furrow our brow. Once again, it seems to be an instance of using a strategy, in this case frowning, which helps the mind activate System 2 rather than respond impulsively.

In short, when people are faced with problems, any strategy enabling System 2 to trump System 1 appears helpful. There can be dangers in making blink-type responses when quick responsiveness prevents full exercise of your accumulated knowledge. There can be advantages in slowing down.

The hard working robot deep inside you

Despite the findings cited earlier, and the examples given in Table 30.1 (above), it would be quite incorrect to gain an impression that Systems 1 and 2 are in natural conflict. Your System 1 is one of the most valuable attributes that you possess. You have spent many years investing in it through your life and your education. It is what enables you to function with ease in your environment, the physical world, but also your social world. In accord with the **social brain hypothesis**, we now appreciate that large areas of cerebral cortex are implicated in enabling your System 1 to read the social universe with remarkable precision and sensitivity.

This is the system that enables you to relax and enjoy life. Why? Because all is going well. In one sense, this robot inside you is the repository of all your past experiences, as expressed in terms of the habits and other learned operations you have been able to master during your lifetime. The robot represents the wealth of your social learning history. Once you have acquired strong knowledge, this is the system that enables you to look at complex situations, to perceive them as an expert, and to respond with speed, accuracy, and nuanced sensitivity.

Being a teacher involves long hours of teaching, and it is your System 1 that enables you to sustain strong and skilful performances over time in what is inherently a highly social situation. You were not born with a functioning System 1 as such. But you were born with the ability to learn from feedback and through exposure to significant models within your life and teaching career.

Your life experiences have provided you with scores of useful habits that are now activated automatically. As a professional teacher, you have the ability to look at a classroom situation and read it quickly, within microseconds (or what has become known as a blink response). This skill has been identified through the research of David Berliner who has found that as teachers increase their level of expertise, so does their ability to instantly read the information that the classroom affords them. Expert teachers rely on feedback cues to inform them as to which strategy to adopt next. Metaphorically, expert teachers watch their students like hawks. But this is not a conscious strategy. It is your robot that requires constant input information to guide your next action. The efficiency and effectiveness of the robot depends strongly on its reading of critical feedback information to keep it on track.

Professor Berliner's research found that experienced teachers, as they teach and move around the classroom, engage in many actions of which they are not consciously aware. If you take time to study a video of yourself teaching, you will notice many surprising aspects. For instance, using recordings, Berliner found that experienced teachers would move around the room, and do things such as touch a student's desk, nod at someone, use expressive hand gestures, and yet be unaware of what they did. For instance, when asked questions such as 'Why did you touch John's desk?', the teachers might look blank and deny such an event. Skilled teachers subtly control their students' behaviour and attention using a rich repertoire of management skills executed automatically. They can no more describe exactly what they did than you can say what angle of elevation your brain computed in throwing a ball, or how many times you adjusted the steering wheel to drive your car in a straight line. The behaviour is performed in context, using procedural knowledge not registered in any conscious memory.

Your inner friendly robot is a highly responsive and sensitive agent. In any familiar situation, you can respond quickly, efficiently, and *without* thinking. There is no need to invest time and effort if the system is doing well. The active mind can move onto important things. This robot is inherently dependable, does not tire easily, and handles routines without demanding much of your energy or attention. Nevertheless, when grilled as to why the teacher might display an act such as touching Johnny's desk, the teacher can look at the video film and immediately explain the reasons. It could be, for instance, 'I touched John's desk because I wanted to gain his attention, and let him know I was watching'.

What is so curious about such examples is that they do imply some level of awareness being active at the time, even though attention was not involved. For example, your arms and hands might be doing a palms-down gesture, to dampen the activity level in the classroom, while your active focal attention is on the information you are about to convey concerning the plight of the Italian nation during World War II. Later, we ask you what you were doing with your hands, and you look blank. But if we now show you the video of what you were doing, you immediately see that your palms-down gesture served as a key managerial tool. System 1 was running part of the show at that point, which enabled your conscious mind to focus on World War II.

But, we still need to 'explain' what the robot did

That people can readily explain something they have done, even if they cannot actually recall the act, is an especially curious phenomenon. We value explanations as things to treasure and respect. There simply has to be a good reason. Research into decision-making has thrown up many curious findings. It has been known since the 1920s that people will readily form attitudes towards target objects without any real understanding of how their attitudes get formed. Market research, for example, established that people show strong brand loyalty to one product, even when the identical product is available elsewhere, more cheaply.

In one classic study, Tim Wilson and Richard Nisbett (1978) asked people to select the best pantyhose of four brands in a market research context. In truth, the products were identical, merely presented differently. People made decisions, and were asked why. Virtually all participants produced viable answers such as 'sheer weave', or 'elasticity' in describing the one chosen. In the event, the real underlying factor was the order of presentation, with strong recency effects evident. The fourth and final one was chosen 40 per cent of the time. But people cannot say they preferred one because it was presented last. Instead, they had no difficulty in generating an answer to fit the context, even though it was straight confabulation.

Such findings help to describe the relationship between Systems 1 and 2 (see Table 30.2). Your System 2 has the job of monitoring, verbalising, explaining, and making sense of it all. Since (a) you do prefer product X to product Y and (b) you clearly are making choices freely, then (c) there must be clear and sensible reasons why you would behave this way. It is necessary to see oneself as a rational human being, even though the principles that govern System 1 inherently are not rational ones. This type of reflective thinking, referred to as an *attributional response*, enters the realm of System 2 functioning. System 1 learns

TABLE 30.2 Contrasting System 1 with System 2 psychological processes

UNDERLYING PROCESS	SYSTEM 1 LOW COST AND FAST PROCESSING	SYSTEM 2 HIGH COST AND SLOW PROCESSING
Level of awareness	Unconscious.	Consciousness expressed in words and feelings.
Target of adjustment	Negotiation of present context in an efficient and timely manner.	Ensuring that future eventualities will transpire successfully, irrespective of current situational pressures.
Nature of learning	Can learn implicitly (i.e. without words) through behavioural conditioning.	Learns more explicitly through using knowledge and thinking strategically.
Mechanism of learning	Associations and contingencies. Learning may be generalised through low-level or surface cues.	Uses associations, but stores these as rule-based principles arrived at through analysis and deep inferential processes.
Activation of memory	Automatic activation within context. Can be a 'blink' response being activated.	Depends on activating content within working memory. Blink responses are evaluated as part of WM contents.
Level of effort	Effort minimal as well-learnt procedures make little demands on focused attention.	Effort high, with danger of overload. Attention is focused on one thing at a time. **Ego-depletion** effects possible.
Overlapping skills	Some level of multi-tasking is possible when performance demands are low.	This mind is designed to focus, and is incapacitated through any attempt to multitask.
Nature of goals being actively pursued	Goals are often implicit or unspoken (such as desire to look good, make friends, or spell correctly). Oriented to present.	Goals are consciously represented and often flagged (such as need to get good grades, buy a nice house, or have a holiday). Oriented to future.
Tactics for solving problems	Heuristic methods such as useful and practical short cuts. Locate the correct steps in terms of well-honed procedural knowledge.	Careful assessment of all available resources, including declarative knowledge and knowledge of how to access external resources.
Hypothesis testing	Does not occur. But experiencing anxiety then activates System 2.	Planning and information gathering allow for several possibilities to be mentally simulated.
Major liability to you	Heuristics have limits. Can induce overconfidence. Also major problem of impulsiveness.	Metacognitive processes are often poorly executed. Also system is lazy, will tire easily (ego depleted), and is inclined to show helplessness symptoms.

through associations, but System 2 relies on the ability to express actions and knowledge in terms of rules, logic, and coherent relationships. Although presentation order effects can be powerful (the last one seen is advantaged), the conscious mind does not know this.

Your System 2 executive

System 2 is the effortful thinking and planning part of your mind. While System 1 enables the past to impact upon the present, System 2 can operate on a more extended time frame. This system enables your present knowledge to be applied to the future, by which we mean the *long-term future*, rather than the pressing issue of negotiating the next few minutes. The beauty of System 1 is that it enables you to cope well with immediate contexts and goals. But it is System 2 that enables you to think, plan ahead, and scheme, and so adjust actions toward serving those goals you harbour that can be more abstract, remote, or deferred. Indeed, impulse control and delay of gratification are typically the natural accomplishments of effective System 2 functioning.

One of the major functions of your conscious mind is to engage in simulations of the future. For instance, you can imagine what would happen if your car breaks down, or if you insult your boss, or win the lottery, or get selected as a model teacher. However, you do not have to have your car break down to find out what you might do. Inside your head there is a *mental model* of reality. You can run this model to simulate reality in terms of 'what if' ideas. The ability to envisage the future, and make goal directed motions in the present, which anticipate outcomes that you have never before experienced, is very much a product of your second mind, your System 2.

As indicated earlier, this system will come into operation once System 1 responding appears unlikely to achieve your goals. You may not always be explicitly aware of goals that your System 1 is following. But a part of your mind is always vigilant. For example, you may not realise that you want to maintain friends with someone until you realise that the interaction with this person is going awry. Alarm bells ring. Suddenly the goal of friendship is seen as an explicit one, and then consciousness kicks in to help you decide if such a goal is worthy of pursuit, and if so, to decide what repairs are necessary.

Here is a scenario as experienced by us all from time to time. It is a social situation, and interactions appear to be going well, with a sense of ease, automaticity, and congeniality. Then you clumsily, unwittingly, 'hit a nerve'. You need to back-pedal. Your System 2 will have certain default skills such as slowing down, inhibiting automatic responses, and can quickly activate social appeasement gestures, such as saying 'sorry', and adopting submissive body language.

In one sense, your inner robot has let you down. Your gaucheness elicits immediate external feedback, which drives the System 2 executive to take over. You may not know what to do, but at this point powerful executive processes can be brought into play. This entails specific mental focus, conscious recognition, explicit evaluation of the most important goal to be pursued, and a redirection, perhaps reversal, of your overt behaviour. Throughout this episode, your heart will have been beating faster, and your pupils dilated. Just by way of interest, there is a significant body of data indicating that successful marriages are characterised by partners' ability to activate such relationship repair strategies.

The crucial differences in how your two mind systems handle the world are shown in Table 30.1. If you study this table you will see how the two systems act in a complementary manner. Most of your life is spent at the level of System 1. You do not need to think, but you can rely on successful habits that you have been building up from birth. However, this system also brings with it a level of rigidity. Times emerge when System 1 no longer provides protection and security. It literally 'runs out' of decent options. The natural human response is then one of increasing anxiety that signals the need to arouse System 2 from slumber.

System 2 initially ascertains that resources are stretched, and orders an immediate contraction of mental energies. *Stop, look, listen,* and *focus* are strategies activated in order to begin the serious appraisal work. Recognition processes are brought to bear almost immediately. *What do I know about this current situation that reminds me of something in the past?* But failures in recognition then drive the mind to acquire additional resources. If declarative knowledge is not available, perhaps you know how to locate external information that can readily be converted into fresh declarative knowledge. If so, the working memory can be brought in to marry new knowledge into the old, and so allow development to proceed.

Over time, this new declarative knowledge is converted into new procedural knowledge, and the need for future System 2 overrides is averted since adjustment is taken over by System 1 again. This is one way in which the mind builds its knowledge base. But notice how this entire process hinges upon being sensitive to the available feedback, and using that feedback to realign and reprogram System 1.

Our necessary mental collaboration

Systems 1 and 2 work in with each other, metaphorically hand in glove. System 1 is successful and reliable as the repository of your life skill. System 2 is needed to support and back up. System 2 has limited energy, but while its energies remain, it has powerful tricks up its sleeve. For one thing, it provides override whenever self-control is needed. You will note the comment in Table 30.2 that this system can be subject to **ego depletion** (see also Chapter 26). Typically, we cannot sustain intensively high levels of effort for much longer than 15 minutes. In children, such ego-depletion effects creep in after short periods of just several minutes' intense concentration.

Hence, although your System 2 is what you will use to restore your life back onto an even keel, it is a system that can never guarantee success. Not only is it limited in the amount of learning and knowledge acquisition it can assimilate, but it is limited in the level of effort available to it within any given period. Metaphorically, it is a muscle. You can will yourself to change, but after a few minutes, you are still the same you, merely with a minor amendment tacked on. You are always stuck with what your System 1 can do for you. Changes to your basic robotic self are achieved only through piecemeal efforts.

If there is any comfort to this notion, try considering the following insight offered to us by Keith Stanovich, a leading researcher in this area: *although we are robots, we are the only robots who are aware of this fact.* If you can understand now what this sentence is attempting to express, then you can be assured that your System 2 has kicked in and is at this moment, being highly responsive.

The story of blink

Blink is the title of a book by Malcolm Gladwell, an American science writer, which became an instant best seller in 2008. We strongly recommend this as an excellent review of research highlighting the role of System 1 processing in a range of decision-making situations. Gladwell interviewed many leading behavioural scientists and was impressed by the quality and volume of research data supporting the idea that we engage in remarkably fast and accurate assessments.

For instance, within split seconds, art experts can evaluate art products, and experienced police officers make assessments of villains' intentions with remarkable insight. In one sense, we are all expert in dealing with others. We all can recognise human faces instantly, and read interpersonal reactions on other people's faces within microseconds. It may be wonderful news to some that there is a surprising literature about the essential validity of speed dating. One well-known finding from the 1950s is that bosses make an assessment about hiring within seconds of meeting a job applicant. There is an impressive body of evidence indicating that, in many contexts humans make decisions within a few seconds.

As teachers, we can note key findings from Nalini Ambady and Robert Rosenthal (of *Pygmalion in the Classroom* fame) that students will form clear judgements about their teachers within 10 seconds of meeting them. This is a serious research finding, called the *thin slice phenomenon*. Perhaps alarmingly, it is known that our students form such judgements by watching our gestures, facial expressions, and body movements, and may do so even before we speak. One disturbing aspect of this research is the finding that such thin slice assessments, as made by students watching brief video films of teachers they did not know, actually correlated with ratings made by the same teachers' own students about their effectiveness as teachers.

Getting blink into perspective

One issue with the blink effect is that it can be overly interpreted. Some writers have interpreted the effect as justifying intuition as a valid strategy for making life decisions. This is a scary and illogical interpretation since such fast and efficient processing is really the domain of people who *already* possess well-developed skills and knowledge. If you buy your next car on the basis of seeing it for a few seconds, you are relying more on the fact that the products on offer are all good ones, rather than displaying a sensible approach to life. Striving to use fast blink responses relies on your being the guest in a benign world, where your System 1 remains unchallenged. Unfortunately, the world is not always of this character, and is populated by many who made fast blink-type decisions unwisely.

Above all, teachers ought *not* to suggest to any student that blink-type responding is inherently a sensible life strategy. When people are young, lacking in knowledge and experience, then impulsiveness is a default position. The notion of impulsiveness is that a person makes errors through responding hastily when additional thinking would have prevented disaster.

When people are in development stages in their lives, the ability to constrain one's impulsiveness, to activate and use System 2, and to exercise willpower judiciously, represent far more important accomplishments than responding quickly, in haste. It is known from the extensive literature into expertise (as described in this book) that although experts can work quickly, they often do not want to, when offered the choice. Experts slow down dramatically whenever they encounter obstacles. This is a lesson in life. Every teacher witnesses impulsive responding in his or her students. It comes with the territory.

IN PERSPECTIVE: Understanding your two selves

A considerable body of accumulated evidence, from physiology, social psychology and cognitive science, indicates the brain possesses two control systems that interact with each other. This cooperative interaction provides us with the intelligence and organisation we need to participate in the world and get on with others who share our genes.

We rely on the automatic and heroic System 1 for the vast bulk of functioning. Nevertheless, this system remains highly sensitive to any feedback suggesting that goals are not being achieved. Whereas System 1 allows us to proceed through our day relatively mindlessly, it has an important resource since it can call in System 2 on a split second's notice. System 2 brings with it increased heart rate, but a slowing down and even a possible cessation of much overt behavioural activity. Consciousness is activated, and hypothetical scenarios need to be run through the

---

head as mental simulations. The ability to simulate reality in the mind, to engage in planful thinking, to divine the future, and entertain 'what-if' possibilities, all become products of high quality System 2 processing.

But System 2, by no means, is a perfect agent. One key problem for our adjustment overall is that System 2 involves effort and is inherently lazy. Its full resources need to draw on years of steady development. It is limited by the knowledge base it can access. It may use 'what-ifs' to generate hypotheses, but still may not test these hypotheses at all well. It requires high levels of effort and investment of resources such as attention and working memory.

Indeed, much of what we hope to achieve within educational institutes can be seen in terms of attempting to equip individuals with the essential tools and resources they need in order for inherent deficiencies within their System 2 minds to be countermanded. Education, by its inevitable purpose and function within our culture, involves reprogramming System 2 functioning at the level of the individual student.

Study guide questions

1 The writers refer to System 1 as functioning as a 'robot', albeit a friendly, hardworking, benign one. Of course, this is metaphorical use of terms. Most probably, you doubted this when you first read it. We are humans, not robots. However, after reviewing the evidence, do you feel this is a suitable metaphor?

2 What does it mean to hold implicit attitudes? Just how do they become known?

3 Does System 1 work in opposition to System 2? Is System 1 driven by impulses that System 2 seeks to control?

4 What direct evidence do we have that these two systems actually exist within the mind?

5 When is System 2 activated?

6 Examine Table 30.1 showing the things each system does well. What are the underlying themes that emerge from the specific examples provided?

7 One odd finding is that difficult-to-read fonts can sometimes produce more intelligent responses than easy-to-read fonts. Explain how such a strange effect becomes possible.

8 The writers suggest that skilled teachers rely on much System 1 functioning. What types of evidence do they cite in this regard?

9 Does System 2 always know what System 1 did? Do you always know why you do things? What does the research tell us about this interesting problem?

10 *Blink* is the title of a well-researched book. One message people get from this book is that humans make effective decisions relatively quickly, within seconds. But this is true only when certain conditions are present. What are these conditions?

11 Why is it that computers, as yet, cannot control cars through city streets? Similarly, why can computers never replace a teacher?

Reference notes

- System 1 and System 2 were terms made salient largely through Keith Stanovich (Stanovich, 1999).

- A major review is found in Daniel Kahneman's influential book, *Thinking Fast, Thinking Slow*, which summarises the lifetime's work of this Nobel prize winner (Kahneman, 2011).

- The mind harbours *both* explicit and implicit attitudes (Olson, Fazio, & Hermann, 2007; T. D. Wilson, Lindsey, & Schooler, 2000).

- Implicit Association Test for adults (Greenwald, Poehlman, Uhlmann, & Banaji, 2009); and for 4-year-olds (Cvencek, Greenwald, & Meltzoff, 2011).

- Cognitive load under stress (Palinko, Kun, Shyrokov, & Heeman, 2010; Van Gerven, Paas, van Merriënboer, & Schmidt, 2004).

- Frowning and reading difficult font makes thinking more deliberate (Alter & Oppenheimer, 2009; Alter, Oppenheimer, Epley, & Eyre, 2007).

- Difficult font helps people realise Moses was never on the Ark (Song & Schwarz, 2008).

- Berliner's studies into automaticity in expert teachers (Berliner, 2004).

- Study into explaining choices between identical products (T. D. Wilson & Nisbett, 1978).

- Relationship repair strategies (B. J. Wilson & Gottman, 2002).

- System 2 and ego depletion (Schmeichel *et al.*, 2003; Vohs *et al.*, 2008).

- Keith Stanovich robot notion (Stanovich, 2004). The actual quotation is 'We are the only robots who have discovered we have interests separate from the interests of the replicators' (p. xii).

- Blink effects described in popular book (Gladwell, 2006).

- Surprising validity of speed dating (Asendorpf, Penke, & Back, 2011).

- We make interpersonal judgements in less than a second (Van Overwalle *et al.*, 2012).

- Thin slices in human judgements and student perception of teachers (Ambady, 2010; Ambady, LaPlante, & Johnson, 2001; Ambady & Rosenthal, 1993).

- Box: The psychology of driving (Vanderbilt, 2008).

31

IKEA, effort, and valuing

What you make, you may come to love. This basic idea, which is behind the **IKEA effect**, is likely to be well known to experienced teachers. You may not, however, have thought of this as a formal scientific principle. The effect refers to this situation: *whenever someone takes an active role in the production of a positive outcome, then he or she is disposed toward valuing that outcome more positively, even to the point of overly inflated assessment, which the person believes is true, fair, and correct.* Having exerted a sincere modicum of effort, for example, in baking biscuits, constructing an essay, painting a wall, or planting a garden, then the responsible individual person takes especial pride in the outcomes of such labour. But the psychological effect itself is more than simple personal pride. The hidden effect is that the person genuinely begins to believe that the product is worth more than would be justified objectively.

The effect has been labelled IKEA by a team of business-oriented psychologists associated with Professor Dan Ariely. In investigating consumer purchasing habits they have documented many interesting trends, including the fact that many companies have become successful through marketing enterprises that require the consumer, as client, to complete certain operations in order to enjoy the final worthwhile product. The effect was named IKEA after the Swedish company, since Dr Ariely had felt much pride in a bookshelf he assembled from purchased flat pack components, even though his family and friends clearly did not value the finished product as much as he did. The crucial element behind the IKEA effect is that the person values the outcome that he or she has created more highly than do other people. Hence, effort has become an automatic value-added component.

We value our work

The IKEA effect is consistent with several other well-known research findings. For example, it has been documented that people are inclined to highly value things for which they had to struggle. Earlier studies showed that on American university campuses, students valued most the groups and clubs that were the hardest ones to join, and they valued grades more highly on those courses in which they had experienced academic difficulties. Similarly, within psychotherapy, clinicians had found improvements in outcomes when clients were required to devote higher levels of effort in meeting their goals. It is also known that the monetary cost of an item can substantially determine how much value people attach to that item. In one study, a discounted energy drink was less effective in refreshing people than the same product when people paid the full price.

It is apparent that when people are working towards difficult goals, they expect to have to achieve them at some cost and effort. As a result, they place a high value upon what they have achieved. Within job satisfaction research it has been found that employees want jobs that demand a level of effort and resulting pride. In the work situation, it may seem curious to note that although people often rate their employment as low in pleasurability, nevertheless it is still rated as high in reward value. To express this in another way, most people will strongly value their work, and what they can achieve there, even though they do not go to work for pleasurable purposes. This fascinating pattern can be seen in stark contrast to other activities, such as watching television, which show the reverse trend, that is, being rated as high in pleasure, but low in personal reward value (i.e., television viewing is pleasurable at the time, but produces no long-term value).

The experimental findings

If you are a teacher responsible for evaluating student work, then it is well worth considering the research on the IKEA effect in some depth. In one experiment, researchers asked a group of university students to assemble an IKEA product, a simple storage box. So how much money would these people be prepared to spend to then take home their completed products? The students who assembled the boxes were prepared to spend, on average, 78 cents. But control group students, who had not participated in the box assembly stage of the experiment, valued the identical boxes at an average of 48 cents. The two groups also differed in how much they said they liked the boxes on a seven-point rating scale. Those who were simply offered a completed box rated it at a mean of 2.5, whereas those who had worked on the boxes rated their liking score at a mean of 3.8 out of 7. Hence, expending effort led to a 50 per cent increase in expressed enjoyment and value.

In another study, the team asked students to make origami models by following an instruction sheet. Even though the resulting products were of poor quality, and rated by the control group students as worth 5 cents, the people who constructed the models rated them as worth 23 cents. To quote the report 'Thus, while the non-builders saw the amateurish creations as nearly worthless crumpled paper, our builders imbued their origami with value' (Norton, Mochon, & Ariely, 2012, p. 11). Using another group of students, it was also found that origami builders believed that the other students would rate their products as highly as they did, at an average of 21 cents. Hence, the builders appeared to believe that their personal evaluations of their inferior products represented a genuine market value.

The IKEA experiments were then replicated using LEGO models, but with an interesting twist. The builders only valued their personally assembled LEGO models highly when allowed to keep the completed model in intact form. When the models were disassembled, they were no longer highly valued, even though the identical components were in the box, and these could have been reassembled quickly. It was found that the effect existed quite independently of whether or not the students considered themselves as 'do-it-yourself' (D-I-Y) people. In one condition of this experiment, it was apparent that the effect did not depend on physically handling the products or their components. Instead, it was the act of completing the assembly successfully that enabled the students to then assay relatively high values onto their own creations.

Additional studies suggested that the IKEA effect can be found only if the participants actually completed their assigned projects. In one condition the researchers asked the participants to stop working before their product was completed. In another condition, the origami instructions were made so difficult that students could not succeed even in finishing low-quality models. Under these conditions, there was no evidence for either the enhanced valuations or enhanced enjoyment that is associated with the behavioural effect. Hence, the IKEA effect appears to be entirely the result of investing energy to complete a worthwhile project and then being able to stand back and admire its successful outcome. Simply working on a project, contributing to it without seeing it through to closure, does not appear to produce the effect at all.

The underlying psychology of IKEA

The IKEA effect apparently cannot be attributed simply to being exposed to, or physically handling, the components involved in the construction of products. So why does viewing the final product result in such an impact? One likely explanation is that the effect is linked directly into the person's memory of the effort involved.

Whenever you appraise a goal or product that you have contributed towards, you recall how difficult it was for you to achieve this goal. This implicates your long-term memory in the following ways.

To get such a commendable product to this final completion point, you needed to make several demanding fine-grain decisions. You had to use certain tools, and make a variety of metacognitive assessments.

You had to sacrifice time, and focus your concentration on a single activity. You had to take charge and be responsible. Hence to you, the entire enterprise represented care and diligence, coupled with personal investments.

Further, there existed a genuine danger, an anxiety, of making an error, of misapplying tools, or of damaging the product being worked upon through accident or ignorance. This did not come cheaply. In some instances self-worth is at stake. Any product that is acceptable is a better outcome than appearing incompetent.

From the perspective of cognitive analysis, we speculate that such memories are activated automatically. You can see the product. You know what effort it took, in terms of skill, investment, and overcoming anxiety. You were responsible. And so, you can experience pride. This is what your memory can do for you, unwittingly, whenever you look at what you have achieved.

A similar process is likely to take place in the minds of your students whenever they complete their work and submit it for assessment. They are aware that it has to be to a good standard. But their standards and that of the teacher may not be totally parallel. Nevertheless, it becomes crucial to recognise the effort and value that students have invested within their work. The IKEA effect will play a hidden but vital role in how your students appraise what they have been able to achieve. Hence, they are asking for their investments to be recognised in the feedback process.

The endowment effect

The IKEA effect is consistent with, but not identical to the **endowment effect**, another principle well known within cognitive psychology. The endowment effect results from valuing your own possessions more highly than can be justified objectively. Hence, by way of illustration, on the open market there is likely conflict between a seller (owner) and a potential buyer when each begins from a different basis of evaluation.

In laboratory experiments it has been found that when people are given an object to keep, for instance a coffee mug, but then are approached to sell that object, they ask for a price higher than they themselves would be prepared to pay for the same item. It was found that such effects are less natural 'greed', but are underpinned by genuine differences in valuations. When it comes to setting values on possessions, it is apparent that ownership adds to the value of that item. Such endowment is one possible explanation for why people are inclined to retain and pay to store possessions when it becomes highly uneconomical. The level of rent-able self-storage space in America is 2.2 billion square feet according to one report, with much of this devoted to objects people are reluctant to sell since the world values such possessions less than the owners. And the owners cannot sell for less than it is worth.

Ownership and effort in the classroom: the psychology of respectful feedback

Now consider this: these two effects, IKEA and endowment, work hand in hand inside the classroom. The IKEA effect stems from the personal contributions and actual work that an individual student puts into achieving a worthwhile goal, project, or product. And the endowment effect works through simple ownership of the finished product. Both effects are natural and inevitable aspects of the human condition. The direct implication is that students will place positive spin upon what they have achieved. But more than this, they will place values on their work that you ought to recognise as high and being somewhat higher than yourself, and others, would otherwise naturally assume to be the case. If you begin to look at student products through their eyes, rather than yours, you will begin to have insight into the efforts and investments that they had to make.

In essence, students will actively assign values onto what they have, what they have achieved, and what they had to do to get there. Indeed, one of the keys in expressing empathy with another person is to recognise that his or her feelings are reflected in the efforts he or she made in order to achieve outcomes. And one of the best ways for you to recognise these efforts will be to take time looking at, and genuinely to appreciate, what has been achieved. After all, the individual you are dealing with has invested time in his or her own products, and thus appreciates it when another individual, especially a teacher, takes time to indicate approval of this same product. The cost may be only a few seconds to you, but the impact on your student can be substantial.

These basic ideas can be tied into our theory of feedback in learning situations (as reviewed in Chapter 8). When we attempt to critique student work, there can be mismatch between feedback we administer and our students' goals. We need to respect that our students are motivated to improve their work, to move forwards, and are looking for constructive feedback. Often, our comments can be seen as overly evaluative, critical, or negative in orientation. We need to ensure that our feedback comments reflect concrete steps that students can take to further develop their worthwhile ideas.

The feeling of being treated (un)fairly

In discussing these effects with beginning teachers, our attention was drawn to yet another twist worth noting. As you train to become a young professional, you need to exert considerable levels of personal effort and investment. The amount of thought and preparation young teachers need to undertake is easily overlooked by their supervisors. Having invested considerable time and energy preparing their programmes, and having taken full responsibilities for running the classroom, the beginning teacher values his or her performance in remarkably positive ways. Hence these young teachers find it confusing when their supervisors begin critiquing them on shallow aspects, such as not moving around the room enough, or not responding quickly to the child with his hand up.

One beginning teacher said to one of us after a field placement, 'If only she had told me I was a doing a good job, I could have taken her advice more seriously.' Human relationships are strengthened when one party actively recognises the other party's elevated appraisals of his or her personal work products. The process of feedback can work more effectively when both parties find agreement in a common starting point, and this involves acknowledgement of value being placed upon achievements. To the beginning teacher, it was important to have her efforts recognised, and when this failed to occur, the credibility of the older supervisory teacher was seriously eroded.

In more general terms, if you fail to recognise the effort that someone has exerted in achieving a product they value, then you cannot expect that individual to take seriously any other feedback you may offer, especially should it involve negative elements. If you fail to appreciate the importance of IKEA effects, if your feedback efforts are seen as too brief or dismissive, you cannot expect to maintain credibility as a strong guiding influence in dealing with that individual.

Two more experiments from the team who brought you the IKEA effect

Here are two more laboratory studies with meaningful results about human motivation and work (Ariely, 2010). In the first study, university students were asked to assemble LEGO models of small robots following precisely detailed instructions. They were paid at a piece rate of two dollars a robot. In one condition, robots were dismantled as soon as they were completed, on the grounds that the parts would be needed if the participant wanted to keep on working. In this condition students completed an average of seven robots. But in another condition, when the robots were not dismantled in front of their eyes, the students completed an average of 11 robots.

In the second experiment students were asked to persevere on a tricky but boring task searching for letters on sheets of paper, earning 50 cents per completed sheet. There were three conditions: students submitted each sheet as completed to a research assistant who either (a) checked for accuracy and showed approval, (b) checked for accuracy but without approval, or (c) put the sheet straight into a shredder without checking accuracy. Obviously, if money provided motivation, then the third condition provides free rein. However, in this condition, students completed only six sheets on average before giving up. In contrast, the non-approval condition average was seven, and the approval condition produced nine sheets on average.

Such findings further confirm a simple truth: *that people will value their labour, and what it produces remarkably strongly, and this goal overpowers other considerations.* Try asking yourself: Would you enjoy going to work if everything you did, or made, was not valued, was rendered meaningless, discarded, or even destroyed, as soon as it was completed? Just how strongly would you exert effort if this was the case? What implications can you see for valuing student work, and for encouraging students to genuinely exert themselves?

IN PERSPECTIVE: Effort can underpin what we value

One of the chief researchers in this area, Dan Ariely (2010, pp. 104–105) summed the findings up neatly in the following four principles:

1 The effort we put into something does not just change the object. It changes the way we evaluate that object.
2 Greater labour leads to greater love.
3 Our overvaluation of the things we make runs so deep that we assume that others share our biased perspective.
4 When we cannot complete something into which we have put great effort, we do not feel so attached to it.

And to this list, we can further add two more key principles:

1 We become precious about what we have, simply because it is ours.
2 Our attitude towards others can depend on how well they treat and respect what we ourselves achieve and value. If someone acknowledges how hard we tried, and the efforts we put in to achieve a worthwhile outcome, then our relationship with that person turns positive. If we are perceived as dismissive of another person's efforts, we cannot expect to maintain a mutually respectful relationship with that person.

In sum, the IKEA effect represents more than just an interesting scientific finding. Such an effect can become relevant in any social context where individuals are expected to be productive or to exert effort. The effect is likely to apply equally to (a) the classroom, factory, office, or the home, and (b) to young children, older students, adolescents, or adults alike.

Study guide questions

1 The IKEA effect involves valuing the product of your labour. But there a sting in the tail. What happens to the person's sense of actual or genuine value? What psychology is involved?
2 Your labour is a value-added component. But is this something the mind sets out to do?
3 It was found that students value grades obtained when they experienced greater difficulties within specific courses. Just why should this be the case?

4   In one study, using LEGO modelling, it was found that enhanced values (IKEA effect) were evident only when the LEGO creations remained intact. What can we infer from this interesting finding?

5   The writers speculate that the IKEA effect is created through the long-term memory. Just what sort of memories are invoked when you cast eye upon a product you have created?

6   There is another well-researched phenomenon called the endowment effect. This is similar to IKEA, but with an important difference. Explain how these two effects, IKEA and endowment work side by side and so reinforce each other in real situations.

7   How do such effects (IKEA and endowment) relate to how we treat student work?

8   Consider just what the student teacher said of her mentor: 'If only she had told me I was a doing a good job, I could have taken her advice more seriously.' Will this comment influence how you treat novices in our profession? Consider the benefits of a moment's kindness, in terms of the notion of 'empathy gap'.

9   The IKEA effect appears to play a role in establishing and maintaining positive relationships between people. How does this occur? What mechanism is at work here?

Reference notes

- Business-oriented research group (Ariely, 2010; Mochon, Norton, & Ariely, 2012; Norton, Mochon, & Ariely, 2012). Dr Ariely is a gifted social scientist and we recommend his website for much serious fun: http://danariely.com.

- Harder to join groups become more strongly valued, a finding that appears true even when the group is boring (Aronson & Mills, 1959; Festinger, 1961).

- Psychotherapy effort exertion improves outcomes (Axsom, 1989).

- Monetary costs increase perceived value. For example, an expensive energy drink 'better' than cheap identical product (Shiv, Carmon, & Ariely, 2005).

- People work hard, and value what they achieve, especially when a task is difficult (Gendolla & Richter, 2010).

- Work is rewarding although not pleasurable: but watching television is the opposite (White & Dolan, 2009).

- Endowment effect: people ask higher prices selling goods they own than they are willing to pay to acquire similar goods (Kahneman, 2011; Morewedge, Shu, Gilbert, & Wilson, 2009).

Glossary

Advance organisers: Information about the nature and structure of information that is to be learnt later. Sometimes advance information will activate prior knowledge, or otherwise prime the mind to react in a certain direction. Other times, such information helps a learner to understand why certain aspects are important to learn thoroughly. Carefully spelled out advance organisers will both organise and motivate a learner.

Aptitude–treatment interactions: Different individuals may respond to different treatments in different ways. This sounds like a truism. However, very few clear examples of such effects have been documented in the literature about human learning, despite a considerable effort of research.

Arrested development: A skill cannot develop any further if simply exercised without specific attention devoted to its improvement through principles of deliberate practice.

Articulatory loop: Sometimes called phonological loop where verbal material can be rehearsed in the mind up to around 2 seconds. If you can say something within 2 seconds, you can keep going on within this rehearsal buffer.

Automaticity: Activity that involves non-conscious control processes. Such behaviours can be initiated and completed virtually without thinking.

Availability, and **ease of access**: Availability refers to accessing and using information from memory that comes to mind with relatively little effort: why trouble yourself working hard on securing the appropriate information, when you have got other information on hand? This immediately available information possesses the property of ease of access.

Backward training: A useful training method to help combat overload. Teach the final elements of a skill sequence firstly so that it is available later when you teach the first steps.

Barnum effect (also known as **Forer effect**): A person appreciates that a given description of personality applies to himself or herself as a unique individual. So does everyone else. Yet it is the same description.

Closeness and conflict: The two base dimensions that underpin relations between social interaction parties, but notably teacher–student relationships.

Cognitive load, cognitive architecture, interacting elements: Terms associated with cognitive load theory which describes how we are resource-limited creatures. The architecture is represented by the various memory systems. The notion of interacting elements means that achieving an understanding of complex events involves understanding how items function as a system rather than as isolated units. For example, understanding how car brakes work involves relationships between multiple elements such as hydraulics, friction, cylinders, and so on.

Cognitive style: Refers to customary and habitual ways of handling information and relating to learning situations that ought not to relate to intellectual capacity.

Cognitive task analysis (CTA): Akin to traditional task analysis, but focus is upon procedural discriminations that the mind must make to negotiate complex decisional situations. This involves exposing the multitude of *if–then* conditional statements that underpin the complex skill, but are frequently hidden from the view or (as in many teaching situations) falsely assumed to be known.

Deliberate practice: Refers to time devoted to learning activities where a skill is being developed under conditions of guidance, specific target goals, corrective feedback, objective assessment, and conscious mental focus.

Digital natives and digital immigrants: The term 'digital native' was introduced into popular vernacular to refer to young people who grew up in the electronic information era, as against those who grew up earlier. Hence, inside the classroom, teachers are the immigrants. But claims made about this generation gap are overblown, and ascribe false attributes to both natives and immigrants alike.

Distraction and deflection strategies for controlling thoughts: In situations needing self-control, you cannot stop yourself thinking a certain thought, if you try not to think this thought. However, one method of thought control is to think about something else. You can interpret a stimulus in a different way by fixating on something you had not attended to earlier. Hence, you might look at a poker chip and instead of seeing it as a means to happiness, note how it does not belong to you, but always is the property of the casino using it to con you. By deflecting your thinking into thinking they own it, by slowly reading the casino's name, you destroy its stimulus power over you.

Duchenne smile: The wide open smile which involves contraction of muscles around the eyes as well as the mouth area.

Ego depletion: After several minutes of self-regulated effort exertion less energy is available and subsequent performances may deteriorate, without the person's conscious awareness. The effect appears strongest when acts involve needing to control impulses, or overriding likely responses.

Ego or performance orientation: The drive to achieve as expressed through the display and recognition of superior levels of performance in a social context. This orientation is coupled with competitiveness and concern over evaluations.

Elaboration: As a mental strategy, this means to add to information as it enters the mind. The source of elaboration is your prior knowledge. The process adds to the encoding of the stimulus and provides an additional set of valuable retrieval cues.

Elaborative reminiscing style and joint talk: Modes of interacting with young children. When parents use richly elaborated language to talk about experiences, the child's memory system is stimulated as words relate to shifting time zones (i.e., past, present, and future). Joint talk refers to the child entering the conversations.

Emotional leakage: This refers to emotional aspects of communication that a sender is attempting to disguise, suppress, or otherwise hide. But such aspects are still detected by an audience.

Encoding: Literally to place something into a code. In psychology it means to interpret, group, or classify an input into a coherent system. Thus if you see 1788, you may encode it mentally as a year.

Endowment effect: Inflated value on a product on account of personal ownership.

Episodic memory: Memory for specific events, such as when you saw a shark. This is often contrasted against **semantic memory** which does not relate to any one context.

Expert blind spot effect: That automaticity and expertise prevents an expert from understanding the experience of someone who does not possess the same ability to process the data so quickly and efficiently.

False memory effect: People can be primed to believe an experience occurred to them when in truth it did not occur. There are several excellent studies showing how this can occur.

IKEA effect: Inflated value placed on a product by person who created it, in the belief others share such a perception.

Implementation intentions (also known as **if-then plans**): A strategy to achieve self-control through planning a response to a problematic situation. For instance shopping from a prepared list and preparing yourself with ideas such as *'If I see the chocolate then I will look down at my fat stomach'*.

Implicit learning: A general term for any form of successful learning outside of natural consciousness. You can still learn implicitly, even though your conscious mind does not register this matter in verbal terms (although it may later, once your 'success' becomes obvious even to yourself).

Impulse control: The ability to make choices which avoid errors in the short-term, in the service of a more worthwhile goal which may not be immediately visible.

Inattentional blindness: When coping with one demanding task, it is possible to miss apprehending other important information within the perceptual field, in a manner that seems inexplicable to observers.

Infantile amnesia: Lack of memory for your earliest years. Thought to reflect absence of language.

Knowledge gaps: The awareness that your understanding of a phenomenon is strong in some aspects, but weak in other aspects. If understanding is to advance, those gaps need to be filled.

Mastery goal orientation: The drive to achieve as expressed through learning new skills, developing one's potential, or having intrinsic interests in a phenomenon.

Method of loci, memory palaces, pegwords: Terms associated with the deliberate use of mnemonic devices to enhance memory capabilities, especially when memorising relatively meaningless lists.

Mind wandering: This highly technical term describes when the focus of the mind no longer reflects the current situation or demand faced by the individual.

Negative escalations, snowball effects, cascades: These terms refer to contexts in which events may turn to the better, or worse, through the operation of natural amplification processes. A related notion is that of the Matthew effect where the presence of a trait leads to an increase in that same or similar trait over time. Thus, a skilful reader may read a good deal and so becomes an even better reader, and increases her vocabulary at the same time.

Ostension, the principle of: This is where one person signals to another that they need to watch with care as important information is about to be shown (i.e. modelled). Teachers may use cues such as hand gestures to signal to students that they need to pay attention to what is about to follow.

Overconfidence: In the absence of feedback, one base presumption is that one is competent and capable. This idea can manifest itself through inflated expectations about one's ability to perform or complete a task. Greg felt he could paint the house given 'a couple of weekends', but it took six months. This is also called the *planning fallacy*.

Plateau: Skills do not develop in neat orderly ways. Increments in skill level never display a linear relationship with time. Large advances in learning appear to occur, followed by periods of apparent minimal growth. In fact, plateaus are important for gains to be consolidated, and for conscious aspects to become automated, such that attention can move to defining higher-level goals.

Posture matching and chameleon effect: When people interact well in a group context they tend to synchronise their actions and mirror each other's gestures. The chameleon effects refers to direct copying of specific gestures, such as rocking in a chair, triggered unconsciously by seeing another person do this.

Primacy and recency: Whenever presented with a sequence, the order in which you receive information affects ability to retrieve it. Advantages exist for the first (primacy) and last (recency) items.

Priming: This is an implicit memory effect where the response to one event is influenced by being exposed to a subtle cue earlier. Thus, having someone smile at you could make you respond positively to a question such as *'What was your holiday like?'* Or seeing a picture of an airliner half an hour earlier might induce you to say *'plane'* when asked to name a vehicle.

Proactive and retroactive interference: The mind is inclined to mix up its memory traces when overloaded. If you learn 20 Spanish words, then 20 French words shortly after, your ability to recall the French terms is inhibited by learning the Spanish words earlier (interference is proactive). Your ability to recall the Spanish is affected by having learnt the French ones later (retroactive interference).

Recitation method, IRE cycle, CDR method: No formal definitions are likely since there are many variations. But the recitation method refers to a style of formal classroom teaching with the teacher controlling many aspects of the classroom interaction process such as the content of instruction, timing of activities, nature of questions, and forms of assessment.

Rehearsal, and **cumulative rehearsal fast finish**: Rehearsal is the most basic memory strategy but its execution can become complex with increasing age. Cumulative rehearsal fast finish is where a person tries to input the initial items reasonably slowly, saying them over, but the final items need to come in fast so that they can get dumped out quickly without disrupting the rehearsal frame set up earlier. With increasing age these strategies become possible.

Repeated reading: The family of teaching procedures whereby a student is provided with opportunities to read material that becomes familiar through repetition. Repetition can seem tiresome to adults, but generally not to young students.

Schema and schema refinement: The basic unit of knowledge above the level of a concept is the schema. Schemata typically consist of concepts organised together. Thus the schema for *birthday party* involves concepts such as presents, sweet food, a host, a sequence of events, and so on. Refinement refers to changes that accrue to schemata over time.

Self-enhancement: The native tendency to evaluate yourself somewhat higher than others would, or in relation to objective standards.

Self-esteem, perceived competencies, self-efficacy, and self-affirmation: The number of terms used to articulate self-processes is daunting. But each has a distinct meaning in the literature. Self-esteem is general and not tied to any one context. Perceived competencies refer to specific areas such that one feels competent in some, but not all areas of one's life. Self-efficacy refers to confidence about coping well in the context that is immediately in the mind's view, right there before you. Self-affirmation relates to statements rehearsed about oneself, for instance, when under stress (e.g., '*I am an honest hard-working person*').

Social brain hypothesis: That the demands of living in social groups selected for (in evolutionary terms) increases in brain capacity. Hence, our brains work so as to lock onto and interpret other people and learn from them. Unconsciously, the brain reacts neurologically to the presence and actions of other species members.

Social comparison: This is where one person uses others as a standard for comparison or judgement.

Spontaneous trait inference effect: On seeing another human being, you unconsciously form a series of judgements about the person, implicating their supposed traits, motives, and personality. This social brain process is unstoppable and psychologically as inevitable as reading the phrase '*I would not do this*' in this sentence.

Spotlight effect: The belief that the self is the centre of attention for other people present in the room.

Strings or serial orderings: Sequences of information to be committed to memory as unit, generally learnt through rehearsal. For instance, your Visa number, or the times tables.

Three degrees of social separation: Smile at one person, and he or she may smile at another. However, the effect appears to wash out by the third person. The effect might apply to range of mimicked action.

Time allocated, instructional, engagement, and academic learning time: Terms used to analyse how time in classrooms unfolds at the level of the individual student. For instance, in the same class, same lesson, one student may accumulate 10 minutes of academic learning time, whereas the student two seats away may accumulate only 1 minute. Academic learning time is indexed through the student displaying a high success level whilst task engaged.

Vigilance decrement: Reduction in attention and concentration, especially when tasks are prolonged and non-eventful.

References

Abbott, A., & Collins, D. (2004). Eliminating the dichotomy between theory and practice in talent identification and development: Considering the role of psychology. *Journal of Sports Sciences, 22*(5), 395–408.

Abel, E. L., & Kruger, M. L. (2010). Smile intensity in photographs predicts longevity. *Psychological Science, 21*(4), 542–544.

Aberson, C. L., Healy, M., & Romero, V. (2000). Ingroup bias and self-esteem: A meta-analysis. *Personality and Social Psychology Review 4*(2), 157–173.

Ackerman, R., & Koriat, A. (2011). Response latency as a predictor of the accuracy of children's reports. *Journal of Experimental Psychology: Applied, 17*(4), 406–417.

Ainley, J., Batten, M., Cherry, C., & Withers, G. (1998). *Schools and the social development of young Australians.* Melbourne: Australian Council for Educational Research.

Albert, D., & Steinberg, L. (2011). Judgment and decision making in adolescence. *Journal of Research on Adolescence, 21*(1), 211–224.

Alfieri, L., Brooks, P. J., Aldrich, N. J., & Tenenbaum, H. R. (2011). Does discovery-based instruction enhance learning? *Journal of Educational Psychology, 103*(1), 1–18.

Allen, J. P., & Brown, B. B. (2008). Adolescents, peers, and motor vehicles: The perfect storm? *American Journal of Preventive Medicine, 35*(3, Supplement), 289–293.

Allen, J. P., Pianta, R. C., Gregory, A., Mikami, A. Y., & Lun, J. (2011). An interaction-based approach to enhancing secondary school instruction and student achievement. *Science, 333*(6045), 1034–1037.

Allington, R. L. (1984). Content coverage and conceptual reading in reading groups. *Journal of Reading Behavior, 16*(2), 85–96.

Alquist, J., & Baumeister, R. F. (2012). Self-control: Limited resources and extensive benefits. *Wiley Interdisciplinary Reviews: Cognitive Science, 3*(3), 419–423.

Alter, A. L., & Oppenheimer, D. M. (2009). Uniting the tribes of fluency to form a metacognitive nation. *Personality and Social Psychology Review, 13*(3), 219–235.

Alter, A. L., Oppenheimer, D. M., Epley, N., & Eyre, R. N. (2007). Overcoming intuition: Metacognitive difficulty activates analytic reasoning. *Journal of Experimental Psychology: General, 136*(4), 569–576.

Ambady, N. (2010). The perils of pondering: Intuition and thin slice judgments. *Psychological Inquiry, 21*(4), 271–278.

Ambady, N., LaPlante, D., & Johnson, E. (2001). Thin-slice judgments as a measure of interpersonal sensitivity. In J. A. Hall & F. J. Bernieri (Eds.), *Interpersonal sensitivity: Theory and measurement* (pp. 89–101). Mahwah, NJ: Lawrence Erlbaum.

Ambady, N., & Rosenthal, R. (1993). Half a minute: Predicting teacher evaluations from thin slices of nonverbal behavior and physical attractiveness. *Journal of Personality and Social Psychology, 64*(3), 431–441.

Anderson, E., Siegel, E., White, D., & Barrett, L. F. (2012). Out of sight but not out of mind: Unseen affective faces influence evaluations and social Impressions. *Emotion*, *12*(6), 1210–1221.

Annear, K., & Yates, G. C. R. (2010). Restrictive and supportive parenting: Effects on children's school affect and emotional responses. *Australian Educational Researcher*, *37*(1), 63–82.

Ariely, D. (2010). *The upside of irrationality: The unexpected benefits of defying logic at work and at home.* New York: Harper.

Ariga, A., & Lleras, A. (2011). Brief and rare mental 'breaks' keep you focused: Deactivation and reactivation of task goals preempt vigilance decrements. *Cognition*, *118*(3), 439–443.

Aronson, E., & Mills, J. (1959). The effect of severity of initiation on liking for a group. *Journal of Abnormal and Social Psychology*, *59*(2), 177–181.

Asendorpf, J. B., Penke, L., & Back, M. D. (2011). From dating to mating and relating: Predictors of initial and long-term outcomes of speed-dating in a community sample. *European Journal of Personality*, *25*(1), 16–30.

Attwood, G. (2011). Attitudes to school and intentions for educational participation: An analysis of data from the Longitudinal Survey of Young People in England. *International Journal of Research and Method in Education*, *34*(3), 269–287.

Ausabel, D. P. (1968). *Educational psychology: A cognitive view.* New York: Holt, Rinehart and Winston.

Autin, F., & Croizet, J.-C. (2012). Improving working memory efficiency by reframing metacognitive interpretation of task difficulty. *Journal of Experimental Psychology: General*, *141*(4), 610–618.

Axsom, D. (1989). Cognitive dissonance and behavior change in psychotherapy. *Journal of Experimental Social Psychology*, *25*(3), 234–252.

Aydeniz, M., & Kotowski, E. L. (2012). What do middle and high school students know about the particulate nature of matter after instruction? Implications for practice. *School Science and Mathematics*, *112*(2), 59–65.

Babad, E. (2005). Guessing teachers' differential treatment of high- and low-achievers from thin slices of their public lecturing behavior. *Journal of Nonverbal Behavior*, *29*(2), 125–134.

Babad, E. (2007). Teachers' nonverbal behavior and its effects on students. In R. P. Perry & J. C. Smart (Eds.), *The scholarship of teaching and learning in higher education: An evidence-based perspective* (pp. 201–261): The Netherlands: Springer.

Babad, E. (2009). Teaching and nonverbal behavior in the classroom. In L. J. Saha & A. G. Dworkin (Eds.), *International handbook of research on teachers and teaching* (pp. 817–827): New York: Springer.

Babad, E., Avni-Babad, D., & Rosenthal, R. (2003). Teachers' brief nonverbal behaviors in defined instructional situations can predict students' evaluations. *Journal of Educational Psychology*, *95*(3), 553–562.

Babad, E., Bernieri, F., & Rosenthal, R. (1989a). Nonverbal communication and leakage in the behavior of biased and unbiased teachers. *Journal of Personality and Social Psychology*, *56*(1), 89–94.

Babad, E., Bernieri, F., & Rosenthal, R. (1989b). When less information is more informative: Diagnosing teacher expectations from brief samples of behaviour. *British Journal of Educational Psychology*, *59*(3), 281–295.

Babad, Y. E., Alexander, I. E., Babad, E., Read, P. B., Shapiro, T., Leiderman, P. H., & Harter, S. (1983). Returning the smile of the stranger: Developmental patterns and socialization factors. *Monographs of the Society for Research in Child Development*, *48*(5), 1–93.

Baker, J. A. (2006). Contributions of teacher–child relationships to positive school adjustment during elementary school. *Journal of School Psychology*, *44*(3), 211–229.

Bandura, A. (1977). Self-efficacy: Toward a unifying theory of behavioral change. *Psychological Review*, *84*(2), 191–215.

Bandura, A. (1986). *Social foundations of thought and action: A social cognitive theory*. Englewood Cliffs, NJ: Prentice-Hall.

Bandura, A., & Schunk, D. H. (1981). Cultivating competence, self-efficacy, and intrinsic interest through proximal self-motivation. *Journal of Personality and Social Psychology, 41*(3), 586–598.

Bangerter, A., & Heath, C. (2004). The Mozart effect: Tracking the evolution of a scientific legend. *British Journal of Social Psychology, 43*(4), 605–623.

Bargh, J. A., & Chartrand, T. L. (1999). The unbearable automaticity of being. *American Psychologist, 54*(7), 462–479.

Baumeister, R. F., Bratslavsky, E., Finkenauer, C., & Vohs, K. D. (2001). Bad is stronger than good. *Review of General Psychology, 5*(4), 323–370.

Baumeister, R. F., Campbell, J. D., Krueger, J. I., & Vohs, K. D. (2003). Does high self-esteem cause better performance, interpersonal success, happiness, or healthier lifestyles? *Psychological Science in the Public Interest, 4*(1), 1–44.

Baumeister, R. F., Hutton, D. G., & Cairns, K. J. (1990). Negative effects of praise on skilled performance. *Basic and Applied Social Psychology, 11*(2), 131–148.

Baumeister, R. F., Smart, L., & Boden, J. M. (1996). Relation of threatened egotism to violence and aggression: The dark side of high self-esteem. *Psychological Review, 103*(1), 5–33.

Baumeister, R. F., & Tierney, J. (2011). *Willpower: Rediscovering the greatest human strength*. New York: Penguin.

Beanland, V., & Pammer, K. (2010). Looking without seeing or seeing without looking? Eye movements in sustained inattentional blindness. *Vision Research, 50*(10), 977–988.

Bechara, A., Damasio, H., Tranel, D., & Damasio, A. R. (1997). Deciding advantageously before knowing the advantageous strategy. *Science, 275*(5304), 1293–1295.

Bellert, A. (2009). Narrowing the gap: A report on the QuickSmart mathematics intervention. *Australian Journal of Learning Difficulties, 14*(2), 171–183.

Benner, A. D., & Mistry, R. S. (2007). Congruence of mother and teacher educational expectations and low-income youth's academic competence. *Journal of Educational Psychology, 99*(1), 140–153.

Bennett, S., Maton, K., & Kervin, L. (2008). The 'digital natives' debate: A critical review of the evidence. *British Journal of Educational Technology, 39*(5), 775–786.

Bergen, L., Grimes, T., & Potter, D. (2005). How attention partitions itself during simultaneous message presentations. *Human Communication Research, 31*(3), 311–336.

Berger, S. M., & Hadley, S. W. (1975). Some effects of a model's performance on observer's electromyographic activity. *American Journal of Psychology, 88*, 263–276.

Berger, S. M., Irwin, D. S., & Frommer, G. P. (1970). Electromyographic activity during observational learning. *American Journal of Psychology, 83*(1), 86–94.

Berk, M. S., & Andersen, S. M. (2000). The impact of past relationships on interpersonal behavior: Behavioral confirmation in the social–cognitive process of transference. *Journal of Personality and Social Psychology, 79*(4), 546–562.

Berliner, D. C. (1987). Simple views of effective teaching and a simple theory of classroom instruction. In D. C. Berliner & B. Rosenshine (Eds.), *Talks to teachers* (pp. 93–110). New York: Random House.

Berliner, D. C. (1990). What's all this fuss about instructional time? In M. Ben-Peretz & R. Bromme (Eds.), *The nature of time in school* (pp. 3–35). New York: Teachers College Press

Berliner, D. C. (2004). Describing the behavior and documenting the accomplishments of expert teachers. *Bulletin of Science Technology and Society, 24*(3), 200–212.

Bernieri, F. J. (1988). Coordinated movement and rapport in teacher-student interactions. *Journal of Nonverbal Behavior, 12*(2), 120–138.

Bernstein, D. M., & Loftus, E. F. (2009). How to tell if a particular memory is true or false. *Perspectives on Psychological Science, 4*(4), 370–374.

Biederman, I., & Shiffrar, M. M. (1987). Sexing day-old chicks: A case study and expert systems analysis of a difficult perceptual-learning task. *Journal of Experimental Psychology: Learning, Memory, and Cognition, 13*(4), 640–645.

Biggs, J. B., & Collis, K. F. (1982). *Evaluating the quality of learning: The solo taxonomy: Structure of the observed learning outcome.* New York: Academic Press.

Billings, L., & Fitzgerald, J. (2002). Dialogic discussion and the Paideia seminar. *American Educational Research Journal, 39*(4), 907–941.

Birkerts, S. (1994). *The Gutenberg elegies: The fate of reading in an electronic age.* Boston, MA: Faber and Faber.

Bjorklund, D. F. (2012). *Children's thinking* (5th ed.). Belmont, CA: Cengage.

Bloom, B. S. (1976). *Human characteristics and school learning.* New York: McGraw-Hill.

Bloom, B. S. (1986). Automaticity: The hands and feet of genius. *Educational Leadership, 43*(5), 70–77.

Bloom, B. S. (Ed.). (1985). *Developing talent in young people.* New York: Ballentine.

Boland, A. M., Haden, C. A., & Ornstein, P. A. (2003). Boosting children's memory by training mothers in the use of an elaborative conversational style as an event unfolds. *Journal of Cognition and Development, 4*(1), 39–65.

Bond, C. F., Jr., & DePaulo, B. M. (2008). Individual differences in judging deception: Accuracy and bias. *Psychological Bulletin, 134*(4), 477–492.

Borko, H., & Livingston, C. (1989). Cognition and improvisation: Differences in mathematics instruction by expert and novice teachers. *American Educational Research Journal, 26*(4), 473–498.

Bowman, L. L., Levine, L. E., Waite, B. M., & Gendron, M. (2010). Can students really multitask? An experimental study of instant messaging while reading. *Computers and Education, 54*(4), 927–931.

Bressan, P., & Pizzighello, S. (2008). The attentional cost of inattentional blindness. *Cognition, 106*(1), 370–383.

Brophy, J. (1981). Teacher praise: A functional analysis. *Review of Educational Research, 51*(1), 5–32.

Brophy, J. (1986). Teacher influences on student achievement. *American Psychologist, 41*(10), 1069–1077.

Bruning, R. H., Schraw, G. J., & Norby, M. N. (2011). *Cognitive psychology and instruction* (5th ed.). Boston, MA: Pearson.

Bryan, W. L., & Harter, N. (1899). Studies on the telegraphic language: The acquisition of a hierarchy of habits. *Psychological Review, 6*(4), 345–375.

Bunce, D. M., Flens, E. A., & Neiles, K. Y. (2010). How long can students pay attention in class? A study of student attention decline using clickers. *Journal of Chemical Education, 87*(12), 1438–1443.

Burton, D. L., & Meezan, W. (2004). Revisting recent research on social learning theory as an etiological proposition for sexually abusive male adolescents. *Journal of Evidence-Based Social Work, 1*(1), 41–80.

Butler, R., & Shibaz, L. (2008). Achievement goals for teaching as predictors of students' perceptions of instructional practices and students' help seeking and cheating. *Learning and Instruction, 18*(5), 453–467.

Caldwell, J. H., Huitt, W. G., & Graeber, A. O. (1982). Time spent in learning: Implications from research. *Elementary School Journal, 82*(5), 471–480.

Caputo, D., & Dunning, D. (2005). What you don't know: The role played by errors of omission in imperfect self-assessments. *Journal of Experimental Social Psychology, 41*(5), 488–505.

Carless, D. (2006). Differing perceptions in the feedback process. *Studies in Higher Education, 31*(2), 219–233.

Carlson, E. N., Vazire, S., & Oltmanns, T. F. (2011). You probably think this paper's about you: Narcissists' perceptions of their personality and reputation. *Journal of Personality and Social Psychology, 101*(1), 185–201.

Carr, N. G. (2010). *The shallows: What the Internet is doing to our brains*. New York: W. W. Norton.

Carroll, A., Houghton, S., Durkin, K., & Hattie, J. A. C. (2009). *Adolescent reputations and risk: Developmental trajectories to delinquency*. New York: Springer.

Cauffman, E., Shulman, E. P., Steinberg, L., Claus, E., Banich, M. T., Graham, S., & Wollard, J. (2010). Age differences in affective decision making as indexed by performance on the Iowa Gambling Task. *Developmental Psychology, 46*(1), 193–207.

Ceci, S. J. (1991). How much does schooling influence general intelligence and its cognitive components? A reassessment of the evidence. *Developmental Psychology, 27*(5), 703–722.

Cervone, D. (2005). Personality architecture: Within-person structures and processes. *Annual Review of Psychology, 56*(1), 423–452.

Chabris, C., & Simons, D. (2010). *The invisible gorilla*. New York: Crown Harper Collins.

Chall, J. S. (2000). *The academic achievement challenge: What really works in the classroom*. New York: Guildford.

Chang, M.-L. (2009). An appraisal perspective of teacher burnout: Examining the emotional work of teachers. *Educational Psychology Review, 21*(3), 193–218.

Chartrand, T. L., & Bargh, J. A. (1999). The chameleon effect: The perception–behavior link and social interaction. *Journal of Personality and Social Psychology, 76*(6), 893–910.

Chartrand, T. L., Maddux, W. W., & Lakin, J. L. (2005). Beyond the perception–behavior link: The ubiquitous utility and motivational moderators of nonconscious mimicry. In R. R. Hassin, J. S. Uleman & J. A. Bargh (Eds.), *The new unconscious* (pp. 334–361). New York: Oxford University Press.

Cheng, C. M., & Chartrand, T. L. (2003). Self-monitoring without awareness: Using mimicry as a nonconscious affiliation strategy. *Journal of Personality and Social Psychology, 85*(6), 1170–1179.

Chi, M. T. H., & Ceci, S. J. (1987). Content knowledge: Its role, representation, and restructuring in memory development. In H. W. Reese (Ed.), *Advances in child development and behavior*, Vol. 20 (pp. 91–142). San Diego, CA: Academic Press.

Chi, M. T. H., Glaser, R., & Farr, M. J. (1988). *The nature of expertise*. Mahwah, NJ: Lawrence Erlbaum.

Chinn, C. A., & Brewer, W. F. (1993). The role of anomalous data in knowledge acquisition: A theoretical framework and implications for science instruction. *Review of Educational Research, 63*(1), 1–49.

Choudhury, S., Blakemore, S.-J., & Charman, T. (2006). Social cognitive development during adolescence. *Social Cognitive and Affective Neuroscience, 1*(3), 165–174.

Clark, D., & Linn, M. C. (2003). Designing for knowledge integration: The impact of instructional time. *Journal of the Learning Sciences, 12*(4), 451–493.

Clark, R. C., Nguyen, F., & Sweller, J. (2006). *Efficiency in learning: Evidence-based guidelines to manage cognitive load*. San Francisco, CA: Pfeiffer Wiley.

Clark, R. E., Kirschner, P. A., & Sweller, J. (2012). Putting students on the path to learning: The case for fully guided instruction. *American Educator, 36*(1), 6–11.

Clark, R. E., Yates, K., Early, S., & Moulton, K. (2009). An analysis of the failure of electronic media and discovery-based learning: Evidence for the performance benefits of guided training methods. In K. H. Silber & R. Foshay (Eds.), *Handbook of training and improving workplace performance: Instructional design and training delivery*, Vol. 1 (pp. 263–297). New York: John Wiley.

Clifasefi, S. L., Takarangi, M. K., & Bergman, J. S. (2006). Blind drunk: The effects of alcohol on inattentional blindness. *Applied Cognitive Psychology, 20*(5), 697–704.

Coffield, F., Moseley, D., Hall, E., & Ecclestone, K. (2004). Learning styles and pedagogy in post-16 learning: A systematic and critical review: (Report from the Learning and Skills Learning Research Centre). Retrieved form: http://lerenleren.nu/bronnen/Learning%20styles%20by%20Coffield%20e.a.pdf (accessed 20 May 2013).

Colvin, G. (2008). *Talent is overrated: What really separates world class performers from everybody else.* New York: Portfolio (Penguin).

Cook, S. W., Yip, T. K., & Goldin-Meadow, S. (2010). Gesturing makes memories that last. *Journal of Memory and Language, 63*(4), 465–475.

Corno, L. Y. N. (2008). On teaching adaptively. *Educational Psychologist, 43*(3), 161–173.

Črnčec, R., Wilson, S. J., & Prior, M. (2006). The cognitive and academic benefits of music to children: Facts and fiction. *Educational Psychology, 26*(4), 579–594.

Csibra, G., & Gergely, G. (2006). Social learning and social cognition: The case for pedagogy. In Y. Munakata & M. H. Johnson (Eds.), *Processes of change in cognitive development. Attention and Performance*, Vol. XXI (pp. 249–274). Oxford: Oxford University Press.

Cuban, L. (1982). Persistence of the inevitable: The teacher-centered classroom. *Education and Urban Society, 15*(1), 26–41.

Cuban, L. (1984). *How teachers taught: Constancy and change in the American classroom, 1890–1980.* New York: Longman.

Cunningham, A., & Stanovich, K. (2003). Reading can make you smarter. *Principal, 83*(2), 34–39.

Cvencek, D., Greenwald, A. G., & Meltzoff, A. N. (2011). Measuring implicit attitudes of 4-year-olds: The preschool implicit association test. *Journal of Experimental Child Psychology, 109*(2), 187–200.

Dalbert, C., & Stoeber, J. (2005). The belief in a just world and distress at school. *Social Psychology of Education, 8*(2), 123–135.

Dalton, P., & Fraenkel, N. (2012). Gorillas we have missed: Sustained inattentional deafness for dynamic events. *Cognition, 124*(3), 367–372.

Danziger, S., Levav, J., & Avnaim-Pesso, L. (2011). Extraneous factors in judicial decisions. *Proceedings of the National Academy of Sciences, 108*(17), 6889–6892.

De La Paz, S., & Felton, M. K. (2010). Reading and writing from multiple source documents in history: Effects of strategy instruction with low to average high school writers. *Contemporary Educational Psychology, 35*(3), 174–192.

Delfabbro, P., & Thrupp, L. (2003). The social determinants of youth gambling in South Australian adolescents. *Journal of Adolescence, 26*(3), 313–330.

Demanet, J., & Van Houtte, M. (2012). Teachers' attitudes and students' opposition. School misconduct as a reaction to teachers' diminished effort and affect. *Teaching and Teacher Education, 28*(6), 860–869.

DeWall, C. N., Baumeister, R. F., Gailliot, M. T., & Maner, J. K. (2008). Depletion makes the heart grow less helpful: Helping as a function of self-regulatory energy and genetic relatedness. *Personality and Social Psychology Bulletin, 34*(12), 1653–1662.

Dimberg, U., Andréasson, P., & Thunberg, M. (2011). Emotional empathy and facial reactions to facial expressions. *Journal of Psychophysiology, 25*(1), 26–31.

Dimberg, U., Thunberg, M., & Grunedal, S. (2002). Facial reactions to emotional stimuli: Automatically controlled emotional responses. *Cognition and Emotion, 16*(4), 449–471.

Dishion, T., Owen, L., & Bullock, B. (2004). Like father, like son: Toward a developmental model for the transmission of male deviance across generations. *European Journal of Developmental Psychology, 1*(2), 105–126.

Driscoll, K. C., & Pianta, R. C. (2010). Banking time in Head Start: Early efficacy of an intervention designed to promote supportive teacher–child relationships. *Early Education and Development, 21*(1), 38–64.

Driver, J. (2001). A selective review of selective attention research from the past century. *British Journal of Psychology, 92*(1), 53.

Dunbar, R. I. M. (2009). The social brain hypothesis and its implications for social evolution. *Annals of Human Biology, 36*(5), 562–572.

Dunbar, R. I. M. (2010). *How many friends does one person need? Dunbar's number and other evolutionary quirks.* London: Faber and Faber.

Duncan, G. J., Dowsett, C. J., Claessens, A., Magnuson, K., Huston, A. C., Klebanov, P., Pagani, L., Feinstein, L., Engel, M., Brooks-Gunn, J., Sexton, H., Duckworth, K., & Japel, C. (2007). School readiness and later achievement. *Developmental Psychology, 43*(6), 1428–1446.

Dunn, R. (1984). Learning style: State of the science. *Theory Into Practice, 23*(1), 10.

Dunning, D. (1995). Trait importance and modifiability as factors influencing self-assessment and self-enhancement Motives. *Personality and Social Psychology Bulletin, 21*(12), 1297–1306.

Dunning, D. (2006). Strangers to ourselves. *The Psychologist, 19*(10), 600–603.

Dunning, D., Heath, C., & Suls, J. M. (2004). Flawed self-assessment. *Psychological Science in the Public Interest, 5*(3), 69–106.

Dunning, D., Johnson, K., Ehrlinger, J., & Kruger, J. (2003). Why people fail to recognize their own incompetence. *Current Directions in Psychological Science 12*(3), 83–87.

Dweck, C. S. (1999). Caution: Praise can be dangerous. *American Educator, 23*(1), 1–5.

Ehrlinger, J., & Dunning, D. (2003). How chronic self-views influence (and potentially mislead) estimates of performance. *Journal of Personality and Social Psychology, 84*(1), 5–17.

Ehrlinger, J., Gilovich, T., & Ross, L. (2005). Peering into the bias blind spot: People's assessments of bias in themselves and others. *Personality and Social Psychology Bulletin, 31*(5), 680–692.

Ehrlinger, J., Johnson, K., Banner, M., Dunning, D., & Kruger, J. (2008). Why the unskilled are unaware: Further explorations of (absent) self-insight among the incompetent. *Organizational Behavior and Human Decision Processes, 105*(1), 98–121.

Eigsti, I.-M., Zayas, V., Mischel, W., Shoda, Y., Ayduk, O., Dadlani, M. B., Davison, M. C., Aber, J. L., Casey, B. J. (2006). Predicting cognitive control from preschool to late adolescence and young adulthood. *Psychological Science, 17*(6), 478–484.

Eisenberger, N. I., Inagaki, T. K., Muscatell, K. A., Haltom, K. E. B., & Leary, M. R. (2011). The neural sociometer: Brain mechanisms underlying state self-esteem. *Journal of Cognitive Neuroscience, 23*(11), 3448–3455.

Ellis, Y., Daniels, B., & Jauregui, A. (2010). The effect of multitasking on the grade performance of business students. *Research in Higher Education Journal, 8*, 1–10.

Emler, N. (2001). *Self-esteem: The costs and causes of low self-esteem.* York, UK: York Publishing.

Engel, C. (2012). Low self-control as a source of crime: A meta-study. *Max Planck Institute for Research on Collective Goods.* Retrieved from http://www.coll.mpg.de/pdf_dat/2012_04online.pdf (accessed 20 May 2013).

Engle, R. W., & Bukstel, L. H. (1978). Memory processes among bridge players of differing expertise. *American Journal of Psychology, 91*(4), 673–689.

Ericsson, K. A. (2008). Deliberate practice and acquisition of expert performance: A general overview. *Academic Emergency Medicine, 15*(11), 988–994.

Ericsson, K. A. (Ed.) (2009). *Development of professional expertise.* Cambridge: Cambridge University Press.

Ericsson, K. A., Charness, N., Feltovich, P. J., & Hoffman, R. R. (Eds.) (2006). *Cambridge handbook of expertise and expert performance.* New York: Cambridge University Press.

Ericsson, K. A., Krampe, R. T., & Tesch-Römer, C. (1993). The role of deliberate practice in the acquisition of expert performance. *Psychological Review, 100*(3), 363–406.

Ericsson, K. A., Roring, R. W., & Nandagopal, K. (2007). Giftedness and evidence for reproducibly superior performance: An account based on the expert performance framework. *High Ability Studies, 18*(1), 3–56.

Eva, K. W., & Regehr, G. (2008). 'I'll never play professional football' and other fallacies of self-assessment. *Journal of Continuing Education in the Health Professions, 28*(1), 14–19.

Evertson, C. M., & Weinstein, C. S. (Eds.) (2006). *Handbook of classroom management: Research, practice, and contemporary issues.* Mahwah, NJ: Lawrence Erlbaum Associates.

Feldon, D. F. (2007a). Cognitive load and classroom teaching: The double-edged sword of automaticity. *Educational Psychologist, 42*(3), 123–137.

Feldon, D. F. (2007b). The implications of research on expertise for curriculum and pedagogy. *Educational Psychology Review, 19*(2), 91–110.

Feldon, D. F., Timmerman, B. C., Stowe, K. A., & Showman, R. (2010). Translating expertise into effective instruction: The impacts of cognitive task analysis (CTA) on lab report quality and student retention in the biological sciences. *Journal of Research in Science Teaching, 47*(10), 1165–1185.

Festinger, L. (1961). The psychological effects of insufficient rewards. *American Psychologist, 16*(1), 1–11.

Finkel, E. J., Campbell, W. K., Brunell, A. B., Dalton, A. N., Scarbeck, S. J., & Chartrand, T. L. (2006). High-maintenance interaction: Inefficient social coordination impairs self-regulation. *Journal of Personality and Social Psychology, 91*(3), 456–475.

Fisher, C. W., Berliner, D. C., Filby, N. N., Marliave, R., Cahen, L. S., & Dishaw, M. M. (1980). Teacher behaviors, academic learning time, and student achievement. In C. Denham & A. Lieberman (Eds.), *Time to learn* (pp. 7–32). Washington DC: National Institute of Education.

Fitzpatrick, M. D., Grissmer, D., & Hastedt, S. (2011). What a difference a day makes: Estimating daily learning gains during kindergarten and first grade using a natural experiment. *Economics of Education Review, 30*(2), 269–279.

Fitzsimons, G. M., & Finkel, E. J. (2011). The effects of self-regulation on social relationships. In K. D. Vohs & R. F. Baumeister (Eds.), *Handbook of self-regulation: Research, Theory, and Applications* (2nd ed., pp. 407–421). New York: Guilford Press.

Fivush, R., Haden, C. A., & Reese, E. (2006). Elaborating on elaborations: Role of maternal reminiscing style in cognitive and socioemotional development. *Child Development, 77*(6), 1568–1588.

Foehr, U. G. (2006). *Media multitasking among American youth: Prevalence, predictors, and parings.* Menlo Park, CA: Kaiser Family Foundation

Foer, J. (2011). *Moonwalking with Einstein: The art and science of remembering everything.* London: Allen Lane.

Foerde, K., Knowlton, B. J., & Poldrack, R. A. (2006). Modulation of competing memory systems by distraction. *Proceedings of the National Academy of Sciences, 103*(31), 11778–11783.

Forrest, W., & Hay, C. (2011). Life-course transitions, self-control and desistance from crime. *Criminology and Criminal Justice, 11*(5), 487–513.

Fowler, J. H., & Christakis, N. A. (2010). Cooperative behavior cascades in human social networks. *Proceedings of the National Academy of Sciences, 107*(12), 5334–5338.

Frith, C. D., & Frith, U. (2012). Mechanisms of social cognition. *Annual Review of Psychology, 63*(1), 287–313.

Furnham, A., & Schofield, S. (1987). Accepting personality test feedback: A review of the Barnum effect. *Current Psychology, 6*(2), 162–178.

Gage, N. L. (2009). *A conception of teaching.* New York: Springer.

Gagne, E. D., Yekovich, C. W., & Yekovich, F. R. (1993). *Cognitive psychology of school learning* (2nd ed.). New York: Harper Collins

Gailliot, M. T., & Tice, D. M. (2007). Emotion regulation and impulse control: People succumb to their impulses to feel better. In K. D. Vohs, R. F. Baumeister, & G. Loewenstein (Eds.), *Do emotions help or hurt decision making? A Hedgefoxian perspective* (pp. 203–216). New York: Russell Sage Foundation.

Gardner, M., & Steinberg, L. (2005). Peer influence on risk taking, risk preference, and risky decision making in adolescence and adulthood: An experimental study. *Developmental Psychology, 41*(4), 625–635.

Gawrilow, C., Gollwitzer, P. M., & Oettingen, G. (2011). If-then plans benefit delay of gratification performance in children with and without ADHD. *Cognitive Therapy and Research, 35*(5), 442–455.

Gendolla, G. H. E., & Richter, M. (2010). Effort mobilization when the self is involved: Some lessons from the cardiovascular system. *Review of General Psychology, 14*(3), 212–226.

Gersten, R., Clarke, B., Jordan, N. C., Newman-Gonchar, R., Haymond, K., & Wilkins, C. (2012). Universal screening in mathematics for the primary grades: Beginnings of a research base. *Exceptional Children, 78*(4), 423–445.

Gersten, R., Jordan, N. C., & Flojo, J. R. (2005). Early identification and interventions for students with mathematics difficulties. *Journal of Learning Disabilities, 38*(4), 293–304.

Gettinger, M. (1986). Issues and trends in academic engaged time of students. *Special Services in the Schools, 2*(4), 1–17.

Geving, A. M. (2007). Identifying the types of student and teacher behaviours associated with teacher stress. *Teaching and Teacher Education, 23*(5), 624–640.

Gigerenzer, G. (2008). *Gut feelings: The intelligence of the unconscious.* New York: Penguin Books.

Gilovich, T., & Savitsky, K. (1999). The spotlight effect and the illusion of transparency: Egocentric assessments of how we are seen by others. *Current Directions in Psychological Science, 8*(6), 165.

Gladwell, M. (2006). *Blink: The power of thinking without thinking.* London: Penguin.

van Gog, T., Paas, F., Marcus, N., Ayres, P., & Sweller, J. (2009). The mirror neuron system and observational learning: Implications for the effectiveness of dynamic visualizations. *Educational Psychology Review, 21*(1), 21–30.

Goldin-Meadow, S., Cook, S. W., & Mitchell, Z. A. (2009). Gesturing gives children new ideas about math. *Psychological Science 20*(3), 267–272.

Goldin-Meadow, S., & Wagner, S. M. (2005). How our hands help us learn. *Trends in Cognitive Sciences, 9*(5), 234–241.

Gollwitzer, P. M., & Oettingen, G. (2012). Goal pursuit. In R. M. Ryan (Ed.), *Oxford handbook of human motivation* (pp. 208–231). New York: Oxford University Press.

Good, T. L., & Brophy, J. E. (2008). *Looking in classrooms* (10th ed.). Boston, MA: Allyn and Bacon.

Good, T. L., Slavings, R. L., Harel, K. H., & Emerson, H. (1987). Student passivity: A study of question asking in K-12 classrooms. *Sociology of Education, 60*(3), 181–199.

Goodlad, J. (1994). *A place called school: Prospects for the future.* New York: McGraw-Hill.

Gottfredson, M. R., & Hirschi, T. (1990). *A general theory of crime.* Stanford, CA: Stanford University Press.

Gough, P. B., & Tunmer, W. E. (1986). Decoding, reading, and reading disability. *Remedial and Special Education, 7*(1), 6–10.

Graham, S., & Barker, G. P. (1990). The down side of help: An attributional-developmental analysis of helping behavior as a low-ability cue. *Journal of Educational Psychology, 82*(1), 7–14.

Grahe, J. E., & Bernieri, F. J. (1999). The importance of nonverbal cues in judging rapport. *Journal of Nonverbal Behavior, 23*(4), 253–269.

Grape, C., Sandgren, M., Hansson, L., Ericson, M., & Theorell, T. (2002). Does singing promote well-being? An empirical study of professional and amateur singers during a singing lesson. *Integrative Physiological and Behavioral Science, 38*(1), 65–74.

Greenwald, A. G., Poehlman, T. A., Uhlmann, E. L., & Banaji, M. R. (2009). Understanding and using the Implicit Association Test: III. Meta-analysis of predictive validity. *Journal of Personality and Social Psychology, 97*(1), 17–41.

Gueguen, N., & Fischer-Lokou, J. (2004). Hitchhikers' smiles and receipt of help. *Psychological Reports, 94*(3), 756–760.

Haden, C. A., Ornstein, P. A., O'Brien, B. S., Elischberger, H. B., Tyler, C. S., & Burchinal, M. J. (2011). The development of children's early memory skills. *Journal of Experimental Child Psychology, 108*(1), 44–60.

Haden, C. A., Ornstein, P. A., Rudek, D. J., & Cameron, D. (2009). Reminiscing in the early years: Patterns of maternal elaborativeness and children's remembering. *International Journal of Behavioral Development, 33*(2), 118–130.

Hallam, S., Price, J., & Katsarou, G. (2002). The effects of background music on primary school pupils' task performance. *Educational Studies, 28*(2), 111–122.

Hamre, B. K., & Pianta, R. C. (2005). Can instructional and emotional support in the first-grade classroom make a difference for children at risk of school failure? *Child Development, 76*(5), 949–967.

Hamre, B. K., Pianta, R. C., Downer, J. T., & Mashburn, A. J. (2008). Teachers' perceptions of conflict with young students: Looking beyond problem behaviors. *Social Development, 17*(1), 115–136.

Harker, L., & Keltner, D. (2001). Expressions of positive emotion in women's college yearbook pictures and their relationship to personality and life outcomes across adulthood. *Journal of Personality and Social Psychology, 80*(1), 112–124.

Harris, L. T., & Fiske, S. T. (2006). Dehumanizing the lowest of the low: Neuroimaging responses to extreme out-groups. *Psychological Science 17*(10), 847–853.

Harris, M., & Rosenthal, R. (2005). No more teachers' dirty looks: Effects of teacher nonverbal behavior on student outcomes. In R. E. Riggio & R. S. Feldman (Eds.), *Applications of nonverbal communication* (pp. 157–192). Mahwah, NJ: Lawrence Erlbaum.

Harris, P. R. (2011). Self-affirmation and the self-regulation of health behavior change. *Self and Identity, 10*(3), 304–314.

Hartwig, M., & Bond, C. F., Jr. (2011). Why do lie-catchers fail? A lens model meta-analysis of human lie judgments. *Psychological Bulletin, 137*(4), 643–659.

Hattie, J. A. C. (2009). *Visible learning: A synthesis of over 800 meta-analyses relating to achievement.* London: Routledge.

Hattie, J. A. C. (2012). *Visible learning for teachers.* London: Routledge.

Hattie, J. A. C., & Gan, M. (2011). Instruction based on feedback. In R. E. Mayer & P. Alexander (Eds.), *Handbook of research on learning and instruction* (pp. 249–271). New York: Routledge.

Hattie, J. A. C., & Timperley, H. (2007). The power of feedback. *Review of Educational Research, 77*(1), 81–112.

Hedrick, A. M., Haden, C. A., & Ornstein, P. A. (2009). Elaborative talk during and after an event: Conversational style influences children's memory reports. *Journal of Cognition and Development, 10*(3), 188–209.

Heerey, E. A., & Velani, H. (2010). Implicit learning of social predictions. *Journal of Experimental Social Psychology, 46*(3), 577–581.

Helt, M. S., Eigsti, I., Snyder, P. J., & Fein, D. A. (2010). Contagious yawning in autistic and typical development. *Child Development, 81*(5), 1620–1631.

Hershey, A. D. (2010). Recent developments in pediatric headache. *Current Opinion in Neurology, 23*(3), 249–253.

Hertenstein, M., Hansel, C., Butts, A., & Hile, S. (2009). Smile intensity in photographs predicts divorce later in life. *Motivation and Emotion, 33*(2), 99–105.

Hickson, G. B., Federspiel, C., Picher, J., Miller, C., Gauld-Jaeger, J., & Bost, P. (2002). Patient complaints and malpractice risk. *Journal of the American Medical Association, 287*, 2951–2957.

Hinds, P. J. (1999). The curse of expertise: The effects of expertise and debiasing methods on prediction of novice performance. *Journal of Experimental Psychology: Applied, 5*(2), 205–221.

Hinds, P. J., Patterson, M., & Pfeffer, J. (2001). Bothered by abstraction: The effect of expertise on knowledge transfer and subsequent novice performance. *Journal of Applied Psychology*, *86*(6), 1232–1243.

Hinsz, V. B., & Tomhave, J. A. (1991). Smile and half the world smiles with you: Frown and you frown alone. *Personality and Social Psychology Bulletin*, *17*(5), 586–592.

Hirschi, T. (2004). Self-control and crime. In R. F. Baumeister & K. Vohs (Eds.), *Handbook of self-regulation: Research, theory, and application* (pp. 537–552). New York: Guilford Press.

Hofmann, W., Baumeister, R. F., Förster, G., & Vohs, K. D. (2012). Everyday temptations: An experience sampling study of desire, conflict, and self-control. *Journal of Personality and Social Psychology*, *102*(6), 1318–1335.

Hofmann, W., Vohs, K. D., & Baumeister, R. F. (2012). What people desire, feel conflicted about, and try to resist. *Psychological Science*, *23*(6), 582–588.

Hoover, W. A., & Gough, P. B. (1990). The simple view of reading. *Reading and Writing*, *2*(2), 127–160.

Hostetter, A. B. (2011). When do gestures communicate? A meta-analysis. *Psychological Bulletin*, *137*(2), 297–315.

Howe, M. J. A. (1999). *Genius explained*. Cambridge: Cambridge University Press.

Howe, M. J. A., Davidson, J. W., & Sloboda, J. A. (1998). Innate talents: Reality or myth? *Behavioral and Brain Sciences*, *21*, 399–407.

Howe, M. L., & Courage, M. L. (1993). On resolving the enigma of infantile amnesia. *Psychological Bulletin*, *113*(2), 305–326.

Hu, Y., & Ericsson, K. A. (2012). Memorization and recall of very long lists accounted for within the long-term working memory framework. *Cognitive Psychology*, *64*(4), 235–266.

Iacoboni, M. (2008). *Mirroring people: The new science of how we connect with others*. New York: Farrar, Straus and Giroux.

Ingvarson, L., & Hattie, J. A. C. (Eds.) (2008). *Assessing teachers for professional certification: The first decade of the National Board for Professional Teaching Standards*. Amsterdam: Elsevier Press.

Jelić, M. (2009). Is self-esteem predictor of in-group bias and out-group discrimination? *Review of Psychology*, *16*(1), 9–18.

Johnson, D. D. P., & Fowler, J. H. (2011). The evolution of overconfidence. *Nature*, *477*(7364), 317–320.

Jones, K. S., & Scmidlin, E. A. (2011). Human–robot interaction: Toward usable personal service robots. *Review of Human Factors and Ergonomics*, *7*(1), 100–148.

Junco, R., & Cotten, S. R. (2012). No A 4 U: The relationship between multitasking and academic performance. *Computers and Education*, *59*(2), 505–514.

Kahneman, D. (2011). *Thinking fast, thinking slow*. New York: Farrar Straus Giroux.

Kämpfe, J., Sedlmeier, P., & Renkewitz, F. (2011). The impact of background music on adult listeners: A meta-analysis. *Psychology of Music*, *39*(4), 424–448.

Karabenick, S. A. (1994). Relation of perceived teacher support of student questioning to students' beliefs about teacher attributions for questioning and perceived classroom learning environment. *Learning and Individual Differences*, *6*(2), 187–204.

Karabenick, S. A., & Newman, R. S. (2010). Seeking help as an adaptive response to learning difficulties: Person, situation, and developmental influences. In P. Peterson, E. Baker, & B. McGaw (Eds.), *International Encyclopedia of Education* (3rd ed., pp. 653–659). Oxford: Elsevier.

Kavale, K. A., & Forness, S. R. (1987). Substance over style: Assessing the efficacy of modality testing and teaching. *Exceptional Children*, *54*(3), 228–239.

Kearns, J. N., & Fincham, F. D. (2005). Victim and perpetrator accounts of interpersonal transgressions: Self-serving or relationship-serving biases? *Personality and Social Psychology Bulletin*, *31*(3), 321–333.

Keating, D. P., & Halpern-Felsher, B. L. (2008). Adolescent drivers: A developmental perspective on risk, proficiency, and safety. *American Journal of Preventive Medicine, 35*(3, Supplement), 272–277.

Keith, N., & Ericsson, K. A. (2007). A deliberate practice account of typing proficiency in everyday typists. *Journal of Experimental Psychology: Applied, 13*(3), 135–145.

Kidd, C., Palmeri, H., & Aslin, R. N. (2013). Rational snacking: Young children's decision-making on the marshmallow task is moderated by beliefs about environmental reliability. *Cognition, 126*(1), 109–114.

Killen, M., & Smetana, J. G. (Eds.) (2006). *Handbook of moral development*. Mahwah, NJ: Lawrence Erlbaum.

Kirschner, F., Paas, F., Kirschner, P. A., & Janssen, J. (2011). Differential effects of problem-solving demands on individual and collaborative learning outcomes. *Learning and Instruction, 21*(4), 587–599.

Kirschner, P. A., Sweller, J., & Clark, R. E. (2006). Why minimal guidance during instruction does not work: An analysis of the failure of constructivist, discovery, problem-based, experiential, and inquiry-based teaching. *Educational Psychologist, 41*(2), 75–86.

Kleinman, G., & Anandarajan, A. (2011). Inattentional blindness and its relevance to teaching forensic accounting and auditing. *Journal of Accounting Education, 29*(1), 37–49.

Knowlton, B. J., & Foerde, K. (2008). Neural representations of nondeclarative memories. *Current Directions in Psychological Science, 17*(2), 107–111.

Konrath, S. H., O'Brien, E. H., & Hsing, C. (2011). Changes in dispositional empathy in American college students over time: A meta-analysis. *Personality and Social Psychology Review, 15*(2), 180–198.

Kraut, R. E., & Johnson, R. E. (1979). Social and emotional messages of smiling: An ethological approach. *Journal of Personality and Social Psychology, 37*(9), 1539–1553.

Krumhuber, E., Manstead, A., & Kappas, A. (2007). Temporal aspects of facial displays in person and expression perception: The effects of smile dynamics, head-tilt, and gender. *Journal of Nonverbal Behavior, 31*(1), 39–56.

LaBerge, D., & Samuels, S. J. (1974). Toward a theory of automatic information processing in reading. *Cognitive Psychology, 6*(2), 293–323.

LaFrance, M. (1985). Postural mirroring and intergroup relations. *Personality and Social Psychology Bulletin, 11*(2), 207–217.

LaFrance, M. (2011). *Lip service: Smiles in life, death, trust, lies, work, memory, sex, and politics*. New York: W. W. Norton.

LaFrance, M., & Broadbent, M. (1976). Group rapport: Posture sharing as a nonverbal indicator. *Group and Organization Studies, 1*(3), 328–333.

LaFrance, M., & Hecht, M. A. (1995). Why smiles generate leniency. *Personality and Social Psychology Bulletin, 21*(3), 207–214.

LaFrance, M., Hecht, M. A., & Paluck, E. L. (2003). The contingent smile: A meta-analysis of sex differences in smiling. *Psychological Bulletin, 129*(2), 305–334.

Lakens, D. (2010). Movement synchrony and perceived entitativity. *Journal of Experimental Social Psychology, 46*(5), 701–708.

Lakin, J. L., Chartrand, T. L., & Arkin, R. M. (2008). I am too just like you: Nonconscious mimicry as an automatic behavioral response to social exclusion. *Psychological Science 19*(8), 816–822.

Laland, K. N., & Rendell, L. (2010). Social learning: Theory. In D. B. Michael & M. Janice (Eds.), *Encyclopedia of animal behavior* (pp. 260–266). Oxford: Academic Press.

Lavie, N. (2010). Attention, distraction, and cognitive control under load. *Current Directions in Psychological Science, 19*(3), 143–148.

Leary, M. R., & Guadagno, J. (2011). The sociometer, self-esteem, and the regulation of interpersonal behavior. In K. D. Vohs & R. F. Baumeister (Eds.), *Handbook of self-regulation: Research, theory, and applications* (2nd ed., pp. 339–354). New York: Guilford Press.

Leinhardt, G. (1987). Development of an expert explanation: An analysis of a sequence of subtraction lessons. *Cognition and Instruction*, *4*(4), 225–282.

Leinhardt, G., & Greeno, J. G. (1986). The cognitive skill of teaching. *Journal of Educational Psychology*, *78*(2), 75–95.

Lewis, R., Romi, S., & Roache, J. (2012). Excluding students from classroom: Teacher techniques that promote student responsibility. *Teaching and Teacher Education*, *28*(6), 870–878.

Lilienfeld, S. O., Lynn, S. J., Ruscio, J., & Beyerstein, B. L. (2010). *Fifty great myths of popular psychology*. Chichester, UK: Wiley-Blackwell.

Litman, J. A., Hutchins, T. L., & Russon, R. K. (2005). Epistemic curiosity, feeling-of-knowing, and exploratory behaviour. *Cognition and Emotion*, *19*(4), 559–582.

Little, M., & Kobak, R. (2003). Emotional security with teachers and children's stress reactivity: A comparison of special education and regular education classrooms. *Journal of Clinical Child and Adolescent Psychology*, *32*(1), 127–138.

Loewenstein, G. (1994). The psychology of curiosity: A review and reinterpretation. *Psychological Bulletin*, *116*(1), 75–98.

Luchies, L. B., Finkel, E. J., & Fitzsimons, G. M. (2011). The effects of self-regulatory strength, content, and strategies on close relationships. *Journal of Personality*, *79*(6), 1251–1280.

Lundeberg, M. A., Fox, P. W., & Punccohar, J. (1994). Highly confident but wrong: Gender differences and similarities in confidence judgements. *Journal of Educational Psychology*, *86*(1), 114–121.

Mabe, P. A., & West, S. G. (1982). Validity of self-evaluation of ability: A review and meta-analysis. *Journal of Applied Psychology*, *67*(3), 280–296.

Macknik, S. L., Martinez-Conde, S., & Blakeslee, S. (2010). *Sleights of mind: What the neuroscience of magic reveals about out everyday deceptions*. New York: Henry Holt.

Mark, G., Gudith, D., & Klocke, U. (2008). The cost of interrupted work: More speed and stress. *Proceedings of the Twenty-sixth Annual SIGCHI Conference on Human Factors in Computing Systems*, 107–110. Retrieved from http://dl.acm.org/citation.cfm?doid=1357054.1357072 (accessed 20 May 2013).

Marsh, H. W., & O'Mara, A. (2008). Reciprocal effects between academic self-concept, self-esteem, achievement, and attainment over seven adolescent years: Unidimensional and multidimensional perspectives of self-concept. *Personality and Social Psychology Bulletin*, *34*(4), 542–552.

Maurer, R. E., & Tindall, J. H. (1983). Effect of postural congruence on client's perception of counselor empathy. *Journal of Counseling Psychology*, *30*(2), 158–163.

Mayer, R. E. (2003). The promise of multimedia learning: Using the same instructional design methods across different media. *Learning and Instruction*, *13*(2), 125–139.

Mayer, R. E. (2004). Should there be a three-strikes rule against pure discovery learning? *American Psychologist*, *59*(1), 14–19.

McVay, J. C., & Kane, M. J. (2010). Adrift in the stream of thought: The effects of mind wandering on executive control and working memory capacity. In A. Gruszka, G. Matthews, & B. Szymura (Eds.), *Handbook of individual differences in cognition* (pp. 321–334). New York: Springer.

Mead, N. L., Baumeister, R. F., Gino, F., Schweitzer, M. E., & Ariely, D. (2009). Too tired to tell the truth: Self-control resource depletion and dishonesty. *Journal of Experimental Social Psychology*, *45*(3), 594–597.

Meehan, B. T., Hughes, J. N., & Cavell, T. A. (2003). Teacher–student relationships as compensatory resources for aggressive children. *Child Development*, *74*(4), 1145–1157.

van Merriënboer, J. J. G., & Sweller, J. (2005). Cognitive load theory and complex learning: Recent developments and future directions. *Educational Psychology Review*, *17*(2), 147–177.

van Meurs, I., Reef, J., Verhulst, F. C., & van der Ende, J. (2009). Intergenerational transmission of child problem behaviors: A longitudinal population-based study. *Journal of the American Academy of Child and Adolescent Psychiatry, 48*(2), 138–145.

Memmert, D. (2006). The effects of eye movements, age, and expertise on inattentional blindness. *Consciousness and Cognition: An International Journal, 15*(3), 620–627.

Meyer, W.-U. (1982). Indirect communications about perceived ability estimates. *Journal of Educational Psychology, 74*(6), 888–897.

Meyer, W.-U. (1992). Paradoxical effects of praise and criticism on perceived ability. *European Review of Social Psychology, 3*(1), 259–283.

Miles, L. K. (2009). Who is approachable? *Journal of Experimental Social Psychology, 45*(1), 262–266.

Mischel, W. (2012). Self-control theory. In P. A. M. Van Lange, A. W. Kruglanski, & E. Higgins, T. (Eds.), *Handbook of theories of social psychology*, Vol. 2 (pp. 1–22). London: Sage.

Mischel, W., Ayduk, O., Berman, M. G., Casey, B. J., Gotlib, I. H., Jonides, J., Kross, E., Teslovich, T., Wilson, N. L., Zayas, V., Shoda Y. (2011). Willpower over the life span: Decomposing self-regulation. *Social Cognitive and Affective Neuroscience, 6*(2), 252–256.

Mlodinow, L. (2012). *Subliminal: How your unconscious mind rules your behavior.* New York: Pantheon Random House.

Mochon, D., Norton, M. I., & Ariely, D. (2012). Bolstering and restoring feelings of competence via the IKEA effect. *International Journal of Research in Marketing, 29*(4), 363–369.

Moely, B. E., & Hart, S. S. (1992). The teacher's role in facilitating memory and study strategy development in the elementary school. *Child Development, 63*(3), 653.

Moffitt, T. E., Arseneault, L., Belsky, D., Dickson, N., Hancox, R. J., Harrington, H., Houts, R., Poulton, R., Roberts, B. W., Ross, S., Sears, M. R., Thomson, W. M., Caspi, A. (2011). A gradient of childhood self-control predicts health, wealth, and public safety. *Proceedings of the National Academy of Sciences, 108*(7), 2693–2698.

Mol, S. E., & Bus, A. G. (2011). To read or not to read: A meta-analysis of print exposure from infancy to early adulthood. *Psychological Bulletin, 137*(2), 267–296.

Monahan, K. C., & Steinberg, L. (2011). Accentuation of individual differences in social competence during the transition to adolescence. *Journal of Research on Adolescence, 21*(3), 576–585.

Moreno, S. (2009). Can music influence language and cognition? *Contemporary Music Review, 28*(3), 329–345.

Moreno, S., Bialystok, E., Barac, R., Schellenberg, E. G., Cepeda, N. J., & Chau, T. (2011). Short-term music training enhances verbal intelligence and executive function. *Psychological Science, 22*(11), 1425–1433.

Morewedge, C. K., Shu, L. L., Gilbert, D. T., & Wilson, T. D. (2009). Bad riddance or good rubbish? Ownership and not loss aversion causes the endowment effect. *Journal of Experimental Social Psychology, 45*(4), 947–951.

Moxley, J. H., Ericsson, K. A., Charness, N., & Krampe, R. T. (2012). The role of intuition and deliberative thinking in experts' superior tactical decision-making. *Cognition, 124*(1), 72–78.

Müller, S., Abernethy, B., & Farrow, D. (2006). How do world-class cricket batsmen anticipate a bowler's intention? *Quarterly Journal of Experimental Psychology, 59*(12), 2162–2186.

Murphy, P. K., Wilkinson, I. A. G., Soter, A. O., Hennessey, M. N., & Alexander, J. F. (2009). Examining the effects of classroom discussion on students' comprehension of text: A meta-analysis. *Journal of Educational Psychology, 101*(3), 740–764.

Musch, J., & Klauer, K. C. (Eds.) (2003). *The psychology of evaluation: Affective processes in cognition and emotion.* Mahwah, NJ: Lawrence Erlbaum.

Myers, S., & Pianta, R. C. (2008). Developmental commentary: Individual and contextual influences on student–teacher relationships and children's early problem behaviors. *Journal of Clinical Child and Adolescent Psychology, 37*(3), 600–608.

Nathan, M. J., & Petrosino, A. (2003). Expert blind spot among preservice teachers. *American Educational Research Journal*, 40(4), 905–928.

Naveh-Benjamin, M., Craik, F. I. M., Perretta, J. G., & Tonev, S. T. (2000). The effects of divided attention on encoding and retrieval processes: The resiliency of retrieval processes. *Quarterly Journal of Experimental Psychology*, 53(3), 609–625.

Neal, D. T., & Chartrand, T. L. (2011). Embodied emotion perception: Amplifying and dampening facial feedback modulates emotion perception accuracy. *Social Psychological and Personality Science*, 2(6), 673–678.

Niederle, M., & Vesterlund, L. (2011). Gender and competition. *Annual Review of Economics*, 3, 601–630.

Nordgren, L. F., Banas, K., & MacDonald, G. (2011). Empathy gaps for social pain: Why people underestimate the pain of social suffering. *Journal of Personality and Social Psychology*, 100(1), 120–128.

Norretranders, T. (1998). *The user illusion: Cutting consciousness down to size*. New York: Viking.

Norton, E. S., & Wolf, M. (2012). Rapid automatized naming (RAN) and reading fluency: Implications for understanding and treatment of reading disabilities. *Annual Review of Psychology*, 63(1), 427–452.

Norton, M. I., Mochon, D., & Ariely, D. (2012). The IKEA effect: When labor leads to love. *Journal of Consumer Psychology*, 22, 453–460.

Nucci, L. P. (1984). Evaluating teachers as social agents: Students' ratings of domain appropriate and domain inappropriate teacher responses to transgressions. *American Educational Research Journal*, 21(2), 367–378.

Nückles, M., Wittwer, J., & Renkl, A. (2005). Information about a layperson's knowledge supports experts in giving effective and efficient online advice to laypersons. *Journal of Experimental Psychology: Applied*, 11(4), 219–236.

Nuthall, G. A. (2007). *The hidden lives of learners*. Wellington: New Zealand Council for Educational Research.

Nysse-Carris, K. L., Bottoms, B. L., & Salerno, J. M. (2011). Experts' and novices' abilities to detect children's high-stakes lies of omission. *Psychology, Public Policy, and Law*, 17(1), 76–98.

O'Connor, E. E., Dearing, E., & Collins, B. A. (2011). Teacher–child relationship and behavior problem trajectories in elementary school. *American Educational Research Journal*, 48(1), 120–162.

Olson, M. A., Fazio, R. H., & Hermann, A. D. (2007). Reporting tendencies underlie discrepancies between implicit and explicit measures of self-esteem. *Psychological Science*, 18(4), 287–291.

Ophir, E., Nass, C., & Wagner, A. D. (2009). Cognitive control in media multitaskers. *Proceedings of the National Academy of Sciences*, 106(37), 15583–15587.

Ornstein, P. A., Coffman, J. L., Grammer, J. K., San Souci, P. P., & McCall, L., E. (2010). Linking the classroom context and the development of children's memory skills. In J. L. Meece & J. S. Eccles (Eds.), *Handbook of research on schools, schooling, and human development* (pp. 42–59). New York: Routledge.

Oveis, C., Gruber, J., Keltner, D., Stamper, J. L., & Boyce, W. T. (2009). Smile intensity and warm touch as thin slices of child and family affective style. *Emotion*, 9(4), 544–548.

Paas, F., & Sweller, J. (2012). An evolutionary upgrade of cognitive load theory: Using the human motor system and collaboration to support the learning of complex cognitive tasks. *Educational Psychology Review*, 24(1), 27–45.

Palinko, O., Kun, A. L., Shyrokov, A., & Heeman, P. (2010). Estimating cognitive load using remote eye tracking in a driving simulator. Paper presented at the Proceedings of the 2010 Symposium on Eye-Tracking Research.

Palmquist, C. M., & Jaswal, V. K. (2012). Preschoolers expect pointers (even ignorant ones) to be knowledgeable. *Psychological Science*, 23(3), 230–231.

Pashler, H., McDaniel, M., Rohrer, D., & Bjork, R. (2008). Learning styles: Concepts and evidence. *Psychological Science in the Public Interest, 9*(3), 105–119.

Peace, V., Miles, L., & Johnston, L. (2006). It doesn't matter what you wear: The impact of posed and genuine expressions of happiness on product evaluation. *Social Cognition, 24*(2), 137–168.

Peter, F., & Dalbert, C. (2010). Do my teachers treat me justly? Implications of students' justice experience for class climate experience. *Contemporary Educational Psychology, 35*(4), 297–305.

Peter, F., Kloeckner, N., Dalbert, C., & Radant, M. (2012). Belief in a just world, teacher justice, and student achievement: A multilevel study. *Learning and Individual Differences, 22*(1), 55–63.

Pianta, R. C., & Allen, J. P. (2008). Building capacity for positive youth development in secondary school classrooms: Changing teachers' interactions with students. In M. Shinn & H. Yoshikawa (Eds.), *Toward positive youth development: Transforming schools and community programs* (pp. 21–39). New York: Oxford University Press.

Pianta, R. C., & Stuhlman, M. W. (2004). Teacher–child relationships and children's success in the first years of school. *School Psychology Review,* 33(3), 444–458

Pietschnig, J., Voracek, M., & Formann, A. K. (2010). Mozart effect–Shmozart effect: A meta-analysis. *Intelligence, 38*(3), 314–323.

Pinker, S. (2011). *The better angels of our nature: The decline of violence in history and its causes.* London: Allen Lane.

Plant, E. A., Ericsson, K. A., Hill, L., & Asberg, K. (2005). Why study time does not predict grade point average across college students: Implications of deliberate practice for academic performance. *Contemporary Educational Psychology, 30*(1), 96–116.

Pollatsek, A., & Rayner, K. (2009). Reading. In L. R. Squire (Ed.), *Encyclopedia of Neuroscience* (pp. 29–34). Oxford: Academic Press.

Pollock, E., Chandler, P., & Sweller, J. (2002). Assimilating complex information. *Learning and Instruction, 12*(1), 61–86.

Prensky, M. (2001). Digital natives, digital immigrants. *On the Horizon, 9*(5), 1–6.

Prensky, M. (2006). Listen to the natives. *Educational Leadership, 63*(4), 8–13.

Prensky, M. (2010). *Teaching digital natives: Partnering for real learning.* Thousand Oaks, CA: Corwin Press.

Pressley, M., & McCormick, C. (1995). *Advanced educational psychology for educators, researchers, and policymakers.* New York: Harper Collins

Price, D. A., & Yates, G. C. R. (2010). Ego depletion effects on mathematics performance in primary school students: Why take the hard road? *Educational Psychology, 30*(3), 269–281.

Provine, R. (2000). *Laughter: A scientific investigation.* New York: Viking.

Provine, R. (2005). Yawning. *American Scientist, 93*(6), 532–539.

Putnam, S. P., Spritz, B. L., & Stifter, C. A. (2002). Mother–child coregulation during delay of gratification at 30 months. *Infancy, 3*(2), 209–225.

Rayner, K. (2001). Eye movements in reading. In N. J. Smelser & P. B. Baltes (Eds.), *International encyclopedia of the social and behavioral sciences* (pp. 5210–5214). Oxford: Pergamon.

Reader, S., & Biro, D. (2010). Experimental identification of social learning in wild animals. *Learning and Behavior, 38*(3), 265–283.

Reed, N., McLeod, P., & Dienes, Z. (2010). Implicit knowledge and motor skill: What people who know how to catch don't know. *Consciousness and Cognition, 19*(1), 63–76.

Reynolds, M., Wheldall, K., & Madelaine, A. (2010). Components of effective early reading interventions for young struggling readers. *Australian Journal of Learning Difficulties, 15*(2), 171–192.

Reynolds, M., Wheldall, K., & Madelaine, A. (2011). What recent reviews tell us about the efficacy of reading interventions for struggling readers in the early years of schooling. *International Journal of Disability, Development and Education, 58*(3), 257–286.

de Ridder, D. T. D., Lensvelt-Mulders, G., Finkenauer, C., Stok, F. M., & Baumeister, R. F. (2012). Taking stock of self-control. *Personality and Social Psychology Review*, 16(1), 76–99.

Rind, B., & Bordia, P. (1996). Effect on restaurant tipping of male and female servers drawing a happy, smiling face on the backs of customers' checks. *Journal of Applied Social Psychology*, 26(3), 218–225.

Risko, E. F., Anderson, N., Sarwal, A., Engelhardt, M., & Kingstone, A. (2012). Everyday attention: Variation in mind wandering and memory in a lecture. *Applied Cognitive Psychology*, 26(2), 234–242.

Ritter, S. M., Karremans, J. C., & van Schie, H. T. (2010). The role of self-regulation in derogating attractive alternatives. *Journal of Experimental Social Psychology*, 46(4), 631–637.

Roberts, W. A. (2002). Are animals stuck in time? *Psychological Bulletin*, 128(3), 473–489.

Roscoe, S. N. (1997). The adolescence of engineering psychology. In S. M. Casey (Eds.), *Human Factors History Monograph Series*, Vol. 1. Retrieved from www.hfes.org/publication maintenance/featureddocuments/27/adolescence.pdf (accessed 20 May 2013).

Rosenshine, B. (2012). Principles of instruction: Research-based strategies that all teachers should know. *American Educator*, 36(1), 12–39.

Rosenshine, B., & Stevens, R. (1986). Teaching functions. In M. Wittrock (Ed.), *Handbook of research on teaching* (3rd ed., pp. 376–391). New York: Macmillan.

Ross, P. E. (2006). The expert mind. *Scientific American*, 295(2), 64–71.

Rowe, K. (2006). Effective teaching practices for students with and without learning difficulties: Issues and implications surrounding key findings and recommendations from the National Inquiry into the Teaching of Literacy. *Australian Journal of Learning Difficulties*, 11(3), 99–115.

Rowe, M. L., & Goldin-Meadow, S. (2009). Differences in early gesture explain SES disparities in child vocabulary size at school entry. *Science*, 323, 951–953.

Rudin, D., Kiss, A., Wetz, R., V., & Sottile, V. M. (2007). Music in the endoscopy suite: A meta-analysis of randomized controlled studies. *Endoscopy*, 39(6), 507–510.

Ryan, A. M., & Shin, H. (2011). Help-seeking tendencies during early adolescence: An examination of motivational correlates and consequences for achievement. *Learning and Instruction*, 21(2), 247–256.

Sabbagh, M. A., & Shafman, D. (2009). How children block learning from ignorant speakers. *Cognition*, 112(3), 415–422.

Sabers, D. S., Cushing, K. S., & Berliner, D. C. (1991). Differences among teachers in a task characterized by simultaneity, multidimensional, and immediacy. *American Educational Research Journal*, 28(1), 63–88.

Samuels, S. J., & Farstrup, A. E. (2006). *What research has to say about fluency instruction* (3rd ed.). Newark, DE: International Reading Association.

Samuels, S. J., & Farstrup, A. E. (Eds.) (2011). *What research has to say about reading instruction* (4th ed.). Newark, DE: International Reading Association.

van Schaik, C. P., & Burkart, J. M. (2011). Social learning and evolution: The cultural intelligence hypothesis. *Philosophical Transactions of the Royal Society B: Biological Sciences*, 366(1567), 1008–1016.

Santinello, M., Vieno, A., & De Vogli, R. (2009). Primary headache in Italian early adolescents: The role of perceived teacher unfairness. *Headache*, 49(3), 366–374.

Schellenberg, E. G. (2011). Examining the association between music lessons and intelligence. *British Journal of Psychology*, 102(3), 283–302.

Schellenberg, E. G., Nakata, T., Hunter, P. G., & Tamoto, S. (2007). Exposure to music and cognitive performance: Tests of children and adults. *Psychology of Music*, 35(1), 5–19.

Schiaratura, L., & Askevis-Leherpeux, F. (2007). The influence of the nonverbal behaviour of examiners on children's psychometric performances. *European Journal of Psychology of Education*, 22(3), 327–332.

Schmeichel, B. J., & Vohs, K. (2009). Self-affirmation and self-control: Affirming core values counteracts ego depletion. *Journal of Personality and Social Psychology*, *96*(4), 770–782.

Schmeichel, B. J., Vohs, K. D., & Baumeister, R. F. (2003). Intellectual performance and ego depletion: Role of the self in logical reasoning and other information processing. *Journal of Personality and Social Psychology*, *85*(1), 33–46.

Schooler, J. W., Smallwood, J., Christoff, K., Handy, T. C., Reichle, E. D., & Sayette, M. A. (2011). Meta-awareness, perceptual decoupling and the wandering mind. *Trends in Cognitive Sciences*, *15*(7), 319–326.

Schwarz, N. (1999). Self-reports: How the questions shape the answers. *American Psychologist*, *54*(2), 93–105.

Schwarz, N., Bless, H., Strack, F., Klumpp, G., Rittenauer-Schatka, H., & Simons, A. (1991). Ease of retrieval as information: Another look at the availability heuristic. *Journal of Personality and Social Psychology*, *61*(2), 195–202.

Scott, C. (2010). The enduring appeal of learning styles. *Australian Journal of Education*, *54*(1), 5–17.

Scriven, M. (1967). The methodology of evaluation. In R. W. Tyler, R. M. Gagne & M. Scriven (Eds.), *Perspectives on Curriculum Evaluation, American Educational Research Association Monograph Series on Curriculum Evaluation*, Vol. 1: Chicago, IL: Rand McNally.

Seger, C. A. (1994). Implicit learning. *Psychological Bulletin*, *115*(2), 163–196.

Senju, A., & Csibra, G. (2008). Gaze following in human infants depends on communicative signals. *Current Biology*, *18*(9), 668–671.

Shermer, M. (2011). *The believing brain: From ghosts and gods to politics and conspiracies: How we construct beliefs and reinforce them as truths*. New York: Times Books.

Shiv, B., Carmon, Z., & Ariely, D. (2005). Placebo effects of marketing actions: Consumers may get what they pay for. *Journal of Marketing Research 42*(4), 383–393.

Shulruf, B., Hattie, J. A. C., & Dixon, R. (2008). Factors affecting responses to Likert type questionnaires: Introduction of the ImpExp, a new comprehensive model. *Social Psychology of Education*, *11*(1), 59–78.

Simons-Morton, B. G., Ouimet, M. C., Zhang, Z., Klauer, S. E., Lee, S. E., Wang, J., Chen, R., Albert, P., Dingus, T. A. (2011). The effect of passengers and risk-taking friends on risky driving and crashes/near crashes among novice teenagers. *Journal of Adolescent Health*, *49*(6), 587–593.

Simons, D. J., & Chabris, C. F. (1999). Gorillas in our midst: Sustained inattentional blindness for dynamic events. *Perception*, *28*(9), 1059–1074.

Siu Man, L., & Hui, W. (2010). Effects of smiling and gender on trust toward a recommendation agent. Proceedings of the Cyberworlds (CW), 2010 International Conference, 398–405. Retrieved from http://ieeexplore.ieee.org/stamp/stamp.jsp?tp=&arnumber=5655223& isnumber=5654996 (accessed 20 May 2013).

Slutske, W. S., Moffitt, T. E., Poulton, R., & Caspi, A. (2012). Undercontrolled temperament at age 3 predicts disordered gambling at age 32. *Psychological Science 23*(5), 510–516.

Smallwood, J., Mrazek, M. D., & Schooler, J. W. (2011). Medicine for the wandering mind: Mind wandering in medical practice. *Medical Education*, *45*(11), 1072–1080.

Smith, F., Hardman, F., Wall, K., & Mroz, M. (2004). Interactive whole class teaching in the National Literacy and Numercy Strategies. *British Educational Research Journal*, *30*(3), 395–411.

Smith, F. W., & Schyns, P. G. (2009). Smile through your fear and sadness. *Psychological Science*, *20*(10), 1202–1208.

Sobel, D. M., & Corriveau, K. H. (2010). Children monitor individuals' expertise for word learning. *Child Development*, *81*(2), 669–679.

Song, H., & Schwarz, N. (2008). Fluency and the detection of misleading questions: Low processing fluency attenuates the Moses illusion. *Social Cognition*, *26*(6), 791–799.

Spilt, J., Koomen, H., & Thijs, J. (2011). Teacher wellbeing: The importance of teacher–student relationships. *Educational Psychology Review, 23*(4), 457–477.

St Clair-Thompson, H., Stevens, R., Hunt, A., & Bolder, E. (2010). Improving children's working memory and classroom performance. *Educational Psychology, 30*(2), 203–219.

Stahl, S. A. (1999). Different strokes for different folk? A critique of learning styles. *American Educator, 23*(3), 1–5.

Stanovich, K. E. (1999). *Who is rational? Studies of individual differences in reasoning.* Mahwah, NJ: Lawrence Erlbaum.

Stanovich, K. E. (2000). *Progress in understanding reading: Scientific foundations and new frontiers.* New York: Guilford Press.

Stanovich, K. E. (2004). *The robot's rebellion: Finding meaning in the age of Darwin.* Chicago, IL: University of Chicago.

Steinberg, L. (2007). Risk taking in adolescence: New perspectives from brain and behavioral science. *Current Directions in Psychological Science, 16*(2), 55–59.

Stel, M., & Vonk, R. (2009). Empathizing via mimicry depends on whether emotional expressions are seen as real. *European Psychologist, 14*(4), 342–350.

Strayer, D. L., Drews, F. A., & Crouch, D. J. (2006). A comparison of the cell phone driver and the drunk driver. *Human Factors: The Journal of the Human Factors and Ergonomics Society, 48*(2), 381–391.

Strayer, D. L., & Watson, J. M. (2012). Supertaskers and the multitasking brain. *Scientific American Mind, 23*(1), 22–29.

Stucke, T. S., & Baumeister, R. F. (2006). Ego depletion and aggressive behavior: Is the inhibition of aggression a limited resource? *European Journal of Social Psychology, 36*(1), 1–13.

Stull, A. T., & Mayer, R. E. (2007). Learning by doing versus learning by viewing: Three experimental comparisons of learner-generated versus author-provided graphic organizers. *Journal of Educational Psychology, 99*(4), 808–820.

Sullivan, P., Clark, D., & O'Shea, H. (2010). Students' opinions about characteristics of their desired mathematics lessons. In L. Sparrow, B. Kissane, & C. Hurst (Eds.), *Shaping the future of mathematics education,* Proceedings of the 33rd annual conference of the Mathematics Education Research Group of Australasia (pp. 531–538). Freemantle: MERGA.

Surawski, M. K., & Ossoff, E. P. (2006). The effects of physical and vocal attractiveness on impression formation of politicians. *Current Psychology, 25*(1), 15–27.

Sweller, J. (1988). Cognitive load during problem solving: Effects on learning. *Cognitive Science, 12*(2), 257–285.

Sweller, J., Ayres, P., & Kalyuga, S. (2011). *Cognitive load theory.* New York: Springer.

Sweller, J., Clark, R. E., & Kirschner, P. A. (2010). Mathematical ability relies on knowledge, too. *American Educator, 34*(4), 34–35.

Takeuchi, T., & Inomata, K. (2009). Visual search strategies and decision making in baseball hitting. *Perceptual and Motor Skills, 108*(3), 971–980.

Tangney, J. P., Baumeister, R. F., & Boone, A. L. (2004). High self-control predicts good adjustment, less pathology, better grades, and interpersonal success. *Journal of Personality, 72*(2), 271–324.

Taylor, J. E. T., Witt, J. K., & Grimaldi, P. J. (2012). Uncovering the connection between artist and audience: Viewing painted brushstrokes evokes corresponding action representations in the observer. *Cognition, 125*(1), 26–36.

Taylor, S. E., & Brown, J. D. (1988). Illusion and well-being: A social psychological perspective on mental health. *Psychological Bulletin, 103*(2), 193–210.

Taylor, S. E., Lerner, J. S., Sherman, D. K., Sage, R. M., & McDowell, N. K. (2003). Portrait of the self-enhancer: Well adjusted and well liked or maladjusted and friendless? *Journal of Personality and Social Psychology, 84*(1), 165–176.

Tervaniemi, M., Rytkönen, M., Schröger, E., Ilmoniemi, R. J., & Näätänen, R. (2001). Superior formation of cortical memory traces for melodic patterns in musicians. *Learning and Memory*, 8(5), 295–300.

Therrien, W. J. (2004). Fluency and comprehension gains as a result of repeated reading. *Remedial and Special Education*, 25(4), 252–261.

Thibault, P., Gosselin, P., Brunel, M., & Hess, U. (2009). Children's and adolescents' perception of the authenticity of smiles. *Journal of Experimental Child Psychology*, 102(3), 360–367.

Thompson, V., & Morsanyi, K. (2012). Analytic thinking: Do you feel like it? *Mind and Society*, 11(1), 93–105.

Thompson, W. F., Schellenberg, E. G., & Letnic, A. K. (2012). Fast and loud background music disrupts reading comprehension. *Psychology of Music*, 40(6) 700–708.

Trehub, S. E. (2001). Musical predispositions in infancy. *Annals of the New York Academy of Sciences*, 930(1), 1–16.

Tsouloupas, C. N., Carson, R. L., Matthews, R., Grawitch, M. J., & Barber, L. K. (2010). Exploring the association between teachers' perceived student misbehaviour and emotional exhaustion: The importance of teacher efficacy beliefs and emotion regulation. *Educational Psychology*, 30(2), 173–189.

Twenge, J. M. (2007). *Generation me: Why today's young Americans are more confident, assertive, entitled, and more miserable than ever before.* New York: Free Press.

Twenge, J. M., & Campbell, W. K. (2009). *The narcissism epidemic: Living in the age of entitlement.* New York: Free Press.

Twenge, J. M., Konrath, S., Foster, J. D., Campbell, W. K., & Bushman, B. J. (2008). Egos inflating over time: A cross-temporal meta-analysis of the Narcissistic Personality Inventory. *Journal of Personality*, 76(4), 875–902.

Tyler, J. M., Feldman, R. S., & Reichert, A. (2006). The price of deceptive behavior: Disliking and lying to people who lie to us. *Journal of Experimental Social Psychology*, 42(1), 69–77.

Uleman, J. S., & Saribay, S. A. (2012). Initial impressions of others. In K. Deaux & M. Snyder (Eds.), *Oxford handbook of personality and social psychology* (pp. 337–366). Oxford: Oxford University Press.

Uleman, J. S., Saribay, S. A., & Gonzalez, C. M. (2008). Spontaneous inferences, implicit impressions, and implicit theories. *Annual Review of Psychology*, 59(1), 329–360.

Underwood, C., Rothman, S., & ACER. (2008). School experiences of 15 and 16 year-olds, LSAY Briefing 16. Retrieved from http://research.acer.edu.au/cgi/viewcontent.cgi?article=1015&context=lsay_briefs (accessed 20 May 2013).

Usher, E. L., & Pajares, F. (2009). Sources of self-efficacy in mathematics: A validation study. *Contemporary Educational Psychology*, 34(1), 89–101.

Van Bavel, J. J., & Cunningham, W. A. (2009). Self-categorization with a novel mixed-race group moderates automatic social and racial biases. *Personality and Social Psychology Bulletin*, 35(3), 321–335.

Vanderbilt, T. (2008). *Traffic: Why we drive the way we do, and what it says about us.* New York: Alfred A. Knopf.

Van Gerven, P. W. M., Paas, F., van Merriënboer, J. J. G., & Schmidt, H. G. (2004). Memory load and the cognitive pupillary response in aging. *Psychophysiology*, 41(2), 167–174.

Van Overwalle, F., Van Duynslaeger, M., Coomans, D., & Timmermans, B. (2012). Spontaneous goal inferences are often inferred faster than spontaneous trait inferences. *Journal of Experimental Social Psychology*, 48(1), 13–18.

Vohs, K. D., Baumeister, R. F., & Schmeichel, B. J. (2012). Motivation, personal beliefs, and limited resources all contribute to self-control. *Journal of Experimental Social Psychology*, 47(3), 379–384.

Vohs, K. D., Baumeister, R. F., Schmeichel, B. J., Twenge, J. M., Nelson, N. M., & Tice, D. M. (2008). Making choices impairs subsequent self-control: A limited-resource account of decision making, self-regulation, and active initiative. *Journal of Personality and Social Psychology, 94*(5), 883–898.

Vohs, K. D., Finkenauer, C., & Baumeister, R. F. (2011). The sum of friends' and lovers' self-control scores predicts relationship quality. *Social Psychological and Personality Science, 2*(2), 138–145.

Vrij, A., Akehurst, L., Brown, L., & Mann, S. (2006). Detecting lies in young children, adolescents and adults. *Applied Cognitive Psychology, 20*(9), 1225–1237.

Vrij, A., Fisher, R., Mann, S., & Leal, S. (2006). Detecting deception by manipulating cognitive load. *Trends in Cognitive Sciences, 10*(4), 141–142.

Walsh, D. G., & Hewitt, J. (1985). Giving men the come-on: Effect of eye contact and smiling in a bar environment. *Perceptual and Motor Skills, 61*(3:1), 873–874.

Watson, J. M., & Strayer, D. L. (2010). Supertaskers: Profiles in extraordinary multitasking ability. *Psychonomic Bulletin and Review, 17*(4), 479–485.

Wendorf, C. A., & Alexander, S. (2005). The influence of individual- and class-level fairness-related perceptions on student satisfaction. *Contemporary Educational Psychology, 30*(2), 190–206.

Westwood, P. (2011). The problem with problems: Potential difficulties in implementing problem-based learning as the core method in primary school mathematics. *Australian Journal of Learning Difficulties, 16*(1), 5–18.

Wheldall, K. (2009). Effective instruction for socially disadvantaged low-progress readers: The Schoolwise Program. *Australian Journal of Learning Difficulties, 14*(2), 151–170.

White, M. P., & Dolan, P. (2009). Accounting for the richness of daily activities. *Psychological Science, 20*(8), 1000–1008.

Wilber, M. K., & Potenza, M. N. (2006). Adolescent gambling: Research and clinical applications. *Psychiatry, 3*(10), 40–48.

Williams, E. F., & Gilovich, T. (2008). Do people really believe they are above average? *Journal of Experimental Social Psychology, 44*(4), 1121–1128.

Willingham, D. T. (2009). *Why don't students like school? A cognitive scientist answers questions about how the mind works and what it means for your classroom.* San Francisco, CA: Jossey-Bass.

Wilson, B. J., & Gottman, J. M. (2002). Marital conflict, repair, and parenting. In M. H. Bornstein (Ed.), *Social conditions and applied parenting, Handbook of parenting*, Vol. 4 (2nd ed., pp. 227–258). Mahwah, NJ: Lawrence Erlbaum.

Wilson, H. K., Pianta, R. C., & Stuhlman, M. (2007). Typical classroom experiences in first grade: The role of classroom climate and functional risk in the development of social competencies. *Elementary School Journal, 108*(2), 81–96.

Wilson, K., & Korn, J. H. (2007). Attention during lectures: Beyond ten minutes. *Teaching of Psychology, 34*(2), 85–89.

Wilson, T. D. (2002). *Strangers to ourselves: Discovering the adaptive unconscious.* Cambridge, MA: Belknap Harvard.

Wilson, T. D., Lindsey, S., & Schooler, T. Y. (2000). A model of dual attitudes. *Psychological Review, 107*(1), 101–126.

Wilson, T. D., & Nisbett, R. E. (1978). The accuracy of verbal reports about the effects of stimuli on evaluations and behavior. *Social Psychology, 41*(2), 118–131.

Winkielman, P., & Cacioppo, J. T. (2001). Mind at ease puts a smile on the face: Psychophysiological evidence that processing facilitation elicits positive affect. *Journal of Personality and Social Psychology, 81*(6), 989–1000.

Winner, E. (2000). The origins and ends of giftedness. *American Psychologist, 55*(1), 159–169.

Wiseman, R. (2007). *Quirkology: How we discover the big truths in small things.* New York: Basic Books.

Wittwer, J., Nückles, M., Landmann, N., & Renkl, A. (2010). Can tutors be supported in giving effective explanations? *Journal of Educational Psychology, 102*(1), 74–89.

Wittwer, J., Nückles, M., & Renkl, A. (2008). Is underestimation less detrimental than overestimation? The impact of experts' beliefs about a layperson's knowledge on learning and question asking. *Instructional Science, 36*(1), 27–52.

Wittwer, J., & Renkl, A. (2008). Why instructional explanations often do not work: A framework for understanding the effectiveness of instructional explanations. *Educational Psychologist, 43*(1), 49–64.

Wittwer, J., & Renkl, A. (2010). How effective are instructional explanations in example-based learning? A meta-analytic review. *Educational Psychology Review, 22*(4), 393–409.

Wolf, M. (2007). *Proust and the squid: The story and science of the reading brain.* New York: Harper.

Wolf, M., & Barzillai, M. (2009). The importance of deep reading. *Educational Leadership, 66*(6), 32–37.

Wulf, G., McConnel, N., Gartner, M., & Schwarz, A. (2002). Quiet eye duration, expertise, and task complexity in near and far aiming tasks. *Journal of Motor Behavior, 34*(2), 197.

Wylie, C., Hipkins, R., & Hodgen, E. (2008). *On the edge of adulthood: Young people's school and out of school experiences at 16.* Wellington: New Zealand Council for Educational Research.

Yates, G. C. R. (2000). Applying learning style research in the classroom. In R. J. Riding & S. G. Rayner (Eds.), *International perspectives on individual differences: Cognitive styles* (pp. 347–364). Stamford, CT: Ablex.

Yates, G. C. R. (2005). How obvious: Personal reflections on the database of educational psychology and effective teaching research. *Educational Psychology, 25*(6), 681–700.

van der Zwaag, M. D., Dijksterhuis, C., de Waard, D., Mulder, B. L. J. M., Westerink, J. H. D. M., & Brookhuis, K. A. (2011). The influence of music on mood and performance while driving. *Ergonomics, 55*(1), 12–22.

Zyphur, M. J., Warren, C. R., Landis, R. S., & Thoresen, C. J. (2007). Self-regulation and performance in high-fidelity simulations: An extension of ego-depletion research. *Human Performance, 20*(2), 103–118.

Index

Note: all page numbers in *italics* relate to entries being referred to in tables.

10-year rule 95

academic confidence: active teaching strategies 224–225; motivational strategies 225–226
academic learning time 36, 37–38, 39–40, 320
academic self-concept 219
academic work, owning 225, 310
acrostics and acronyms 171, *172*
active response to source of learning 47–48; misconceptions concerning 77ff
advance organisers 115, 315
aptitude-treatment interaction 181, 315
arrested development 315; and role of automaticity 97–99
articulatory loop 121, 315
assessment for teaching 69
associative stage of skill development *98*
associative thinking 291–292
attention 48, 286, 287; *see also* inattentional blindness (IB)
auditory learners 115, 176
automaticity 52ff, 84, 133, 147, 315; and arrested development 97–99; a conservation strategy 97–98; lack of 53, 59; and mathematics 57–59; and multitasking 190; and practice 93–95, 97; and skill development 100; teaching 59–61; and time 61
autonomous stage (of skill development) *98*
availability and access (in memory) 6, 98, 108, 131, 141, 221, 230, 236, 294, 315

backward design 149
backward training 133, 315
'bad is stronger than good' 5, 65, 140
Barnum effect (personality profile), also called Forer effect 232, 315
Beginning Teacher Evaluation Study (BTES) 38, 39

blink effects 27–28, 31–33, 296, 297, 299, 302–303
bodily synchronism (interpersonal) 272–273
body language 266, 273, 278

cascading inattention 48
CDR method 44, 45–46, 319; *see also* recitation method
chameleon effect 238, 274–275, 319; as built in 275–276; and social interactions 278
character assessment 32
chess champions 33, 87, 232
chunking 123, 124, 161; and expertise 86, 88
classroom management 18, 108, 250
closeness 17–18, 19, 21, 315
cognitive architecture 146–147, 316
cognitive load 8, 48, 59, 78, 79, 146, 147, 148, 235, 287, 316; and aids to learning 153; and collaborative groups 152; and gestures 142; and inattentional blindness 283, 284–285; and mimicry 274; and multimedia 150; and problem-solving 151–152; reducing 149–150; sources of 148–149; and teaching 153–154; and worked examples 151–152; and working memory 149–150, 152, 153, 154
cognitive style 178ff, 316
cognitive task analysis 75–77, 316
communicating: and action 26–27; with beginners 12–13
competitiveness 239
completion examples 152
comprehension 264–265
computer literacy 196–197, 199–200
computer as metaphor for mind 122, 188
concentration spans 114
conditional knowledge 132
confidence 8–9, 59, 215–216, 221, 224
conflict 17–18, 21, 315

contagion effect 261–262, 265, 273
content knowledge 11, 107
conversation, and memory acquisition 158–159, 161
coping strategies 119–120
CRIME (chunking, rehearsal, imagery, mnemonics, elaboration) 123–124
critical thinking 134
cueing 12–13, 32, 73, 162, 163
cumulative rehearsal and fast finish 123, 319
curiosity 6
curriculum knowledge 14
'cut and paste' approach 199, 201

deception and self-deception 229
decision-making 298, 302, 303
declarative knowledge 126, 301
declarative stage of skill development *98*
deep learning; and recitation method 47; and time 40–41; *see also* System 2
deflection strategies for controlling thoughts 254, 287, 316
deliberate practice 40, 93, 96, 97, 99, 100, 105, 169, 197, 316
depression 237
descriptive stage model of skill development 97, *98*
desirable traits, and memory 230
didactic instruction 49
DIE model for teaching 108
differential treatment 291
digital immigrants 196, 316
digital natives 120, 187, 196, 197–198, 203, 316
direct instruction, explicit teaching, 60, 72ff
discovery leaning process 77–79
disequilibrium 130
distraction strategies for controlling thoughts *see* deflection strategies
distress indicators 26–27
distributed practice 114
divide-and-conquer strategies 59
document analysis 74–75
driving performance: and background music 207; and phone using 190–191, 195
dual systems theory 290–291, 303–304; evidence for 293–294; origins of 291–292; *see also* System 1; System 2
Duchenne smile 262–264, 316
dumb-and-dumber effect *see* Dunning–Kruger effect
Dunbar's number 135
Dunning–Kruger effect 32–33, 233–235; and memory 235–237

e-reading 202
early talent indicators 99

effort 225; and IKEA effect 306–308; and memory 308–309; ownership of 309–310; and praise 68–69; and recognition 309–311; and System 1 *299*; and System 2 *299*
ego depletion 48, 61, 248–249, 317; and mental work 249–250; negative effects of 250–251; and self-control 249–250, 301–302; and System 1 251; and System 2 251, *299*, 301–302
ego/performance orientation 29–30, 239, 317
egotism 239–240
elaboration 115, 123–124, 161, 162, 317; CRIME 123–124
elaborative reminiscing style 159, 317
emotional leakage 18, 29, 317
empathy 21, 240, 255, 310
empathy gap 14, 16, 20, 21, 65
encoding 161, 316
endowment effect 309–310, 317
engaged time 36, 37, 39
episodic memory 157, 317
errors of omission 236–237
evolutionary perspective 7, 55, 73, 79–81, 124, 135, 262, 277
expert blind spot effect 13, 317
expert-novice contrast 85
expertise xvi, 11, 12, 13, 73, 166, 303; 10-year rule 95; the Bloom report 93–95, 97; and chunking 86, 88; and deep-level processing 87; and deliberate practice 40; domain-specificity 85–88; and inattentional blindness 285; and mental models 131; research into 84–85, 103–104, *104*; and self-monitoring skills 88; and short-term memory 88; speed and accuracy 86; sports training 88, 90; traits of 85–87, 90; and unconscious processing 89–90; use of time to think hard 87–88; and working memory 86–87, 88–89; *see also* teacher expertise
extraneous cognitive load 148–149
eye movements, and inattentional blindness 284; and reading 53, 89–90; and gaze 266, 272

facial expression 266; classifying 260; inferring personality from 267; and mirror neuron theory 277; and self-control 276
fair treatment 26, 310–311, 312
false memory effects 117, 317
family support 20, 94
far transfer 208–209
feedback 75, 128, 133; an common starting point 311; and confidence 215–216; corrective 73, 78, 105, 225; and deliberate practice 96; disconfirmation 140; effective 66–67, 69–70; goal recalibration 239; and IKEA effect 310–311, 312; informational

68; and knowledge level 65–66; and overconfidence 119; and perceived competencies 218; and posture matching 32; and recitation method 45, 46–47; respectful 309–310; and self-assessment 231; student vs. teacher views 64–65; and System 2 300–301; on teacher impact 69
feedback cues 150, 264–265, 297
field dependent, field independent 178
first impressions 27–28, 31–33, 266–267
first letter mnemonics 172
flip teaching 149
forgetting, rates of 116–117
frowning 296
FUTON bias 204

gambling, pathological 246
gestures: aids in thinking and communicating 141–142; and cognitive load 142; impact on children 142–143; and implicit knowledge 140–141; and implicit learning 143; and language acquisition 142; and mirror neuron theory 277, 278; and smiles/smiling 266
goals: recalibration of 239; setting 119, 120; and System 1 299, 300–301; and System 2 299, 300–301; of teachers 30
Goldilocks principle xiii, 67, 211, 221
golf players' quiet eye 87–88
'grammar' of schooling 44
gratification delay 244, 245–246, 253
grouping strategies 161

healthy attributions 225
hidden costs 189–190, 193
high maintenance interaction (effects of) 248–249
history teaching strategies 74–75, 77
human factors research 48, 189, 281
human nature: continuity of 204; and digital native theory 197–198, 203
human skill levels, changes in 95–96

iconic store 122–123
ideas 127, 129–130
identification 253
if–then procedures 76, 132; if–then thinking (hypothetical) 131; if–then plans (self-control) 254, 318
IKEA effect 306, 317; and effort 306–308; and endowment effect 309–310; and feedback 310–311, 312; psychology of 308–309; research findings 307–308
imagery 162; CRIME 123–124
implementation intentions (if–then plans) 254, 318
Implicit Association Test 291

implicit attitude 290–291
implicit learning 136–137, 139–140, 143, 317
implicit mimicry 32, 274–278
impulse control 249–250, 317
impulsiveness 31–33, 303
in-group bias effect 217–218
inattentional blindness (IB) 281–282, 318; in the classroom 285–287; and cognitive load 283, 284–285; and eye movements 284; and expertise 285; implications of 285–287; research findings 282–283; and training 283–284
inattentional deafness 285
individuality 180, 184, 225; and classification 267–268
infant–parent bonding 206
infantile amnesia 157, 318
inflation effect 218
information processing 136, 146; and recitation method 47–49
innate talent 99
Innocence Project, The 117
instructional explanations (problems with) 47, 48
instructional time 36ff
interacting elements 147–148, 316
interference 114, 188; and memory 118
intergenerational transmission 253, 257, 259
Internet: and knowledge acquisition 202–203; and shallow thinking 201–203; as source of information 204
interpersonal interactions: posture matching 273–274; timing 272–273
interpersonal reactions, measuring 271–272
interpersonal sensitivity, and teacher expertise 108–109
intrusion 117
invisible gorilla studies 79, 203, 282, 283, 284, 287
invulnerability hypothesis 21
IQ (intelligence quotient) 177–178; and self-control 247; tests 207
IRE cycle (initiation-response-evaluation) 44–45, 319; see also recitation method
isolated knowledge 41

job satisfaction 306–307
joint talk 159, 317

keyword mnemonics 173
kinaesthetic learners 176
knowledge acquisition: and Internet 202–203; six principles of 113–115
knowledge building, and the self 77–79
knowledge gap 6–7, 70, 78, 223, 318
knowledge transmission 78, 79; and evolution 79–80

language: and memory 157–158; time-shifting process 158–159
language acquisition, and gestures 142
learners, categories of 177
learning: and active mind 115; as cumulative 225; and mental resources 119; as pleasant 119; and System 1 *299*; and System 2 *299*; time, effort and motivation 114–115; an unconscious activity 138–139
learning style assessment 176–177; empirical research 181–183; field development 177–179; match hypothesis 181, 182–183, *184*; questionnaires 179–180
learning styles 114: as preferences 179–180, 183, *184*; and rhetoric 183–184, *184*; use of term 176–177; VAK model 176, 178–179, 181
lesson participation, opting-out 47
lesson plans 108
literacy levels 56
long-term memory 89, 122, 123, 146, 147, 161, 162, 201, 308
look-back 53
look-say-cover-write-check 129
lying, detection of 27, 28–29

managerial competence 231
mastery goal orientation 29–30, 30, 318
matching hypothesis (in learning styles) 181, 182–183, *184*
mathematics: and automaticity 57–59; computer programs 60–61; times tables 57
Me generation 239–240
meaningfulness 115, 129–130
means-end thinking 59
memory 7, 8–9; acquisition, and conversation 158–159; a constructive process 117; and desirable traits 230; and Dunning–Kruger effect 235–237; and effort 308–309; and interference 118; mental training program 167–168; role of language 157–158; and schooling 160–162; and self-efficacy 221, 222; skills, teaching 162–164; and System 1 *299*; and System 2 *299*
memory championships (memory athletes) 166–169, 174
memory palaces 167, 169, 171, 318
memory retention, six principles of 116–118
mental development, and music practice 210
mental models *127*, 130–132
mental switching 189–190, 193
mental work, and ego depletion 249–250
method of loci 167, 318
mind wandering 48, 114, 318
mirror neuron theory 276–277; implications of 277–278
misconceptions 48–49, 78, 114, 118

mnemonic-based card counting system 169
mnemonics 116, 123, 161–163; championship 167–168; content-related 171–173; CRIME 123–124; first letter mnemonics 172; in contextual training experiences 174; keyword mnemonics 173; limits of 174; Major system 167–168; mental training program 167–168; need for 168–169; pegword scheme for memorisation 171, 172, 318; in perspective 169–170; teaching 162–163, 170–171; whole-class level 173–174
moral righteousness 27
Morse code operators 84
motivation 29–30, 311; *see also* IKEA effect
Mozart effect 114, 207–208
multi-modal input 115
multi-store theory 120–122
MULTILIT (making up for lost time in literacy) 60
multimedia, and cognitive load *150*
multimedia input 115
multitasking 99, 120, 191–192, 287; and automaticity 190; as helpful 192–193; use of term 187–189
music, background 191–192, 209; and driving performance 207; effect on the brain 207–208; effects of 206–207; medical settings 207, 209
music instruction: and personal control/self-discipline 209, 210; universal benefits of 208–209

narcissism 217, 229, 238, 239–240
National Board for Professional Teacher Standards (NBPTS) 107
negative escalations 16, 18, 59, 318
negative information 138, 140
negative traits (not admit to self) 229, 232, 235

observational learning 72–73, 78–79, 82, 115
omniscience principle 80
oral language facility 54; and accurate reading 55–56
orbicularis oculi 260
ostention, principle of 73, 80, 318
overconfidence 119, 120, 122, 215, 223, 318
overestimation 105, 220, 231, 233, 234
overload 48, 114, 118–120, 133

pacing (ability to control) 150
Paideia model 49
parental conversational style 158–159, 161
perceived competencies 216, 218–219, 220, 221, 320
personalisation 150
personality (in teacher role) 26–27

phonetic analysis 52, 54, 57
plateaus in learning 100, 318
positive escalations 21
positive feelings 59
posture matching 32, 273–274, 319
practice: and automaticity 93–95, 97; deliberate
    40, 93, 96, 97, 99, 100, 105, 169, 197, 316;
    role of time in 100; and skilfulness 96–97;
    types of 95–96
practice makes perfect 93
praise 67–68, 69–70, 71; discourages effort
    68–69
pre-instructional experience 149
presentation mannerisms 28
primacy 89, 116, 319
priming 260, 294, 319
prior knowledge 7, 114–115, 120, 122, 123,
    124, 126, 129, 131, 149, 225
proactive interference 118, 319
problem-solving 131, 132, 133, 151–152, 248,
    296, 299
procedural knowledge 126, 127, 132–133, 301
professional development: and teacher–student
    relationships 17, 19; timescale 105
public knowledge principle 80
punitive models 18

Quicksmart program 60–61
quiet eye period 87–88, 91

reading: computer programs 60–61; and eye-
    movement 53, 89–90; and font type 203,
    205, 294–296; literacy levels 56; and oral
    language skills 55–56; repeated 60; simple
    theory of 55, 56–57, 62; speed 53–54; and
    System 1 296; and System 2 294–296
reading problems 53–57, 59–61
recall 6, 89, 116, 117; record for recalling pi
    167
recency effect 89, 116, 298, 319
recitation method 44, 162, 319; advantages and
    disadvantages 46–47; and deep learning 47;
    and feedback 45, 46–47; and information
    processing 47–49; and prior knowledge
    48
reciting 123
recognition 116, 235, 301, 309–311
redundancy effect 48, 150, 153
reflective thinking 291–292
rehearsal 123, 161, 162, 319; CRIME 123–124
relevance, principle of 80
reminiscing styles 159
repeated reading 60, 319
repetition 128, 153
retroactive interference 118, 319
risk assessment in adolescents 21–23, 27
rote learning 116, 123, 128

saccades 53, 89–90
savings principle of 118
schemata 127, 130, 131, 146–147, 148, 151,
    153, 170, 221, 225, 319
schemata development or refinement 41, 130,
    133
school: attitudes to 4–5; as buffer 18–19, 20
science class 75–77
scripts 130
selective attention 136, 191
self-affirmation 220, 222, 320
self-assessment 237; and chronic self-views 232;
    and feedback 231; possibility of 230–232
self-centredness 239
self-control 243, 287; continuity of 246–247; as
    developmental trait 245–246; and dietary
    control 248, 251; and ego depletion 249,
    249–250, 301–302; and facial expression
    276; gradients 247; and IQ 247; mental
    cooling strategies 254; and music
    instruction 209, 210; neurological evidence
    for 246; proactive mode 251–252; and
    social interaction 248, 255; and System 2
    301–302; a trait in adulthood 247–248;
    theory, shifts in 244–245
self-deception 229
self-doubt 69
self-efficacy 5, 216, 219–221, 224, 320; and
    memory 221, 222; origins of 221–222; test
    procedures 220; and verbal exhortation
    221–222; vicious cycles 223
self-enhancement 218, 228–229, 231, 237, 239,
    240, 319; reasons for 229–230
self-esteem 67, 216–217, 218–219, 220, 221,
    223–224, 238, 239, 320; cracks in theory
    217–218; questionnaires 216; and social
    pathology 217
self-fulfilling prophecy 291
self-image: and reality 238–239; and social
    interactions 237, 238
self-knowledge 238
self-monitoring skills, and expertise 88
self-presentation 32–33, 228
self-regulation 48, 66
self, the, and knowledge building 77–79
self-worth 239
sensory memory 121, 146
sensory recognition knowledge 126–128, 127
serial orderings see strings
serial position effects 116
shallow thinking: and the Internet 201–203; see
    also System 1
short-term memory 121, 123, 168, 201; and
    expertise 88
simple theory of reading 55, 56–57, 62
skill development 96–97, 98, 100; timescale
    114–115

smiles/smiling: Botox smile 263; and comprehension 264–265; and contagion effect 261–262, 265, 273; Duchenne smile 262–264, 316; effects of 268–269; and eye gaze pattern 266; facial muscle movement 260–261, 266; flexible nature of 266; and gestures 266; and head angle 266; a natural language 262; and negative emotions 263–264; patterns 262–263, 268; and professional persona 265–266, 278; research findings 259–260; responsive 269; and shoulder positioning 266; and sincerity 262–264; a social sign 261, 262; timing 266; types of 260–261, 262
snowball effects *see* negative escalations
social brain hypothesis 7–8, 80, 124, 135, 296, 320
social chameleons *see* chameleon effect
social comparison 65, 79, 137, 226, 320
social interaction 132–133; and chameleon effect 278; and self-control 248, 255; and self-image 237, 238
social learning history 252–253
social modelling 72–73, 78, 79, 82, 140, 253, 259; neurological basis for 277
social pathology: family model 253; and self-esteem 217
social responsibility 218
social rules 27
Socratic questioning 49
SOLO (structure of observed learning outcomes) 133–134
spatial learning 140
speed reading 54
spontaneous trait inference effect 267, 320
sports training, and expertise 88, 90
spotlight effect 237, 320
stereotypes 268, 291
story chaining 172
stress from ego depletion 250–251
strings (simple associations) *127*, 128–129, 171, 320
striving: calibrating 222–223, 239; with confidence 221
student voice 49
switching costs (in multitasking) 189–190, 193
System 1 9, 97, 137, 290, 292, 294, 302, 303–304; actions *295*; and car driving 292–293; and decision-making 302; and effort *299*; and ego depletion 251; and goals *299*, 300–301; hypothesis testing *299*; and immediacy 300–301; level of awareness *299*; a liability *299*; mechanism of learning *299*; and memory *299*; nature of learning *299*; overlapping skills *299*; problem-solving *299*; psychological processes

298–300; and reading 296; target of adjustment *299*; and teaching 296–298
System 2 5, 9, 59, 137, 251, 290, 292, 293–294, 303–304; actions *295*; deficiencies 304; and effort *299*; and ego depletion 251, *299*, 301–302; and feedback 300–301; and goals *299*, 300–301; hypothesis testing *299*; and impulsiveness 303; level of awareness *299*; a liability *299*; and long-term future 300–301; mechanism of learning *299*; and memory *299*; nature of learning *299*; overlapping skills *299*; problem-solving *299*; psychological processes 298–300; and reading 294–296; and self-control 301–302; target of adjustment *299*

tactile learners 115
task analysis 75, 133
task difficulty, underestimating 12
teacher expertise 103–105, *104*; and interpersonal sensitivity 108–109; laboratory studies 105–107; observing 107–108; teacher impact 69
teacher–student relationships: and closeness 17–18, 20, 21; and conflict 17–18, 21; and developmental trajectories 19; emotional climate 28; and interaction 19–20; long-term importance of 20–22; low teacher expectations 20; positive 16–17, 18, 19; and professional development 17, 19; a protective factor 19; student expectations 31; trust 30; unfair treatment of students 26–27
teacher talk 45–46, 47–48, 49
teachers: as activator 72, *73*; as facilitator 72, *73*; goals and intentions 30; students' expectations of 31
temporal contiguity 150
thin slice phenomenon 31–32, 302; *see also* blink effects
three degrees of social separation 262, 320
time: academic learning time 36, 37–38, 39–40, 320; and automaticity 61; and deep learning 40–41; engaged 36, 37, 39; instructional 36, 37, 39; and practice 100; stating the obvious 36, 41–42
time allocated 36, 37, 38, 39, 41, 320
time analysis, conceptual basis of 36–38
time-shifting process, language 158–159
times tables 57
tone of voice 266–267
trust 29–30

unconscious processing, 12, 118, 138ff, 262, 264, 272–275, 290ff; and expertise 89–90, 90, 106
under-confidence 223

unfair treatment 26–27, 310–311, 312

VAK model 176, 178–179, 181
verbally based instructions 47, 78, 79, 132
vigilance decrement 192–193, 320
visual learners 115, 176
VL synthesis xi, xiii, xv, 13, 65, 66, 67, 72ff, 198

willpower 243, 251–252, 303; and social
    learning history 252–253
word association 53, 172
work ethic 94

worked examples 47, 51–152, 132–133, 149,
    150, 155, 208, 222–223; and cognitive load
    151–152
working memory 121, 123, 128–129, 131, 146,
    147, 168, 287, *299*; and cognitive load
    149–150, 152, 153, 154; and expertise
    86–87, 88–89; and interacting elements
    147–148, 316

'yawning is contagious' 273

zygotmaticus major 260